Fast Forward

Fast Forward

Work, Gender, and Protest in a Changing World

Torry D. Dickinson and Robert K. Schaeffer

Artwork by Teresa Schmidt

ROWMAN & LITTLEFIELD PUBLISHERS, INC.
Lanham • Boulder • New York • Oxford

ROWMAN & LITTLEFIELD PUBLISHERS, INC.

Published in the United States of America
by Rowman & Littlefield Publishers, Inc.
4720 Boston Way, Lanham, Maryland 20706
www.rowmanlittlefield.com

12 Hid's Copse Road, Cumnor Hill, Oxford OX2 9JJ, England

Copyright © 2001 by Rowman & Littlefield Publishers, Inc.

Teresa Schmidt's image on the cover and page 159 was based on a photograph by Eugene Richards, "May in the Morning, 1991" and her rendering is published by permission of the photographer.

Teresa Schmidt's image on page 273 was inspired by a news photo and is published by permission of Michael Shulman, Archive Photos.

All rights reserved. No part of this publication may be reproduced, stored in a retrieval system, or transmitted in any form or by any means, electronic, mechanical, photocopying, recording, or otherwise, without the prior permission of the publisher.

British Library Cataloguing in Publication Information Available

Library of Congress Cataloging-in-Publication Data
Dickinson, Torry D.
　Fast forward : work, gender, and protest in a changing world / Torry D. Dickinson and Robert K. Schaeffer.
　　p. cm.
　Includes bibliographical references and index.
　ISBN 0-7425-0894-3 — ISBN 0-7425-0895-1 (pbk.)
　　1. Working class. 2. Social movements. 3. Discrimination in employment. 4. Working class women. I. Schaeffer, Robert K. II. Title.

HD4854 .D53 2001
331.13'3–dc21　　　　　　　　　　　　　　　　　　　　　　　　　　2001019011

Printed in the United States of America

∞™ The paper used in this publication meets the minimum requirements of American National Standard for Information Sciences—Permanence of Paper for Printed Library Materials, ANSI/NISO Z39.48-1992.

*To Joy MacCarthy, Henry Paul Schaeffer,
Patricia Plank Dickinson, and Walter (Dick) Dickinson,
rebels all.*

Contents

Preface: Looking Back, Moving Forward		ix
Part I Seeing Global Change		1
1 An Introduction to Work, Gender, and Protest		3
Part II Worker Households, Businesses, and States		21
2 The Meaning of Work		23
3 The Changing World of Work		36
4 The Redistribution and Reorganization of Work in the Core		49
5 The Submerging Periphery		82
6 Reverses in the Semiperiphery		114
7 Welfare States Cut Worker Benefits		138
Part III The Changing Ground for Working Households		159
8 Households, Class Transformations, and the Emergence of Women-Centered Labor Movements		161
9 The Degradation of Social and Natural Work Environments		186
Part IV Change and Protest		203
10 Institutional Struggles: Female and Male Workers Challenge Business		205
11 Institutional Struggles: Workers Challenge States		224
12 Diversifying Struggles: Redefining Work and Society		252
Part V Conclusion		273
13 Fast Forward		275
Selected Bibliography		291
Index		295
About the Authors		303

Preface:
Looking Back, Moving Forward

When we began our research for this book, we asked, How do changes in wage work, micro-entrepreneurial activities, unpaid household work, and state support of workers relate to women's and men's political struggles? As we investigated this question, we discovered that, just as household work and wage work intersect, "women's politics" and "men's politics" intersect at many points and transform each other.

Our approach called for a historically grounded, materialist analysis of laboring people's relationships around the world. We decided to examine the changing connections among work and working people's political cultures. This preliminary effort would provide a holistic analysis of labor's paid and unpaid work efforts, including those engaged in by women and men. By combining our knowledge about gender divides, global ethnic divides, informal and formal work relations, and global economic change, we could situate work and social movements in a broad context. To understand social movements, it is crucial to understand the changing work and cultural contexts in which they emerge.

It soon became obvious that across the world-economy vast work-based disparities exist between the poor and the rich, women and men, and people of color and people culturally defined as "Whites." Social problems abound, and the needs of the world's female and male working people have been unmet. So how do working people address these problems, given the failure of national and global institutions to attack global poverty, gender and racial injustice, and economic and political inequality? To answer this question, we decided that we needed a comprehensive theoretical framework that incorporated the fact that women do most of the world's work. And most of these women are women of color living in the global South. By placing women's work and feminist ideas at the heart of our investigation, we could examine sexism, racism, and inequality. Of course, it is impossible to study these forms of inequality without also exploring the lives and work of men.

Work and social identities are complex and overlapping. Men are gendered, just like women. "Whites" are racialized, just like people of color. This book examines how working people are trying to address the changing but somewhat fixed class, gender, age, and racial structures that limit people's efforts to make decisions and to define life-sustaining and meaningful work. The book explores how businesses and states transform work, what these changes mean for women and men in households, and how social movements try to influence global institutions. Some of these movements use the household as a base for creating extra-institutional change.

Changing the world requires intense human involvement by people who work and live in diverse family arrangements. This book is more than a study of today's gendered world; it is a call for greater participation in an analysis of the contemporary world and the ways that people can create change. As you read this book, we invite you to think about how to create a more egalitarian and democratic world. We encourage you to consider these questions: (1) What social relations would best meet the economic, social, cultural, and political needs of working people? (2) What new social relations are needed to make that happen? and (3) How will global structural change and social movements transform work, community, and society? We have only begun to answer these questions in the following chapters.

As we complete this book, we acknowledge that our study of history and our own experience as activists have made us aware that global change is chaotic and that social-movement activists may not know the best strategies to address chaotic change. Social movements do not act alone. They operate in a global environment where other forces and actors shape change. For example, environmental destruction, ethnic conflict, famine and hunger, migration, and crime syndicates and bandits are important sources of change. This has been a sobering realization. In this context, it may take decades before better ways of living are developed and institutionalized. It is important to recognize that there is no single approach, no single theory, no universal strategy that social movements should all adopt. Adverse developments will block some progressive efforts. But when progress is blocked, movements may develop new strategies for circumventing obstacles.

As the diverse pool of global movements now confronts these obstacles, their actions identify and also eliminate various social options. The choices people make now eliminate possible pathways of human development in the immediate future. So the choices people make today are very important. This is one reason why democratic involvement is such an important issue in the world today. This is particularly true if we are at a juncture of dramatic systemic change, which we think is the case.

If the choices made today help shape future developments, it is best that these choices be made by democratic majorities rather than by elite minorities. The future belongs to all of us. It is not enough to leave crucial development decisions to business and state managers who have promoted global polarization. This book is written for those thinkers and activists who are interested in understanding the world around them and who want to make some kind of conscious effort to improve it. People like you can bring about democratic participation in collective governance.

As historical sociologists and participatory social action researchers in feminist, labor, and environmental movements, we want to thank those mentors, support groups, friends, and relatives who have nurtured us and brought us to this project. Torry Dickinson thanks Milo Smith, her mentor in women's employment, education, and training work, and a cofounder of the California and U.S. Displaced Homemaker movement. Over the years, Torry has grown from intellectual partnerships with colleagues and friends associated with SUNY-Binghamton's Fernand Braudel Center and sociology department. Terence K. Hopkins and Beverly Silver deserve our thanks for first asking us to present a paper on work around the world. Special thanks also go to Kathie Friedman Kasaba, William G. Martin, Immanuel Wallerstein, Anna Davin, S. O. Y. Keita, Jean A. Smith, Richard Allen (RAP IV), M'eliz Maatta, Derry O'Connor, and Rink Dickinson, as well as to coauthor, Robert, and to their children, Jazz and Jeffree.

As this book unfolded, Torry was actively involved in trying to end U.S. campus violence against women and in establishing a university mentoring and research program for students of color and other disadvantaged students. Working with Talat Rahman, Mordean Taylor-Archer, Dorinda Lambert, Susan Allen, other committee members, and women's studies students provided political momentum as she did her research. The women's studies and American ethnic studies staff, including Vera White, Patrisha Swanigan, Anthony Wallace, Lory Stone, and Todd Nicewonger, provided assistance and friendship during much of the project. It was also a great pleasure for Torry to get to know and to work with KSU artist Teresa Schmidt, who exhibits such passion for working people and social-change makers. Moreover, she thanks her parents and Robert's parents for introducing their children to the importance of meaningful work, intellectual inquiry, social justice, and democracy.

Robert Schaeffer thanks a number of people for influencing or supporting his work. Immanuel Wallerstein, Jesse Lemisch, Giovanni Arrighi, Marcus Rediker, William Friedland, Jim Mellon, Marianne Massenberg, and John Judis made important contributions to Robert's thoughts about work. And the owners, managers, coworkers, organizers, and bureaucrats at the *Shopping News,* Postal Instant Press, *Freedom News, Daily Jacket,* Container Corporation of America, Union Street Gallery, *East Bay Voice, In These Times,* Office of Appropriate Technology, Friends of the Earth, District 65 of the United Auto Workers, *Maine Times, Nuclear Times,* Greenpeace, San Jose State, and unemployment insurance and food stamp programs in California and Maine contributed to his understanding of the diverse meanings of work and politics.

Let us now turn to the diverse meanings of work and protest for people the world over.

Part I
SEEING GLOBAL CHANGE

Women are assuming greater work burdens in households and
are taking the lead in protests against global change.

Chapter 1

An Introduction to Work, Gender, and Protest

This broad, historically based, systemic examination of work, gender, and protest shows how working people today respond to and shape the world around them. A study of work, gender, and protest reveals both the world-constructing forces of global capitalism and the world-reshaping forces of popular protest. Through the study of work, gender, and protest, processes of global integration and disintegration are revealed. In this book we outline the development of key problems that affect women, men, and children around the world and identify ways that working people address systemic problems and advance a broad range of possible solutions.

In this preliminary examination of contemporary relationships between people's work, the gendered components of work and activism, and the many forms that working people's protests take, we focus on working-class formation, de-formation, and transformation in the world-economy. Rather than simply analyze the integration of the global ruling class (the subject of most globalization studies), this study examines transformations of the global working class. It employs a global framework that developed out of a world-system analysis of capitalism and antisystemic movements.

Capitalism is not simply commodifying the world; it is also marginalizing much of the world. This is not new. Uneven development has always been a hallmark of capitalism. But uneven development today is beginning to place people outside of the capitalist system. At this point in its development, capitalism has both strengthened labor's reliance on wage labor and market consumption in some parts of the world and, simultaneously, forced laboring households to rely more on their own capacities in other parts of the world.

Although other scholars have documented and analyzed trends relating to business, the state, and the worldwide system, this study is primarily concerned with changes in the global working class. What does a broadly defined study of work, gender structures, and multifaceted protests reveal about the system as a whole? Where is working-class politics taking people, the system, and future societies?

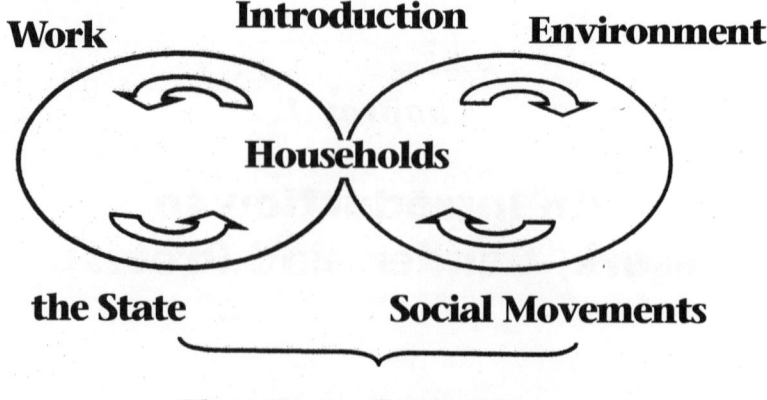

A *visual depiction of the structure of* Fast Forward.

To answer these questions, this study examines labor's formal relations with businesses and states; labor's more informal, "on-the-ground," work-based relations; and protests related to work and politics. In particular, it uses a broad exploration of gendered work and protest to analyze the system, class transformations, and alternative social constructions. The diagram illustrates the structure of the book.

First, we discuss what it means to be part of the global working class in the contemporary period. Then we will examine how changes in businesses and states have affected labor in different parts of the world. This will constitute our first circuit of inquiry. After we have completed our analysis of the impact of the world-economy's dominant institutions on labor, we will analyze informal household relations on the ground, and how laboring households organize work and conduct politics in changing social and environmental contexts. As part of this second circuit of inquiry, we examine labor movements and protests that have emerged in relation to business and the state and movements that operate outside of dominant institutions. After completing this second circle of analysis, we will reexamine our initial concerns, review contemporary institutional change, and reconsider the social significance of worker protests and class transformations.

GLOBAL WORKERS' LIVES ARE CONNECTED

Working people in a class-based global society are directly connected to each other, though many ignore, deny, or resist this mutual interdependency. Today the relationship between worker households in the well-off, global North and those in the poorer, global South is often indirect. Their connection can perhaps be illustrated by the kind of relations exhibited in restaurants. When worker households in the

North dine out, they consume food and drink made by others far away. Farmers, vintners, brewers, ranchers, and fishers produce food for the table in different settings around the world and receive small (and shrinking) sums for the goods they make. Diners are served by a small army of cooks, busboys, waiters, and washers who labor for low wages, scramble for tips, and wait silently by. The meal on the table is also made possible by the work of people who keep food-industry and service workers fed, clothed, washed, and trained to work for others. The work that women, wives, children, and elders do is not paid, but without their labor, farmers could not harvest food and waiters could not lay the table. Diners, of course, ignore these servants and concentrate instead on the cuisine and conversation at their table. But every bite that diners enjoy, every sip they take is made possible by the exploitation of paid and unpaid workers, near and far.

Yet although diners benefit from the exploitation of farmers and fishers, cooks and waiters, children and wives, they do not themselves organize this work or profit from it. Capitalist firms—the restaurateurs but also the companies that purchase grain, process beef, ship produce, supply napkins, scrutinize accounts, and draw up ads—organize the people who work in the food-processing and food-service industries. It is they who profit from the exploitation of paid and unpaid workers, from the sale of food to worker-consumers. Everyone in the restaurant, diners and servants and their off-stage assistants scattered across the globe, was brought together by capital. It is capital's mediating presence that shapes the whole scene.

Working people from the South, who are hidden by global market operations, have been forced or persuaded to toil for corporations and banks in the North so that the relatively well-off minority can continue to dine well. When household members in the wealthy core countries close their eyes for a cozy eight hours of sleep, downy nighttime covers are pulled up by the hands of hardworking moms in the world-economy's impoverished periphery, or by bonded child laborers, by teenage girls who make sneakers, by migrating dads who send money home, and by grandparents and aunts who vend gum and cigarettes. After the global North goes to sleep, the global South can slumber; before the North awakes, the South rises. Although formal slavery on plantations has been outlawed, a freer form of economic subordination now allows core workers to forget that they have been holding hands with and standing on the backs of peripheral workers for five hundred years. During this time, workers in the North and South have made few efforts to team up. They have not done so because the entire global system is set up to cultivate the demands of workers and consumers in the North, paying them the highest wages (though at unequal levels) and allowing them to imagine what college they should attend, what car they should buy, what house they should furnish, and what vacation they should take when they retire, even if these goods were secured through bank credit and consumer indebtedness.

Workers' destinies have been intertwined through divisive class relations and through related, but mutually unacknowledged, rebellions for the last five hundred years. At this conjuncture in history, we need to ask: Will laboring people in the North and South be able to work together for their own collective good?

THE GEOGRAPHY OF CONTEMPORARY SCHOLARSHIP

For this study, the analytical scope of the literature was wide and deep, leading to a broad examination of many related literary terrains and geographies of scholarship and observation. This topographical approach to literature review was needed to cover the historical and social-relational scope of this study, consisting of the capitalist world-economy at the end of the twentieth century and the beginning of the twenty-first, and the recent creation of external relations and working women and men who survive outside of the world market. Although many types of literature explore end-of-century capitalism in various parts of the world, there is a dearth of information on working women and men in external, nonsystemic arrangements, whether they are located in regions where the world-economy continues to dominate or in new, external areas. To consider class transformations in the contemporary context, we turned to many sets of literature for conceptual and empirical guidance.

A central goal in this analysis is to provide a more comprehensive account of the context in which social movements and spontaneous protests have developed in the last decade.

Although we conduct feminist, environmental, labor, and antiracist research, we are primarily students of world-system analysis. This school has a multidisciplinary, flexible, and evolving framework, which grew out of the intellectual and political movements of the late 1960s, including women's studies, Black studies, Chicano studies, and Third World studies. Furthermore, the world-systems framework has continually developed, as scholars analyze history and deepen their understanding of social change.

In our study of contemporary social change, we developed our ideas in a friendly but critical relationship with globalization, postmodernist, postcolonial, and post-structuralist literature. We felt it was important to learn from the strengths of literature that identifies and analyzes the outcomes of global and regional historical processes and then to include these insights in our analytical framework. We see many types of social-change literature, including feminist, as compatible and complementary with world-systems analysis.

Although postmodernist and post-structuralist scholars emphasize fragmentation and diversity, as a way of understanding the inequality that results from classism, imperialism, sexism, racism, ageism, and other forms of inequality, they fail to provide a full account of how these divisions historically emerged. For example, some social-change researchers only identify the effects, symptoms, or by-products of a global division of labor, without seeing how and why these divisions emerged on a global scale. They often do not appreciate the importance of global structural integration and fail to acknowledge that the global division of labor includes different economic zones that shape unequal social relations. Many scholars do not use or provide an explanatory framework for the study of inequality and social change. So far, world-systems scholars have been alone in developing an open, evolving, comprehensive framework that can be used to explain how the world has been transformed and how it is changing.

We think that academic scholars and community-based activists should learn from each other. The need for multicultural and multisituational intellectual thought rings out. The thick boundary separating the university from other centers of learning, which is rooted in everyday life and in a variety of professions, requires reexamination, if scholars, activists, and other thinkers are to understand social change more clearly.

Even though literature's boundaries are being crossed, multidisciplinary endeavors are highly underdeveloped. For example, although feminist scholarship has begun to take antiracist analysis seriously, these two types of literature have been largely unintegrated into many theoretical explorations of the world-economy, globalization, and post-structuralism. Somehow, researchers have been able to talk about transnational take-overs and market consumption without noticing who is working (for low wages or for no pay) to uphold the whole structure. Many researchers, who continue to see the study of sexism and racism as add-ons to "real" theories, fail to realize that sexism and racism tell us what the global system is about.

Unfortunately, global processes have been studied in fragmented ways, as new schools of thought have emerged and as theoretical specialization has been cultivated. Labor studies often became separated from antiracist and antisexist research. Scholars sometimes saw women as nonworkers, except during the times that they were engaged in wage labor; they treated men as full-time wage laborers even though men spent a large portion of their lives outside of paid employment. As a result, there is a lack of strong, sustained, and theoretical analysis of the global organization of labor as a group that includes both wage and nonwage workers.

The gendered component of world economic organization has generally been underexplored in studies of the world-economy, globalization, post-structural cultures, and social movements, even though it is crucial to any understanding of the world today. By combining feminist and world-system analysis, we see the whole in a different way. Feminist insights, if placed within a world-economic framework, help redefine all relationships within global society and evolving cultures. They do not simply "add to" an understanding of a fixed whole. A gender-conscious analysis of work shows how and why the whole structure is being constructed and contested. When we started this study, we knew that we would see things differently if we integrated feminist and world-system analyses. But at the end of the research process, we recognized that this synthesis also contributed to a new understanding of working-class transformations.

An analysis of gender inequality and gendered resistance must be located within a transformative analysis of global society. Both world-economy studies and feminist studies need to form part of a common scholarship. On their own, feminist ideals cannot be understood outside of the global, historical system, nor can they, by themselves, lead to a full understanding of society and its transformations. If world-systems analysis is defined in an open and evolving way, it provides a framework in which feminist studies can be situated.

Although we benefited from exposure to different types of literature, we became aware of an important shortcoming in many schools of thought. Most writers on globalization cultivate images of the universal spread of wage work and the unbridled and universal growth of market consumption. We agree that the world-economy has expanded and deepened through commodification. But while labor, products, land, resources, and capital are continually created as "products" that are sold on the market, commodification has not resulted in global homogeneity.

Although postmodernist, post-structuralist, and some postcolonial thinkers stress the importance of social constructions, they have overemphasized the social divisions that separate working people from each other. In contrast, world-systems researchers emphasize social processes and social construction, yet they also show how conflicts between labor and capital express themselves through divisions within these global classes. Postmodernist and post-structuralist studies typically examine labor's fragmentation without reference to an integrated global class analysis.

Although postmodernist and post-structuralist schools focus on cultural conflict, they typically avoid considering how work and cultural conflicts are related. The interplay between economic inequality and cultural divisions is often left untouched, preventing scholars from explaining social movements and social transitions. Postmodernist and post-structuralist scholars see culture in relationship to patriarchy, racism, and postcolonial developments, but they generally fail to examine a global historical system. Rather, they see social relations as regional or national constructs that emerge within the context of specific colonial, postcolonial, or noncolonial arrangements.

In innovative multidisciplinary inquiry, which includes women's studies, African studies, social movements, and cultural studies, some social movement scholars have turned to historical analysis and gathered fresh empirical evidence on new movements. A whole body of literature now examines work relations, materialistic culture, cultural divides, and social movements.[1] In this broad literature, some feminists consider women's struggles about wage and nonwage work. Some social movement literature addresses welfare and immigrant rights issues.

Environmental scholars look at global social change issues, including social movements. But many environmentalists accept what we call the "radical globalization" framework. They maintain that a globalization steamroller is running across the planet, flattening biological and cultural diversity and paving the way for homogeneous commodified relations. For the "radical globalization" group, the commodification process is seen as strengthening the North's hold over the South and the rule of powerful, transnational global organizations over labor everywhere.

While we respect the political intentions of "radical global thinkers," there is less economic uniformity than they imagine. Although some workers find themselves producing goods on the global assembly line, many other workers live in areas with less economic investment. These thinkers may notice economic expansion in the North and in export enclaves, yet they fail to note the severe economic contraction that has affected many parts of the world. Granted, it is important to recognize processes of global integration, but there are problems with analyses that omit processes that disinvest, differentiate, and impoverish.

Disciplinary-based social movement theory typically fails to look at social movements within a historical, materialistic, world-economic, or global way. In disciplinary-bound social movement analyses, theoretical frameworks are often developed within an ahistorical or case-study context. The full context of social change is typically eliminated and the "movement organization" is separated from its social and historical context. In most cases, scholars treat movement categories as given. For example, they automatically reuse the category of the "women's movement" in different historical settings, perpetuating the notion that women are engaged in only a discrete set of political activities, denying that women's struggles can overlap with other kinds of issues and social groups. In many cases, social movements have not been subjected to a historical, relational analysis.

Once scholars sever movement organizations from the broad social context in which they have emerged, they then dissect internal movement processes and interactions, by discussing leadership approaches, various organizing strategies, the impact of bureaucratic tendencies, the ability to mobilize resources, and a host of other nonglobal, ahistorical, and nonrelational issues. There is little examination of how social movements develop in relation to each other and to the world-system as a whole.

In writings on social movements, we are often left with the picture that movements function in an autonomous way. However, when movements and protests emerge, they are shaped by multiple layers of conflicting relations that develop within a region and within the world-economy. And some of these conflicts reflect labor's struggles against firms, states, and sometimes even other laboring groups. As global scholars who study social movements work within the framework of a changing world-economy and its unequal patterns of chaotic development, they should always consider relationships between particular movements and the whole family of movements.[2]

THE STRENGTHS OF WORLD-ECONOMY STUDIES: THEORY AND METHOD

World-systems theory and method can be used to study how the modern world has changed, who has been affected by change, and who has been fighting for change. This theoretical framework also contributes to an identification of differentiated outcomes of these historical processes. No other literature explains why the world has changed in the ways that it has. And only world-systems literature shows how the world's integrated parts have changed in differentiated and unequal ways.

World-systems methodology differs from other research approaches because it is involved with studying the ever-changing modern world, which has exhibited both continuities and discontinuities. Time and place are key elements in world-economy research. The basic unit of analysis is the world, which has been integrated together by the world-economy. Spatial relations are considered in relationship to the three zones of the capitalist world-economy, which are spatial expressions of class relations. Temporal changes are followed by studying the historical system and its structures, long-term structural transitions of about 150 years in length, medium-term economic waves of expansion and contraction of about 50 years in length, and short-term and seasonal change.

Although world-economy scholars debate when capitalism began, many define capitalism as a historical system with its own natural history, with a beginning and an end. The dominant center of the system emerged during the collapse of Western European feudalism, and the Western European enterprises and states (later accompanied by elites in the United States and Japan) fueled capital accumulation by conquering and colonizing almost all of Latin America, Africa, and Asia between 1500 and the twentieth century. The global system expanded in long-term structural phases. These long-term bursts of unequal development brought new countries to hegemonic dominance and ushered in new patterns of global accumulation. Shorter periods of global expansion and contraction established these fairly fixed structures and served as the "breathing mechanism" of the global system.[3]

By 1950, firms, backed by powerful states, had incorporated almost all areas of the world into this class-based system. The world has been divided into the core (the rich countries that have conquered others), the periphery (the poorest countries that have almost always suffered from colonization and its cumulative impact), and the semiperiphery (which includes a small number of "middle-income" countries that may have experienced downward or upward mobility within the world-economy's hierarchy).

In recent years, an intense global class polarization has become more evident. Since 1970, the global pattern has changed in three notable ways: no new hegemonic power has emerged; economic expansion has been restricted to particular parts of the world; and for the first time a new cycle of economic expansion is not based on direct forms of (colonial) political rule by the core. In subsequent chapters, we will explore what these historical divergences may mean for people living on the planet.

In this study, we are using world-economy analysis to examine female and male workers and contemporary social movements. To do this, we went back to 1945 and traced developments in the post–World War II period, when the United States was the hegemonic power. Although we went back as far as 1945, we concentrated on the period since 1970, especially events in the last five years.

As we did our research, we employed historical and comparative methods. Gender and class relations are at the center of this study. We used a dialectical analysis to explore the network of gender and class relations and the contradictions expressed within them.

Studying global change requires extensive data gathering and analysis. The five-year process of considering changes in work, gender, and protest is only partly recorded in this book. We started by recognizing that our views of work and politics would affect our study. Intellectual openness about global working-class politics required extensive research, questioning, and historical and comparative analysis. It required us to step away from narrow political understandings, distance ourselves from predictable exhortations from social change publications, and establish a more independent way of identifying protests.

Our collective primary research included trips to study social movements in the United States, Western Europe, and Eastern Europe, as well as extended participatory action research on informal work, labor organizing, feminism, antiracism, and environmentalism. This activist research provided us with analytical skills that helped us approach social protest in new ways. Knowledge acquired from activist engagement, practical experience as social change professionals, and archival research helped guide our relational analysis of social movements. Eventually, our study of movements allowed us to assess movements and their relational connections to world-economic institutions, and not just according to given work site, gender, and ethnic identifications. This enabled us to see concrete connections and cross-overs between various movements, which was an important breakthrough in our research.[4]

Like other world-system scholars, we relied heavily on our analysis of others' published research. Just as we subjected our primary research to extensive analysis, we did the same for published studies. We supplemented our primary, secondary, and historical research with others' ground-level observations on changes in everyday life. Because we wanted to examine the last five years in considerable detail, we used many sources documenting social change processes to supplement other scholars' published research (which could be five to ten years out of date). Documentary filmmakers and activist feminists at international conferences, who are often five years ahead of most academicians, provided important ground-level evidence. Journalists acted as another set of eyes for us, providing up-to-date details about people and communities. Publications by activist and educational organizations and papers presented at professional meetings and international peace conferences were also helpful.

We used both deductive and inductive reasoning to identify crucial global changes. We also analyzed relations between dominant global institutions (businesses and states) and ground-level institutions (households, gender, and ethnicity), where working-class households organized home-based work, survival strategies, and political protests. Changing environmental contexts affected ground-level relationships, and working people often fought to improve the environment around them. Although we started our study with an understanding of the historical system of capitalism, we moved from the specific (e.g., women's nonwage work in the late twentieth-century United States) to the general (e.g., the basic structures and processes of the world-system and post-1990s global developments), and then back to the specific (e.g., the rise in U.S. immigrants' unionization efforts, and women's environmental movements throughout the world).

WORKING PEOPLE'S LIVES IN A GLOBAL, SYSTEMIC FRAMEWORK

In the global society, almost all people have been created as workers who receive pay for a small portion of the work they do. A very small group of people have controlled enough resources to get others to work for them. In this system, the hiring (and also previously enslaving) group, usually based in the rich countries, has often acquired its resources through inheritance. In global society, the bulk of the world's work is unpaid or worker-organized. In the rich countries of the global North, most of this unpaid and self-organized work is largely invisible, and most of the workers who do it are invisible, too. These workers are rarely acknowledged, even though the work they do indirectly sustains consumer culture. Labor's relations of interdependency have been largely hidden from public view by the household, a much ignored but central world-economic and gendered institution.

The states and businesses of the capitalist world-economy have created laboring households as the world's basic work unit. Labor also reproduces this work unit in its different ways. For example, it typically reproduces household patriarchy. Wage labor and less-visible nonwage work is organized through the household, a multidimensional work unit. In a systemic sense, "individual wage workers" and "individual unpaid workers" rarely actually exist. In fact, systemic forces often stamp out individualism, free expression, and self-fulfillment, except when individuality promotes consumerism, productivity increases, and corporate growth.

Individuals actually are organized as members of long-term, multigenerational households and occasionally as members of short-term, domestic survival networks. Over the multigenerational course of a household life cycle, most workers either contribute to or benefit from intrahousehold income and resource transfers. As will be shown, the world's women tend to contribute much more than they receive. If only one person is earning wages in a household at any given moment, for example, then that wage is stretched to meet the needs of perhaps five or even ten people. Only the richest workers in the North earn wages that can sustain an entire household of working people. But even these households supplement consumer purchases with some household work. Most of the world's workers receive individual-level wages or wages that are so low that wage-stretching covers very few necessities. Most workers survive and reproduce themselves by doing a lot of collective household work. Household "work units" generate their own supplemental income and they meet most of their own needs.

Household members have their social consciousness shaped by the household work unit, by its connections with other households, by their work at production sites, and by their connections with other groups of workers around the world. In the rich countries of the North, household members rarely acknowledge the connections between women and men in households, between workers in different ethnic groups, and between workers in imperial and postcolonial countries, North and South.

Systemic class relationships are expressed through a triad of polar oppositions—Black vs. White, South vs. North, and female vs. male—that simultaneously ties working households together and imposes divisive economic and political conditions on them. A small minority of the world's workers (about one-seventh of the world's population) is located in the wealthy countries of the core. Although these households constitute the world minority in population terms and often in ethnic terms, they constitute the dominant culture in global labor and hold considerable power. World-majority households, those that make up six-sevenths of the world's population and that collectively comprise a diverse ethnic majority, are located in the South. Although households in the North tend to rely heavily on wages, state transfers, and market consumption, low-wage households in the South rely heavily on their own income-generating capabilities. Of course, extensive labor migration takes place from the South to the North (as well as migration within these zones). This means that the North's laboring population increasingly consists of "world-majority" people, or people of color.

In global society, laboring people in the North and South are intimately connected through their different ties to wage labor and to paid and unpaid household work. These global relations are created by businesses and states, which are functional to capital accumulation in the core. Working people in the North and South also are intimately related through their various social movements, which can demonstrate labor's power on a world stage.

Although corporations profit from wage labor, corporations and worker households depend on paid labor *and* on the unpaid work of household members to sustain workers and maintain the system as a whole. But the largest profits are generated by workers in the South. Although they are paid next to nothing, workers there sustain themselves and the world-economy by doing tremendous amounts of unpaid and informal work.

Household members in the core have sometimes failed to appreciate the magnitude of global inequality or recognize that a direct relationship exists between well-being in the North and dire poverty in the South. Still, during the forty years after World War II, many households in North America and Western Europe became very disturbed by the brutal system of apartheid in South Africa, where a small White minority (less than 15 percent of the population) subjugated an ethnically diverse Black majority (about 85 percent of the population). The White minority used its control of the legal and economic system to obtain ownership of more than 85 percent of the most fertile land. The Black majority was left only with access to less than 15 percent of the country's poorest land. The system of apartheid also made it illegal for Black labor to vote, move from one location to another, live together as families, live in many parts of cities, set up shantytowns, travel without government ID cards, move from government-assigned "homeland" areas (*bantustans*) without permission, obtain jobs reserved for Whites, and earn decent wages.

Most workers around the world recognized that apartheid in South Africa was a terrible injustice, that it created severe inequality. But apartheid was not as atypical as many people imagine. In many respects, apartheid was a model of the global system of inequality that has existed for the last five hundred years. Like the Afrikaner minority, the North consists of less than 15 percent of the world population and demands the vast majority of the available economic and natural resources. Like the ethnically diverse "Black" majority in South Africa, the South is home to 85 percent of the world's population but claims only a fraction of the available economic and natural resources. The North, like the Afrikaner regime, has been able to maintain this unequal distribution of wealth because it controls powerful economic institutions (the International Monetary Fund, World Trade Organization, transnational corporations) and political institutions (strong states and their military forces, the Group of Seven, NATO). These organizations, like apartheid, ensure that the unequal distribution of resources and the system of global inequality remain intact.

Economic and political elites in the North insist that the world's vast majority of workers earn the lowest wages, work the longest hours, perform the most unpaid and informal work, receive the fewest benefits, live in the poorest conditions, obtain the most modest education, face the meanest states, and wield the least amount of economic or political power. The high profits generated in the South directly enrich corporations and indirectly sustain their employees in the North. Each and every day, workers in the North are endowed by workers in the South. It is not simply that households in the North purchase jeans produced by poorly paid workers overseas. The entire material basis of life in the North is endowed with the hard, underpaid, and unpaid work done by the world's economically subjugated majority.

Commercial life shapes culture, as globalization and post-structuralist scholars emphasize. Household members in the North have been encouraged to be introspective, assume likable identities, develop their personalities (often with the assistance of expensive therapists), and explore their "individual" potential. But as income and state benefits declined for core workers after 1970, it became difficult for middle-class workers to realize commercialized dreams and individualistic aspirations. Materialistic dreams never had been realized in any sustained way by poorer worker households in the North. Today, during the limited expansion of the world-economy, an even smaller proportion of the core's working households will be able to realize their material and cultural expectations.

Global corporations and states in the core have worked for five hundred years to ensure that households in the South would toil for little or no pay. This system has allowed corporations to pay working-class households in the North much higher wages and to distance the world's high-paid worker minority from the low-paid worker majority. But while global elites have divided global workers, the North–South labor divide will not last forever, particularly if free-thinking workers visualize their connections with other workers, change their behavior, and transform the relations between them.

The growing global gap between rich and poor affects relationships between households that depend heavily on wage income and state benefits in the core and households that depend primarily on nonwage income in the periphery. Wages in the periphery usually do not even cover the cost of maintaining one household member. Given the fact that wages and state benefits have declined in the South, more than half of the income that worker households receive is generated by work that is self-organized by employed and unemployed household members. This compares sharply with middle-class worker households in the core, where workers have come to expect that 75 to 80 percent of their household's needs will be provided by wages and state benefits.

The few households that work for wages in the periphery have helped capitalists intensify global production. But most worker households in the periphery have been marginalized and excluded from wage work. Because capitalist firms in the core are intensifying development in the core, they need fewer workers in the periphery. So employers may instead recruit workers from the semiperiphery and from the core's internal "Third World colonies." If corporations draw on labor from households in the core, labor in the North may become even more exploited, while labor in the South, which has long sustained the core, may be marginalized. This kind of global change could create considerable disorder.

Global class stratification has meant that women also have joined with people of color in the South to help sustain White households in the North. Although women comprise 50 percent of the population, they have been socially constructed as highly productive labor, like people of color in the core and workers in the South. Women do over two-thirds of the world's work, most of it low-paid or unpaid. Because women have done almost all of the household work, in addition to wage labor and informal work, they work from sixteen to eighteen hours a day, from the time they get up to the time they go to sleep. Most men in the North and South have not appreciated this aspect of global inequality.

Although the global redistribution of wages is concealed and mediated by capital, people of color and women workers in the world-economy indirectly work "for" the North's high-paid, mostly male laborers and their household-based work units. In much the same way that the low-paid and unpaid work done by peripheral households sustains middle-class and wealthy households in the North, people of color in the core help sustain White families living on the other side of town. In much the same abstract or indirect way, female-headed households sustain male-headed households that live next door, whether male-headed work units are in the periphery or core. Male laborers have come to view their entitlement to high wages and political power as "natural," that they should be paid more than the world's majority. But if and when wage workers recognize that the modern world is socially manufactured by wage and nonwage workers alike, by women and men, Blacks and Whites in the North and South, will they replace assumptions about the "natural superiority" of a few workers with demands for greater equity for all?

Many female workers in the South have begun to question the multilayered structure of inequality in the world-system. They have been joined by female workers around the world, who have been pressed into service by the global system in recent years. Whether they live in the South or North, women have sustained worker households and the rich countries of the North. This means that the underpaid labor and unpaid work done by most women have made it possible for the structure of global inequality to remain intact. The system has socially segregated workers by ethnicity, gender, and geography. This has divided workers culturally and politically. Yet because workers also have shared multidimensional identities, it has become possible for workers to construct overlapping movements. Women's paid and unpaid work has actually increased as a result of declining global wages, state benefits, and subsidies. But because their work burden has grown, women have emerged as strong leaders of overlapping global movements for social change.

THE HISTORICAL REPRODUCTION OF
GLOBAL CLASS RELATIONSHIPS

In the global system of capitalism, both the ruling class (capital) and the working class (labor) are created and reproduced on a global scale. However, most scholars fail to explore class relationships as global or as two-sided and hierarchical (with both exploiters and exploited). Globalization literature's "big-tent" approach has tended to blur the global class divide. For example, certain conservative, liberal, and radical globalization scholars argue that the organization of global corporations, banks, and transnational agencies can lead to real development for all areas of the world and not just widespread underdevelopment for most working people.

Although globalization scholars place emphasis on the creation of a transnational capitalist-class and transnational ruling-class organizations, they often start their analysis with events that mark new stages of intercapitalist and trans-state cooperation. These new moments of cooperation often are abstracted from historical processes and from the cross-generational, cyclical, and secular development of the creation of global capital. Organizations are stressed, and these are seen at one moment in time. Scholars often do not understand how ruling elites are reproduced in the long run through households, elite schools, intermarriage, and monopolistic networks.

Although they usually define capital as a global class, globalization scholars typically do not see that labor is also a global class. Instead, labor is often studied within regional or national contexts. In most radical globalization analyses of labor's exploitation, the study of labor is often limited to wage laborers from specific ethnic groups who work on the global assembly line within one or two branches of industry. By defining labor as simply the group that appears on the factory floor at a particular moment in time, globalization scholars usually only recognize working-class protests that relate to factory-floor and union-organizing issues. Other issues relating to the reproduction of households and to the rise of working-class protests tend to be erased from view.

Although world-systems analysis has invited scholars to study the formation of the global laboring class in relation to global capital,[5] most world-systems scholars have failed to employ and develop the household as the basic reproduction unit for each global class. Although domestic labor and household scholars began to examine how labor was reproduced during the 1970s and 1980s, many critical thinkers have been reluctant to pursue this research because postmodernist and some feminist scholars argued that it did not stress resistance enough. But continued work in this area is crucial if work and protest are to be understood in a comprehensive way.

Just as global capital has reproduced itself through households and social networks, global labor also reproduces itself through households and social networks. And just as the global ruling class includes more than the people who currently control and run capitalist enterprises, the global laboring class includes not just people who work on the assembly line or in other paid employment. Global capital includes all those who once accumulated, are accumulating, and are being prepared to accumulate, or who sustain others who have, are, or may accumulate. Likewise, global labor includes all those who once worked for wages, are working for wages, may work for wages, or sustain others who once labored, are laboring, or may eventually labor. The reproduction of global class relationships has meant that people have been cultivated to fit into the work-centered class system. At this historical moment, scholars should ask both how class relations are being reproduced and whether the reproduction of these class relations is being disrupted, subverted, and overturned. It is only by understanding the holistic changes in working-class reproduction that contemporary labor struggles can be fully appreciated.

In summary, global labor includes all members of the world's working class. Because workers' wages rarely cover the full cost of maintaining workers and their multigenerational households (even in the core), unemployed working people (including youth, people in their middle years, and elders) all help sustain wage laborers and other household members through their nonwage work and income transfers. Global labor is comprised of the whole pool of laboring people who will either work as wage laborers at some point in their lives or who will help reproduce wage laborers by supplementing their wages with nonwage income, goods, and/or services.

Global labor is a multigenerational class, just like global capital. Global labor's basic unit—the laboring household—is reproduced over an extended period of time, usually fifty to seventy-five years. In this sense, global labor is far larger than the number of people currently earning wages, which is the definition commonly provided by most scholars. Global labor is also larger than the group of people who have worked for wages at some point in their lives. Some members of laboring households never work for wages themselves. Rather, they help sustain household members who are working or may eventually work for wages by doing nonwage work (such as providing child care and elder care, cooking food, and remaking clothes, or engaging in petty-producing).

In the global labor class, household members have diverse responsibilities at any given moment. If working people help to reproduce actual or potential wage laborers for capitalist producers, they form part of the global labor class. In some historical circumstances, all household members may be called upon to do wage labor for some part of their lives. But today, many household members (especially in low-income areas) engage in wage labor for only short or sporadic periods of their lives, and some never are brought directly into capitalist wage labor. During the present period, a large portion of global labor consists of people who may never work for business or the state. We expect that growing numbers of nonwage workers will choose to step out of the system on their own. If workers are expelled from the world-economy, then they will have to reproduce themselves through new family, work, and community arrangements.

In summary, global labor consists of all working-class people who, over the multigenerational household life cycle, engage in at least one of these activities: sustain other potential and actual wage-laborers through nonwage contributions, work for wages within a capitalist production unit, or rely on another household member's wage labor for a portion of their lives. Some members of the global labor class have worked for wages at some point of their lives, and others have relied on wages provided by other members of the unit. Global labor consists of the huge pool of the world's working people who have either cycled through wage employment or have helped others work for wages by supporting them with unpaid and self-organized work. This supplementary and crucial nonwage work has created and sustained the system's full-time, part-time, and temporary wage workers.

The global organization of production is difficult to discern because household work units almost always overlap with emotional, family units. The work that families do for "love" is mixed up with the unpaid and low-paid self-organized work that households undertake to sustain themselves. This work also maintains the global system of inequality. Because the work people do crosses the boundaries set by emotional attachment and economic necessity, by private firms and public institutions, by formal and informal networks, by neighbors and intimates, it has been difficult to appreciate the totality of work and the importance of households.

Within a global capitalist division of labor, the distinction between private and public is not only socially created, but it became rearranged to such an extent that it is difficult for workers to appreciate the fact that public and private spheres are inextricably joined. It was not until women began addressing these issues that labor struggles acquired more diverse, comprehensive strategies, which together fully addressed the multiple dimensions of the global, capitalist division of labor.[6] Feminist scholarship shows that laboring women are an integral part of global labor, whether they bring in wages, receive state transfers that contribute to the household income pool, or do nonwage work that provides in-kind and monetary income.

To compete in an anarchic world-economy, firms and states consciously and unconsciously reshape households and their work activities. A central part of class struggle in rich and poor zones relates to household makeup, the extent of household co-residentiality, and the proportion of wage and nonwage work. In the contemporary world-economy, the separation between adult males and adult females is an integral part of the restructuring of work environments.

Some wage and nonwage work is being degraded or transformed, and some is becoming obsolete. Although the world-system has provided the basic motor of these changes, laboring people around the world are now taking major steps to direct development and to shape social and economic processes of household, community, and regional reproduction. As labor's wage and nonwage work environment is changing in dramatic ways, so, too, are working people's survival strategies, political struggles, and the ways that social movements and alternative institutions may collide, overlap, or unite.

As worldwide capitalist relations assume both established and new directions, and as the ties between the North and parts of the South become redefined as part of these processes, work structures will become recast in both formal and informal realms. We are primarily interested here in the ways that groups of laboring people respond to and organize against the new global frontiers of work, identifying alternative ways of economic and political life. To begin this process, we turn to the different kinds of work that people do to survive.

NOTES

1. For multidisciplinary studies that explore the historical, heterogeneous, institutional, and extra-institutional roots of contemporary movements, refer to: Susan Eckstein, ed., *Power and Protest: Latin American Social Movements* (Berkeley: University of California Press, 1989); Sonia E. Alvarez and Arturo Escober, eds., *The Making of Social Movements in Latin America* (Boulder, Colo.: Westview Press, 1992).

2. According to Wallerstein, the "family of anti-systemic forces must move at many speeds in constant reformulation of the tactical priorities . . . a coherent, nonunified [multi-front] family of forces can only emerge if each group has a democratic structure." Immanuel Wallerstein, *After Liberalism* (New York: New Press, 1995), 249.

See also Immanuel Wallerstein, *Utopistics: Or Historical Choices for the Twenty-First Century* (New York: New Press, 1998).

For a historical analysis of the "worldwide family of anti-systemic movements," see Giovanni Arrighi, Terence K. Hopkins, and Immanuel Wallerstein, *Anti-Systemic Movements* (London: Verso, 1989), 115.

3. An analysis of recurring cycles of expansion and contraction suggests that it is as if we live inside a historically bounded, living system. This global system breathes in a huge gulp of air every twenty or twenty-five years, and then, in a similar period of time, it breathes old air out. Cycles of expansion and contraction can be seen as "the breathing mechanism of the capitalist organism, inhaling the purifying oxygen and exhaling poisonous waste" (p. 34). Global recessions expel economic inefficiencies, and economic expansions reallocate capitalist resources and increase global accumulation. Immanuel Wallerstein, *Historical Capitalism with Capitalist Civilization* (London: Verso, 1996).

4. As we went through the process of studying work, gender, and politics, we increasingly identified, as Tarrow does, more instances of the "ferocious, uncontrolled and widely diffused aspects" of social movements. But unlike Tarrow, we rarely felt that these movements were "ephemeral" or capable of being "institutionalized" by the system. Sidney Tarrow, *Power in Movement: Social Movements and Contentious Politics* (Cambridge: Cambridge University Press, 1998), 210.

5. The idea of a global continuum of laboring households is presented in Terence K. Hopkins and Immanuel Wallerstein, and Working Group Members, "Patterns of the Development of the Modern World-System," *Review* 1, no. 2 (Fall 1977): 111–145. In this formulation, laboring households that exhibit a growing, established reliance on wage income are undergoing increased proletarianization. As areas of the world were incorporated within the capitalist world-economy, and as capitalist development proceeded over four to five centuries, households faced increasing levels of proletarianization.

As we did our research, we thought more about the reverse of the process of proletarianization: deproletarianization. We began to posit that if laboring households exhibited an established and ongoing drop in their reliance on wage income (and on middle-class entitlement transfers, or necessary, survival-related income transfers), then these households would be undergoing deproletarianization. The formulation of proletarianization in "Patterns of Development" shaped our thinking about the formation, de-formation, and transformation of global labor.

6. As we decided how to study changes in work, gender, and protest, we were guided by the analysis of the world-economy's institutions in Immanuel Wallerstein, "The States in the Institutional Vortex of the Capitalist World-Economy," *International Social Science Journal*, UNESCO, 32, no. 4 (1980): 743–751. According to this formulation, the world-economy

has four basic institutions: classes/capitalist firms, states, ethnic groups, and households. We have added gender/age to this list. We saw this set of multilayered, interpenetrating institutional relationships as upholding the capitalist world-economy. For us, if these institutions supported the world-system, then antisystemic movements must destabilize the system by attacking these institutions. Our study of changes in work, gender relations, and social movements followed from our initial analysis of global institutions.

Part II

WORKER HOUSEHOLDS, BUSINESSES, AND STATES

Households enlist all their members to survive.

Part II

WORKER HOUSEHOLDS, BUSINESSES, AND STATES

Chapter 2

The Meaning of Work

When most people think of "work," they imagine men with paid jobs. But this is the narrowest possible conception of work. What is left out of this picture is the fact that different kinds of people work, not just men, and they do different kinds of work. Actually, women do most of the world's work, and much of it is unpaid. Neglected, too, is the work done by children, youth, elders, and unemployed men, much of it unpaid and unappreciated. Work cannot be understood without examining how gender is embedded in all social relations. Furthermore, workers' protest cannot be understood without appreciating the gender-based organization of paid and unpaid work.

Work is hard. Everybody works. People work hard at different things to survive. And how people work shapes the ways they participate in politics.

The world of work is vast and varied. But in general, people do four different kinds of work. Some of the work people do helps them *subsist* as workers. Some of it involves *sharing* with others. Some of it helps them earn money on their own account, by being *enterprising*. And some of it involves working for others, finding jobs that pay *wages*. The range of activities that comprise the contemporary world of work can be illustrated by a brief description of each kind of work.

To subsist as workers, people work together. They prepare meals, raise children, wash clothes, attend school, and care for their parents. Take the siblings in the Mitchell family. Audrey, Mildred, and Charles Mitchell care for their ninety-five-year-old mother, Eldora, in Durham, North Carolina, with help from Sheila Parker, Charles Mitchell's girlfriend. "Some of my friends say they admire what I'm doing," Charles says. "I say, 'Well, this is mom. I don't have but one.' She brought me up and looked after me. I feel I should do the same. I feel everybody should."[1]

This kind of work is common in the United States, where family members provide 80 percent of all home care for the elderly.[2] And it is even more prevalent in other countries, where responsibility for children and parents falls almost entirely on family and friends.

Throughout much of the world, people in households work hard to meet basic subsistence needs. They draw water and cultivate crops, even when they live in cities. Urban gardeners, for example, supplied 20 percent of the diet for people living in African cities and 90 percent of the vegetables consumed in Chinese cities.[3] Women and men also tend animals and hew firewood. "We have some shelter, some food. And now we are chopping wood so we don't die from the cold," Sedia Nuspahic, a resident of Bihac, Bosnia-Herzegovina, told reporters as she gathered wood in the fall of 1996.[4]

The Mitchell siblings and Sedia Nuspahic do this kind of work for themselves, for family and friends, without compensation, to subsist as workers, to survive as families.

Women and men also do another kind of work. They share, swap, and barter with relatives, friends, and neighbors. And they transfer, give, and bequeath goods, property, services, and money to other household members and people in the community.

Around the world it is common practice to lend a hand.[5] In Sedia Nuspahic's case, three family friends helped her split the five hundred cubic feet of wood she needed to warm her two-room apartment for the winter.[6] For Lazare Koffi, a tailor who owns a clothing business in Abidjan, Ivory Coast, sharing with others is a social obligation. "I pay my rent, the lease for my shop, and my electricity," he reports. "Whatever is left over, I must give to my family. Our traditions require us to help out as much as we can."[7]

In the same spirit, Dean Moffett, a guidance counselor in Maumee, Ohio, buys tuition credits so that his grandchildren, Ali and Jacob Haubner, can afford to attend college when they grow up.[8] It also works the other way around. Felipe Morales, a Mexico City resident, relies on the $100–200 that his son sends him each month from New York City, where he works in construction.[9] People share with family and friends because their mutual survival depends, in part, on cooperation, goodwill, and the exchange of scarce resources.

Moreover, people rent rooms and repair houses, make and recycle goods, and sell goods and services from their homes or vend them on the streets, for domestic and sometimes even foreign markets. Women and men organize work on their own initiative all over the world. The diverse character of this enterprising work can be illustrated with examples from New York City.

In some New York City neighborhoods, 80 percent of the homes have been "unlawfully subdivided" so that homeowners can rent out rooms.[10] Gilberto Medina, for instance, rents out three cubicles in his basement, each for $70 a week, so he can help pay off his family's mortgage.[11] Other homeowners have subdivided their dwellings into multiple apartments and makeshift flats. Some do the remodeling themselves; others hire independent construction workers to do the job, many of them immigrants from places like Bangladesh.[12]

Homes can not only provide income from rent, they can also be a place to make goods and provide services. Antonia Rivas made papusas, tamales, and sweetbreads and served them to customers in her home before she opened a restaurant.[13] Leida

Fermin bought four used sewing machines and turned her small apartment into a garment factory, making party dresses for young girls.[14] Many residents have turned their homes into makeshift laundries, pharmacies, or bodegas, while others arranged marriages or extracted teeth.[15] Gilberto Cordova, for example, an unlicensed dental technician, treated more than one thousand patients in his home, extracting teeth at a fraction of the cost of a licensed dentist.[16]

Many of the goods produced at home are sold at flea markets and farmer's markets. And vendors sell wares they make or purchase on the streets from carts and makeshift stalls.[17] Although street vending is not as common as it once was, it persists despite determined efforts by city officials to restrict, regulate, and prohibit it. But the streets are still a place where people work in large numbers, sometimes as urban recyclers. Juanita Rosario, her husband, Cesar Diaz, and their eight children scour the streets for cans, bottles, and newspapers that they redeem at the We Can recycling center, earning $300–400 a week from their efforts.[18] Tonya White, meanwhile, shifts through neighbors' trash and local garbage dumps—a practice called "junking"—for items that she can sell through consignment shops, which pay her 70 percent of any sale. "There's so many people looking through the garbage, it's hard to find anything good," she complains.[19]

Some of the goods produced by enterprising workers even find their way to foreign markets. Bargain hunters from the United States and Asia comb flea markets for used blue jeans, leather jackets, and rock-and-roll memorabilia, which are sold to markets in Asia. Nat and Lucky Wongchaiwat bought 10,000 pairs of used jeans from flea markets and local dealers to supply their store in Bangkok.[20] Buyers for Japanese markets ship 100,000 pairs a month.

Meanwhile, out in the New York City suburbs, Hank Dam traps raccoons, which are thriving.[21] He sells the carcasses for $3 each to outdoorsmen and Southerners who eat raccoon meat and peddles the pelts to fur merchants, who ship them to markets in Russia and China. When the economic crisis in Russia recently disrupted the fur market, the price for raccoon pelts dropped from $27 to $16.

In New York City, it is evident that women and men organize diverse kinds of work on their own initiative. Although the amount of enterprising work they do is substantial, it is even more common elsewhere. In Latin American cities, more people work for themselves than are employed by licensed businesses and government agencies.[22] In Africa, South Asia, and the former Soviet Union, much if not most of the work being done is organized by enterprising workers themselves.

This kind of work is called different things. In New York, immigrants from El Salvador describe this work, much of it illegal, as *bajo del agua* or "underwater" work.[23] In Italy, economists describe it as *l' economic sommersa* or the "submerged economy."[24] Cubans describe self-organized work as *inventando* or "inventing."[25] Some economists describe it as the "self-service," "underground," "clandestine," or "informal economy," while others call it the "black market."[26] But whatever the name given to enterprising work, people organize it to obtain the money they need, purchase the goods and services they cannot make themselves or obtain from family and friends, and pay the fares, fees, and taxes that governments everywhere demand.

Invisible Work and the State

Official government attitudes toward self-organized, enterprising work vary enormously, ranging from open hostility to indifference. In communist countries, officials outlawed and long suppressed enterprising work, regarding it as proto-capitalist and therefore inimical to the construction of a socialist state. That view changed with the fall of communist governments in the Soviet Union and Eastern Europe. As a result, enterprising work there has flourished, as it has with the adoption of market reforms in residual communist countries, such as China, Vietnam, and Cuba. However, communist officials still view this work with suspicion. In China, officials recently banned door-to-door sales, a measure that affected 2.6 million people who pounded on doors for a living.[27]

In the United States, by contrast, the attitude and policy of federal government officials varies, depending on the work's legal and tax status. The attitude of local government officials, who more closely monitor and police enterprising work, also varies. In New York, for instance, city officials send inspectors to check houses for occupancy and rental-code violations and for the unlicensed production of goods or provision of services. These efforts pose a threat to a homeowner like Gilberto Medina, a home-based seamstress like Leida Fermin, a domestic restaurateur like Antonio Rivas, and an unlicensed dentist like Gilberto Cordova. Officials have also taken a dim view of raccoon trapper Hank Dam, arguing that trapping is "inhumane," and they have threatened to adopt prohibitive legislation. City officials have instructed police to cite unlicensed vendors and enforce antiloitering, panhandling, and recycling ordinances, which prohibit scavengers and "junkers" from searching through trash or collecting from curbside recycling bins. Local, state, and federal officials have also outlawed a wide range of enterprising activities, particularly those involving the sale of drugs and sex, assault, and theft. They have also used tax inspectors to assist police investigations of unlicensed or illegal activities in workers' homes and on the streets. The irony of this is that state officials often invite low-income workers to be more self-reliant and enterprising, to "pull themselves up by their own bootstraps," while at the same time doing everything possible to tie workers' bootstraps in knots.[28]

In Third World countries, the official view may be changing. Some economists now argue that the informal economy "is one of the most socially stabilizing factors in Latin America," largely because it provides work in a setting where jobs in the formal sector are scarce.[29] "You can't afford to crack down on these people," Peruvian economist Hernando de Soto has argued. "They are in the informal sector because they have no choice. I think it's safe to say that if you didn't have the informals, you would have riots in the streets."[30]

The work people organize for themselves in the "underwater," "submerged," "informal," or, as we prefer, "enterprising economy" is distinct from the kind of work people do for others, for pay. Wage work in the "formal" or wage-based economy is the work women and men perform for landlords, owners, employers, corporations, and governments. This is the kind of "work" most people imagine when they think about work. People work for others to obtain the wages and salaries that "jobs" in the "labor force" provide. The work people do for others is also extremely diverse. The U.S. Department of Labor lists dozens of general work categories and thousands of "occupations" in the labor force. The list keeps growing because employers commonly divide and subdivide tasks, to increase the efficiency of the technical division of labor in the workshop, or what the economist Adam Smith long ago called the "division of labor." Since he wrote at the end of the eighteenth century, the social division of labor, which includes the technical division of labor, in the wage-based economy has grown more and more complex.

People perform all of the tasks for others that they do for themselves, and many others besides. They cultivate, husband, mine, manufacture, sell, service, rent, repair, exchange, transport, and distribute goods, services, people, and products on a vast scale, across the globe. Many of these activities would be impossible for families, communities, even whole countries to do on their own. The effort to put men on the moon, for example, enlisted the energies and resources of so many skilled people across the United States and was an enterprise so vast, complex, and expensive that no other country has ever tried to duplicate it. As a result, the world of work now ranges from the prosaic to the interplanetary. It includes the search for firewood and the exploration of outer space. It ranges from the work women, men, girls, and boys do for themselves, for family and friends, without any monetary compensation, to the work people do for others, for pay. Most people do each kind of work, at some point in the lives. And some people work at all of them. Cindy Funderbunk, a resident of Florien, Louisiana, tends chickens and cows on her farm, sells beauty products out of her home, and peddles them door-to-door. She drives a school bus for the district, and she shares her income from her many work tasks with her college-bound daughters.[31] She works across the spectrum, from subsistence, to sharing, to enterprising, to wage work on a daily basis. This is not unusual. It is common practice for hundreds of millions of people like her around the world.

A century ago, working people did a lot of the first three kinds of work, what might collectively be called "improvising work," and a little of the last, what we will call "wage work." In global terms, wage work was relatively scarce, located as it was primarily in the urban manufacturing centers of western Europe and North America. It was difficult then for most workers, particularly women and African Americans, to obtain wage work.[32] Since then, however, wage work has become more widely available around the world. More and more working people have acquired access to it. In recent years, women's access to wage work has increased dramatically.[33] So today, working people, especially women, do more wage work, though, of course, many continue to do improvising work. Although more people today work for wages than they did a century ago, few people subsist, survive, or thrive on wages alone. Indeed, the number of people who survive only on wages, using their income from wages to purchase all the goods and services they need so that they do not have to perform any subsistence tasks, is extremely small. As one man in Cuba remarked, "Here, no one lives on their salaries alone."[34] And this is true generally, not only in Cuba but throughout most of the world. "Even today, over the world as a whole, most work takes place outside of regular jobs," sociologists Chris and Charles Tilly argue.[35] We wholeheartedly concur.[36]

HOUSEHOLD SURVIVAL AND OPPRESSION

People do not live by wage work alone. Nor do they typically work alone. Most people live in households, which join together different workers and separate kinds of work. The household is the organizational unit for working people the world over. In households, workers reproduce and sustain themselves.

Of course, many of these households do not center around the male household or a married couple. Female-headed households are on the rise almost everywhere. The household is an institution of the world-economy, an institution created by firms, states, and workers themselves. One of the main ways that many laboring men have shaped household structures is by insisting that household members accept patriarchal authority, which is enforced by male violence.

In this book, we will use both *households* and *families* to describe the groups that people organize to survive collectively, though we prefer the term *households*, because it is an economic unit of survival and because it is more inclusive.[37] The *family*, which suggests a kin group consisting of people related by marriage or blood, is fairly restricted. Sometimes it includes people who do not carry out survival and social reproduction strategies together for an extended period of time. Nor does the *family* easily include intimate groups that are made up of members not related by marriage. Roommates, unmarried partners, and friends are not comfortably included in discussions of "family." Nor does the common definition of *family* adequately capture the enormously diverse character of household groups around the world or identify their changing structures. Some families, for example, draw members only from one or two generations, while others have three or more generations living together. Some families average two to four members, others have as many as twenty. Some families are headed by men, others by women, some by straight or gay unmarried couples, and others by single women.[38] And these diverse arrangements are everywhere changing. "The idea that the family is a stable and cohesive unit in which the father serves as economic provider and mother serves as emotional care giver is a myth," argues Judith Bruce, a researcher who has studied households around the world for the Population Council. "The reality is that trends like unwed motherhood, rising divorce rates, smaller households, and the feminization of poverty are not unique to America but are occurring worldwide."[39]

It is important to recognize that "households are not isolated entities but rely instead on a social constellation of relatives, friends, and neighbors to get and provide help and favors on a daily basis and during emergencies."[40] Because the term *household* can more easily accommodate the diverse character and changing structure of intimate worker groups, we prefer it to the *family* as a descriptive construct.

People in households typically work hard at different things. They pool and redistribute tasks, resources, and income from household members, other households, neighboring communities, and the state to make collective ends meet. The ability to pool and redistribute resources and income, which helps household members survive, is a major reason, though not the only one, why people organize their lives in small groups. For the last five hundred years, the institutions of the world-economy have smothered communities as a survival unit and tried to replace them with single households. But while households everywhere distribute tasks and redistribute pooled resources, in most cases they do not do so equitably.

In their study of households in seventeen countries around the world, the Population Council found that women tended to work longer hours than men, both at home and in paid employment.[41] Nowhere did men provide as much child care as women. They also found that women usually contributed a larger share of their income to the household than men, while men kept a greater percentage of income for their own personal use.[42]

In Mexico, for example, economists found that women contributed 100 percent of their earnings to the family budget, while men contributed only 75 percent of theirs. "It is not uncommon for children's nutrition to deteriorate while wrist watches, radios, and bicycles are acquired by adult male household members," the World Bank reported.[43]

Although households may redistribute pooled income unequally, they are still redistributive. Some scholars, like Kathryn Ward, have argued that the household is not a useful concept because researchers who use it "ignore inequality between women and men *in* their households as well as in the economy."[44] But the household is still a useful concept, so long as it is understood that households redistribute pooled income, but do so unequally, and that their redistributive patterns are shaped by the hierarchical gender and age patterns of the global society and of households in different social, cultural, and economic settings.[45]

States also play an important role for working people the world over. Like households, states pool and redistribute resources and income. They collect revenues from workers, employers, and other sources, then redistribute revenue as benefits to different groups, working households among them. Most readers in the United States are familiar with "welfare" and other "poverty" programs that distribute resources, income, and benefits to poor workers. But readers may be less familiar with the benefits provided to farmers, soldiers and veterans, students, homeowners, investors, and elderly workers (not to mention wealthy people and corporations). The benefits provided to these groups dwarf benefits granted to the poor. And like households, governments in the United States and elsewhere do not redistribute pooled income equitably, though some do so in a more equitable fashion than others. Still, the benefits provided by states to workers can be significant, even where they are unequally given.

Around the world, people work hard at different things. Their individual efforts are assisted by household members, friends, and neighbors, as well as by states, which redistribute pooled resources. All this together makes it possible for workers to survive, and sometimes even thrive, economically. But in most cases, men have prevented the emergence of household equality and have instead insisted on the maintenance of household patriarchy and inequality.

THE SOCIAL MEANINGS OF WAGE AND NONWAGE WORK

Although women and men work hard at many tasks, the work they do has different social meanings. Some of this work is privileged and celebrated, while much of it is ignored or demeaned. The particular meaning of work is shaped decisively by three things: (1) Who organizes the work? (2) Who does the work? and (3) How is it rewarded or compensated?

When work is organized by employers (landlords, businesses, corporations, or governments), and when it is rewarded with monetary wages, it is relatively privileged. Accordingly, wage work is often seen as the only kind of "real" work. But when work is done for oneself, for family, or for friends; when effort is rewarded with thanks or with payments in kind or in cash, then it is typically ignored or demeaned by dominant institutions and groups, and sometimes even criminalized by governments. Nonwage work is greatly undervalued and those who do it are deprecated. But nonwage work supports the entire global system of wage work.

This unequal treatment of wage and nonwage work is true even for the same general type of work activity. Caring for a child, baby-sitting for a friend, or providing day care for your neighbors are common practices. In 1987, 75 percent of children in the United States were cared for in this fashion.[46] But none of this effort is regarded as "work" or treated as a "job," by employers, the state, and often men, even if it is hard, consumes long hours, or provides resources or income to workers. Yet if this same task is performed for an employer, at Kindercare or Head Start, and is regulated and taxed by government officials, it is regarded by society as "work" because it contributes to income and profits and enlarges the "Gross National Product."[47] Not only is nonwage work excluded from the social ledger, economists object even to suggestions that nonwage work be included in any public account of work. Some economists and legislators say that "there is no sensible way to attach a price tag to unremunerated work, and that doing so would compromise the integrity of economic statistics by freighting them with political assumptions."[48]

The social meaning of work is also significantly shaped by who does the work. When work is done by a woman, it has been assigned a different social meaning by dominant institutions and actors than it does when the identical task is performed by a man. This unequal treatment—of neglect and preference—can even be expressed in numerical terms. Economists regularly measure the fact that a woman, working in the U.S. labor force, is paid, on average, less than 75 percent as much as a man for the same job.[49]

But numbers alone cannot adequately describe the different values attributed to work. If a poor woman receives government assistance, the work she does to care for her children is not only devalued but demeaned. Carol Gagnon, who received welfare to help care for her seven-year-old daughter, began shopping at midnight to avoid abusive shoppers who yelled at her when she used food stamps to pay for her groceries. "There's so much more [yelling] now, I've started going [shopping] in the middle of the night," she said. "We already have very little self-esteem, so the last thing we need is to have the country turn around and point the finger at us and say we're the problem . . . suddenly we're responsible for everything from schools to the deficit. It's like ethnic cleansing. That's what it feels like."[50]

Even William Julius Wilson, a sociologist sympathetic to the plight of poor women, describes them as part of a "nonworking class."[51] He argues that they are poor because there is no "work" for them to do. "For the first time in the twentieth century," he says, "most adults in many inner-city ghetto neighborhoods are *not working* in a typical week [emphasis added]."[52]

Of course, by this Wilson means that they are not working for others, for wages. This may be true. But this does not also mean that the poor do not work. They do. They just do so for themselves, for family and friends. That even a sympathetic scholar like Wilson could suggest that they do not "work" shows just how impoverished, how narrow the vocabulary of work has become.

Still, we agree with Wilson that many urban people are poor because income from wages and, more recently, state benefits have declined. This is a problem not only for the urban poor in American ghettos but for workers the world over. It is not that workers don't work "when [wage] work disappears," to use Wilson's phrase, but that workers work harder at other things when this occurs, though they may work in ways that are not commonly regarded as legitimate, valuable, or meaningful.

The social meaning of work is shaped not only by gender, ethnicity, and class but by age. Work done by children has a different social meaning than it does when performed by adults. In many countries, governments prohibit, discourage, or regulate work when it is done by children but not when the same tasks are done by adults.

The social meanings and values assigned to work, which are often associated with gender, class, ethnicity, and age—are the product of social and historical developments going back a long way. These meanings also vary considerably from one setting to the next. The social value of work done by women in many countries is measurably less than it is in Western Europe and North America. In some places it is valued even less than that of male children. In Afghanistan, for instance, the Taliban government prohibits, discourages, and outlaws work done by adult women, while it permits work done by male children.

The widely held view that wage work is significantly different and more important than improvising (nonwage) work is counterintuitive. After all, both kinds of work can be equally difficult and consume great amounts of time. But while most workers know instinctively that different kinds of work may be equally hard, they, too, may be reluctant to equate the work they do for employers in the paid labor force with the work they organize themselves. They tend to privilege wage labor because the income they receive from employment gives them a kind of power in the market that most other kinds of work cannot provide. And access to employment and wages confers both status and power to people who obtain them. As Nobel Prize–winning economist Amartya Sen has pointed out, men's institutionalized access to employment and wages increased their bargaining power with women and other household members. The bargaining power given to men by their wages explains, in part, why households tend to distribute pooled income and resources unequally, typically to men's advantage.[53]

We recognize that work has different social meanings, not only for employers, investors, government officials, and economists, but also for workers. So we think it important to view work in its entirety and bridge the social divides between different kinds of work. It is essential that we examine work in its entirety and not just focus on its socially privileged and paid variety, for five related reasons.

First, much of the work people do in their lives is not paid. To ignore the unpaid work they do is to discount workers' work lives, neglect their strenuous efforts, and ignore their significant achievements. It is important to recognize workers' "work ethic" and appreciate their capacity for initiative, self-reliance, and cooperation.

Second, workers do not live by wage work alone. The work they do outside the paid labor force helps workers survive as individuals, households, communities, and classes.

Third, much of the improvising (subsistence, sharing, enterprising) work that women and men do makes it possible for some of them to work for others in field, shop, factory, and office. Self-organized work makes wage work possible and profitable for employers.

Fourth, when household members take care of children and elders, prepare their own food, take in boarders, and make or sell goods and services on informal markets, they are doing two things simultaneously. They are helping themselves survive as workers, but they are also making it possible for employers to pay workers wages that are lower than the cost of maintaining worker households.[54] Employers count on households, usually on women in households, to do the work that enables households to survive without adequate wages. This "indirect exploitation" makes it possible for employers to pay the workers they hire less than their work is worth, a form of "direct exploitation." The direct exploitation of workers by employers is made possible by the indirect exploitation of worker households. As Margaret Bentson has argued, "[Women's] unpaid labor in the home is necessary if the entire system is to function."[55] This arrangement, where laboring households work without pay to sustain the system of work for pay is a problem because workers "exploit" themselves so they can be "exploited" by others.

Fifth, as women workers have begun to place more value on their nonwage work, new working-class priorities and politics have emerged. Nonwage work is essential to the functioning of the wage-identified economy as a social institution and the reproduction of unequal class relations. In our view, the world-economy is not just the sum of work done for others. It is the sum of all the work people do, across the spectrum. Without improvising work, the formal economy would not long survive.

Finally, to appreciate the important changes that affect work and understand how workers respond to contemporary change in different settings, it is essential that we examine different kinds of work together. Change that affects one kind of work inevitably affects the others. This is particularly true of wage work, the most visible kind of work. In recent years, wage work, nonwage work, and state benefits have all been transformed by important global developments. The changes associated with work and the state have had dramatic consequences not only for female and male wage workers, but also for people in households who work across the spectrum. We now turn to some of those changes and to the formation of the gendered politics related to change.

NOTES

1. Sara Rimer, "Tradition of Care Thrives in Black Families," *New York Times*, March 15, 1998.
2. Esther B. Fein, "Relatives Burned Out Caring for Aged at Home," *New York Times*, December 19, 1994. This practice varies from one group to another. "Older blacks are twice as likely as whites to receive care from family members when their health declines," reported the National Institute on Aging. Rimer, "Tradition of Care."
3. Barbara Crossette, "More People Grow Food in Cities, Report Says," *New York Times*, February 18, 1996.
4. Mike O'Connor, "Besieged Now by Cold and Hunger," *New York Times*, October 19, 1995.
5. Frank Levy and Richard C. Michel, *The Economic Future of American Families: Income and Wealth Trends* (Washington, D.C.: Urban Institute Press, 1991), 99.
6. O'Connor, "Besieged Now by Cold."
7. Howard W. French, "Does Sharing Wealth Only Promote Poverty?" *New York Times*, January 14, 1995.
8. Sana Wiwolop, "More Grandparents Grab the Tuition Tab," *New York Times*, January 12, 1997.
9. Brendan M. Case, "Cashing in on Immigration," *New York Times*, September 14, 1996.
10. Frank Bruni and Deborah Sontag, "Behind a Suburban Facade in Queens, a Teeming, Angry Urban Arithmetic," *New York Times*, October 8, 1996.
11. Bruni and Sontag, "Behind a Suburban Facade."
12. Somini Sengupta, "Bangladeshi's Brownstone Heights," *New York Times*, July 6, 1996.
13. Doreen Carvajal, "Salvadorans Trying to Make Ends Meet by Creating an Economic Nether World," *New York Times*, December 13, 1994.
14. Deborah Sontag, "Reshaping New York City's Golden Door," *New York Times*, June 13, 1993.
15. Carvajal, "Salvadorans Trying to Make Ends Meet"; Don Terry, "Makeshift Pharmacies Are Dispensing Death," *New York Times*, March 29, 1999.
16. Carvajal, "Salvadorans Trying to Make Ends Meet."
17. Michael de Courcey Hinds, "Inner City Market Blossoms," *New York Times*, May 14, 1994; *New York Times*, "Fewer Produce Peddlers Tread Baltimore Streets," *New York Times*, November 12, 1995.
18. Robin Pogrebin, "Now the Working Class, Too, Is Foraging for Empty Cans," *New York Times*, April 29, 1996.
19. Joseph Berger, "Scavengers' Discoveries Offer a Peek at Excess in Affluent America," *New York Times*, December 20, 1998.

20. Sallie Hofmeister, "Used American Jeans Power a Thriving Industry Abroad," *New York Times*, August 22, 1994.

21. Charlie Le Duff, "The Man to See for Raccoon Pie," *New York Times*, February 19, 1999.

22. "The informal economy represents up to 40 percent of urban employment in many countries, and in Peru economists say the figure is closer to 70 percent. This implies total employment [in the informal economy in Latin America] at close to 40 million," reported the *New York Times*. Nathaniel C. Nash, "Latin Informal Economy Saves Day," *New York Times*, March 21, 1992.

23. Carvajal, "Salvadorans Trying to Make Ends Meet."

24. Joan Smith and Immanuel Wallerstein, "Households as an Institution of the World-Economy," in Joan Smith and Immanuel Wallerstein, eds., *Creating and Transforming Households: The Constraints of the World-Economy* (Cambridge: Cambridge University Press, 1992), 3.

25. James C. McKinley, Jr., "In Cuba's New Dual Economy, Have-Nots Far Exceed Haves," *New York Times*, January 11, 1999.

26. Nigel Thrift, "The Geography of International Economic Disorder," in R. J. Johnston and P. J. Taylor, eds., *A World in Crisis? Geographical Perspectives* (London: Blackwell, 1986), 42; Torry D. Dickinson, *CommonWealth: Self-Sufficiency and Work in American Communities, 1830–1993* (Lanham, Md.: University Press of America, 1995), 3, 22; Chris Tilly and Charles Tilly, *Work under Capitalism* (Boulder, Colo.: Westview, 1998), 32.

27. Seth Faison, "A Smile, a Shoeshine and a Scam in China," *New York Times*, May 27, 1998.

28. Dickinson, *CommonWealth: Self-Sufficiency and Work in American Communities, 1830–1993*, 197.

29. Nash, "Latin Informal Economy."

30. Nash, "Latin Informal Economy."

31. Allen R. Myerson, "The Death of Some Salesmen," *New York Times*, April 28, 1996.

32. Dickinson, *CommonWealth: Self-Sufficiency and Work in American Communities, 1830–1993*, 15, 198–199.

33. Dickinson, *CommonWealth: Self-Sufficiency and Work in American Communities, 1830–1993*, 5, 12.

34. Le Duff, "The Man to See for Raccoon Pie."

35. Tilly and Tilly, *Work under Capitalism*, 22.

36. "First, few modern households in the modern world, anywhere, can afford over a lifetime to ignore any of these [different] sources of income. Secondly, wage income, even for households who are thought of as fully 'dependent on it' remains only one of [many] components, and as a percentage rarely approaches, even today, a massive proportion of the total," argue sociologists Joan Smith and Immanuel Wallerstein. Smith and Wallerstein, "Households as an Institution of the World-Economy," 10.

37. Dickinson, *CommonWealth: Self-Sufficiency and Work in American Communities, 1830–1993*, ii.

38. Peter T. Kilborn, "Shifts in Families Reach a Plateau, Study Says," *New York Times*, November 27, 1996.

39. Tamar Lewin, "The Decay of Families Is Global, Study Says," *New York Times*, May 30, 1995.

40. Mercedes González de la Rocha, *The Resources of Poverty: Women and Survival in a Mexican City* (Oxford: Blackwell, 1994), 128.

41. Lewin, "The Decay of Families Is Global."

42. Lewin, "The Decay of Families Is Global."

43. Lester Brown, *State of the World 1993* (New York: Norton, 1993), 64; Jane Perlez, "For Women, Lion's Share of Work," *New York Times*, December 2, 1991; Susan Greenhalgh, "Intergenerational Contracts: Familial Roots of Sexual Stratification in Taiwan," in Daisy Dwyer and Judith Bruce, eds., *A Home Divided: Women and Income in the Third World* (Stanford: Stanford University Press, 1988), 48–49.

44. Kathryn B. Ward, "Reconceptualizing World System Theory to Include Women," in Paula England, ed., *Theory on Gender/Feminism on Theory* (New York: Aldine De Gruyter, 1993), 43, 53; Judith Bruce and Daisy Dwyer, "Introduction," in Dwyer and Bruce, *A Home Divided*, 2–3.

45. Dickinson, *CommonWealth: Self-Sufficiency and Work in American Communities, 1830–1993*, 198–200.

46. Tilly and Tilly, *Work under Capitalism*, 152.

47. "Why should conversation, song, decoration and so on count as work when performed as commercial services but not when carried on for the benefit of friends and relatives?" ask Chris and Charles Tilly. Tilly and Tilly, *Work under Capitalism*, 152.

48. *New York Times*, "The 'Nonworking Class,'" *New York Times*, August 25, 1996.

49. Tamar Lewin, "Gender Pay Gap Widens," *New York Times*, September 15, 1997.

50. Melinda Hennegerger, "Welfare Bashing Finds Its Mark," *New York Times*, March 5, 1995.

51. *New York Times*, "The 'Nonworking Class.'"

52. William Julius Wilson, "Work," *New York Times Magazine*, August 18, 1996, 27; William Julius Wilson, *When Work Disappears: The World of the New Urban Poor* (New York: Knopf, 1996), xiii. Wilson later notes, "To be officially unemployed or officially outside the labor market does not mean that one is totally removed from all forms of work activity. Many people who are officially jobless are nonetheless involved in informal kinds of work activity, ranging from unpaid household work in the informal or illegal economies that provide income." *When Work Disappears*, 74.

53. Louise A. Tilly, *Industrialization and Gender Inequality* (Washington, D.C.: American Historical Association, 1993), 4.

54. Household work that supplements inadequate wages, Immanuel Wallerstein has written, has allowed some businesses "to remunerate their work force at lower rates, thereby reducing the cost of their production and increasing their profit margins." Immanuel Wallerstein, *Historical Capitalism* (New York: Verso, 1983), 27.

55. Margaret Bentson, "The Political Economy of Women's Liberation," in Rosemary Hennessy and Chrys Ingraham, eds., *Materialist Feminism* (New York: Routledge, 1997), 23.

Chapter 3

The Changing World of Work

The world of work has changed for female and male workers of the world. The most important change in recent years was this: the income that workers received from wages and from state benefits has everywhere declined, since the 1970s in the North and since the 1980s in the South.

Falling income has been modest for some workers, dramatic for others. In the United States, decline has been relatively modest in global terms. Between 1979 and 1995, the median income fell 4.6 percent, a wage cut amounting to about $100 a month.[1] But incomes did not decline at the same rate for all. For the millions of workers who received the minimum wage, real income declined 16 percent.[2] Farm workers saw their incomes fall even further, as much as 20 percent.[3] In real terms (in terms of what workers can buy with each dollar), millions of unskilled workers in America earned less in 1995 than they did in 1955.[4] This despite the much-heralded economic growth in the 1990s.

For workers in the vast regions once known as the "Third World" and what was called the communist "Second World," income loss has been more dramatic. Incomes have declined to levels that workers received decades ago. A 1996 UN study found that wages in 89 countries were lower than they were in the 1980s. Income in 70 of these countries was lower than it had been in the 1960s or 1970s, and income in 19 countries was lower than it had been in 1960.[5] As a result, more than three billion people on the planet earn less than $2 a day.[6] Another billion people are unemployed or underemployed.[7]

In Mexico, minimum wages declined by nearly 60 percent in the 1980s and 1990s, and the number of workers in poverty increased by five million in 1995–1996 alone.[8] Similar reversals have accompanied recent economic crises in Indonesia, Brazil, and Russia.[9] In Russia, income from wages has not only fallen off an economic cliff, but wages due are often unpaid for months at a time, forcing workers to borrow money and discount their wages due to shopkeepers so they can purchase food.[10] The situation for workers across Russia is similar to that of sailors in the British navy during the eighteenth century. Sailors then toiled for months, even years, without being paid their wages. So they were forced to make ends meet by promising their wages at a discount to shopkeepers and landlords.[11] This practice has become common in contemporary Russia. Today, 44 million people, one-quarter of Russia's population, live below the poverty level, which is reckoned at $32 a month.[12]

Falling wages have been accompanied in many countries by shrinking state benefits. States in the core (Western Europe, North America, Japan, and Australia) have cut benefits to some groups of workers, as the U.S. government has done to women on welfare and also immigrants. Many other "entitlement" programs are being reviewed or assaulted throughout the core. Rich countries have generally provided benefits to some groups of workers. To make sure that only the intended beneficiaries receive state support, governments in the core usually erect large and costly bureaucracies to administer them. The practice of governments in poor countries is rather different. Instead of creating targeted entitlement programs, they generally subsidize the price of some goods, thereby providing benefits that are universally available. For example, many peripheral governments subsidize the cost of food, energy, public transport, or housing. Subsidies lower the price of these goods, not just for the poor but for everyone. Although rich people who do not need government subsidies can obtain them, officials choose not to restrict benefits to the truly needy because it would be necessary to create a large and costly bureaucracy to administer benefits. The problem for workers has been that economic crises of various sorts have forced governments around the world to reduce subsidies for many goods, substantially lowering benefits and standards of living.[13] And while income from wages and state benefits have declined, the cost of many goods that workers need to survive has increased.

For workers in the core, the price of housing, utilities, health care, education, and taxes has increased in recent years.[14] Since 1970, the cost of a single family house in the United States has increased 44 percent, and increases have been even more dramatic along the coasts and in big cities.[15] In New York City, for example, the average cost of a co-op apartment in Manhattan has risen from $24,500 per room to $85,565 per room.[16] When housing costs rise at this rate, it is not surprising that people like Gilberto Medina subdivide their houses and rent them out. Nor should it be surprising that many families moved into low-cost mobile homes in the 1980s.[17]

Wage workers get fewer health benefits from their employers, and fewer workers can afford to purchase health insurance on their own. The number of workers without health insurance in the United States grew by 12 million in the last decade, from 31 million in 1989 to 43 million in 1999.[18] The cost of a college education has also increased, as state governments reduced their subsidies and raised tuition. The tax burden for working households has also modestly increased, at a time when taxes on wealthy households have substantially declined.[19]

Working women and men in the periphery pay higher prices for somewhat different goods. The withdrawal of government subsidies for food, energy, public transport, and housing has increased the price of each. In Mexico, for example, the government's 1999 decision to eliminate its $1 billion annual tortilla subsidy increased the price of this dietary staple from 15 to 20 cents a pound, a significant increase because the average Mexican consumes nearly 300 pounds of tortillas a year.[20] Rising prices for staple foods—wheat bread in Egypt, which the government now plans to adulterate with corn; ramen noodles in South Korea—are important daily reminders of change.[21]

As in the core, worker households in the periphery have also seen rents increase. In Egypt, rising rents on agricultural land will affect 900,000 tenant households.[22] Governments around the world have also increased taxes on workers by raising tolls, fares, and license fees. When countries fall into debt or face a currency crisis, global financial institutions usually insist that they raise taxes.[23] And in many countries, government officials have illegally levied fees, demanded payments, and collected bribes that increased tax burdens for many workers.[24]

The recent wave of currency devaluations in countries around the world has also contributed to rising prices for some imported goods. Where it has increased the cost of luxury goods such as imported cars, televisions, or alcoholic beverages, the effect on workers has been negligible. But where it has increased the cost of essential goods such as imported wheat in Egypt, where half of the wheat consumed is imported and where each worker consumes 400 pounds annually, or where it has increased the price of cooking kerosene or fuel oil, the consequences for workers can be devastating.[25]

As a result of falling income and rising prices, workers the world over have seen real living standards fall, slightly for some, dramatically for many. Changes that affect one kind of work—in this case, wage labor—reverberated across the work world, altering the life and work of workers everywhere. To replace lost income from wage work and state benefits, workers have intensified their efforts across the work spectrum. Several common responses have become evident in recent years. First, workers have intensified their search for wage work. This search has brought women into the paid labor force in large numbers and has led women and men to leave home and migrate in search of paid employment. Second, for those unable to find paid work, many have organized their own microbusinesses. Third, household members have worked harder at home to cut costs and do or acquire for themselves what they can no longer afford to purchase from the market. For many workers, cost-cutting efforts can mean consuming less or reducing household size.

WOMEN SUPPORT HOUSEHOLDS

As income began to fall in the 1970s and 1980s, workers intensified their search for paid employment. One expression of this has been the entry of women, in large numbers, into the labor force. By finding more paid work in the 1970s and 1980s, women have kept household incomes from falling as far as they would have if workers had to depend entirely on male wages alone.[26] In Mexico City, for example, where male income from wages fell 35 percent in the mid-1980s, total household incomes fell only 11 percent because women's wage earnings made up much, but not all, of the difference.[27] In the United States, 37 million women work for low-to-modest wages, and "their wages serve as a cushion between welfare and getting by."[28]

In their search for paid work, women, men, and teens have traveled far and wide. Considerable attention has been paid to the press of immigrants across national borders and the tides of political refugees fleeing from one country to another, nearly 50 million, according to UN estimates. But while it has attracted less attention, migration within states is more prevalent and more significant than movement across borders.[29] In China alone, 100 million men and women migrate to jobs on a seasonal basis, a group twice as large as the number of political refugees worldwide.[30] The migration of rural inhabitants to big cities in China, Russia, Cuba, and Israel has become so severe that authorities have imposed huge fees for people seeking urban residence ($11,600 for a residency license in Beijing). They have also adopted tough regulations that allow police to evict, fine, and "expel" internal migrants from Beijing, Hong Kong, Moscow, Havana, and Jerusalem and "deport" them to towns and villages in rural provinces.[31] In the United States, meanwhile, the Immigration and Naturalization Service has forced immigrant workers from their jobs (sometimes without trying to deport them), even if they have children who are U.S. citizens. "The intent is to really change the dynamics, change the climate, and change the decision-making process of these migrants," INS Commissioner Doris Meissner said of the 5.5 million people living illegally in the United States.[32]

In addition to seeking wage work, female and male workers have organized enterprising work of their own. A UN study of Latin America and the Caribbean found that as employment in the paid labor force fell during the 1970s, workers turned to informal and enterprising kinds of work, and the amount of work organized by workers now exceeds the amount of work provided by employers.[33] Although fewer workers organize their own work in core countries, the same kind of shift is evident. As income from wage work fell in the 1970s, the size of the informal economy grew substantially in the United States, from 7.7 percent of GNP in 1973 to 9.1 percent of GNP in 1981.[34] U.S. corporate managers have even encouraged workers to become more self-directed and less reliant on businesses for jobs. "People need to look at themselves as self-employed, as vendors who come to this company to sell their skills," argued AT&T resource manager James Meadows. "In AT&T, we have to promote the whole concept of the workforce being contingent."[35]

This means, of course, that the diverse types of work organized by enterprising workers have everywhere expanded. In Baghdad it means that educated households peddle their private library collections on the streets for cash, urban gardeners in Russia vend their produce from sidewalk stalls, and young boys pick pockets in Chinese border towns that were once noted for being "crime free."[36]

Workers have also responded to falling wages by cutting their costs. One way to cuts costs has been to consume less. The average household in Africa now consumes 20 percent less than it did twenty-five years ago, a 1998 UN study found.[37] For many, this has meant eating less meat and milk, grain, or vegetables.[38] For some, it means cutting back on education. When the economic crisis hit Indonesia in 1998, Josisna Banu took her daughter Juliana out of school to save on uniform and school fees. "We just couldn't afford [the $2 uniform fee]," she explained.[39] For some, it has meant sharing space with others. When Antonio Da Motta's rent in New York City jumped 30 percent in 1996, he put up a wall, creating an extra bedroom, and took in a roommate, Web Tysner, to cut costs.[40] In Salinas, California, meanwhile, ten migrant workers shared a single room at the Westwind Motel and divided the $200 a week rent between them. "When it comes to the rent, it's much more economical this way," explained Reyna Fernandez, a worker in nearby strawberry fields.[41]

DOWNSIZING HOUSEHOLDS

Another way to cut costs has been to reduce household size. Demographers have long argued that birth rates and family size declined as incomes rose, a conclusion based largely on observations of workers in the core during the last century. But some evidence now exists that falling incomes can have the same effect in some settings.

During the Great Depression, for example, birth rates and household size dropped dramatically in many U.S. cities.[42] And in recent years, birth rates and household size have experienced another sharp decline in the United States.[43] In other settings, declines have been dramatic. Birth rates in Russia have fallen from 13.4 per 1,000 population in 1990 to 8.6 per 1,000 in 1997, one of the lowest rates in the world.[44] Much, though not all of it, has been due to the deepening economic crisis and the collapse of household incomes. During this period, the number of single mothers has increased. "There is so much economic uncertainty and real fear," Marina Kiyenya, a single mother explained. "Men feel humiliated that they cannot provide for their families, and they just walk away."[45] But it is not just fathers who have walked away. Increasingly mothers have, too. About two million Russian children lack families, two-thirds of them live on the streets, and the number of parentless children now surpasses the number orphaned after World War II.[46] Although there are fewer orphans in the United States, an equal number—two million children under thirteen—nonetheless have no adult supervision before or after school.[47]

Credible evidence now suggests that falling birth rates and household size are due in large measure to falling incomes. In Brazil, the Catholic Church and the government have long opposed family planning. But falling incomes in the 1980s and 1990s have convinced Brazilians generally to have fewer children and reduce family size as a way to cut costs. As Canadian demographer George Martine observed, "In the absence of any government birth control program . . . Brazil has experienced the largest self-induced drop in human history . . . compressing 100 years of fertility decline into 20 years."[48]

PEOPLE WORK HARDER

Household members also worker harder at home to do or acquire for themselves what they can no longer afford to purchase from the market. A good example of this is health and child care in the United States. As the cost of health care has increased, and the number of workers covered by health insurance has declined, workers have increasingly cared for their own, in their homes. The number of people providing free care to a family member or friend has tripled in the last ten years, from 7 million in 1987 to 21 million in 1998.[49] And much the same is true of child care. In the last decade, the number of children in their grandparent's care has increased 50 percent.[50] There are now 1.4 million children in "skip-generation" households, most of them headed by grandmothers who are home alone.[51]

Contemporary change has been a discriminatory process. Falling incomes and rising costs affected workers everywhere. But they affected some more than others. Wages and state benefits have fallen further and faster for workers in poor countries than for workers in rich countries, more for unskilled workers than skilled ones, more for males than females.

As incomes declined in Indonesia, for instance, parents took their children out of school to save money. But this did not affect girls and boys equally. "Parents are afraid that their money will run out, so they are pulling girls out of school," explained Marianna Kulla. "People say it's better for girls to stay at home so that they can save money for boys."[52] For girls in Indonesia, change has had uneven, discriminatory consequences. This has been the common pattern.

In the United States, more workers have provided home health care to family members because they cannot afford to pay for health-care services. But most of this care is provided by women, usually daughters. Many daughters have to quit their jobs to provide care for elderly parents.[53] The rising cost of health care has burdened women more than men.

Many people imagine that change affects everyone in much the same way. They assume that a new technology, like the personal computer, will provide similar benefits to all. But we take a different view. For us, change is more like the weather. A change in the weather—falling pressure—may create a storm. But a low-pressure system can have very different consequences for people who live along its path. The storm may bring rain to people living in the plains, snow to people in the mountains, and clear skies to people in the valleys beyond. It can inflict fog, flood, hail, or avalanche. As a result, people visited by the same weather system may experience change in very different ways.

IMMISERATION DIVIDES LABOR

One of the insights Amartya Sen made in his landmark study *Poverty and Famine* was that change does not affect everyone in the same way. Sen found that food-related change affected people from equally poor backgrounds in very different ways. During the Great Bengal Famine of 1944, everyone living in the region experienced the same important change: the rising price of rice. But when Sen examined the effect of rising rice prices on equally poor people in rural villages, he found that wage workers and sharecroppers were affected in different ways. It seems that wage workers could not increase their incomes to keep pace with rising prices. Sharecroppers, meanwhile, were less affected by rising rice prices because they were due a portion of the crop, no matter what its price. The particular social circumstances of workers in the same village turned out to have important consequences. Wage workers starved; sharecroppers survived. The same change—rising rice prices—meant different things: death for some, life for others.

Although famine is a traumatic consequence of dramatic change, it illustrates how change can be discriminatory. Economic change is much the same. Falling income from wage labor and state benefits has meant different things for different people in different places. It has different meanings, depending on one's gender, age, ethnicity, skill, education, location, and citizenship. Workers experience change in different ways. This makes it hard for workers to develop a common response to change.

Falling incomes and resources, or the "immiseration" of workers, do not necessarily produce a collective response by impoverished workers, though some social scientists have thought that this would. Karl Marx, for instance, assumed that immiseration would provoke the workers of the world to cast off their chains. They sometimes did but not always or everywhere. Later, the Italian socialist Antonio Gramsci tried to complicate this theory by arguing that the social and political organizations of "civil society" occluded worker recognition of their shared interests, thereby preventing them from acting in concert. But while this was an important insight, theories or expectations of worker response to economic change need to be examined further. Change often results in the creation of separate economic interests and social identities for different groups of workers. These interests and identities may prevent workers from developing a common response to shared problems or persuade them to respond to change in ways that injure the interests of other workers or even harm their own interests.

WORKER STRATEGIES KEEP WORKERS DIVIDED

One reason that workers have adopted separate interests and identities is that they have been encouraged or required to do so by businesses, states, and markets. Worker interests and identities as *consumers* are a good example of this. Consumer interests and identities have been encouraged by the advertising industry, which increased spending in the United States from $198 per capita in 1950 to $498 in 1989.[54] In the year 2000, businesses in the United States spent $235.6 billion to advertise their wares.[55] The introduction of mass media technologies—particularly, radio and TV—encouraged the spread of consumer interests. As Juliet Schor has found, "For every hour of television watched weekly, [individual] spending rose $208."[56]

Government policies have also played an important role. In the United States, tax and monetary policies in the postwar period were designed to give workers a role as consumers and persuade them to purchase certain kinds of goods. By granting a tax deduction for interest payments on home loans, for example, the government gave workers a material interest in being consumers of homes, encouraging them to identify themselves as members of a "middle class," a class defined more by how one spent than by how one worked. The more recent tax deduction for Individual Retirement Accounts (IRAs) likewise gave workers an economic interest in the stock market and a new social identity as "investors." This kind of government policy paved the way for advertisers, who used television to sell mutual funds to workers across the country. These developments have encouraged, even required, workers to adopt new economic interests and social identities. But this has been difficult to achieve. As the economist John Maynard Keynes pointed out in the 1930s, most people's desire to save was stronger than their inclination to consume. This being the case, Keynes urged government officials to adopt economic policies designed to persuade workers to consume, so that high levels of consumer demand would sustain relatively high levels of employment.[57] In Japan, the government has only recently tried to persuade workers to spend and promote job growth.

Women who work as housewives in Japan have been notoriously thrifty. They typically keep household accounts and control household income, keeping a careful eye on saving money. Women are responsible for managing budgets in nearly 80 percent of Japanese households.[58] "My wife keeps the accounts very strictly," Morikazu Lkuyama complained. "I can't even cheat one yen from her."[59] This tightfistedness was long celebrated because it produced world-high savings rates in Japan (12–15 percent annually). Worker savings were then used to finance the expansion of industry in postwar Japan. To appreciate the historical thrift of Japanese housewives, compare the roughly $100,000 saved by the average Japanese household with the meager $3,000 saved by the average American household.[60]

But this long-celebrated thrift is now under attack, as it has been for many years in the United States. Because the Japanese economy has been mired in recession, the government has tried to stimulate worker interest in consumption and undermine thrifty habits. Recently, officials distributed $6 billion in shopping vouchers to Japanese households in a campaign to persuade housewives to shop, shop, shop. Housewives cannot deposit the coupons in their savings accounts because the coupons expire after a few months. Housewives are encouraged to become consumers, not savers.[61]

The pressure to consume in the United States has become especially dangerous. Here, spendthrift consumer identities have become so pronounced that American workers did not acquire any net savings in 1998, the first time since the Great Depression.[62] Some misguided economists have even celebrated this "urge to splurge." "This is not the time to tell people to stop spending," argued Harvard economist Gregory Mankiw.[63] U.S. workers have been urged to shop despite the fact that the average consumer debt per household almost doubled in the last decade, rising from $38,734 in 1990 to $65,796 in 2000.[64]

Some scholars have argued that consumerism is an expression of workers' "false consciousness." But consumer identities are not simply false or unwitting, they represent real material interests. If workers did not pursue them, their interests as workers might be injured. The worker who can become a homeowner or open an IRA, but does not, is made a fool.

Part of the problem is this: having been persuaded, even required to adopt consumer interests and identities, workers may act in ways that indirectly injure other workers, frustrate government policy, and even undermine their own interests as workers.

If workers pursue their interests as investors and purchase stocks for their IRA accounts, they help finance corporate mergers that result in worker layoffs. They may, in effect, contribute to their own unemployment. If workers buy cheap foreign goods to cut their costs, they may increase trade deficits, which can trigger currency devaluations and lead to higher domestic interests rates, increased consumer debt, economic recession, and widespread unemployment. If workers protect themselves from currency devaluations by exchanging domestic currency for dollars, as workers in Argentina and Russia have done (60 percent of all bank deposits in Argentina are in dollars; $15 billion in U.S. currency is now circulating in Russia), they may frustrate government monetary policies designed to manage the economy and increase employment. Workers might unwittingly contribute to the kind of exchange rate instability that they themselves are trying to avoid and might thus create a two-currency economy, which may be beneficial to some workers who can obtain dollars but injurious to other workers who cannot easily acquire hard currencies.[65] When workers have multiple interests and identities as both workers and consumers, their activities as consumers may injure their status as wage workers.

Much the same could be said of other worker interests and identities, those associated with gender, age, ethnicity, location, skill, or citizenship. These separate interests and identities make it difficult for working people to develop a single, uniform response to a common problem, like falling wages and benefits. Under the circumstances, it seems unreasonable to expect (as Marx did) that they would adopt a single class identity. To understand how workers respond to common problems, when they have multiple, separate, and diverse interests and identities, we need to examine change in its entirety, looking at work across the spectrum on a global scale. Only then can we analyze how change affects the world of work, identify how it affects workers around the world, and appreciate their different responses to change.

In the following chapters, we will explain why incomes for wage workers are falling, how this affects wage and nonwage workers in different settings, and how workers have responded to change. One common response has been for households to intensify their search for wage work while at the same time increasing their nonwage work activities. It is important that women have played a major role for households, entering the labor force and assuming a greater work burden at home. The central role of women in the wage-based economy and in worker households has given rise to political movements in which women play significant roles.

NOTES

1. John Cassidy, "Who Killed the Middle Class?" *The New Yorker* (October 16, 1995): 114; Paul Ryscavage, *Income Analysis in America: An Analysis of Trends* (Armonk, N.Y.: Sharpe, 1999), 91.
2. Alan B. Krueger, "The Truth about Wages," *New York Times*, July 31, 1997; Louis Uchitelle, "Minimum Wage and Jobs," *New York Times*, January 12, 1995.
3. Steven Greenhouse, "U.S. Surveys Find Farm Worker Pay Down for 20 Years," *New York Times*, March 31, 1997.
4. Uchitelle, "Minimum Wage and Jobs"; Ryscavage, *Income Inequality in America*, 83.
5. Barbara Crossette, "U.N. Survey Finds World Rich–Poor Gap Widening," *New York Times*, July 15, 1996.
6. Crossette, "U.N. Survey Finds World Rich–Poor Gap Widening."
7. *New York Times*, "U.N. Report Shows Billion Adults Unemployed or Underemployed," *New York Times*, November 26, 1996.
8. Mercedes Gonzáles de la Rocha, *The Resources of Poverty: Women and Survival in a Mexican City* (Oxford: Blackwell, 1994), 270; Anthony De Palma, "Income Gulf in Mexico Grows and So Do Protests," *New York Times*, July 20, 1996.
9. Timothy L. O'Brien, "Indonesians Visit U.S. Seeking Help with Debt," *New York Times*, July 9, 1998; Philip Shenon, "U.S. Officials, in Indonesia, Warn Rulers to Respect Rights," *New York Times*, August 2, 1998.
10. Alessandra Stanley, "Today's Battle of Stalingrad: Trying to Collect a Paycheck," *New York Times*, December 25, 1996; Michael Wines, "Resignedly, Russians Work Ever Harder for Even Less," *New York Times*, August 25, 1998; Steve LeVine, "In Former Soviet Republic, Bribes Light the Night," *New York Times*, February 7, 1999.
11. Robert K. Schaeffer, *The Chains of Bondage Broke: The Proletarianization of Seafaring Labor, 1600–1800* (Ph.D. dissertation, State University of New York at Binghamton, 1984), 238–240.
12. *New York Times*, "Younger Workers in Russia Found More Likely to Barter," *New York Times*, November 19, 1998.
13. On the eve of the Pope's visit to Cuba in 1998, Mrs. Elba Gonzáles, a resident of Rancho Veloz, said she was hungry. But it wasn't from fasting. She has seen her income from the government evaporate, and her situation has become desperate. "We wake up in a bad mood and go to sleep in a bad mood," she explained. Mirta Ojito, "'Where's the Joy of Life?' The Dirt Poor in Cuba Wonder," *New York Times*, January 23, 1998.
14. Cassidy, "Who Killed the Middle Class?" 119.
15. Michael Wallace, "Downsizing the American Dream: Work and Family at Century's End," in Dana Vannoy and Paula J. Dubeck, eds., *Challenges for Work and Family in the Twenty-First Century* (New York: Aldine de Gruyter, 1998), 33.
16. Cassidy, "Who Killed the Middle Class?" 120.
17. Kevin Sack, "Mobile Homes Go Upscale: One Pet per Plot, Please," *New York Times*, February 23, 1997; William Finnegan, "Prosperous Times, Except for the Young," *New York Times*, June 12, 1998.
18. Peter T. Kilborn, "Third of Hispanic Americans Do without Health Coverage," *New York Times*, April 9, 1999; Ryscavage, *Income Inequality in America*, 76.
19. Frank Levy, *Dollars and Dreams: The Changing American Income Distribution* (New York: Russell Sage Foundation, 1987), 66.
20. Ginger Thompson, "Tortilla Rises: Must Belts Tighten?" *New York Times*, January 4, 1999.

21. Sheryl WuDunn, "South Korea's Mood Swings from Bleak to Bullish," *New York Times*, January 24, 1999; Douglas Jehl, "Egypt Adding Corn to Bread: An Explosive Mix?" *New York Times*, November 27, 1996.

22. Douglas Jehl, "Egypt's Farmers Resist End of Freeze on Rents," *New York Times*, December 27, 1997.

23. Nora Lustig, *Mexico: The Remaking of an Economy* (Washington, D.C.: Brookings Institution, 1992), 106.

24. LeVine, "In Former Soviet Republics, Bribes Light the Night"; Patrick E. Tyler, "No Rights Mean No Incentive for China's Farmers," *New York Times*, December 15, 1996.

25. Jehl, "Egypt Adding Corn to Bread."

26. Cassidy, "Who Killed the Middle Class?" 118; Lester C. Thurow, "The Boom That Wasn't," *New York Times*, January 18, 1999.

27. De la Rocha, *The Resources of Poverty*, 273.

28. Peter T. Kilborn, "More Women Take Low-Wage Jobs Just So Their Families Can Get by," *New York Times*, March 13, 1994.

29. Barbara Crossette, "This Is No Place Like Home," *New York Times*, March 5, 1995; John Darnton, "U.N. Faces Refugee Crisis That Never Ends," *New York Times*, August 8, 1994; John Darnton, "Crisis-Torn Africa Becomes Continent of Refugees," *New York Times*, May 22, 1996.

30. Elisabeth Rosenthal, "100 Million Restless Chinese Go Far from Home for Jobs," *New York Times*, February 24, 1999.

31. Patrick E. Tyler, "Beijing to Impose Huge Fees to Limit Migrants in the City," *New York Times*, September 15, 1994; Edward A. Gargan, "Illegal Chinese Race to Get Toehold in Hong Kong," *New York Times*, May 23, 1997; Celestine Bohlen, "Moscow Jobs Beckon, but Let the Migrant Beware," *New York Times*, June 13, 1998; Rachel L. Swarns, "Moscow Sends Homeless to Faraway Hometowns," *New York Times*, October 15, 1996; Larry Rohter, "Cuba's Unwanted Refugees: Squatters in Havana," *New York Times*, October 20, 1997; Meil MacFarquhar, "Israel's New Poor: Foreigners Replace Arab Labor but Make Many Uneasy," *New York Times*, August 19, 1996.

32. Sam Howe Verhovek, "Illegal Immigrant Workers Being Fired in I.N.S. Tactic," *New York Times*, April 2, 1999.

33. Nathaniel C. Nash, "Latin Informal Economy Saves Day," *New York Times*, March 21, 1992.

34. Levy, *Dollars and Dreams*, 219.

35. Chris Tilly and Charles Tilly, *Work under Capitalism* (Boulder, Colo.: Westview, 1998), 224.

36. Barbara Crossette, "Where People Go Hungry, the Arts Are Starved Too," *New York Times*, February 4, 1998; Serge Schmeman, "How Can You Have a Bust If You Never Had a Boom?" *New York Times Magazine*, December 27, 1998, 29; Seth Faison, "Hidden China, a Swarm of Pimps and Pickpockets," *New York Times*, March 30, 1999.

37. Barbara Crossette, "Most Consuming More, and the Rich Much More," *New York Times*, September 13, 1998.

38. De la Rocha, *The Resources of Poverty*, 76.

39. Nicholas D. Kristof, "As Asian Economies Shrink, Women Are Squeezed Out," *New York Times*, June 11, 1998.

40. Julie V. Iovine, "As Rents Move up, Roommates Move in," *New York Times*, March 20, 1997.

41. By saving money on rent, workers like Mr. Fernandez, who earned only $5.15 an hour, could save money to send home to their families in Mexico. "It's difficult thinking it might

be a year or two before I see my family," one worker said. "But it's good that we can earn and save some money here." Steven Greenhouse, "As Economy Booms, Migrant Workers' Housing Worsens," *New York Times,* May 31, 1998.

42. "Rapid falls in the birthrate are historically associated with bad times, when money is tight." Kathleen Stanley and Joan Smith, "The Detroit Story: The Crucible of Fordism," in Joan Smith and Immanuel Wallerstein, eds., *Creating and Transforming Households: The Constraints of the World-Economy* (Cambridge: Cambridge University Press, 1992), 37, 49–50.

43. Kathleen Gerson, "Gender and the Future of the Family: Implications for the Post-Industrial Workplace," in Vannoy and Dubeck, *Challenges for Work and Family,* 16.

44. Celestine Bohlen, "Russian Women Turning to Abortion Less Often," *New York Times,* March 29, 1999; Abraham Brumberg, "Free Fall," *Los Angeles Times Book Review,* March 21, 1999.

45. Alessandra Stanley, "Russian Mothers, from All Walks, Walk Alone," *New York Times,* October 21, 1995.

46. "Younger Workers in Russia Found More Likely to Be Poor," *New York Times,* November 19, 1998.

47. Lester C. Thurow, "Companies Merge; Families Break up," *New York Times,* September 3, 1995.

48. James Brooke, "Births in Brazil Are on Decline, Easing Worries," *New York Times,* August 8, 1989.

49. Ian Fisher, "Families Providing Complex Medical Care, Tubes and All," *New York Times,* June 7, 1998.

50. Jason DeParle, "As Welfare Rolls Shrink, Load on Relatives Grows," *New York Times,* February 21, 1999.

51. DeParle, "As Welfare Rolls Shrink."

52. Kristof, "As Asian Economies Shrink, Women Are Squeezed Out." In rural China, only 20 percent of girls are enrolled in school, while 40 percent of boys attend. Elisabeth Rosenthal, "School a Rare Luxury for Rural Chinese Girls," *New York Times,* November 1, 1999.

53. Judy Singleton, "The Impact of Family Caregiving to the Elderly on the American Workplace: Who Is Affected and What Is Being Done?" in Vannoy and Dubeck, *Challenges for Work and Family,* 203.

54. Alan Durning, "Asking How Much Is Enough," in Lester R. Brown, *State of the World 1991* (New York: Norton, 1991), 163.

55. Stuart Elliott, "Advertising: The Media Business," *New York Times,* June 28, 2000.

56. Louis Uchitelle, "Keeping up with the Gateses?" *New York Times,* May 3, 1998.

57. See John Maynard Keynes, *The General Theory of Employment, Interest and Money* (New York: 1935).

58. Mary C. Brinton, *Women and the Economic Miracle: Gender and Work in Postwar Japan* (Berkeley: University of California Press, 1993), 94. "As primary keepers of family finances, Japanese women are the bedrock of consumption. They put their husbands on a monthly allowance, decide when to replace the family car, and generally manage the household account," one observer has argued. Nicholas D. Kristof, "Japan Is a Woman's World Once the Front Door Is Shut," *New York Times,* June 19, 1996.

59. Kristof, "Japan Is a Woman's World."

60. Stephanie Strom, "Shopping for Recovery," *New York Times,* May 29, 1998.

61. Sheryl WuDunn, "To Revive a Sick Economy, Japan Hands Out Coupons," *New York Times,* March 14, 1999.

62. Sylvia Nasar, "Economists Simply Shrug as Savings Rate Declines," *New York Times*, December 21, 1998.

63. Nasar, "Economists Simply Shrug"; Robert Skidelsky, "Two Cheers for Consumerism," *New York Times*, August 14, 1998.

64. Saul Hansell, "We Like You. We Care about You. Now Pay Up." *New York Times*, January 26, 1997.

65. Michael Specter, "Forget the Rubles! Russians Obsessed with U.S. $100 Bills," *New York Times*, November 4, 1995; Clifford Krauss, "Buck Doesn't Stop: Now Argentina May Adopt It," *New York Times*, February 25, 1999.

Chapter 4

The Redistribution and Reorganization of Work in the Core

For workers in the core, two important changes have affected wage work, the primary source of work and income for most households during the postwar period. First, a significant share of the wage work available to men in manufacturing industries has been *redistributed*, much of it from the United States to industries located in other core states. Second, much of the wage work performed in U.S. manufacturing and service industries has recently been *reorganized*, a process that has spread to industries based in other core states. In other words, some manufacturing jobs have been sent overseas, and the labor process in many firms has been transformed. The redistribution and reorganization of wage work in the core have had important consequences for household incomes and gender relations.

Before 1970, the global redistribution of work generally provided jobs and raised wages for workers across the core. But after 1970, men in U.S. manufacturing industries saw many jobs disappear and watched their incomes decline. Women helped compensate, in part, for male income losses in heterosexual households by finding jobs in growing service industries.

The subsequent reorganization of work by U.S. firms during the 1980s and 1990s has also resulted in job loss and declining wages, not only in manufacturing but also in service industries. These losses were concealed by U.S. economic growth in the 1990s, when U.S. industries made gains at the expense of Japanese and Western European industries. In this period, the reorganization of work made U.S. industries more competitive, while economic crises in Japan and Western Europe made industries there less competitive. So the reorganization of work helped redistribute work again, this time to U.S. advantage. But when industries in Western Europe and Japan eventually reorganize work along lines pioneered in the United States, they will likely recover some of the wage work they have lost in recent years. When that occurs, many of the apparent gains made by U.S. workers in the 1990s will likely evaporate. Moreover, any new redistribution of work would result in renewed job loss in the United States. Workers in Western Europe and Japan would also experience job and income loss because industries that reorganize along U.S. lines generally shed manufacturing and service workers.

The redistribution and reorganization altered gender relations in the core. The exit of men from manufacturing and the entry of women into service industries have transformed economic, political, and social roles for men and women. This development was apparent first in the United States but has become evident more recently in Western Europe and Japan. Indeed, it is a common development throughout the periphery and semiperiphery, though it has occurred there for somewhat different reasons, as we will see in subsequent chapters.

To appreciate these developments, we will examine the redistribution and reorganization of wage work in the core and assess the impact of change on jobs, incomes, and gender relations in different regions.

REDISTRIBUTING WORK, 1950–1970

After World War II, male wage workers in the United States produced most of the manufactured goods consumed in Western Europe and Japan; male and female farm households in the United States produced most of the food consumed in Western Europe and Japan. But that changed during the next twenty-five years. By 1973, the United States produced only one-fifth (21.9 percent) of the world's manufactured goods, down from more than half (56.7 percent) in 1948. Other core states, meanwhile, doubled their share of world manufacturing, from 15 to more than 30 percent.[1] So by 1973, most of the manufactured goods in Western Europe and Japan were made by indigenous male wage workers, not by North Americans. About the same time, Western Europe became self-sufficient in food, and its consumption of agricultural produce grown in the United States declined substantially. Essentially, a significant share of the wage work available in manufacturing and in agriculture had shifted from the United States to Western Europe and Japan. Governments, businesses, and consumers all adopted policies and practices that shifted the location of jobs in manufacturing and agriculture from the United States to other locations in the core.

U.S. policies played a crucial role in the postwar redistribution of wage work. While U.S. policies were designed to promote political and military cooperation and foster economic growth within the core, they also contributed to the redistribution of wage work. Here's how.

First, the U.S. government provided public aid worth billions of dollars to its allies through the Marshall Plan and related programs.[2] It also directed vast quantities of military aid to Western Europe and Japan, aid amounting to as much as $2 trillion between 1950 and 1970.[3]

Public aid provided capital that Allied governments used to rebuild wrecked infrastructure and rebuild industries destroyed by war, creating jobs for demobilized servicemen in construction and manufacturing. Western Europeans needed this infusion of capital because much of their available capital had been moved by investors to the United States during the war, creating a capital shortage in postwar Europe.[4] U.S. military spending overseas provided numerous benefits to core allies. Because the military purchased goods for overseas U.S. bases from local suppliers, U.S. defense spending created jobs in defense-related industries. U.S. purchases of French aircraft for NATO, for example, created jobs in an industry that would later compete with U.S. aircraft manufacturers.[5] The hundreds of thousands of U.S. servicemen stationed in Western Europe and Japan spent their wages there, creating jobs for local businesses and injecting dollars, a scarce and important commodity, into local economies. These practices provided capital that was used to create national and local manufacturing and service industries in Western Europe and Japan. And by serving abroad, U.S. soldiers released young men in Western Europe and Japan from military obligations, so they could take jobs in rebuilding industries.

Second, the U.S. government allowed its allies to levy high tariffs (taxes on goods they imported from the United States) and establish strict controls on capital movements. These policies encouraged U.S. firms to invest heavily in Western Europe. General Electric, for example, quadrupled the number of factories it operated in Western Europe between 1949 and 1969.[6] The $78 billion that U.S. firms invested in Western Europe during the 1950s and 1960s was used to create jobs and produce goods there, rather than import goods made by wage workers in the United States.[7] Private U.S. investments in this period may have resulted in the loss of two million jobs in the United States.[8] This practice, which was encouraged by government policies in the United States and Western Europe, contributed to the redistribution of wage work in manufacturing industries.

Third, U.S. officials established a global system of fixed exchange rates during the war. The Bretton Woods agreement, as it was called, allowed Western European and Japanese firms to compete as equals in U.S. markets, even though they were not yet competitive with U.S. firms.[9] Generous postwar exchange rates, which made Western European and Japanese goods seem cheap in U.S. markets, and low U.S. tariffs on imported goods encouraged worker-consumers in the United States to purchase toys, sewing machines, radios, and alcohol from Western Europe and Japan. Exchange rates also persuaded U.S. workers to travel abroad. The $4.8 billion that U.S. worker-tourists spent overseas, most of it in Western Europe, created jobs in service industries and injected dollars into Allied economies.[10] As a result, worker-consumers in the United States also helped to send U.S. jobs to Western Europe and Japan.

For their part, governments in Western Europe and Japan made the most of opportunities provided by U.S. policies, business practices, and consumer behaviors. U.S. public aid, military assistance, private investment, and consumer spending provided them with capital and markets that they used to create jobs and rebuild industries. Governments in Western Europe and Japan also adopted policies that tapped another important resource: their own domestic wage workers.

Generally speaking, governments in Western Europe and Japan adopted monetary, trade, and tax policies designed to discourage consumption by their own wage workers, encouraging them instead to save. By making it difficult for them to purchase imported goods or buy big-ticket items such as houses or cars, they persuaded, even required, workers to save a high percentage of their earnings. Japanese worker households, for example, put aside nearly 20 percent of their income in the 1950s and 1960s.[11] The money deposited by workers in banks and postal accounts, which paid very low rates of interest, was then collected by banks and the government and used to finance investment in manufacturing industries.[12]

To reward worker-consumer thrift and maintain the lower standards of living that modest consumption entailed, governments in Western Europe and Japan adopted rather different approaches. In Western Europe, governments compensated thrifty workers by providing generous social welfare benefits to workers: pensions, health care, unemployment compensation, and vacations. The "welfare states" established in Western Europe tapped the economic resources of domestic workers and created electoral support for conservative governments. (This contrasted with the United States, where the social benefits provided by the "welfare state" created electoral support in the postwar period for "liberal" government.)

The Japanese government took a rather different approach. It offered worker-consumers few social benefits, which were much less generous than programs in Western Europe or the United States. Instead, the government provided generous financing to industries, which provided male workers in manufacturing and service industries with "lifetime employment" (*shushin koyo*) and a seniority-based wage system (*nenko joretsu seido*).[13] Women employed by large firms were typically hired only on a "temporary" basis and were assigned the status of "miscellaneous workers" even if they worked full-time for many years. Women were thereby largely excluded from the benefits designed to compensate households for their thrift, though it was women who kept households thrifty, as we have seen. The rewards offered male workers were nevertheless sufficient to persuade worker households to support conservative government throughout the postwar period.

Policy makers in the United States could encourage and permit a redistribution of wage work in the core, a process that resulted in the distribution of U.S. jobs to manufacturing industries located elsewhere in the core, because a considerable amount of work needed to be done. Workers were recruited to rebuild whole economies in Western Europe and Japan, wage wars in Korea and Vietnam, fashion weapons and vehicles for arms and space races with the Soviet Union, build houses and supply durable goods for baby-boom households that had scrimped during the Depression and saved during the war, and supply postcolonial states with goods financed by the World Bank and foreign-aid programs. There was so much work to be done that the United States could surrender a significant share of the available wage work to its allies and still provide wage work to most males. So much work was available that industries could even offer jobs to large numbers of minorities, women, and immigrants.

In the United States, the lure of paid work in the North and West, and the pain of institutional racism in the South, persuaded five million African American workers to leave Southern farms for jobs in big cities, where many found wage work in manufacturing and service industries.[14] At war's end, many women were forced out of manufacturing industries to make room for returning servicemen. But while the percentage of women in the labor force dropped from 34.7 percent in 1944 to 31.1 percent in 1954, the decline was small (the number of women who worked for wages actually increased slightly), and women retained a claim on a significant share of the available wage work.[15] U.S. industries even provided work for a large number of immigrants, one million in the late 1940s, 2.5 million more in the 1950s, and another 3.3 million in the 1960s. Agricultural firms also annually recruited another 300,000 to 445,000 workers from Mexico through the government's Bracero Program.[16]

Western Europe experienced such a large demand for wage work that industries could provide virtually full employment for domestic males, provide jobs to eight million ethnic Germans who were forced to migrate from Eastern Europe and the Soviet Union after the war, give jobs to another three million Germans who fled East Germany before the Berlin Wall was built in 1961, and also recruit millions of other workers from Spain, Portugal, southern Italy, Yugoslavia, Greece, and Turkey (each country donated about one million workers to the labor force in Western Europe) through various "Guest Worker" programs during the 1950s and 1960s.[17]

In Japan, meanwhile, industry provided full employment for men; jobs for many women, though on unequal terms; and jobs for another 2.6 million Japanese "immigrants," who migrated from areas occupied by Japan during the war, much as ethnic Germans had done.[18]

Because the demand for wage work was so strong, wages rose across the core, though at different rates. In the United States, wages doubled between 1950 and 1970. Wages rose at an even faster rate in Western Europe and Japan. By 1970, they had become comparable to wage levels in the United States.[19]

But while wages rose more rapidly for workers in Western Europe and Japan, their standards of living did not measure up to the living standard of U.S. workers. Policies that discouraged consumption and promoted savings in Western Europe and Japan forced workers to pay high taxes, spend more of their income on food, and made it difficult for them to purchase cars or homes that were comparable to those available, at a lower cost, to worker households in the United States. One striking measure of different living standards is this. In 1970, 96 percent of U.S. worker households had flush toilets in their homes. But only 9.2 percent of worker households in Japan had flush toilets in their homes or apartments.[20]

During the twenty-five years after the war, wage work was widely available, wages rose, wage differentials narrowed, and standards of living improved, though at different rates, for most worker households in the core. Under these conditions, the redistribution of wage work in manufacturing industries was regarded as unproblematic, even beneficial. For U.S. policy makers, the provision of "U.S. jobs" to industries in Western Europe and Japan was a relatively small price to pay for military unity, political cooperation, and economic growth in the core. But this would change after 1970, when the price of redistributive policies became apparent to wage workers in the United States.

REDISTRIBUTION AND DEINDUSTRIALIZATION, 1971–1979

In 1971, the United States posted a modest trade deficit, its first since 1893. Though small, the $2.3 billion trade deficit signaled that the United States had already lost a significant share of wage work to industries located elsewhere in the core. During the next twenty years, U.S. job losses and trade deficits would mount, and much of the wage work previously performed in U.S. manufacturing industries would be redistributed abroad.

The redistribution of wage work in the core, a process known in the United States as "deindustrialization," accelerated in the 1970s because economic conditions had changed. In the early 1970s, the demand for wage work in the core declined. It fell because the United States withdrew from the war in Vietnam and slowed the pace of the arms and space races with the Soviet Union. It fell, too, because the OPEC oil embargo forced up energy prices, and poor Soviet grain harvests raised food prices. As energy and food prices rose, consumers cut back, and demand weakened, triggering a global recession.

Meanwhile, the global supply of manufactured goods had steadily increased. The recovery and growth of manufacturing industries in Western Europe and Japan increased supplies from the core. The expansion of new manufacturing industries located in the periphery and semiperiphery, which was a product of the "import-substitutionist" policies adopted by capitalist and communist states in these zones during the postwar period (see chapters 5 and 6), greatly increased the supply of manufactured goods produced by wage workers around the world. Under these conditions, the battle for a share of global markets and a claim to a share of the available wage work in manufacturing industries intensified. As they did, many important manufacturing industries in the United States lost markets, and the jobs these industries had provided were redistributed to industries located elsewhere, typically in other core states.

Why was wage work in U.S. manufacturing industries redistributed during the 1970s? There is no single answer. The reasons varied from one industry to the next. A brief look at government policies, industry practices, and consumer behavior in three important manufacturing industries—steel, autos, and aircraft—illustrates some of the different reasons why wage work was redistributed.

Steel

According to Benjamin Fairless, head of U.S. Steel in 1950, the U.S. steel industry was "bigger than those of *all* other nations on the earth put together."[21] But the steel industry declined slowly in the 1960s and then rapidly in the 1970s, victimized by U.S. government policy and its own business practices.

During the postwar period, successive U.S. presidents worked hard to keep steel prices low. They did so to prevent steel price increases from triggering inflation and to ensure that the other U.S. industries that used steel—auto makers, appliance manufacturers—paid low prices for it. When U.S. steel companies announced price hikes, Presidents Kennedy, Johnson, and Nixon attacked the steel industry, lobbied its leaders to rescind price increases, and ordered federal agencies to purchase steel from low-price competitors.[22] But government efforts to keep prices low lowered profit rates and made it difficult for the steel industry to use its earnings to modernize aging plants.[23] The government also used antitrust suits to prevent mergers and promote competition. This helped keep prices low, though mergers might have helped the industry reorganize and increase its efficiency. Ironically, this policy led officials to reject proposed mergers among U.S. firms but allowed the firms to be acquired by *foreign* firms.[24] When steel-industry firms asked the government to levy tariffs on steel imports or prosecute foreign firms' producers that illegally "dumped" cheap steel in U.S. markets, officials repeatedly refused.[25]

For their part, industry leaders were slow to adopt new, energy-efficient technology, relying instead on aging plants and outmoded technologies because they wanted to pay for these before investing in new capacity. In 1978, 45 percent of U.S. plate mills were more than twenty-five years old, while only 5 percent of comparable Japanese mills were this old.[26] The industry's acrimonious relations with labor unions also triggered a series of long strikes in the 1950s, forcing the industry to raise worker pay. The industry might have afforded wage increases if it had invested in new technology and increased productivity, but the government's low-price policies made this difficult to do.[27]

Business consumers also played a role in the steel industry's decline. U.S. businesses that used steel wanted cheap steel, so they lobbied hard against steel-industry efforts to raise prices or secure government protection against unfair foreign competition. General Motors, for instance, argued that actions against countries that dumped low-price steel in the United States "will have a negative effect on the prices [General Motors pays] for finished products with high steel content."[28] Then in the 1970s, as inflation pushed up steel prices, businesses began using plastic and aluminum materials to replace steel in cars and appliances.[29] This reduced the demand for steel, both foreign and domestic.

The U.S. steel industry was among the first U.S. industries to experience deindustrialization. As early as 1959, the United States imported more steel than it exported. By 1970, the U.S. share of world steel production had plummeted to 20 percent, down from 50 percent in 1945. Steel production then fell from 130 million tons in 1970 to 88 million tons in 1985. Today, the industry does not produce enough steel to meet domestic demand, and the United States is "the only major industrial nation that is not self-sufficient in steel."[30]

Autos

The decline of the U.S. auto industry in the 1970s was due less to government policy than it was to business practices and consumer habits. Its decline was significant because at present 7.5 million people build, sell, or repair cars and trucks in the United States.[31]

The Volkswagen "Beetle" was the first import to make inroads in the U.S. market in the 1960s, largely because its size, price, and durability were unmatched by models made in Detroit. By 1970, it had captured 15 percent of the U.S. market.[32] During the 1970s, it was superseded by Japanese models. Japanese cars captured U.S. markets for a variety of reasons. Car makers in Japan adopted new technologies like the system of "just-in-time production," or "*kanban*," which reduced inventory costs and unitized body construction, which made cars stronger and used less steel. Japanese manufacturers developed amicable relations with wage workers in Japan, which helped increase production and improve quality. So when oil prices rose in the 1970s, cost-conscious worker-consumers in the United States turned to high-mileage, inexpensive, durable cars from Japan. They bought 4 million Japanese cars in 1970, 12 million in 1980.

For their part, U.S. auto makers were slow to adopt new technologies and develop cheap, high-quality, fuel-efficient models that could compete with imports. Their acrimonious relations with workers and their unions prevented the industry from significantly improving productivity or quality in the 1960s and 1970s.[33] In 1980, the four major U.S. auto makers lost $4 billion and Chrysler was on the verge of bankruptcy.[34]

Still, unlike the steel industry, U.S. auto makers were not without means. In the 1950s and 1960s, Ford had opened factories in Western Europe, building cars and employing workers there. In the 1970s and 1980s, other U.S. car makers followed suit, opening factories overseas, particularly in Latin America. By 1980, the industry had itself moved 37.2 percent of its production abroad. Wage work in the U.S. auto industry was redistributed partly because other core firms captured U.S. markets with the assistance of U.S. worker-consumers but also because U.S. firms themselves redistributed work to other settings.

Aircraft

Unlike steel or autos, U.S. policy makers provided massive aid to the aircraft industry, which they viewed as essential to national defense. In the 1940s, the government built dams that provided cheap electricity to smelt aluminum, the essential raw material for modern aircraft, and purchased hundreds of thousands of planes from private manufacturers during the war.[35] After the war, the military poured billions of dollars into the industry, financing new technology and designs and providing demand for the development of new military and commercial aircraft. The government's purchase of a transport plane from Boeing enabled the company to launch its first successful commercial aircraft, the 707.[36] As a result, the industry captured 90 percent of the world market, a position it held well into the 1970s.

But U.S. dominance did not go unchallenged. In 1965, aircraft firms in Western Europe organized Airbus, a consortium that used government aid to develop commercial aircraft. Government subsidies and private investment from European and American banks enabled Airbus to develop its first plane (with wings from Britain, cockpit from France, tail from Spain, edge flaps from Belgium, body from West Germany, and, more important, engines from the United States).[37] Unlike its U.S. competitors, the plane ran on two engines rather than three and required two pilots, not three, which saved fuel and lowered operating costs. These were important considerations for Eastern Airline, which made the first significant purchases of the new plane.[38] By 1988, Airbus had captured 23 percent of the world market. It wrested markets and jobs first from weak U.S. firms like Lockheed and McDonnell Douglas. During the next decade, it began challenging Boeing, the world leader. And in 1999, for the first time ever, Airbus received more orders for new planes than Boeing did.[39] Although the deindustrialization of the U.S. aircraft industry came later than it did to the steel and auto industries, the effect was much the same. "Every time a $50 million airplane is sold by Airbus instead of Boeing," one expert observed, "America loses about 3,500 high-paying jobs for one year."[40]

DEINDUSTRIALIZATION AND GENDER ROLES

The redistribution of wage work in the core resulted in job loss and falling wages in U.S. manufacturing industries. Deindustrialization *dis*organized labor because union membership in the United States was concentrated in manufacturing, making it difficult for both unionized and nonunionized workers to raise wages and keep pace with rising prices.[41] Deindustrialization ruined cities built around manufacturing industries. Philadelphia, Chicago, and New York lost 60 percent of their manufacturing jobs in the 1970s.[42] In Youngstown, a city devastated by deindustrialization, the mayor observed, "I shouldn't be saying this, but if I were looking for a future, I wouldn't look for it here."[43]

Not surprisingly, urban deindustrialization triggered a massive migration. Between 1970 and 1979, 11.7 million people left the Northeast and northern Midwest, moving to the South and West.[44] But more important, deindustrialization transformed gender roles.

In the United States, deindustrialization eliminated jobs long reserved for men. When the steel, auto, and aircraft industries surrendered markets and ceded jobs to overseas competitors, they laid off the men who smelted steel, assembled cars, and fabricated aircraft. Except for a brief time during World War II, few women worked in these industries. During the postwar period—indeed, for most of this century—wage work in manufacturing had given men economic power in the labor force (largely through labor unions), political power in public life (primarily through the Democratic Party), and social authority in households (based largely on their role as "breadwinners"). The loss of wage work in manufacturing undermined male power in public life and male authority in private life.

Of course, job loss has not always resulted in the erosion of male power and authority. During the Great Depression, men lost manufacturing jobs in droves. But because few women were employed in manufacturing or service industries, and those who were lost their jobs, too, male job loss did not significantly alter gender roles. In the 1970s, however, male job loss was accompanied by the entry of women into service industries. It was the combination of these two simultaneous developments—the exit of men from manufacturing and the entry of women into service industries—that transformed gender relations.

During the 1970s, a growing number of women secured work in service industries. This is somewhat surprising. One might think that the end of the war in Vietnam, the demobilization of servicemen, and the recession triggered by rising oil and food prices would have resulted in the expulsion of women from the labor force, much as it had after World War II. But women were not expelled because the number of returning servicemen was small, because few women worked in manufacturing industries, and because the service industries where women were employed in large numbers were actually growing in this period.

Women entered the labor force in large numbers during the 1970s for two reasons. First, women needed to secure wage work to maintain household incomes in an inflationary-recessionary, job-and-income-loss environment. In a sense, deindustrialization pushed women into the labor force. Second, the service industry, which historically had reserved jobs for women, needed workers as the demand for its goods and services increased. Growing demand was the product of several related developments. Massive advertising and widely available credit encouraged U.S. workers to spend, not save. Worker households that spent an increasing percentage of their disposable income on consumption, increased the demand for services from the private sector. Increased government spending on social service-welfare programs also increased the demand for public service-sector workers, and women found jobs as teachers, health-care workers, and social service administrators.[45] Moreover, as women left home to take private- and public-sector service jobs, worker households began buying services that women could no longer or easily provide as "housewives." This further stimulated the demand for women workers and also teenagers in service industries.[46] In 1964, for example, only 1.7 million Americans worked in restaurants and bars. But 7.1 million did so in 1994.[47] So the expansion of the service industry helped pull women into the labor force.

As a result of economic push and pull, the percentage of women in the paid workforce increased from 38 percent in 1970 to 43 percent in 1980. This increase was comparable to the rapid gains made by women during World War II. Women continued to enter the labor force, though at a slower rate, after 1980, rising to 45 percent by 1990.[48]

Of course, women who took paid jobs did not stop working at home. They still shouldered substantial nonwage workloads.[49] So women's total work (unpaid household work plus wage work) increased substantially in this period, from an average of about 1,400 hours in 1969 to 1,700 hours in 1987.[50]

Finding paid work was not the only tactic that worker households adopted in response to change. Many also organized their own work. "[B]eginning in the early 1970s, self-employment [which had declined since 1955] began an almost spectacular revival," as workers searched for alternative sources of income.[51] Women played an increasingly important role in these activities. The percentage of women among the self-employed increased from 14 percent to 22 percent during the 1970s.[52] This strategy was particularly important for poor and minority households, which had long relied on self-employment as a significant source of income.[53]

While women assumed more prominent economic roles, they also began playing a larger role in public and private life. Feminism and the emergence of the women's movement in the 1970s encouraged women to play a more visible role in politics and public life. The social status given women by wage income and the autonomy provided by new reproductive technologies and legal rights (the Pill, divorce law reform, abortion rights) made it possible for many women to assume new roles in worker households. Of course, changing economic, political, and social roles for women and men frequently increased tensions between women and men, resulting in high divorce rates and the rise of female-headed households.

This development was perhaps first apparent for poor African American worker households. During the 1950s and 1960s, black men and women had migrated from the South to northern cities, and men found wage work in heavy industries. Because black men were heavily "concentrated in industries like steel" and in cities where manufacturing industries made their home, deindustrialization in the 1970s had a catastrophic impact on jobs and employment industries for African American males.[54]

The exit of black men from manufacturing, and the entry of black women into service industries and government welfare programs, transformed gender relations and contributed to the rise of female-headed households. But while this development has often been portrayed as symptomatic of problems unique to African American households, it can be more usefully understood as the early expression of problems common to most worker households in the United States. The problems evident in African American households were not an aberration but a harbinger. As it turned out, the exit of men from manufacturing and the entry of women into service industries has become a common, global development in recent years. It has not only transformed gender relations for African American households but has also, as we shall see, altered gender relations in worker households throughout the United States, across the core, and around the world.

The ongoing redistribution of work in the core was joined in the 1980s and 1990s by another development: the reorganization of the labor process. This reorganization would have important consequences for the redistribution of work, and for workers, throughout the core.

THE UNITED STATES STRIKES BACK, 1979–1992

The redistribution of wage work, particularly of male wage labor in manufacturing, which generally came at U.S. expense, did not go unnoticed or unchallenged. In the 1980s, U.S. officials, alarmed about the loss of U.S. hegemony, adopted monetary and trade policies designed to reassert U.S. control over the redistributive process, stem manufacturing losses, and reclaim some of the wage work available to industry in the core.

As a first step, U.S. policy makers raised interest rates in 1979. Then in 1985, they again devalued the dollar in relation to the currencies of other core states (they had first done so in 1971). And in 1986, they initiated a series of trade negotiations with members of the General Agreement on Tariffs and Trade (GATT) and with neighboring states in North America.[55]

High U.S. interest rates in the early 1980s persuaded investors in Western Europe, Japan, and Latin America to purchase U.S. treasury bonds. In 1980, for example, foreign investors bought $71 billion worth of U.S. bonds, with two-thirds of the money coming from Western Europe and Japan and most of the rest from Latin America.[56] The subsequent dollar devaluation in 1985 had much the same effect, encouraging investors from Western Europe and Japan to buy U.S. assets (corporations, real estate, and raw materials) and open factories of their own in the United States. In 1987, Japanese firms built or acquired 239 factories in the United States, up from only 43 in 1984. Total foreign investment in the United States, most of it from other core states, increased from $184 billion in 1985 to $304 billion in 1988.[57]

Prior to 1980, public resources and private investment in the core had generally traveled in one direction, from the United States to Western Europe and Japan. But U.S. monetary policies in the 1980s altered investment traffic patterns in the core. As Western European and Japanese investment in the United States increased (first buying public and then purchasing private assets), investment became multilateral, not unilateral. The emergence of a multilateral or "globalized" investment, however, was generally restricted to the core. It did not extend to the periphery or semiperiphery. Only about one-quarter of U.S. aid and investment found its way to countries in the periphery and semiperiphery, a point we will examine in subsequent chapters.[58]

Much the same was true of trade. U.S. trade negotiations in the late 1980s and early 1990s were designed to reduce core barriers to U.S. exports. By persuading Western Europe and Japan to reduce trade and other barriers, U.S. officials hoped to increase U.S. exports and change the direction of trade flow. In the 1970s and 1980s, trade goods had been moving from Western Europe and Japan to the United States. The trade agreement adopted by GATT members in 1994 helped stimulate the flow of U.S. goods to its main trading partners, thereby multilateralizing trade, along with investment.

Taken together, U.S. monetary and trade policies helped attract core investment to the United States and force U.S. allies to open their doors to some U.S. goods. Essentially, these measures rescinded the economic advantages that U.S. policy makers had given Western Europe and Japan in the late 1940s, when generous monetary and trade policies were used to promote economic recovery and political cooperation during the Cold War. But while these steps helped level the economic playing field in the core, they did not greatly improve U.S. performance on the field. The redistribution of wage work continued in the 1980s, though at a slower pace than it had in the 1970s.

U.S. monetary policies also had adverse consequences for some wage workers in the United States and in Western Europe and Japan, as well as a devastating impact on governments, businesses, and workers in the periphery and semiperiphery, developments that will be more fully explored in subsequent chapters.

In the United States, high interest rates in the early 1980s clobbered interest-rate-sensitive industries, particularly housing and agriculture, leading to job losses for workers in construction, banking, farming, and the many industries associated with them.

Housing

As interest rates rose, consumers withdrew money from their accounts with savings and loan companies (S&Ls) and purchased government securities, which offered higher rates than S&Ls were allowed to pay.[59] To protect S&Ls from massive losses (almost $22 billion in 1981), the government in 1981 allowed them to raise interest payments to depositors. But this meant that S&Ls were paying depositors more in interest than the banks were earning on the interest paid by borrowers, who had contracted for home loans at low, long-term, fixed rates. So S&Ls began losing money, and the industry was threatened with widespread bankruptcy.

To prevent S&Ls from going under, the government in 1982 allowed them to make commercial loans and offer consumer credit, like commercial banks, so they could increase their earnings (commercial loans and credit cards pay much higher interest than home loans) and thus restore their profitability. But massive investments in commercial real estate led to a glut of office buildings. When the commercial real estate market collapsed in 1985, the S&L industry was driven into bankruptcy. By 1990, 40 percent of the industry was bankrupt, forcing the government to spend more than $200 billion to bail out depositors in failed S&Ls.

The collapse of the S&L industry crippled the residential construction industry, which had long relied on S&Ls to finance home construction. The construction industry, which had already been slowed by high interest rates and recession, found itself hard pressed to obtain financing as S&Ls reduced home loans and increased their investment in commercial real estate. And the construction industry was hammered when S&Ls went bankrupt and its primary source of financing evaporated. In 1984, the construction industry built only 1.7 million homes, down from 2.4 million a decade earlier, when the population was smaller and the demand for housing was weaker.[60]

As S&Ls collapsed and the construction industry withered, jobs in both industries were lost, adversely affecting the 4.4 million men employed in construction, the most labor-intensive industry in America, and the millions of other men and women in banking, timber, furniture, landscape, hardware, plumbing, electrical, heating and air conditioning, flooring, carpeting, drapery, home furnishings, and roofing.[61] Because the residential housing industry has not since recovered, the gap between demand and supply has continued to grow, forcing up prices and rents for worker-consumer households across the country.[62]

Agriculture

High interest rates also clobbered farmers, many of whom had borrowed heavily in the 1970s to expand production and reap the high prices associated with repeated

Soviet crop failures.[63] When Soviet harvests recovered and world food prices fell, and interest rates rose, many U.S. farmers were driven into bankruptcy. Although the number of farmers ruined by rising interest rates and falling commodity prices was relatively small (400,000 went bankrupt in the early 1980s), their demise had a significant impact on other businesses and workers in rural communities.

Farm bankruptcy had a widespread impact because farm households are really big consumers. The average farm household consumes more in a year than a steelworker household consumes in a lifetime. A farm household might borrow $100,000 each year to buy what it needs to grow food; a steel-worker household might borrow that sum to buy a house only once every thirty years. So the ruin of even a few farmers had a devastating impact on small businesses and the workers they employed in rural towns. Moreover, the entry of men and women from bankrupt or struggling farm households into local labor markets usually depressed wages for the jobs that remained.

U.S. monetary policies not only had an adverse impact on U.S. workers in housing and agriculture, they also affected some groups of workers in Western Europe and Japan. Although workers in Western Europe and Japan generally gained from the redistribution of work, they did not escape the effects of new monetary policies unscathed. High interest rates triggered a global recession in the early 1980s. As recession took hold, governments in Western Europe forced hundreds of thousands of immigrant "guest workers" back to their countries of origin in southern Europe. This prevented recession from hitting domestic wage workers full force. But by emptying their labor force of "surplus" immigrant workers in the 1980s, they would have no buffer to shield domestic workers from the next recession, which appeared in the 1990s.

In Japan, the recession was milder because manufacturing industries were generally able to increase their exports to the United States during the 1980s. Where industries did have to cut back, they laid off "temporary workers," most of them women. Temporary women workers in Japan, like immigrant wage workers in Western Europe, bore the brunt of recession in the early 1980s. But when recession appeared again in the 1990s, Japanese industries, having shed their "temporary" workers, would have to begin laying off men in secure, "lifetime" jobs.[64]

THE REORGANIZATION OF WORK IN THE CORE

Although U.S. monetary and trade policies may have leveled the playing field of global work, they did not improve U.S. performance on it. But it turned out that other, largely unappreciated policy changes did have an enormous impact on work and workers in the United States and, eventually on work and workers across the core. When U.S. officials amended social security, income tax, and antitrust programs in the early 1980s, they created conditions for a large-scale reorganization of work in manufacturing and service industries. This reorganization helped U.S. industries regain markets and increase their share of wage work in the 1990s, when industries in Japan and Western Europe slumped. For wage workers in the United States, this reorganization resulted in "downsizing" and income loss. But these losses were concealed, at least for a time, by U.S. economic growth in the late 1990s.

The massive reorganization of work in the United States was propelled by small but important policy changes in the early 1980s. In 1981, the Reagan administration passed legislation to reform Social Security. As part of the package, officials made Individual Retirement Accounts (IRAs) more widely available to worker households.[65] Workers rushed to take advantage of the tax breaks given to IRA accounts, and deposits in IRAs increased from $30 billion in 1980 to $370 billion in 1990, a more than ten-fold increase. Much of the money deposited in IRA and 401(k) accounts, which also grew rapidly, was invested in the stock market, typically through mutual funds. In 1982, less than 10 percent of U.S. households owned stocks. But tax-free accounts encouraged millions to invest in the stock market, and by 1998, nearly 49 percent of U.S. households owned stocks.[66]

In the mid-1980s, worker-investors were joined by wealthy households and foreign investors. Wealthy Americans used money given them by tax cuts (the Reagan administration cut taxes on wealthy households from 70 percent to 28 percent in the early 1980s) to invest in the stock market. Foreign investors rushed to purchase U.S. stocks after the dollar was devalued in 1985 (the devaluation cut the price of U.S. assets for foreign buyers), and foreign investment in the stock market totaled $176 billion in 1986.

While government policies pushed investors toward the stock market, Wall Street exerted its own pull. The market was able to attract investors from worker, wealthy, and foreign households because stock prices were rising for the first time in a decade. The market's initial rise was given a jump start by two new government policies. First, corporate income-tax cuts allowed businesses to increase their dividends to shareholders, making them more attractive to investors. Second, and more important, the Reagan administration abandoned antitrust enforcement. This allowed businesses to merge with other firms, cut costs, increase profits, and raise dividends. This made them even more attractive to investors.

As new investment was pushed and pulled into Wall Street, stock prices rose, bid up by growing demand. Rising stock prices in turn put enormous pressure on U.S. corporations to boost profits and increase their pay-outs to investors, who expected dividends to keep pace with rising stock prices. To keep up with the Dow Joneses, corporate managers reorganized work. They merged with other firms, rearranged production, introduced new technology, and laid off or downsized workers in an unrelenting effort to raise productivity, cut costs, and increase profits. Higher profits could then be used to increase shareholder dividends, and this would help boost stock prices.

Between 1982 and 1987, the Dow Jones Industrial Average rose from 777 to 2,722, a three-fold increase. This bull market came to an end on October 19, 1987, when prices fell 508 points, a 22-percent decline that resulted in a $1 trillion loss for investors. But the market soon recovered because the demand for stocks did not evaporate, as it had after the 1929 crash. Demand remained strong because worker-investors who held stocks in IRAs and 401(k)s could not easily withdraw their money without incurring stiff tax penalties. Worker households were, in effect, forced by the tax code to stay in the market and prop up prices. When other investors realized that the government and worker households had built a floor under the stock market, below which prices could not easily fall, investment resumed. By 1990, investment had returned to pre-crash levels and prices began to rise again. Stock prices then surged upward, and the Dow climbed from 3,000 in 1990 to more than 11,000 in 1999, the longest bull market in U.S. history. As stock prices rose, the reorganization of work accelerated.

For businesses, rising stock prices put enormous pressure on managers to increase their profits so they could pay higher dividends to investors.[67] Firms that failed to do so were punished by investors, who sold off stock and drove down its price. When that happened, managers were fired and the firm became prey to others. To prevent this and survive in an inflationary stock-price environment, managers have adopted two strategies to increase profits, pay-outs, and share prices. Both strategies typically resulted in job loss for workers.

The first strategy has been to reorganize the firm by merging with other firms, sometimes divesting parts to relieve themselves of unprofitable burdens or to raise cash for other parts. By merging with other firms, managers tried to create economies of scale or obtain control of markets that would enable them to increase profits. Of course, this strategy only became feasible because the federal government stopped enforcing antitrust laws.[68]

In 1980, the year before the current merger wave began, corporations announced mergers worth $33 billion. Since then, businesses have merged and merged again. On just one day in 1998 (November 23), corporate managers announced mergers worth $40 billion, a sum greater than the value of all mergers in 1980.[69] Between 1981 and 1996, firms arranged mergers worth $2 trillion. And the pace has since accelerated, with mergers worth $1 trillion recorded in 1997 and $1.6 trillion in 1998.[70] All told, there were 151,374 mergers worth $13 trillion between 1980 and 2000. "We're in the greatest merger wave in history," said John Shepard Wiley, a professor of antitrust law at UCLA "There has been a sea change in [public] attitudes toward large mergers."[71]

A second strategy has been to reorganize production, introduce new technology, lay off workers, and cut costs to increase productivity. For example, managers at Caterpillar, a heavy equipment manufacturer, closed nine plants and spent $1.8 billion to modernize its remaining factories. As new technology was introduced, the firm cut its workforce from 90,000 to 54,000 and increased production. "We've almost doubled our productivity since the mid-1980s," Caterpillar executive James Owens enthused.[72]

Business efforts to increase productivity have not been limited to manufacturing industries. Computer, phone, fax, and other electronic technologies—scanners, automatic tellers, and so on—have enabled managers to reorganize service-sector firms, where it had long been difficult to deploy technology as a way of increasing productivity. The demand for technology that can improve productivity has spawned the growth of the computer industry, which in turn has transformed service industries. In 1995, experts predicted that "half of the nation's 59,000 branch banks will close and 450,000 of the 2.8 million jobs in the banking industry will disappear [by the year 2000]" as a result of new bank technologies like automated tellers.[73] As Carl Thur, president of the American Productivity Center, put it, "The trick [for U.S. business] is to get more output without a surge in employment."[74]

In the 1970s and early 1980s, productivity in U.S. firms increased slowly. But by combining firms, reorganizing business, introducing new technologies, laying off workers, and cutting costs, managers were able to increase the productivity of their firms. Between 1982 and 1994, "productivity increased about 19.5 percent."[75] Since then it has recently increased at high annual rates: 2.8 percent in 1996, 2.5 percent in 1997, and 3.0 percent in 1998. These rates are significantly higher than the 1.1 percent annual increases reported from 1973 to 1989.[76]

Increased productivity helped U.S. firms raise profits. Between 1983 and 1996, annual corporate profits nearly quadrupled, from less than $200 billion to $736 billion.[77] Higher profits made it possible to increase dividends to shareholders. This in turn has increased the value of corporate stock, drawn new money into the stock market, and driven stock prices higher, and higher still.

For workers, the reorganization of work, which was driven by the stock market, has resulted in massive job loss or, as it came to be known, "downsizing." Like other phrases used in the 1980s and 1990s—"involuntary force reductions," "right-sizing," "repositioning," "deselection," "reducing head count," "separated," "severed," "unassigned," and "reductions in force"—downsizing has meant one thing: "You're fired."

Mergers resulted in job loss because some jobs in combined firms overlapped. Merged banks did not need two branches on the same street, merged manufacturing firms did not need two sets of accountants to keep the books, much less two assembly lines making the same goods under different brand names.

Between 1981 and 1991, 4 million workers at Fortune 500 companies lost their jobs, and total employment in these large firms fell from 16 to 12 million workers.[78] By 1998, the 800 largest U.S. firms employed only 17 percent of the workforce, down from nearly 26 percent in 1978.[79] Firms throughout the economy accelerated the pace of layoffs: 1.42 million workers were laid off in 1980, 3.26 million in 1995.[80] Of course, new jobs were also created, but many of them were on a part-time, temporary, or contractual basis. Some firms even "leased" their workers to other firms to cut costs and evade labor-law restrictions.[81] As many as 30 million workers are now employed on a part-time, temporary, or contractual basis.[82]

Previous waves of change affected male workers in manufacturing: steel, autos, aircraft, construction. But contemporary downsizing has affected men and women, in manufacturing and service industries. It has affected skilled workers and college graduates, not just workers with high school diplomas.[83] It has affected White workers, not just Blacks and Hispanics. It has affected managers in offices and assembly-line workers in factories. It has created two-tier workplaces, where permanent employees work alongside temporary or "permatemp" workers, who do the same jobs but receive very different salaries and benefits.[84] The only groups of workers that have been relatively immune from downsizing have been government workers and public-sector employees like teachers.

Ongoing job loss and the rise of temporary and part-time employment have made it extremely difficult for workers to raise wages, even though their productivity has increased and profits have grown. This contrasts sharply with the early postwar period, when productivity gains enabled firms to increase profits. Corporations raised wages both because they could afford to do so and because widespread union membership helped workers insist that productivity gains be shared. But this has changed. The reorganization of work *dis*organized workers and weakened unions. Today, the percentage of unionized workers in private industry (only 9.4 percent) is what it was in 1929.[85] Unions would have to recruit 15 million new members to regain their postwar strength.[86] While the reorganization of work has weakened worker claims on the profits created by productivity increases, it has strengthened investor claims on corporate profits. Because the reorganization of work is now being driven largely by the stock market, investors can now insist that any gains be shared with stockholders and managers, not with workers. As a result, workers have not been able to increase wages, despite the fact that corporations could afford to do so.

There is serious irony here. Workers who invested in the stock market to provide for their retirement helped fuel the stock-price inflation that forced corporations to reorganize and, in the process, downsize workers. As investors, many workers benefited from rising stock prices and the corporate distribution of profits to shareholders. But as workers, many investors experienced job and income loss, which resulted from the reorganization of work and redistribution of profits. One *New York Times* writer captured this irony for workers in a headline, which read, "You're Fired! (but Your Stock Is Way Up)."[87]

The reorganization of work led to job loss and declining wages. Labor's share of the national income declined, and the wealth it once claimed has been redistributed upward.[88] The richest 2.7 million Americans now claim as much wealth as the bottom 100 million Americans, and in 1999, 215 million American workers took "home a thinner slice of the economic pie than [they did] in 1977."[89]

Moreover, men and women are working longer hours. Juliet Schor, author of *The Overworked American*, estimates that the hours worked by wage workers in the United States increased to 1,966 in 1999, surpassing the Japanese by 70 hours and Europeans by 320 hours (or almost nine full work weeks). "Excessive working time is a major problem," she concluded.[90]

Because men and women are working longer, many workers have less time for family, friends, or vacations. Working parents today spend "40 percent less time with their children than they did 30 years ago," MIT economist Lester Thurow reported.[91] Friendships also suffer from heavy workloads. Kim Sibley, who juggles two jobs in Flint, Michigan, was asked by a reporter whether her friends also had dual careers. "I don't have time for friends," she replied.[92]

Vacations are also a disappearing entity. In 1996, 38 percent of all worker families in the United States did not take any vacation, an increase from the 34 percent who did not vacation in 1995. And the average length of vacations for those who do manage to enjoy time off has declined from five days to four days in the last ten years.[93]

Increased workloads can sometimes be fatal. The number of workers asked to work evening or night shifts has increased 30 percent since 1985, and 15 million workers now work night shifts. As a result, the number of fatigue-related auto accidents has increased. Government highway safety officials estimate that 1,500 traffic deaths and 40,000 injuries are caused annually by fatigued workers, particularly those with late shifts.[94]

BOOM AND BUST IN THE CORE

The reorganization of work resulted in job and income loss for both women and men in the United States. But it also helped manufacturing and service industries increase productivity and profitability, which helped industry increase investment in research and development.[95] These developments improved the performance of U.S. industries in the 1990s in redistributive battles with industries based in other core states. The gains made by U.S. businesses in the 1990s promoted overall economic growth, providing jobs for downsized wage workers, at least for a time, though on a more casual and lower-paid basis.

U.S. businesses expanded and unemployment rates fell after 1992 as a result of several developments in the core, the periphery, and the semiperiphery. Slumping economic development in these regions weakened manufacturing and service industries based there, providing reorganized U.S. industries with the opportunity to make redistributive gains. U.S. businesses did well in the 1990s because businesses in Japan, Western Europe, the periphery, and the semiperiphery did not.

In the early 1990s, Japan and Western Europe both experienced economic crises. Although the crises had different origins in each, both regions were confronted with their first real setbacks since World War II, problems that persisted throughout the decade.

In Japan, problems began in 1985. The devaluation of the dollar eventually doubled the value of the yen, increasing the value of assets held by Japanese banks, which more than doubled in the late 1980s. Banks and workers invested this newfound wealth in the stock market and in real estate. The flood of new investment bid up stock and real estate prices. The Nikkei Index (the Japanese stock market) rose from 12,000 in 1986 to 38,916 in 1990, a three-fold increase.[96] The price of residential and commercial real estate quadrupled between 1985 and 1990.[97] It was said in 1990 that the value of land in Tokyo alone was worth more than all the land in the United States. Japanese worker-consumers had so much money to burn that they even poured money into the market for pet insects, particularly for rare beetles called *ohkuwagata*. In 1990, single bugs sold for $7,000 at department stores, and one huge specimen sold for $30,000.[98]

But too much money can cause problems. The money pouring into the stock and real estate markets drove prices to unsustainably high levels. In the stock market, prices soared while dividend yields fell.[99] The "bubble" of high stock prices burst in 1990. Prices fell one-half by 1991 and continued falling. Between 1990 and 1992, the Nikkei Index registered a 61-percent decline.[100] Stock prices did not recover from the crash in Japan, as they had in the United States after the 1987 crash, because worker-investors fled the market and did not return.

The real estate market soon followed. In 1990, some worker households in Japan found they would need to use the wages of a lifetime just to buy one *tsubo* (six feet by six feet) of land in Tokyo.[101] When owners discovered they could not sell high-priced property, the residential and commercial real estate markets collapsed and prices plummeted, bankrupting individuals, businesses, and banks that had used land as collateral for other loans. The pet insect market also collapsed. Bugs that sold for $7,000 during the beetle-mania of the 1980s were marked down to only $300 in 1999.[102]

For workers, the recession led to widespread layoffs and rising unemployment rates, which doubled in the 1990s. This came as a great shock to workers in a country where businesses routinely provided lifetime employment and regular wage increases to many of their workers, most of them male. Corporations began laying off workers, hiring "temporary" workers, eliminating seniority-based pay systems, and introducing "merit pay."[103] "For years, everyone's pay increased as they got older," observed Shoji Hiraide, general manager of a Tokyo department store. "It made everyone think that we are all in the middle class. But lifetime employment is crumbling and salaries are based more on merit and performance. In seven or eight years, Japanese society will look much more like Western society, with gaps between rich and poor that can be clearly seen."[104]

The recession fell most heavily on female workers, who were long treated as "temporary workers" by corporations that guaranteed lifetime employment only to men. Women in temporary jobs were dismissed first. The government disguised rising employment for women by recording them as "housewives," not "unemployed workers." This practice understated real unemployment rates. The fact that Japanese businesses downsized even men in lifetime positions meant that they had already laid off a great many women. "Somehow, although I've done nothing wrong, I feel like a criminal," Kimiko Kauda said after being fired from her job of thirty years. "I have never heard of people being fired in my neighborhood or among my friends."[105]

Western Europe also became mired in recession during the 1990s, though for different reasons than Japan. The 1989 collapse of the communist government in East Germany led to German unification. The German government then spent $600 billion to rebuild the region's economic infrastructure, provide benefits to workers, purchase voter loyalty, and prevent a "widespread social explosion" by workers laid off as the East deindustrialized.[106] Because spending on this scale—$600 billion for a small region with the population of New York state—can trigger inflation, the government raised taxes and the Bundesbank, which controls monetary policy, raised interest rates to reduce inflationary pressures. These measures triggered a sharp recession and widespread job loss.[107] In the early 1990s, unemployment rates doubled from 6 percent to 12 percent in Germany and were twice this rate in the East, where deindustrialization and recession were joined. Faced with high unemployment rates, German unions agreed to substantial pay cuts (10 percent in 1997), benefit reductions, shorter vacations, and work-rule concessions. "Corporations want to abolish the social consensus in Germany," union negotiator Peter Blechschmidt said of the 1997 wage cuts. "They are trying to change this into a different country."[108] A country more like the United States.

The situation in Germany was not unique. Countries throughout Western Europe also experienced recession and rising unemployment, partly due to the cost of European unification. In 1991, most Western European states agreed at Maastricht, in the Netherlands, to adopt a common currency (the United Kingdom has so far abstained). To prepare for the introduction of a single currency in 1999, governments in the European Union set a number of common economic goals: reducing budget deficits, stabilizing exchange rates, and, most important, reducing inflation. To meet this last goal, member governments raised interest rates. As in Germany, high interest rates triggered a regional recession, and unemployment soared throughout Europe. Unemployment rose to 12 percent in France and Italy, 13 percent in Ireland, 22 percent in Spain, and even more in regions like southern Italy.[109]

Although recession and job loss affected workers throughout Western Europe, women were the big losers, particularly in eastern Germany. Nearly 60 percent of the four million who had been employed in 1989 lost their jobs during the next four years.[110] Only half as many men lost their jobs in the same period. Young people have also been affected in disproportionate numbers. Like Japan, Western European industries had strong seniority systems. So when recession hit, they laid off younger workers. In general, young people were unemployed at twice the rate (21.8 percent) as workers over twenty-five years old.[111]

While economies in Japan and Western Europe languished, communist economies in Eastern Europe and the Soviet Union collapsed, and economies across the periphery and semiperiphery staggered under debt-crisis burdens, developments that will be examined in subsequent chapters. Slumping economies weakened manufacturing and service industries located in the core, periphery, and semiperiphery, providing opportunities for reorganized industries based in the United States.

Of course, by the late 1990s, governments and industries in Western Europe and Japan responded to renewed U.S. competitiveness by reorganizing work. They did so by adopting measures pioneered in the United States. For a start, governments and businesses have tried to increase the role played by investors and stock markets. In Germany, for instance, worker-consumers are being encouraged to adopt an *Aktienkulture*, or "stock culture," and invest their substantial savings in the stock market.[112] To facilitate this, the government plans to cut capital gains taxes on German corporations, which would make it easier for them to reorganize and consolidate industry.[113] And business has increased advertising expenditures to encourage stock market investment. Deutsche Telekom recently spent $150 million on a campaign to advertise a $10 billion stock offering, which was then used to purchase Telecom

Italia, one of the first big cross-border mergers in Western Europe.[114] These policies and practices are helping jump-start the *Aktienkulture*, not only in Germany but across Europe.[115]

Mergers play an important role in the reorganization of work. The value of annual mergers in Western Europe jumped dramatically in the second half of the 1990s, growing from about $150 billion in 1994 to more than $600 billion in 1999.[116] As businesses merged and modernized, they typically downsized workers, just like their corporate counterparts in the United States. This has helped keep unemployment rates high. Downsizing, together with efforts to curb seniority-based pay systems and exact wage concessions from unionized workers, has kept wages from rising, as they had in the past.

Of course, if industries in Western Europe and Japan successfully reorganize along U.S. lines (the process currently appears more rapid in Western Europe than in Japan), they will likely increase their ability to compete in redistributive battles with the United States and reclaim some of the wage work obtained by U.S. industries in the 1990s. This would again redistribute work, raise unemployment, and reveal the job losses incurred by wage workers as a result of the reorganization of work in the United States.

The redistribution and reorganization of work have resulted in job and income loss for wage workers across the core. But while wage workers face many of the same problems, they do so with different resources at their disposal.

In the United States, worker households are heavily indebted. To maintain their standards of living, they have spent down their savings. The year 1998 was a turning point. This was the first year since the Great Depression that U.S. workers did not acquire any net savings.[117] As savings declined, household debts increased. The average consumer debt per household nearly doubled in the last decade, rising from nearly $39,000 in 1990 to $66,000 in 2000. And since 1973, debt has grown as a percentage of income from 58 percent to 85 percent.[118]

Although much of the $5.5 trillion in total household debt is in the form of home loans, worker households owe $350 billion on their credit cards.[119] Not surprisingly, bankruptcies are at record levels: one in 100 households annually declares bankruptcy.[120] "There is a lid on earnings, but meanwhile, people's cost of living and their desire for fancier lifestyles go unabated," observed A. Stevens Quigley, a Seattle bankruptcy lawyer.[121] Student debt also grew from $18 billion to $33 billion between 1991 and 1997, and graduates owe $18,000 on average when they leave college.[122]

Although worker households are up to their ears in debt, some can tap other resources that are not typically counted in savings-rate/debt-burden ledgers. The generation of workers that accumulated savings, pensions, and houses during the 1950s and 1960s has transferred important assets to its children, the heavily indebted baby-boomers. Some economists estimate that as much as 25 percent of worker-household income comes from parents and relatives.[123] Essentially, the postwar generation has helped the current generation of wage workers survive. In addition to income from this source, worker households that used IRAs to invest in the stock market have generally seen the value of their stocks rise, which would boost their real savings.[124] But even after adjusting for income from these two sources, which are not available to most worker households, U.S. worker households are still heavily indebted.

Compare the condition of worker households in the United States with worker households in Japan and Western Europe. Although savings rates in Japan and Western Europe have recently declined, as workers used up some savings during the recession and retired workers spent their accumulated savings, they still save a large percentage of their income.[125] In Japan, households saved, on average, 12 percent of their disposable income in 1999 and had $100,000 in the bank.[126]

In the United States, workers are heavily indebted and household account balances are in the "red." But in Japan and Western Europe, where workers have substantial savings and few debts, household account balances are in the "black." As a consequence, households in Japan and Western Europe are in a much better position to weather changes associated with the redistribution and reorganization of work than their peers are in the United States. So while worker households across the core now have comparable incomes and face similar problems, they confront economic change with different resources. Thus, when new economic storms emerge, their fortunes may diverge.

LONG-TERM TRENDS

Since World War II, wage work in the core has been redistributed and reorganized. Initially, the redistribution of work was managed largely by government policies—exchange rates, tariff barriers, defense spending, and foreign aid. But today, the redistribution of work is directed increasingly by the cross-border corporations that formed when industries reorganized: Mercedes-Chrysler; Ford-Volvo; Renault-Nissan; Aegon TransAmerica-Deutsche Telekom-Telecom Italia; Volkswagen-Rolls Royce, and MCI-British Telecom. These cross-border corporations (XBCs) differ from their transnational corporation (TNC) predecessors. TNCs were firms based in one core state, which conducted business through subsidiaries in other states (in the core, the periphery, and the semiperiphery). XBCs, by contrast, are firms with origins in more than one core state, usually formed by mergers, which conduct business in other states. Of course, government policies played an important role in initiating and facilitating the reorganization and the emergence of XBCs. But because XBCs now manage the redistribution of work as a process internal to the corporation, government policies that used to shape the redistributive process now play a less significant role in determining outcomes.

It is important to note that the redistribution of wage work, managed first by governments and more recently by XBCs, generally resulted in the redistribution of work *within* the core. Jobs in U.S. industries were redistributed to industries in Western Europe and Japan, not to industries in the periphery and semiperiphery. Ford workers in Detroit lost jobs to Toyota workers in Yokohama and Volkswagen workers in Munich;

Boeing workers in Seattle lost jobs to Airbus workers in London, Paris, Milan, and Hamburg. Of course, some wage work in the core was redistributed to industries in the periphery and semiperiphery, but not much. With a few exceptions, which we will examine in subsequent chapters, the redistribution and reorganization of wage work, two processes that define contemporary "globalization," have been generally confined in the core. As such, we think that "globalization" should be understood as a "selective," not "ubiquitous," process, which best characterizes developments in the core, not in the periphery and semiperiphery.

During the twenty-five years after World War II, the redistribution of wage work in the core was relatively unproblematic, occurring as it did during a vigorous expansion of the world-economy. But it became a more onerous process between 1970 and 1992, when the world-economy slumped. During this period, wage workers in the United States bore the brunt of change. The reorganization of work, which began in the United States during the 1980s, allowed U.S. industries to regain some control of the redistributive process in the 1990s, when the world-economy entered a new expansionary phase.

The current expansion of the world-economy, however, differs in important respects from the postwar boom. The current expansion is weaker than it was after World War II because the global demand for goods and services is not as strong, and the supply of goods is potentially greater.

The expansion of the world-economy depends first on a growing demand for goods and services by businesses and working people. Demand expanded in the 1990s because worker households in the United States used their savings and borrowed money to shop and buy. "The American consumer has taken the globe from deep contraction back to flatness to recovery," one investment analyst observed.[127] Demand grew, too, because worker households in Western Europe and Japan increased their consumption somewhat, though they still save more and consume less than workers in the United States.[128] And demand grew in the periphery and semiperiphery because workers began buying imported goods long denied them by capitalist and communist dictatorships that insisted they purchase only domestic manufactures.

But while demand has grown, it is weak compared to the period after World War II, largely because U.S. worker households are tapped out. It will be difficult for U.S. working-class households to continue spending at current rates as their debts mount and their wages stagnate, a direct result of the reorganization process. Back in the 1950s, wartime savings and rising wages enabled worker households to consume more. Rising consumer demand in turn helped fuel the expansion, a synergy described by economists as "Fordism." But the current reorganization of work is "anti-Fordist" because it does not permit wage increases and relies instead on debt, not savings, to fuel expansion. Without wage increases, it will be difficult for worker households to increase consumption, strengthen demand, and fuel continued economic expansion.[129]

States in the core and throughout the periphery and semiperiphery also constrain economic growth because they have cut back on military spending and social-welfare spending (a development we will examine in detail in chapter 7). The end of Cold War arms and space races, debt crises, and shrinking tax revenues have forced states to cut back.

Demand is also weak because potential consumers in the periphery and semiperiphery cannot easily obtain the economic resources they need to finance increased consumption. For much of the postwar period, states and businesses in the periphery and semiperiphery could obtain money from the core. Core states, private investors, and global financial institutions such as the World Bank, International Monetary Fund, and Eurocurrency market were eager to lend money and provide aid as a way to finance increased consumption. But with the onset of the debt crisis, and the increasing reluctance of core states, investors, and global institutions to provide inexpensive, long-term financing, it has become difficult for states and businesses in the periphery and semiperiphery to increase consumption levels very much. There is no effort on the part of core states to provide the kind of financing they did after World War II, which might have been used to assist democratizing and postcommunist states in the periphery and semiperiphery. Markets in the Third World will remain small and demand from these regions will probably remain weak.

Of course, the deindustrialization that occurred in indebted and democratizing states across the periphery and semiperiphery during the 1980s and 1990s reduced the global supply of goods and services available to the world-economy.[130] The collapse of industry there made it possible for core industries to expand their production of goods and services for the world-economy. Because the United States reorganized work in manufacturing and service industries during this period, firms were able to supply goods more readily than their business counterparts in Western Europe and Japan.

But while the collapse of suppliers in the periphery and semiperiphery was comparable in real terms to the destruction of industries during World War II, it is a lot easier for manufacturing and service industries in the core to increase supplies, pick up the slack, and meet any growing demand.

New supplies are more readily available today than they were after 1945 because industries in the core are intact and they are using new production technologies to increase supplies. Because core industries were not generally disturbed by the debt crisis, they can quickly expand to meet growing demand.

Although the world-economy is expanding, its demand side is weaker, and its supply side is stronger, than it was during the postwar period. Because the forces that combined to promote sustained growth (strong demand, inadequate supplies) are not in evidence today (weak demand, strong supplies), the current expansion will likely be shorter and less intense. For wage workers, who have profited little from the expansion in the 1990s, a quick end to a modest expansion would result in serious losses, particularly for heavily indebted households in the United States. And the end could come abruptly if there is any severe deflation of stock prices on Wall Street, where price/equity ratios have increased dramatically and turnover rates have quickened.[131] These developments are probably unsustainable in the long run because they depend on workers to invest and consume, workers whose ability to invest and consume is being undermined by the reorganization of work.[132] Workers in a gendered workforce, who also participate in gendered household work, may respond to further intercore job redistribution, and possible economic breakdown, in dramatic and unanticipated ways.

NOTES

1. Bertrand Bellon and Jorge Niosi, *The Decline of the American Economy* (Montreal: Black Rose, 1988), 29.
2. T. E. Vadney, *The World since 1945* (London: Penguin, 1992), 73.
3. Ruth Sivard, *World Military and Social Expenditures, 1987–88* (Washington, D.C.: World Priorities, 1987), 37.
4. Eric Helleiner, *States and the Reemergence of Global Finance: From Bretton Woods to the 1990s* (Ithaca, N.Y.: Cornell University Press, 1994), 58–59.
5. Henry C. Dethloff, *The United States and the Global Economy since 1945* (New York: Harcourt Brace, 1997), 72.
6. Richard J. Barnet and John Cavanah, *Global Dreams: Imperial Corporations and the New World Order* (New York: Touchstone, 1994), 113; Peter Dicken, *Global Shift: The Internationalization of Economic Activity* (New York: Guilford Press, 1992), 67.
7. Ikeda Satoshi, "World Production," in Terence K. Hopkins and Immanuel Wallerstein, eds., *The Age of Transition: Trajectory of the World-System, 1945–2025* (London: Zed, 1996), 48; A. G. Kenwood and A. L. Lougheed, *The Growth of the International Economy, 1820–1990* (London: Routledge, 1992), 250; Ernst Mandel, *Europe vs. America: Contradictions of Imperialism* (New York: Monthly Review Press, 1970), 13; Cynthia Day Wallace and John M. Kline, *EC 92 and Changing Global Investment Patterns: Implications for the U.S.–EC Relationship* (Washington, D.C.: Center for Strategic and International Studies, 1992), 2; Barnet and Cavanah, *Global Dreams*, 42.
8. This is a rough estimate. Economists calculate that $1 billion of U.S. investment overseas results in the loss of 26,500 domestic jobs. So investments worth $78 billion would result in the loss of more than two million jobs in the United States, the number of people living in Boston, Kansas City, Miami, and San Francisco.
9. Robert K. Schaeffer, *Understanding Globalization: The Social Consequences of Political, Economic, and Environmental Change* (Lanham, Md.: Rowman & Littlefield, 1997), 43–44; Shigeto Tsru, *Japan's Capitalism: Creative Defeat and Beyond* (Cambridge: Cambridge University Press, 1993), 49–51, 78.
10. Saskia Sassen, *Globalization and Its Discontents* (New York: Harcourt Brace, 1997), 39, 79.
11. Jon Halliday, *A Political History of Japanese Capitalism* (New York: Pantheon, 1975), 279.
12. Shigeto, *Japan's Capitalism*, 109; Halliday, *A Political History of Japanese Capitalism*, 273; Michael J. Piore and Charles F. Sabel, *The Second Industrial Divide: Possibilities for Prosperity* (New York: Basic Books, 1984), 161.
13. Halliday, *A Political History of Japanese Capitalism*, 224–227. In 2000, one woman successfully sued her employer for job discrimination because managers denied her a pay raise for twenty-one years. Howard W. French, "Women Win a Battle, but Job Bias Still Rules Japan," *New York Times*, February 26, 2000.

14. Nicholas Lehman, *The Promised Land: The Great Black Migration and How It Changed America* (New York: Knopf, 1991), 6.

15. Ruth Milkman, "Union Responses to Workforce Feminization in the United States," in Jane Jenson and Rianne Mahon, eds., *The Challenge of Restructuring: North American Labor Movements Respond* (Philadelphia: Temple University Press, 1993), 229.

16. Lawrence Mishel, Jared Bernstein, and John Schmitt, *The State of Working America, 1998–99* (Ithaca, N.Y.: Economic Policy Institute, Cornell University Press, 1999), 182; Paul Hirst and Grahame Thompson, *Globalization in Question: The International Economy and the Possibilities of Governance* (Cambridge: Polity Press, 1996), 26; Sassen, *Globalization and Its Discontents*, 35; Richard B. Craig, *The Bracero Program: Interest Groups and Foreign Policy* (Austin: University of Texas Press, 1971), 102–103.

17. Saskia Sassen, *Losing Control? Sovereignty in an Age of Globalization* (New York: Columbia University Press, 1996), 81; Faruk Tabak, "The World Labour Force," in Hopkins and Wallerstein, *The Age of Transition*, 94; Robert K. Schaeffer, *Power to the People: Democratization around the World* (Boulder, Colo.: Westview, 1997), 66–67, 189.

18. Shigeto, *Japan's Capitalism*, 68.

19. B. J. McCormick, *The World Economy: Patterns of Growth and Change* (Oxford: Philip Allan, 1988), 188.

20. Juliet B. Schor, *The Overworked American: The Unexpected Decline of Leisure* (New York: Basic Books, 1991), 111; Lehman, *The Promised Land*, 111; Halliday, *A Political History of Japanese Capitalism*, 231.

21. Judith Stein, *Running Steel, Running America: Race, Economic Policy, and the Decline of Liberalism* (Chapel Hill, N.C.: University of North Carolina Press, 1998), 7.

22. Paul R. Lawrence and Davis Dyer, *Renewing American Industry* (New York: Free Press, 1983), 72; Stein, *Running Steel*, 209, 223.

23. Stein, *Running Steel*, 210.

24. Stein, *Running Steel*, 290.

25. In 1967, for example, the Japanese steel industry charged Japanese customers $116 a ton for steel but charged U.S. customers only $96 a ton, a clear case of illegal dumping. Stein, *Running Steel*, 218, 257.

Despite evidence that foreign producers were dumping steel and seizing U.S. markets, officials refused to take action, arguing that doing so would increase domestic prices or undermine political relations with its allies. President Clinton recently rejected tariffs on cheap steel imports from Russia, despite obvious dumping, because, he said, it would jeopardize U.S.–Soviet political relations and deprive them of the earnings they needed to repay their debts to the West. "It's extremely important that we not cut off one of the few sources of raising hard currency that the Russians have right now," one adviser said. David E. Sanger, "U.S. Says Japan, Brazil Dumped Steel," *New York Times*, February 13, 1999.

26. Ira C. Magaziner and Mark Patinkin, *The Silent War: Inside the Global Business Battles Shaping America's Future* (New York: Vintage Books, 1990), 309.

27. Stein, *Running Steel*, 16.

28. Leslie Wayne, "American Steel at the Barricades," *New York Times*, December 10, 1998.

29. Lawrence and Syer, *Renewing American Industry*, 72.

30. Stein, *Running Steel*, 295, 303; Frank Levy, *Dollars and Dreams: The Changing American Income Distribution* (New York: Russell Sage, 1987), 91; Dethloff, *The United States and the Global Economy*, 124.

31. Tom Redburn, "A Revolution Built in Mr. Ford's Factory," *New York Times*, January 2, 2000.

32. William J. Abernathy, Kim B. Clark, and Alan M. Kantrow, *Industrial Renaissance: Producing a Competitive Future for America* (New York: Basic Books, 1983), 47, 54; Magaziner and Patinkin, *The Silent War*, 5–7.

33. James A. Geschwender, *Racial Stratification in America* (Dubuque, Iowa: Wm. C. Brown, 1978), 224, 236–237.

34. Lawrence and Syer, *Renewing American Industry*, 18; Kim Moody, "Labor Givebacks and Labor Fightbacks," in Robert Cherry, ed., *The Imperiled Economy. Book II. Through the Safety Net* (New York: Union for Radical Economics, 1988), 161.

35. Dethloff, *The United States and the Global Economy*, 44.

36. William Greider, *One World, Ready or Not: The Manic Logic of Global Capitalism* (New York: Simon and Schuster, 1997), 125; Ian McIntyre, *Dogfight: The Transatlantic Battle over Airbus* (Westport, Conn.: Praeger, 1992), 2.

37. McIntyre, *Dogfight*, 44–45; Magaziner and Patinkin, *The Silent War*, 230, 244, 251–252.

38. McIntyre, *Dogfight*, xx, 44; Magaziner and Patinkin, *The Silent War*, 255.

39. John Tagliabue, "A Yankee in Europe's Court," *New York Times*, February 11, 2000; Magaziner and Patinkin, *The Silent War*, 232.

40. Magaziner and Patinkin, *The Silent War*, 257.

41. Michael Goldfield, *The Decline of Organized Labor in the United States* (Chicago: University of Chicago Press, 1987), 9–10; Joe Rogers, "Don't Worry, Be Happy: The Postwar Decline of Private-Sector Unionism in the United States," in Jenson and Mahon, *The Challenge of Restructuring*, 55; Ian Robinson, "Economistic Unionism in Crisis: The Origins, Consequences, and Prospects of Divergence in Labour-Movement Characteristics," in Jenson and Mahon, *The Challenge of Restructuring*, 35.

42. Levy, *Dollars and Dreams*, 108; William Julius Wilson, *When Work Disappears: The World of the New Urban Poor* (New York: Knopf, 1996), 29–30.

43. Lawrence and Dyer, *Renewing American Industry*, 78.

44. Barnet and Cavanah, *Global Dreams*, 99.

45. Wilson, *When Work Disappears*, 32–33. Many of the women who found public sector jobs were organized by unions. The growth of public sector unions, representing predominantly female workers, prevented unions from declining more sharply than they did. Indeed, unions were much more successful organizing women than men after 1970. Milkman, "Union Responses to Workforce Feminization," 237, 239.

46. Shor, *The Overworked American*, 26.

47. David Cay Johnston, "The Servant Class Is at the Counter," *New York Times*, August 27, 1995.

48. Milkman, "Union Responses to Workforce Feminization," 229.

49. Shor, *The Overworked American*, 87–88.

50. Shor, *The Overworked American*, 29.

51. Robert L. Aronson, *Self-Employment: A Labor Market Perspective* (Ithaca, N.Y.: ILR Press, 1991), 2–3; Robert B. Reich, *The Work of Nations: Preparing Ourselves for 21st-Century Capitalism* (New York: Vintage Books, 1992), 95.

52. Aronson, *Self-Employment*, 4.

53. Aronson, *Self-Employment*, 74, 91.

54. Stein, *Running Steel*, 306, 316; Barnet and Cavanah, *Global Dreams*, 54.

55. For a detailed discussion of these policies, see Schaeffer, *Understanding Globalization*, chapters 3, 4, and 9.

56. Bill Orr, *The Global Economy in the 90s: A User's Guide* (New York: New York University Press, 1992), 287.

57. Edward M. Graham and Paul R. Krugman, *Foreign Direct Investment in the United States* (Washington, D.C.: Institute for International Economics, 1991), 14, 21; Neil Reid, "Japanese Direct Investment in the U.S. Manufacturing Sector," in Glenn D. Hook and Michael A. Weiner, eds., *The Internationalization of Japan* (London: Routledge, 1992), 66; Alan Scott, ed., *The Limits of Globalization: Cases and Arguments* (London: Routledge, 1997), 141.

58. Arthur A. Alderson, "Globalization and Deindustrialization: Direct Investment and the Decline of Manufacturing Employment in 17 OECD Nations," *Journal of World-Systems Research* 3, no. 1 (1997): 5.

59. See Schaeffer, *Understanding Globalization*, 74–80.

60. Warren W. Wagar, review of Steven K. Sanderson, "Civilizations and World Systems: Studying World-Historical Change," *Journal of World-System Research* 3, no. 1 (1997): 149–150; Richard P. Appelbawm, "A Progressive Housing Program for America," in Sara Rosenberry and Chester Hartman, eds., *Housing Issues of the 1990s* (Westport, Conn.: Praeger, 1989), 314.

61. Jan Jindy Pettman, "An International Political Economy of Sex," in Eleonore Kofman and Gilliam Youngs, eds., *Globalization: Theory and Practice* (London: Cassell, 1996), 193; Lawrence Mishel and David M. Frankel, *The State of Working America, 1990–91* (Armonk, N.Y.: Sharpe, 1991), 104.

62. In 1970, a median-income household would have had to use the money earned in 29.5 months to purchase a home, but by 1998 it would have to use the money earned in 32 months to purchase a home. Louis Uchitelle, "The American Middle, Just Getting by," *New York Times*, August 1, 1999.

63. See Schaeffer, *Understanding Globalization*, chapter 8.

64. International Labor Office, *World Employment 1996/1997: National Policies in a Global Context* (Geneva: International Labour Office, 1996), 50; McCormick, *The World Economy*, 141.

65. See Schaeffer, *Understanding Globalization*, chapter 7.

66. Richard W. Stevenson, "Fed Says Economy Increased Net Worth of Most Families," *New York Times*, January 19, 2000; Mishel, Bernstein, and Schmitt, *The State of Working America, 1998–99*, 268.

67. Floyd Norris, "Dividends Rise, but Not as Fast as Stocks," *New York Times*, January 3, 1997.

68. In the 1980s, Republican administrators abandoned antitrust because they believed mergers would increase business efficiency and make U.S. companies stronger and more competitive with mega-firms in Western Europe, where antitrust laws are weak, and in Japan, where they are virtually nonexistent.

69. Laura M. Holson, "A Day for Mergers, with $40 Billion in Play," *New York Times*, November 24, 1998.

70. Stephen Labaton, "Merger Wave Spurs a New Scrutiny," *New York Times*, December 13, 1998. Laura M. Holson, "The Deal Still Rules," *New York Times*, February 14, 1999. Bankers and lawyers received more than $2 billion in fees for arranging the Exxon-Mobil merger in 1998. *New York Times*, "Costs of Exxon-Mobil Deal to Top $2 billion," *New York Times*, April 6, 1999.

71. Stephen Labaton, "Despite a Tough Stance or Two, White House Is Still Consolidation Friendly," *New York Times*, November 8, 1999.

72. James Sterngold, "Facing the Next Recession without Fear," *New York Times*, May 9, 1995.

73. Saul Hansell, "Wave of Mergers Is Transforming American Banking," *New York Times*, August 21, 1995.

74. Stanley Aronowitz and William DiFazio, *The Jobless Future: Sci-Tech and the Dogma of Work* (Minneapolis: University of Minnesota Press, 1994), 3.

75. John Judis, "Should an Economist Be in Charge of the Economy?" *The New Republic*, June 7, 1999.

76. Michael Wallace, "Downsizing the American Dream: Work and Family at Century's End," in Dana Vannoy and Paula J. Dubeck, eds., *Challenges for Work and Family in the Twenty-First Century* (New York: Aldine de Gruyter, 1998), 23; Mishel, Bernstein, and Schmitt, *The State of Working America, 1998–99*, 29.

77. Robert J. Samuelson, "Economic Mythmaking," *Newsweek*, September 8, 1997; Mishel, Bernstein, and Schmitt, *The State of Working America, 1998–99*, 69.

78. Robert D. Hershey, Jr., "Survey Finds 6 Million, Fewer Than Thought, in Impermanent Jobs," *New York Times*, August 19, 1995.

79. Hershey, "Survey Finds 6 Million, Fewer Than Thought, in Impermanent Jobs."

80. Louis Uchitelle and N. R. Kleinfield, "On the Battlefields of Business, Millions of Casualties," *New York Times*, March 3, 1996. See the critique of this in John Cassidy, "All Worked Up," *New Yorker* (April 22, 1996): 52–53; Davil L. Brich, "The Hidden Economy," *Wall Street Journal*, June 10, 1998, 23, and the *Times*' response: Louis Uchitelle, "Despite Drop, Rate of Layoffs Remains High," *New York Times*, August 23, 1996.

81. Christopher D. Cook, "Workers for Rent," *In These Times*, July 22, 1996; Barry Meier, "Some 'Worker Leasing' Programs Defraud Insurers and Employers," *New York Times*, March 20, 1992.

82. Chris Tilly, "Short Hours, Short Shrift: The Causes and Consequences of Part-Time Employment," in Virginia L. duRivage, ed., *New Policies for the Part-Time and Contingent Workforce* (Armonk, N.Y.: Sharpe, 1992), 15, 17; Hershey, "Survey Finds 6 Million."

83. One in five college graduates now works in a low-wage job that does not require a college degree. Sylvia Nasar, "More College Graduates Taking Low-Wage Jobs," *New York Times*, August 7, 1992.

84. Steven Greenhouse, "Equal Work, Less-Equal Perks," *New York Times*, March 30, 1998.

85. Steven Greenhouse, "Growth in Unions' Membership in 1999 Was the Best in Two Decades," *New York Times*, January 20, 2000; Robinson, "Economistic Unionism in Crisis," 35.

86. Andrew Hacker, "Who's Sticking to the Union?" *New York Review of Books*, February 18, 1999; Steven Greenhouse, "Union Membership Slides Despite Increased Organizing," *New York Times*, March 22, 1998.

87. Floyd Norris, "You're Fired! (but Your Stock Is Way Up)," *New York Times*, September 3, 1995.

88. Louis Uchitelle, "As Class Struggle Subsides, Less Pie for the Workers," *New York Times*, December 5, 1999.

89. David Cay Johnston, "Gap between Rich and Poor Found Substantially Wider," *New York Times*, December 5, 1999.

90. Steven Greenhouse, "So Much Work, So Little Time," *New York Times*, September 5, 1999. Median-income worker households with two wage earners worked harder, with adults laboring 20 percent more hours in 1997 than they did in 1979. Uchitelle, "The American Middle, Just Getting by."

91. Lester Thurow, "Companies Merge; Families Break Up," *New York Times*, September 3, 1995.
92. John Foren, "Spotlight on Moonlighters," *San Francisco Chronicle*, May 31, 1992.
93. Edwin McDowell, "The Abbreviated Tourist," *New York Times*, July 31, 1997. Edwin McDowell, "More Work or Less Work Can Equal No Time Off," *New York Times*, July 6, 1996.
94. "Sleep-Depriving Jobs Linked to Accidents," *New York Times*, June 4, 1999.
95. From 1994 to 1999, R&D spending increased from $97.1 billion to 166 billion, far more than R&D outlays in Japan, which totaled $95 billion in 1998. William J. Broad, "U.S. Back on Top in Industrial Research," *New York Times*, December 28, 1999; Louis Uchitelle, "The $1.2 Trillion Spigot," *New York Times*, December 30, 1999.
96. Sheryl WuDunn, "The Heavy Burden of Low Rates," *New York Times*, October 11, 1996; Gretchen Morgenson, "Beware of Japanese Bearing Promises," *New York Times*, June 21, 1998; Charles P. Kindleberger, *World Economic Primacy 1500 to 1900* (Oxford: Oxford University Press, 1996), 206–207.
97. Sheryl WuDunn and Nicholas D. Kristof, "Crisis in Banking Is Japanese, but Implications Are Global," *New York Times*, June 27, 1998. Kevin Phillips, *The Politics of Rich and Poor: Wealth and the American Electorate in the Reagan Aftermath* (New York: Random House, 1990), 151.
98. Nicholas D. Kristof, "Long Mandibles, Sleek Carapace. A Steal at $300," *New York Times*, April 10, 1999.
99. Kindleberger, *World Economic Primacy*, 207.
100. Kindleberger, *World Economic Primacy*, 207.
101. Shigeto, *Japan's Capitalism*, 169; Rob Steven, "Structural Origins of Japan's Direct Foreign Investment," in Hook and Weiner, *The Internationalization of Japan*, 52.
102. Kristof, "Long Mandibles."
103. Stephanie Strom, "Japan's New 'Temp' Workers," *New York Times*, June 17, 1998; Andrew Pollack, "Japanese Starting to Link Pay to Performance, Not Tenure," *New York Times*, October 2, 1993; Sheryl WuDunn, "When Lifetime Jobs Die Prematurely," *New York Times*, June 12, 1996; Stephanie Strom, "Toyota Is Seeking to Stop Use of Seniority to Set Pay," *New York Times*, July 8, 1999; Howard W. French, "Economy's Ebb in Japan Spurs Temporary Jobs," *New York Times*, August 12, 1999; David E. Sanger, "Look Who's Carping about Capitalism," *New York Times*, April 6, 1997.
104. Stephanie Strom, "Tradition of Equality Fading in New Japan," *New York Times*, January 4, 2000.
105. Andrew Pollack, "Jobless in Japan: A Special Kind of Anguish," *New York Times*, May 21, 1993.
106. Stephen Kinzer, "Help Wanted: One Mayor, Please," *New York Times*, March 13, 1995.
107. John Judis, "Germany Dispatch: Middle of Nowhere," *New Republic*, November 29, 1999.
108. Alan Cowell, "German Workers Fear the Miracle Is Over," *New York Times*, July 30, 1997; Nathaniel C. Nash, "In Germany, Downsizing Means 10.3% Jobless," *New York Times*, March 7, 1996; Ferdinand Protzman, "VW Offers Its Workers 4-Day Week or Layoffs," *New York Times*, October 29, 1993.
109. Sylvia Nasar, "Where Joblessness Is a Way of Making a Living," *New York Times*, May 9, 1999; Roger Cohen, "Europeans Consider Shortening Workweek to Relieve Joblessness," *New York Times*, November 22, 1993; Mishel, Bernstein, and Schmitt, *The State of Working*

America, 1998–99, 386; Celestine Bohlen, "Italy's North–South Gap Widens, Posing Problem for Europe, Too," *New York Times*, November 15, 1996.

110. Sabine Lang, "The NGOization of Feminism: Institutionalization and Institution Building within the German Women's Movement," in Joan W. Scott, Cora Kaplan, and Debra Keates, eds., *Transitions, Environments, Translations: Feminisms in International Politics* (New York: Routledge, 1997), 104.

111. Niels Thygesen, Yutaka Kosai, and Robert Z. Lawrence, *Globalization and Trilateral Labor Markets: Evidence and Implications* (New York, Paris, and Tokyo: Trilateral Commission, 1996), 94–95; Edmund L. Andrews, "The Jobless Are Snared in Europe's Safety Net," *New York Times*, November 9, 1997. Ethnic groups and workers in particular regions have also suffered. North African immigrants in France have extremely high rates of unemployment. And workers in southern Italy are unemployed at twice the national rate. Bohlen, "Italy's North–South Gap."

112. Edmund L. Andrews, "Making Stock Buyers of Wary Germans," *New York Times*, October 17, 1996; John Tagliabue, "European Giants Set to Close Deal," *New York Times*, April 20, 1999.

113. Edmund L. Andrews, "Germany Proposes Some Tax-Free Stock Sales, Lifting the Market," *New York Times*, December 24, 1999.

114. Andrews, "Making Stock Buyers of Wary Germans"; Tagliabue, "European Giants Set to Close Deal."

115. John Tagliabue, "Resisting Those Ugly Americans," *New York Times*, January 9, 2000.

116. Rich Miller, "Euro Forces Europe into Industrial Transformation," *USA Today*, July 19, 1999.

117. Sylvia Nasar, "Economists Shrug as Savings Rate Declines," *New York Times*, December 21, 1998.

118. Saul Hansell, "We Like You. We Care about You. Now Pay Up," *New York Times*, January 26, 1997. Mishel, Bernstein, and Schmitt, *The State of Working America, 1998–99*, 275.

119. Juliet B. Schor, *The Overspent American: Upscaling, Downshifting, and the New Consumer* (New York: Basic Books, 1998), 72; Maria Fiorini Ramirez, "Americans at Debt's Door," *New York Times*, October 14, 1997.

120. Saul Hansell, "Personal Bankruptcies Surging as Economy Hums," *New York Times*, August 25, 1999.

121. Hansell, "Personal Bankruptcies Surging."

122. "Debt-Load Growing for College Graduates," *New York Times*, October 24, 1997; Ethan Bronner, "College Tuition Rises 4%, Outpacing Inflation," *New York Times*, October 8, 1998. Robert D. Hershey, Jr., "Graduating with Credit Problems," *New York Times*, November 10, 1996.

123. Marilyn Fernandez and Kwang Chun Kim, "Dominant and Minority Couples: An Analysis of Family Economic Well-Being," in Vannoy and Dubeck, *Challenges for Work and Family*, 76–77.

Some economists estimate that older generations may transfer $10 trillion to younger generations during the next fifty years. But estimates about the size of intergenerational transfers are the subject of considerable dispute. One study estimated that the older generation may transfer a much greater amount, between $41 trillion and $136 trillion. See David Cay Johnston, "A Larger Legacy May Await Generations X, Y and Z," *New York Times*, October 20, 1999.

124. Klaus Friedrich, "The Real American Savings Rate," *New York Times*, May 4, 1999.

125. Kindleberger, *World Economic Primacy*, 205.

126. Stephanie Strom, "Japan's Investors Become Bullish on Merrill Lynch," *New York Times*, January 6, 2000; Stephanie Strom, "Shopping for Recovery," *New York Times*, May 29, 1998.

127. Gretchen Morgenson, "U.S. Shoppers Shoulder the Weight of the World," *New York Times*, June 20, 1999.

128. Edmund L. Andrews, "Wal-Mart Lowers Its Prices at Stores across Germany," *New York Times*, January 4, 2000.

129. Louis Uchitelle, "As the Good Times Roll, the Marxists Are Mellowing," *New York Times*, January 16, 2000.

130. See Schaeffer, *Power to the People*.

131. Gretchen Morgenson, "Investing's Longtime Best Bet Is Being Trampled by the Bulls," *New York Times*, January 15, 2000; Floyd Norris, "Growing Number of Corporations Choose Not to Offer Dividends," *New York Times*, January 4, 2000.

132. See, for example, the scenarios outlined by John Cassidy, "That's the Way the Money Goes," *The New Yorker*, May 15, 2000.

Chapter 5
The Submerging Periphery

Workers in the vast periphery have been affected by three crucial developments in the last twenty years. First, and most important, commodity prices have fallen. This has reduced incomes for workers, businesses, and states, which rely on the production and export of agricultural goods, raw materials, and unfinished industrial goods for their livelihood. Falling prices have affected nearly 75 percent of the people on the planet.[1]

Second, manufacturing industries, which produced goods for domestic markets in the periphery, have collapsed and disappeared. The destruction of manufacturing industries in the 1980s and 1990s reduced wage work and income for workers, particularly urban males.

Third, there has been an expansion of some export manufacturing in "free trade" enclaves, often called *maquiladoras* (after zones in Mexico), and the growth of service industries, particularly tourism, in recreational enclaves. Both industries have provided a substantial number of jobs for women and girls. But the apparent gains made by women in these industries have not offset the massive job and income losses in agriculture, mining, and domestic manufacturing and service industries.

This is a familiar pattern. In the periphery, as in the core, jobs have been lost and wages have fallen. But they did so at different times. During the 1970s, workers incomes fell in the core but actually increased in the periphery. Economically, the 1970s were good times for workers in the periphery. It was the only time during the postwar period when their incomes substantially improved. But the 1970s were difficult politically, because most workers in the periphery labored under the direction of dictators, juntas, and one-party regimes.[2] Then in the 1980s, peripheral incomes fell, and did so dramatically. Economically, this was the worst of times. But the collapse of dictators in the 1980s improved political conditions for workers the world over.

There is another important pattern. In the periphery, as in the core, men have lost jobs and income, while women have acquired some low-paying waged jobs. But in both the core and periphery, increased participation of women in the paid workforce did not compensate for the loss of male jobs and income. Yet although the pattern is similar, the reasons for change are different. In the core, deindustrialization, job loss, and falling wages were due to competition and inflation. In the periphery, deindustrialization and falling commodity prices were due to the debt crisis and technological change in the core. But whatever the source of change, worker households in the periphery and in the core responded to economic crisis by cutting back on consumption and intensifying enterprising and subsistence activities. Because less wage work is available in the periphery than in the core, workers in the periphery have come to rely increasingly on nonwage work to survive. Indeed, nonwage work now occupies more people than wage work in the periphery.

One way that households in the periphery have cut back has been to bear fewer children. Fertility rates have fallen, in some regions dramatically, in response to deteriorating economic conditions. This contrasts with the core, where *improving* economic conditions were held responsible for falling birth rates and the "demographic transition." In the periphery, *deteriorating* economic conditions have reduced fertility rates and family size.

As in the core, members of households in the periphery have migrated in search of jobs and nonwage opportunities. But they have done so in far greater number, migrating not only en masse to domestic cities but also across national borders, often to core countries. Like worker households in the United States, which have borrowed heavily to maintain living standards, worker households in the periphery have also gone into debt.

But debt has a different meaning in the core and in the periphery. In the core, households are responsible for debts they contracted and for the national debts contracted by their elected representatives. In the periphery, by contrast, households are responsible not only for repaying their own debts, but also for the debts of dictators and private businesses, which were contracted without worker consent, participation, or approval. Throughout the periphery, worker households have been forced to pay higher taxes and higher prices for essential goods and services to make good the losses of others.[3]

Debt in the periphery also has a rather different meaning. For very poor worker households, which have been driven by debt crisis and falling commodity prices from subsistence toward extinction, borrowed money has enabled some family members to survive. But it has also required them to "work off" debt in charcoal furnaces, brick foundries, carpet factories, or sex-industry brothels, a form of debt bondage akin to slavery, which has no counterpart in the core.[4]

For worker households in the periphery, falling commodity prices, deindustrialization, and the rise of manufacturing and service enclaves have had important consequences. In general, households now work harder, earn less, and owe more. Workers had hoped that the improved political conditions associated with widespread democratization would also improve their economic fortunes. But this has not happened. Instead, worker households in the periphery have seen their economic fortunes deteriorate significantly. This not only threatens their political gains but also defers the prospect of economic improvement to the distant future. How distant?

Some economists estimate that it would take decades, centuries, or even millennia for peripheral countries to catch up with the core, given current rates of growth. Surinam would take 58 years; Thailand 102 years; Indonesia 229; the Congo 1,054; and Sri Lanka 2,000 years to "catch up."[5] Even these estimates may be too optimistic, given the recent slow-down in peripheral rates of growth. Events in recent years have not contributed to an "emerging world" but instead to a vast region of the world that is "submerging."

COMMODITY PRICES IN THE PERIPHERY, 1950–1979

During the 1950s and 1960s, commodity prices fell, but they did so slowly. They fell because producers across the periphery planted more sugar, cotton, and coffee; mined more copper, tin, and gold; and pumped more oil.[6] Increased production swelled world supplies. Postwar economic recovery and growth in the core increased demand for these commodities but did not quite keep pace with growing supplies, so prices gradually fell. Early on, scholars and government officials in the periphery recognized that commodity prices would fall and worried that the incomes of countries that relied on commodity exports would deteriorate, worsening the terms of trade between core and periphery. In the 1950s, the prominent Latin American economist Raúl Prebisch argued that a long-term decline in the terms of trade for commodity producers was "not casual or accidental, but deeply ingrained in the world trading system itself."[7]

Across the periphery, government officials, many of them employed either by capitalist or communist dictators, heeded the warnings of Prebisch and other "dependency theorists." They took two steps to protect themselves from falling commodity prices, which threatened to undermine their economic growth and development. First, they built manufacturing industries that produced goods for domestic markets. They hoped that by producing goods for domestic consumers, these industries could reduce the need to import expensive goods manufactured in the core, a process described by economists as "import substitution."[8] Domestic manufacturing industries helped dictatorships reduce their spending on imported goods, provide jobs for domestic male workers, and provide income and revenue for the state, which could be reinvested in the economy and used to provide jobs in the regime's bureaucracy and army. To protect newly established industries from competition with core firms, regimes slapped high tariffs on imported goods and provided generous subsidies to private and state-owned firms to get them up and running. This strategy was widely adopted by capitalist dictatorships and communist regimes alike.

As a second step, officials tried to organize commodity cartels. They tried to persuade officials from countries that produced particular commodities to join organizations or cartels that could limit supplies and establish supply quotas among members. By agreeing to limit supplies, peripheral producers hoped to strengthen their bargaining position with core buyers, which were dominated by large, postcolonial transnational corporations, and thereby stabilize or even increase the commodity prices they received. The Organization of Petroleum-Exporting Countries (OPEC), which was founded in 1960, became the most famous of these commodity cartels. But it was not alone. Producers of coffee, sugar, tin, and tropical timber also organized cartels.[9] Yet cartels had little success in this period. OPEC, for example, was unable to stabilize oil prices, which fell from $5.38 a barrel in 1951 to only $2.09 in 1970. OPEC's first attempt to embargo oil during the 1967 Arab–Israeli war was a conspicuous failure.[10] But OPEC fortunes, and those of commodity producers throughout the periphery, would improve dramatically in the 1970s.

In 1971, President Richard Nixon devalued the dollar. This cut prices for oil producers because they were paid for their oil in dollars. To deal with falling prices, OPEC reorganized, enlisting the support of oil-producing countries like Indonesia and Nigeria, which had ignored its call for an embargo in 1967. During the 1973–1974 Yom Kippur War, OPEC members agreed to cut their oil deliveries to the West, a move that drove prices up to $16.48, an eight-fold increase.[11] Meanwhile, Soviet grain shortages reduced food supplies, which helped increase the price of agricultural and other commodities to levels not seen since World War II.[12]

Rising prices were generally good for commodity producers in the periphery, particularly for oil-producing states. But for poor countries without any oil of their own, skyrocketing oil prices were a great hardship. Still, while rising oil prices created an economic crisis for many poor countries, they also provided a solution to the problems they caused. Oil-producing countries deposited their flood of oil revenues in banks in Western Europe, creating a giant and growing pool of money in the "Eurodollar market." The Eurodollar market grew from $110 billion in 1970 to $1.5 trillion by 1980.[13] To earn money and repay depositors, core banks then loaned much of this money—$810 billion between 1970 and 1983—to borrowers in the periphery and semiperiphery. Regimes in the periphery used borrowed money to pay for higher-priced imported oil. They also used it to provide low-cost food and services to working people, which helped to purchase some political support for dictatorships, increase military spending to contain any domestic opposition, and expand commodity production to take advantage of unusually high prices.[14]

Although workers in the core experienced the global inflation of the 1970s as a period of relative "scarcity," workers in the periphery experienced it as a time of relative "plenty."[15] In the periphery, economic growth accelerated, state revenues increased, and worker incomes grew in real terms, for the first time in a generation. Economists described events in the periphery as "miraculous," arguing that the periphery had finally found a path to real development.[16]

But the U.S. decision to raise interest rates in 1979 triggered an economic crisis of hurricane proportions in the periphery and semiperiphery. This storm would sweep away all of the economic gains made in the 1970s and wreck the dictatorships that had used borrowed money to finance growth. The winds it generated created waves of change that buffet the periphery still.

Higher interest rates increased costs for peripheral borrowers, who had converted their fixed, low-interest loans to loans with floating rates in the late 1970s at the insistence of core lenders.[17] So when interest rates rose sharply in the early

1980s, interest payments increased five-fold, draining money out of peripheral countries. Investors in the periphery also purchased high-interest U.S. securities. This flow of money out of the periphery, what was called "capital flight," reduced the hard currency stocks that businesses and states needed to repay loans.[18]

While higher interest rates drained money from the periphery, they also triggered a recession in the core. This reduced demand in the core for goods from the periphery and pushed down commodity prices. Because their (interest payment) costs increased at a time when their (commodity) income fell, regimes soon ran out of hard currency reserves and faced bankruptcy. The crisis was felt first in Jamaica and Peru (1979), then in Nicaragua (1980), then in Poland and Bolivia (1981), then in Mexico (1982), and soon thereafter in countries throughout the periphery and semiperiphery.[19] This acute economic crisis combined with various political crises to force dictators from power during the next decade. Regimes transferred power to civilian democrats, who were forced to adopt measures designed to repay debt. Democratization (a political good) was joined with austerity or "structural adjustment programs" (an economic evil). Austerity programs then contributed both to the collapse of commodity prices and to the deindustrialization of import-substitutionist manufacturing industries in the periphery.

COLLAPSING COMMODITY PRICES, 1980–2000

After 1980, commodity prices fell heavily. This placed an increasing burden on poor households, particularly on women. They collapsed because peripheral commodity supplies increased while demand in the core weakened. Peripheral supplies increased for a variety of reasons. During the 1970s, supplies increased because peripheral states used borrowed money to expand production so that firms could take advantage of high prices. For example, world coffee production increased from 3.8 million tons in 1970 to 4.9 million tons in 1979, world cotton production grew from 11 to 14 million tons, and world sugar production increased from 585 to 754 million tons.[20] Then in the 1980s, as peripheral countries searched desperately for ways of earning the hard currency they needed to repay debt, they redoubled their efforts. The austerity programs developed by core creditors and adopted by democratizing states played an important role in expanding peripheral supplies because the programs required states to increase exports to earn the money they needed to pay their bills. Between 1980 and 1988, "the volume of primary products exported by developing countries rose by over 20 percent," the economist Alfred Maizels observed.[21] But growing supplies only glutted markets and produced no real gain for commodity producers in the periphery.

Core states and transnational corporations also played a role in expanding commodity supplies. They frequently financed the expansion of commodity production to diversify their sources of supply, secure long-term supply relations, and weaken the ability of producers in the periphery to organize commodity cartels. So, for instance, TNCs and core states financed projects to grow coffee in Thailand, where it had not previously been cultivated, and soybeans in Brazil, and prospect for oil outside OPEC-member regions. Their discovery of new oil fields in the North Sea, for instance, which was controlled by Norway and the United Kingdom, neither of which belonged to OPEC, helped weaken OPEC's ability to set prices in the 1980s.

But while austerity programs are widely held responsible for impoverishing peripheral economies, they were not wholly to blame. Deflationary policies of core states, the introduction of new core technologies, and changing consumer behavior in the core also played critical roles. They helped reduce core demand for peripheral commodities just when supplies were expanding.

In the early 1980s, the demand for peripheral commodities fell because deflationary policies (high interest rates) forced core economies into a recession. This "slowed down substantially the growth of demand for all industrial inputs, including primary commodities."[22] But when core economies recovered and began to grow again in the mid- to late-1980s, demand in the core did not revive. It did not because the introduction of new technologies in the 1970s and 1980s enabled core producers to replace peripheral commodities with goods made in the core, a process of "substitution" or "dematerialization."[23] Dematerialization occurs when fewer raw materials are needed to produce the same quantity of goods, a kind of raw materials "conservation."[24] In 1984, for example, Japan "consumed only 60 percent of the raw materials required for the same volume of production in 1973."[25]

Product substitution and dematerialization were not entirely new developments. Earlier this century, coal tar distillates were used to create industrial dyes, which replaced vegetable and mineral dyes; vegetable oils were used to make margarine, which replaced butter; oil-based technologies were used to make synthetic rubber to replace natural rubber and synthetic fibers, which replaced cotton, wool, jute, and sisal. But the invention and adoption of a new set of technologies in the 1970s and 1980s set the stage for the widespread replacement of peripheral commodities. New technologies in hand, core producers did more with less.[26]

To illustrate this process and its impact on peripheral commodity producers and workers, let us briefly describe how new technologies affected the demand for a few important peripheral products: sugar, copper, oil, and gold. In each case, men of color lost jobs and income, and in the case of sugar, women of color also lost jobs and income.

Sugar

In the mid-1960s, scientists in Japan and the United States developed enzymes to produce fructose sugar from the starch in corn. The new high fructose corn sweeteners (HFCS) replaced cane and beet sugars in many products. HFCS technology was taken off the laboratory shelf when world sugar prices quadrupled in the 1970s, and core producers began using HFCS instead of cane and beet sugar. The decision by Coca-Cola and Pepsi in the early 1980s to use HFCS in their beverages was a turning point. In the 1970s, U.S. per capita consumption of HFCS was only 0.7 pounds. But it grew to 29.8 pounds by 1983, and in 1985 reached 60 pounds, equaling the consumption of cane and beet sugar for the first time ever.[27]

The demand for cane and beet sugar was undermined not only by HFCS technology, but also by new dietary sweetener technologies, particularly aspartame, which captured 13 percent of the U.S. sugar market by 1988. As core producers switched from cane and beet sugars to HFCS and dietary sweeteners, U.S. imports of sugar grown in the periphery dropped, falling from 4.8 million metric tons in 1970–1971 to only 1.7 mmt in 1989–1990.[28]

Copper

In the mid-1960s, the electrical industry in the core began using aluminum to replace copper wire, and aluminum cables captured 2 percent of the market by 1974. But because aluminum is also a peripheral product, the use of aluminum to replace copper in some goods resulted in the substitution of one peripheral product for another. More important for copper producers has been the development of fiber-optic cable, wireless communication, and recycling technologies in the core.

In 1970, Corning scientists began developing glass fiber that could transmit laser light efficiently enough to make "wave guides," fiber-optic cables that could transmit phone calls and other electronic communications. Still, it would be twelve years before Corning would sell fiber-optic cable in quantity, largely because the phone giant AT&T was not ready to junk its copper-wire phone system and replace it with new fiber-optic cable. But the 1982 breakup of AT&T's phone monopoly and the rising cost of copper, which had doubled in price during the inflationary 1970s, encouraged AT&T's new competitors to build new communications networks using fiber-optic cable. Demand for the new cables has become so great since then that core producers have trouble keeping pace.[29] The subsequent adoption of wireless cellular phone and data networks has meant that businesses have eliminated the need for copper wire for many uses. In addition, core producers have developed new conservation and recycling technologies that enable them to reuse the copper they already possess, rather than purchase new copper from primary producers. By 1985, the United States obtained half of the copper it needed from recycled copper scrap. Although copper is still used, new technologies have replaced copper for many uses, and world demand has weakened dramatically.

Oil

Successive oil embargoes and skyrocketing oil prices stimulated the development and introduction of myriad new oil-replacing technologies. Government tax credits encouraged industries and households in the core to adopt new energy-conservation technologies for transport, manufacturing, office buildings, and dwellings, improvements described by some as a "negawatt revolution."[30] Auto makers, after much delay, improved gas mileage. Electric utilities found ways to meet new demand with existing energy systems. Architects and builders redesigned offices and homes and developed new lighting and refrigeration systems that reduced office and residential energy consumption 16 percent between 1973 and 1985. Overall, U.S. demand for energy fell 20 percent in this period and fell even more in Western Europe and Japan.

Gold

Even gold is not immune from technological innovation. For centuries gold was seen as a repository of value, the "ultimate form of payment."[31] But the development of other monetary instruments—U.S. securities, stocks, and corporate bonds, as well as more sophisticated and obscure ways to store value (money market funds, mutual funds, hedge funds, etc.)—which are essentially new monetary *technologies*, have persuaded many investors, even private banks and central government banks, to dispense with gold, which is mined primarily by men of color in the Third World. Central banks in Argentina, Belgium, the Czech Republic, England, and the Netherlands sold off some of their gold reserves in recent years. Even the Swiss and the International Monetary Fund have announced plans to shed gold assets. As one money manager argued, gold "has essentially been de-monetized by the modern financial economy."[32] The weakening demand for gold by central banks and other investors in the core has further eroded the price that peripheral producers, particularly in South Africa, could obtain for the not-so-precious metal. When the Bank of England sold 25 tons of gold from its vaults—the first lot of a planned sale of 415 tons—South African miners picketed the British embassy in Pretoria. They demonstrated because falling gold prices between 1997 and 1999 had cost 103,000 Black male workers their jobs in South African gold mines. In London, gold dealers opposing the sale hung a banner that read: "Precious Metal, Give Away Prices."[33]

Three important points can be made about substitutionist technologies. First, the introduction of new technologies was spurred by high commodity prices. This means that attempts by peripheral producers to raise prices will likely contribute to the development and introduction of technologies that help the core abandon these goods, thereby weakening demand and forcing down prices. Second, while new technologies reduced the demand for primary goods, they did not wholly eliminate them. Synthetic rubber has not eliminated the need for natural rubber in large truck and airplane tires; synthetic fabrics have not eliminated the demand for cotton denims; HFCS has not replaced cane sugar in baked goods, confectionery, and candies; and new energy technologies have not yet eliminated the demand for oil, which continues to grow as the world car fleet expands. This means that the core will still need some peripheral commodities, though not as much as it once did. Third, because core producers have vast public and private research infrastructures at their disposal, they have the means to invent and deploy new substitutionist technologies. The patent protection provided investors by core states and new free trade agreements mean that core producers can reap the benefits of new substitutionist technologies.[34] The new technologies also helped core firms mine other advantages. HFCS technologies enabled U.S. firms to use domestic corn as their raw material, which strengthened the demand for this important U.S. crop.

Core demand for peripheral products has been reshaped not only by new technologies but also by worker-consumers in the core. In recent years, changed consumer preferences and diets have reduced the demand for many peripheral goods. U.S. worker-consumers drank less coffee—per capita consumption dropped one-third between 1975 and 1991.[35] Although they drink less coffee, they increasingly prefer "more subtle, higher quality arabica coffees" that are lower in caffeine than robusta.[36] This is good for producers of "fine" arabica coffees but bad for robusta growers, particularly in Africa, where robusta is the principal coffee variety.[37]

Changed dietary preferences have also reduced the demand for peripheral goods while increasing the demand for core substitutes. Diet-conscious worker-consumers in the core have increasingly shunned fat-heavy tropical oils and switched to low-cholesterol temperate oils grown in the core; they have abandoned sugared gum for sugarless gums that use aspartame. In the United Kingdom, for example, sugarless gum's share of the market increased from only 6 percent in 1977 to 60 percent in 1993.[38] Health-conscious worker-consumers have sound medical reasons for adopting diets that are lower in caffeine, sugar, and fat. But what is good for worker health in the core is bad for workers in the periphery, who had come to depend on the jobs provided by the export of tropical products to the core.

The growing supply of peripheral commodities and the falling core demand for those goods have combined to slash prices. Real commodity prices fell 50 percent between 1980 and 1992. They fell another 20 to 30 percent in the late 1990s, as demand in failing East Asian economies contracted.[39] Losses for peripheral producers in this period were greater than they were during the Great Depression. In the 1930s, prices fell heavily for peripheral producers, but they also fell for core manufacturers. By contrast, in the 1980s and 1990s, prices fell only for peripheral commodities, not for manufacturers in the core. So the current deflation is selective, affecting the periphery but not the core, and it is worse than any other downturn in this century.[40]

Plummeting commodity prices have had catastrophic consequences for workers and states in the periphery. Once you know that 50 million people in the periphery work in the sugar industry, and 20 million grow coffee, the impact of new HFCS technology and changed consumer diets and preference in the core becomes evident.[41] Although social scientists exclaim at the changes associated with new computer and electronic technologies, their global impact is small compared to the changes associated with more prosaic HFCS technologies or worker-consumer habits.

Of course, the impact of falling commodity prices on work and gender in the periphery varies enormously, depending on how different commodity-producing industries organize work. Falling prices have their biggest impact on labor-intensive industries like sugar, which requires up to six workers per ten hectares in cane fields. In Brazil, the world's largest sugar producer, the number of people working in the industry fell by almost half, from 1.2 million to only 700,000 in the 1990s.[42] During the 1980s, for example, 400,000 sugar workers lost their jobs in the Philippines. A 1985 Catholic Church study found that "an overwhelming majority of the displaced sugar plantation and mill workers . . . are suffering from severe malnutrition, starvation, disease, and lack of medical care, decent clothing and shelter. . . ."[43] In Trinidad and Tobago, two small islands where 8,000 sugar workers lost their jobs, the prime minister argued, "If current conditions are maintained, we shall be confronting a situation that could lead to the destruction of the sugar industry in most developing nations."[44]

Other labor-intensive commodities, like rubber and vanilla, are also threatened by substitutionist technologies and falling prices. If in vitro production of natural rubber becomes a reality, as scientists expect, the jobs of 12 to 16 million workers in East Asian rubber plantations will be put at risk.[45] The development, meanwhile, of artificial vanilla threatens the livelihood of the 100,000 natural vanilla farmers in Madagascar, where most of the world's supply is grown by women and men in independent farming households.[46]

In commodity-producing industries like copper, oil, and gold, the number of workers affected by falling prices is much smaller because they are much more capital-intensive. But the impact has been much the same. In Chile, copper mines have been shut down, workers have lost jobs, and those who still work have seen wages fall. Mario Olivares earned $400 a month mining copper ore, but after being laid off he earned only a dollar a day as a street vendor.[47] In South Africa, the number of gold miners fell by half—from 514,000 to 180,000—in the last decade, and widespread unemployment in mining districts has contributed to increased rates of violence, rape, and divorce.[48] Layoffs in the mining industries of Chile, South Africa, Poland, Russia, and Zambia have devastated the workers most responsible for demanding an end to dictatorship, apartheid, and communism in those countries. Falling prices and economic change have crippled one of the main political constituencies for democratization in the periphery.

The impact of falling commodity prices is not restricted only to the periphery and semiperiphery. Falling copper prices have also affected male miners and oil workers in the United States and Canada. Since 1980, the number of workers in U.S. gas and oil fields fell by more than half, from 425,000 to less than 200,000.[49] Falling oil prices threw 25,000 wildcatters out of work in Wyoming and tens of thousands more in Texas, where they organized a "Starving Oil Workers March" on the state capitol in 1999.[50] And higher oil prices in 2000 did little to increase prospecting or job creation. Still, the number of core workers affected by falling commodity prices is relatively small compared to the periphery, where vast numbers of workers labor in commodity-producing industries.

In the periphery, falling prices have different consequences for men and women workers. Where goods are produced on large-scale plantations (sugar, rubber, soybeans) or in capital-intensive mines (copper, gold, oil), men make up most, if not all, of the workforce. In these industries, men lose jobs and wages as prices fall. But where goods are produced primarily by independent small farmers, who rely much more heavily on female participation (sisal, jute, palm oil, vanilla), falling prices directly affect male and female workers.[51] In Africa, women constitute 47 percent of the workforce in agriculture, 40 percent in South Asia and the Caribbean, and 18 percent in Latin America.[52]

Falling prices not only have reduced worker incomes but have ruined businesses, particularly those with higher production costs. As prices fell, the first firms affected were ones that had poorer soils, deeper mines, poorer ore, thicker oil, and, therefore, higher costs. So falling prices gradually shifted the location of production, from high-cost copper producers like Mexico and Peru to lower-cost producers in Indonesia and Papua New Guinea; from high-cost oil producers in Wyoming and Texas to lower-cost producers in Saudi Arabia and Nigeria.

Falling prices also reduced revenues for peripheral states. In Saudi Arabia, the state's oil revenues fell 40 percent, or $20 billion, during the 1990s, and the government ran a $13 billion budget deficit in 1999.[53] "The boom days are over," Crown Prince Abdullah complained, "and they will not come back."[54] Chile was forced to cut $685 million from its budget in 1998 as copper prices and export earnings fell.[55] And in South Africa, economists estimated that the government lost $200 million in revenue for every $10 fall in the price for an ounce of gold.[56] As revenues fell, it was more difficult for governments to repay their foreign debts or provide services and benefits to domestic workers (a development we will explore further in chapter 6). World Bank economists concluded in 1998 that lower commodity prices "may produce an increase in the financial vulnerability of [commodity-dependent peripheral and semiperipheral] countries."[57]

The expansion of agricultural commodity production has also contributed to hunger and migration. As peripheral farmers devoted more land to the production of export crops (cotton, bananas, sugar, coffee, fresh fruits, and flowers), less land was available for the production of subsistence foods (wheat, corn, millet, rice, beans, and potatoes), which local populations consumed as a central part of their diet. As the supply of subsistence foods fell, prices rose, and people found it harder to purchase the food they needed. In addition, the use of "Green Revolution" agricultural technologies on these export crops typically increased productivity and consolidated land in the hands of large farmers who have access to the credit needed to purchase these inputs. The consolidation of land forced farm households to seek work as wage laborers on large-scale farms and plantations or migrate. Dispossessed workers either moved to urban areas, where their search for work depressed wages in local labor markets, or they moved to marginal rural lands, where their attempts to wrest food from jungle forests and desert fringes wreaked environmental havoc.[58]

DEINDUSTRIALIZATION IN THE PERIPHERY

In addition to falling commodity prices, workers in the periphery have also experienced widespread deindustrialization. For wage workers, the destruction of domestic manufacturing industries has resulted in massive job losses for urban males.

Before 1980, dictators in the periphery used foreign investment (much of it provided by core firms to their subsidiaries in the periphery) and loans (from the Eurodollar market) to build domestic manufacturing industries that provided jobs and produced goods for domestic markets. Governments used high tariffs on manufactured goods imported from the core to protect domestic industries from foreign competition and force domestic worker-consumers to purchase domestic goods. This set of policies and practices, which was supposed to reduce dependence on the core and promote indigenous economic development, was known as "import-substitutionist industrialization." Many of these domestic industries were owned and managed by the state, often by the military, which controlled most peripheral states in this period. Government officials used this industrial sector to create jobs, generate income and revenue for the state, and, frequently, enrich corrupt elites. A few states in East Asia—South Korea, Taiwan, and Singapore—even managed to produce goods that could be exported to markets in Japan and the United States. But manufacturing industries in most peripheral states produced goods that could only be sold to captive domestic consumers.

After 1980, the conditions that allowed domestic manufacturing industries to flourish in the periphery were fundamentally changed by debt crisis, deflation, and democratization. When dictators fell, the newly installed civilian governments adopted a common set of economic policies that they believed would help them repay debt, solve their economic problems, and lay the ground for real development sometime in the future. The neoliberal policies adopted by peripheral and also semiperipheral states had three important features. First, they opened peripheral economies to foreign investment and trade. Second, they sold public or state assets to foreign and domestic entrepreneurs, a process known as "privatization." And third, they cut military spending and demilitarized their economies.[59] Unfortunately, the neoliberal policies they adopted (some policies were required as a condition of IMF austerity programs, some were adopted voluntarily by domestic free-market enthusiasts) led to the widespread deindustrialization of the domestic manufacturing sector, which had long provided jobs for urban men.

Opening Economies

Peripheral states opened their economies to foreign investment and trade by easing restrictions on private investment and capital flow and slashing tariffs on imported manufactured goods. Officials hoped that these measures would encourage foreign investment and force domestic firms to increase the quality of their goods, so that they could survive in a more competitive environment. But foreign investment generally failed to materialize. Investors either continued to invest heavily in the core or invested selectively in just a few countries: East Germany, China, and, to a lesser extent, Brazil and Mexico. As tariffs fell, domestic worker-consumers rushed to buy "higher quality" imported goods. Across Latin America, where average tariffs fell from 39 to 15 percent between 1989 and 1992, the new policy "unleashed a consumer boom, as Latin Americans . . . flocked to snap up imported goods."[60]

In the periphery, as in the core, worker-consumers played an important role in economic developments, often to their own detriment. In Mexico, for instance, binge buying by worker-consumers created a $23 billion trade deficit in 1994. The government then devalued the peso to increase the cost of imports and slow consumer purchases of foreign goods. But this made foreign investors lose confidence in the economy, and they withdrew their money. This further lowered the value of the peso and threatened the government with ruin. Financial crisis was averted when the U.S. government intervened with a $50-billion rescue plan. One element of this plan was that the Mexican government had to raise interest rates to restore foreign-investor confidence. But higher interest rates caused a recession and increased debt payments for worker households that had borrowed money. The buying binges of Mexican worker-consumers eventually contributed to recession, job loss, and a debt crisis for heavy-spending worker households. This would become a common pattern for peripheral and semiperipheral countries in the 1990s (as we shall see in the next chapter). Tariff reduction and binge buying would lead to financial crises but also, more important, to deindustrialization.

When worker-consumers started buying "high quality" imports, they stopped purchasing domestic goods they regarded as inferior. Many domestic industries, when confronted with competition from goods from the core, unceremoniously collapsed. Particularly hard hit were the male-dominated domestic steel and auto industries, which had been the pride of peripheral industrialization.[61]

In Latin America, for example, the proportion of the workforce employed by large manufacturing firms "fell from 44 percent to 32 percent between 1980 and 1990."[62] In Tanzania, domestic industrial production declined by as much as 80 percent.[63]

Privatization

State officials throughout the periphery sold state and public assets to private investors. They hoped to use the money they raised from the sale of state firms to repay debts and balance budgets, and they believed that private management would improve efficiency and quality. Between 1989 and 1992, Brazil sold 92 firms and a port for $52 billion, while Argentina and Mexico together sold 173 companies for $32.5 billion.[64] National banks, airlines, telephone companies, shipping lines, trucking firms, steel mills, cement factories, and port facilities were commonly offered for sale.

But the widespread sale of public assets created a glut on global markets, and many went unsold. Of the 123 firms put on the market by the new democratic government in the Philippines, only 58 were sold, and they earned the government considerably less than their book value.[65]

In many countries, the sale of state firms was accompanied by currency devaluations. Peripheral states commonly devalued their currencies, either to promote exports (so they could repay debts) or to slow binge buying by worker-consumers. But currency devaluations made domestic goods cheaper for foreigners, not for domestic buyers. So when states offered domestic firms for sale, devaluations cut their real price for foreigners, and they were snapped up by foreign investors. As the economist Andre Gunder Frank explained, "The real market value of [peripheral] properties and goods is suffering a classical and severe deflation in terms of world currencies, [so that] property and land . . . can be and is bought by Westerners 'for a song.'"[66]

Across the periphery, core investors creamed off the best manufacturing industries and dissolved the rest. In Argentina, for example, U.S. investors—Citicorp Equity—bought the government's Acros Zapla steel plant. In 1992, Citicorp began modernizing the plant but also cut its workforce, from 5,000 to only 709.[67] The same thing happened when the government's oil company was privatized. Between 1990 and 1996, 4,500 workers lost their jobs; only 500 remained.[68]

Demilitarization

Where civilian governments took power, they quite sensibly cut military spending. They did so to make it harder for the military to mount coups and intervene in political affairs and to reduce the heavy burden of military spending on weak economies. They recognized that military spending had contributed to heavy debt loads and had done little to promote economic growth. They agreed with the findings of scholars like A. F. Mullins, who concluded, "In general, those states that did best in GNP growth . . . paid less attention to military capability than others."[69]

Across the periphery, states reduced the size of armed forces, cut military spending, and privatized firms that were controlled by the army.[70] Military spending in Latin America, for example, fell by one-quarter in the late 1980s. But while reductions in military spending were beneficial for democratic governments and ailing economies, they also resulted in job loss for the males who were conscripted or enlisted to serve in the armed forces. As a result, demilitarization also contributed to male job loss.

Neoliberal policies led to widespread deindustrialization, particularly for manufacturing firms that had been owned by the state. Firms that were subsidiaries of businesses based in the core—and a large number of these were in Latin America— fared better. They took advantage of their access to foreign capital to expand their operations, taking over the local markets of collapsing enterprises. But while they continued to provide jobs for male urban workers, most of the other economic benefits were captured by core firms.

The decline of many manufacturing industries in the periphery resulted in high levels of unemployment and falling wages for male workers employed in the firms that survived.[71] In Argentina and Brazil, unemployment in manufacturing rose to nearly 20 percent by the late 1990s, a three-fold increase.[72] "The recession is only going to get worse," Moises Selerges, Jr., a member of a manufacturing union in Brazil, explained. "We're in the boat. Water's coming in, and we're sinking."[73]

ENCLAVE MANUFACTURING AND TOURISM

Falling commodity prices and the deindustrialization of domestic manufacturing in the periphery resulted in massive job and income losses for workers, primarily men in rural and urban settings. These two developments have been accompanied by a third, which has frequently been seen as beneficial for workers and states in the periphery. The expansion of export manufacturing in "free trade" enclaves, or *maquiladoras*, and the growth of service industries, principally tourism, have provided new jobs, primarily for women, and income for worker households and states.

But the gains made by women in export manufacturing and tourist enclaves have not offset the loss of jobs and income in the primary-commodity and domestic-manufacturing industries.

Maquilas

Export-manufacturing in free trade enclaves in the periphery has been around for decades. Mexico was among the first to do so. After the United States ended its "Bracero Program" in 1964 (see chapter 4), U.S. officials encouraged Mexico in 1965 to set up export-processing *maquiladoras* along its northern border to provide jobs for the 200,000 Mexican workers who had been expelled from jobs in U.S. agriculture.[74] Employment in *maquilas* grew from 3,087 in 1965 to 56,253 in 1975, and then to 500,000 in 1990.[75] At first, *maquilas* produced clothing, toys, luggage, and furniture, but they eventually produced electrical appliances, electronics, and auto parts in large quantity.[76] The U.S. and Mexican firms that operated *maquilas* mostly hired women, and they "constituted about 85 percent of the workforce" in the first decade.[77] The percentage of women in *maquilas* has since declined, to 64 percent in 1988, but this is still a very high percentage compared to women's employment in other manufacturing industries in Mexico.[78]

Maquilas in Mexico employ about one-third of the total number of workers in *maquila* industries around the world.[79] Worldwide employment in export-manufacturing zones grew from 866,000 in 1983 to 1.3 million in 1986.[80] They grew rapidly in this period because states wanted to expand the production of export goods so they could earn the hard currency they needed to repay their debts.[81] As in Mexico, the *maquilas* in most peripheral states employ women to manufacture apparel and electronic goods.

Although employment for women has grown rapidly in the *maquilas* of Mexico and other peripheral states, it has not compensated for the loss of male jobs in primary-commodity and domestic-manufacturing industries.[82] Given the fact that export-manufacturing firms employ only 10 percent of all manufacturing jobs in Mexico and, on average, only 2 percent of manufacturing jobs in the 48 peripheral countries that have *maquilas*, it is easy to see why they cannot.[83] What's more, because export-manufacturing firms are owned primarily by transnational firms from the core, manufacturing profits are captured by others. *Maquilas* do provide hard currency earnings for peripheral states, but states also agree to forego considerable tax revenues—these zones are, by definition, duty free—when they are established.

For workers, *maquilas* provide jobs for women and income for worker households, income that may be sorely needed, particularly where men have lost jobs and seen their income fall. But because *maquilas* pay low wages and provide employment for only short periods of time—usually for women workers between eighteen and twenty-five years of age—the income provided women workers is small and the relief it can provide households is temporary. In Indonesia, the sociologist Diane Wolf found that wages did not even cover the cost of subsistence for the young female workers employed in factories. Their parents' households actually had to subsidize their employment.[84] But they did so because employment provided cash wages, which they could not otherwise obtain in rural subsistence economies, cash they needed to pay taxes and purchase goods that they could not make themselves or obtain through barter.

Tourism

Faced with falling prices, widespread deindustrialization, and the limited gains provided by export manufacturing, it is not surprising that officials in many peripheral states have come to view tourism as a panacea. Many have spent heavily to promote this important service industry, which is now said to provide more jobs worldwide than any other industry.

Like export manufacturing, tourism takes place in enclaves, near sunny beaches and important historical-cultural sites. Like *maquilas*, tourism provides considerable employment for women.[85] Like export manufacturing, employment in the tourist industry grew rapidly in recent years. But unlike *maquilas*, tourism provided jobs in much greater number. Worldwide, the number of people working in the tourist industry increased from 197 million in 1990 to 250 million in 1999.[86] In 1999, worker-tourists spent $4.2 trillion, a level of spending that promised enormous benefits to the workers, businesses, and states that could capture the attention of tourists. Unfortunately, try as they might, peripheral workers, businesses, and states have not captured much of the benefits that the industry provides. Why? There are several reasons.

Most of the world's tourists are workers from core states. Although they spend a lot—U.S. worker-tourists spent $52.6 billion on travel abroad in 1996—they spent most of it in other core countries.[87] Core states captured 65 percent of all international arrivals and 72 percent of all tourist receipts in 1989.[88] Because core tourists traveled primarily to other core states (France, the United States, Spain, Italy, and Britain were the top five destinations), they provided jobs and income for workers and businesses there. More tourists visited Disney's Epcot in Florida than all of Latin America and the Caribbean, excluding Mexico. Even if peripheral countries spent heavily to develop their tourist industries, they would find it difficult to compete with high-tech destinations in the core, like EPCOT, or the European "homelands" of White ethnic groups in the United States, who yearn to visit the lands of their immigrant forebearers. It is important to note, too, that the declining number of vacation days for core workers, a consequence of downsizing and the growth of part-time and temporary employment in the core, probably means that tourism will not grow as rapidly in the future as it has in recent years (see chapter 4).

When worker-tourists from the core do travel to peripheral destinations, most of the money they spend will be captured by airlines, hotels, and cruise lines, which are generally owned by transnational firms based in the core. For example, 97 percent of all tourists flying to the Bahamas "arrived on an American-owned airline," 90 percent of them stayed at hotels owned by transnational corporations, and most of the food and drink they consumed was imported from the core.[89] Access to tourist destinations is largely controlled by travel agents and package-tour companies in the core, so it is difficult and expensive for peripheral states to market their destinations to the worker-consumers who travel.[90] When they arrive in the periphery, tourists spend a relatively small percentage of their vacation dollars on goods or services provided by local workers, businesses, or states. This is particularly true when they travel on cruise ships or stay in all-inclusive resorts, which prevent dollars or deutschemarks from leaking out into local economies.

The expansion of tourist industries in the periphery has also created a glut of beach resorts and hotels. So the industry is subject to the same diminishing returns as other commodity-producing industries. Some countries can attract more tourists if they devalue their currencies. Worker-tourists in the core look for bargains, traveling to countries where the local currency is weak and the hard currencies they earn go far. But while currency devaluations may sometimes increase travel to peripheral countries, they also reduce the value of the industry as a hard-currency earner. Worker-tourists like cheap destinations. But they shun places where poverty is rampant and the infrastructure is decayed—the condition of most peripheral states today. The influx of hard currency into tourist enclaves is also a problem because it creates a two-tier economy. Workers employed in the tourist industry have access to dollars. They typically use the dollars they earn to bid up the price of domestic goods. This behavior creates miniature, selective periods of inflation that hurt workers who do not have access to dollars and are paid only in local currencies. Nor does work in tourist industries replace the jobs lost in other industries. In the Caribbean, for example, more jobs were lost in the declining sugar cane industry than were created in the tourist industry.

Finally, of course, where tourism is linked to the sex industry, it contributes to the degradation and exploitation of the women and children it "employs." In East Asia, between three and four million women and children work in the sex industries of Thailand, South Korea, the Philippines, Taiwan, and Japan.[91] Most of these women, perhaps one-third of them children under seventeen, are held in debt bondage by employers, who often purchase young women from poor households or lure or force them into brothel service, where they are held as slaves until they become ill or aged (twenty-five years old).[92] They are then thrown out, without any savings, and are saddled with the negative stereotypes that make it difficult or impossible for them to find work or marry. Of course, many are also exposed to sexually transmitted diseases, particularly AIDS.

GROWING POVERTY FOR THE MAJORITY

For workers in the periphery, falling commodity prices and widespread deindustrialization have resulted in huge job and income losses, which have not been made good by increased employment in the export-manufacturing and tourist industries. Although women with jobs in *maquilas* and tourism have increased their contribution to household income, they have not been able to prevent income from falling significantly, and worker households have been swept into poverty and debt.

As income from commodity production and wages fell—for example, by 40 percent in Mexico and 65 percent in Tanzania during the 1980s—poverty increased.[93] Half of Peru's 24 million people live in poverty, and the number of poor workers in Latin America increased by 60 million between 1980 and 1993, "leaving 46 percent of the population, nearly 200 million people, living in poverty."[94] More poor people live in India—312 million in 1994—than in all of Latin America and Africa combined.[95] Where malnutrition is rampant, infectious diseases have made a comeback: cholera in Latin America; plague in India.

Like worker households in the United States, which borrowed heavily to maintain standards of living, many middle-income worker households in the periphery borrowed money to purchase homes, buy consumer goods, or start businesses. But when interest rates rose (they rose in the early 1980s when the United States lifted interest rates, and they rose in the 1990s when currency crises forced peripheral governments to raise domestic interest rates to attract foreign investors and prevent capital flight), worker households that had borrowed money were ruined. In a sense, the debt crisis of peripheral states became also a debt crisis for individual worker households. Teresa and Guillermo Lasso, a middle-income couple, owned a beauty parlor and veterinary practice in Mexico. They borrowed $79,000 to build a house. But as the economy worsened, "people were just letting their [pet] dogs and cats die," Dr. Lasso explained. His practice collapsed, and the interest payments on their mortgage increased from $660 a month to $2,125, considerably more than their $1,250 monthly income. Because Mexican banks can charge interest on outstanding interest, they now owe the bank $113,000. They stand on the verge of bankruptcy and risk losing everything.[96]

Workers who borrowed money to purchase less-expensive consumer goods—cars, motor bikes, televisions—have also been affected by domestic interest-rate hikes. As a result, most households have cut back. "Everybody is working the maximum to spend the minimum," explained Luiz Henrique Afonso, a government worker in Brazil. "I don't know anybody whose budget isn't being pinched or who isn't cutting back in some way or another," he said in the wake of currency-crisis interest-rate hikes.[97] For some, this meant cutting back on consumer purchases or food. Ricarda Martínez de Suárez and her husband, who survive on a pension in Mexico, stopped buying chicken heads and feet from the market and started raising chickens to provide meat.[98] For others, it meant cutting back not only on consumer goods but also on the number of children they bear.

Fertility rates in countries across the periphery have fallen dramatically in recent years. Women have decided to have fewer children in Moslem countries like Bangladesh, Egypt, and Indonesia, and in Catholic countries like Colombia and Mexico.[99] Demographers attribute change to a combination of events: economic crisis, television, and contraceptives. In Mexico, declining fertility rates were closely associated with economic crisis, falling from 6.5 births per woman just before the onset of the debt crisis in 1980 to 3 births per woman in 1995.[100] "Small families live better," Gloria Muñoz Castro said, explaining her decision to stop reproducing after having two children. "We didn't want to spend all our money just to feed and clothe children." Her sister-in-law concurred, saying she would not have any children because "food is expensive, the oil is running out, water is scarce. The future's just too bleak."[101]

The general decline in fertility rates reflects this economic assessment. In one survey, nearly one-half of all Mexican households decided "to stop or postpone having children" between 1982 and 1988.[102] Demographers studying the rapid decline of fertility rates in Brazil, which "has experienced the largest self-induced drop in human history," have argued that women reduced family size because their incomes declined (largely as a result of the debt crisis) at a time when their economic expectations rose (partly as a result of watching TV).[103] They were able to have fewer children because they began using contraceptives or had themselves sterilized. To get more with less, women have, in effect, downsized their immediate families by having fewer children, this despite opposition from the Catholic Church and the absence of any family-planning programs sponsored by the state.[104]

For the very poorest workers in the periphery, debt may not only mean cutting back on consumption or family size; it may also mean entering into debt-bondage or slavery. When extremely poor worker households in Bolivia, Brazil, India, or Thailand lose a crop or a job and face ruin and starvation, they can sometimes borrow money to stave off extinction. But because they have no assets or credit, they can only borrow under extremely disadvantageous and onerous conditions. Lenders typically require the children, adults, or entire families to work in charcoal furnaces, brick foundries, carpet factories, or brothels until their debts are repaid.[105] Social scientist Kevin Bales estimated that 27 million people worldwide are "enslaved," most of them by debt.[106] In India, for example, between 300,000 and one million children are held captive in carpet factories to repay household debts, working between twelve and sixteen hours a day.[107] Because lender-owners keep the accounts and refuse to let illiterate workers or borrowers review them, they can keep the children in thrall until they are no longer useful. Unlike slavery in the colonial era, workers today are not enslaved for life but are instead discarded when their productivity declines.[108] This practice is particularly evident in industries where children and young girls are held in debt bondage, in carpet factories and in sex-industry brothels.

Across the periphery, tens of millions of workers are persuaded by falling commodity prices, deindustrialization, and the expansion of enclave manufacturing and tourism to migrate in search of work. The overwhelming majority of migrants moves from rural to urban settings within the same country. There are 70 to 100 million workers who migrate within China alone.[109] A small number moves in the opposite direction, from fertile agricultural areas to remote marginal lands: the Amazon in Brazil, the mountain jungles in Peru and Central America, desert fringe areas in the Sahel, interior jungles in Central Africa, remote islands in the Indonesian archipelago.[110] There they practice swidden agriculture and subsistence farming, mining, or forestry. Of those who move from rural to urban areas, a small number migrates across international borders, seeking work in the core. If they evade capture and deportation and find work, they typically send money to worker households back home.

Contrary to popular belief, immigration provides important economic benefits to core countries. A 1997 National Academy of Science study found that "immigration added perhaps $10 billion a year to the U.S. economy."[111] But perhaps more significantly, migrant worker remittances provide a vital source of income for households and states in the periphery, where they benefit from hard-currency inflow. Indeed, migrant worker remittances may be one of the very few ways that real development is actually promoted in the periphery. In some countries—the Philippines, Cuba, Vietnam—migrant workers provide more money for investment than transnational corporations, banks, and the World Bank combined.[112] Unlike the investments and loans made by core businesses and banks, which go to their subsidiaries and peripheral businesses and states, the money sent by workers goes directly to households, which use the money carefully. A good example is provided by migrants from Chinantlan, Mexico.

In 1945, two brothers from Chinantlan hitch-hiked to New York City, where they found jobs mopping floors.[113] Pedro and Fermín Simón established a base there for other relatives, who traveled singly or in groups to join them in New York over the next fifty years. There they helped each other find work, shared apartments, pooled income, and, more important, sent money home. They tithed a portion of their earnings and formed a committee to raise money for specific development projects in Chinantlan. They bought bricks for the town square and spent $100,000 for a new potable water system. "Our priority is to give this little town its most basic needs," explained Abel Alonso, the New York committee's president. By the late 1990s, the New York–based migrant community sent Chinantlan $2 million each year and its leaders functioned like a government-in-exile. "We have no other source of income besides New York," Chinantlan's mayor Dr. Francisco R. Calixto explained.

The migrants returned regularly to the town for vacations and holiday celebrations, and many built homes and retired there. Their Social Security checks and pensions provided an ongoing source of hard currency for the local economy and helped create jobs in local small businesses. Could the World Bank, U.S. corporations, or the indebted Mexican state have done as much for the development of this small town? Perhaps. But they never tried.

CHINESE EXCEPTIONALISM?

China is unlike other countries in the periphery in three respects. First, although it produces raw materials, it does not export them but consumes them itself. So falling commodity prices have not affected China as they have other export-dependent peripheral countries. Second, because China borrowed relatively little money from core creditors, it did not experience a severe debt crisis and was not forced to impose extensive austerity programs like so many other peripheral states. Instead, it has been the recipient of massive foreign investment, $77 billion between 1979 and 1991, $251 billion between 1992 and 1995, capturing about one-third of all the investment going to peripheral countries.[114] This investment helped stimulate rapid economic growth during the 1980s and 1990s, at a time when most peripheral economies were contracting. Third, the communist regime has remained in power, after it massacred demonstrators demanding democratization in 1989, unlike dictators and communist regimes in most other peripheral states.

Still, like governments in other peripheral states, Chinese officials adopted common neoliberal policies, opening the economy to foreign investment and trade, privatizing state assets, and demilitarizing the economy. By opening China's economy, the government encouraged investment from the core, from neighboring Taiwan and overseas Chinese communities, and, after it reincorporated Hong Kong and Macao, from investors there. Tourism also provided an important source of income, as overseas Chinese toured the mainland in growing numbers.[115] Foreign investors financed the expansion of export manufacturing, which created jobs and earned hard currency from the sale of manufactured goods to core markets, principally the United States.

The Chinese government began to privatize state assets in the late 1970s, when it essentially privatized rural agricultural land. By giving farmers control of land, China increased grain production dramatically (grain production doubled between 1978 and 1984), which helped feed its still-growing population.[116] By paying farmers higher prices for their crops and letting them sell surpluses on open markets, China increased farm income. These policies secured new political support for the regime in the countryside but not in the cities, where rising food prices eroded the real incomes of urban workers and government employees. This was why many urban residents supported antigovernment demonstrators in Tiananmen Square.

Then in the 1990s, the government began privatizing domestic manufacturing industries that produce goods for Chinese markets, selling off more than 10,000 of the state's 300,000 firms.[117] As happened elsewhere in the periphery, this resulted in widespread deindustrialization and, for the first time in China, massive job loss, what the Chinese now call *xia gang*, which means to "step down from one's post."[118] The railway system laid off 1.1 million workers, the textile industry 1.2 million workers, the coal industry 400,000 workers, and the government more than 8 million employees.[119] Some economists estimate that "another one-third of China's 100 million workers need to be shed if surviving companies are to pay their own way."[120] Because many factories in China are located in rural areas, deindustrialization has contributed to large-scale rural-urban migrations, with as many as 100 million workers migrating annually across the country in search of work. As many as three million workers live illegally in Beijing, where they work as vendors, street sweepers, construction workers, building guards, and maids.[121]

The government has also demilitarized the economy somewhat, reducing the size of the army by one million men, cutting its budget, and selling many of the businesses it operated, partly to combat the extensive smuggling operations run by the military.[122]

These three policies promoted rapid economic growth in the 1980s and 1990s. Much of the government's success was due to massive foreign investment, on a scale unique among peripheral states. Not only was the scale of foreign investment atypical, it was unusual because it was directed at a communist regime, one of the few left anywhere in the world. The effort to use investment as a means to transform communists into capitalists has become a kind of evangelical economic project, pursued with almost missionary zeal by private investors and government officials in the core.

But while China has stood apart from the periphery in many respects, it still faces difficult problems. The gains made by agricultural reforms in the 1970s have slowed, and China can no longer expect to double food production in a few short years. If it begins importing food in large quantities, as many experts believe it will do soon, then it will spend more on imports and perhaps run trade deficits. For agricultural workers, poverty has again increased, and between 60 and 100 million workers live on the edge of starvation.[123]

Meanwhile, widespread deindustrialization and inflation have resulted in massive job losses and declining real incomes for urban workers. Today, between 12 and 22 million urban residents live in "absolute poverty," meaning they cannot afford basic food, clothing, or shelter.[124]

The incorporation of Hong Kong and Macao initially funneled new investment into China, but they have also recently become a conduit for capital flight out of China, an estimated $65 billion in 1996, which has undermined the country's economic position.[125] Hong Kong and Macao are also preferred destinations for Chinese migrants, though the government has tried to prevent migrants' entry into these urban manufacturing enclaves.[126]

The growth of export manufacturing, which was financed by massive foreign investment and upon which the "transition to a market economy" and so much else depends, has recently slowed, and economic growth declined by half, from 15 percent in 1997 to 7 percent in 1998.[127] Exports have slowed because the crisis in other Asian countries resulted in the devaluation of their currencies, which made their goods more competitive with Chinese products in overseas markets.

Under these conditions, if foreign investment were to fall off, or export sales weaken, or the government imported more food, or consumers binged on goods from abroad, or U.S.–Chinese relations frayed, slowing U.S. investment or blocking access to U.S. markets, the wheels could come off and China could look less like an exception and more like the rule among peripheral states.

SELECTIVE GLOBALIZATION

Worker households in the periphery have adopted different strategies that they hoped would promote economic development and close the yawning gap between people in rich and poor countries. But they have repeatedly failed, and the distance between periphery and core countries has widened. Some government officials and scholars now hope that "globalization," the neoliberal policies adopted by most peripheral states in the 1980s and 1990s, will promote development. But it is unlikely to do so because economic growth requires, at a minimum, substantial private or public investment. For most peripheral states, this investment will not be forthcoming.

During the 1950s and 1960s, the periphery received some private investment and public aid from the core. In 1960, about 32 percent of all foreign investment flowed into peripheral economies.[128] But notice that the bulk of global investment—68 percent—was invested in the core. Of the money invested in the periphery, much of it was concentrated in only a few states. The $18.6 billion invested by the United States in South Korea and Taiwan between 1962 and 1978 was greater than U.S. investment and aid to all of Africa ($6.89 billion) and India ($9.6 billion) or to all of Latin America ($14.8 billion).[129] Still, with relatively few external resources, many peripheral states managed to construct domestic manufacturing industries that provided jobs for urban male workers and produced goods for domestic markets.

Then in the 1970s, peripheral economies received a boost from two sources. First, they receive a massive influx of money in the form of loans. This money was made available to them because OPEC had raised oil prices and deposited its oil revenue in Eurodollar markets, which was then loaned by core banks to peripheral borrowers. Second, commodity prices rose (along with rising oil and food prices), raising their incomes substantially. The money from loans and the income from high commodity prices provided jobs, increased wages, and provided substantial benefits to workers in the periphery, for the first time in the postwar period. But it did not last. Deflationary policies in the core increased the cost of borrowed money. And the expansion of commodity production by peripheral states created gluts, which began to force down prices. The crisis that ensued has not yet been ameliorated. The debt owed by peripheral states continues to mount—peripheral debt doubled from $639 billion in 1980 to $1,341 billion in 1990—while peripheral states' income from commodities continues to fall.

During the 1980s and 1990s, peripheral states opened their economies, sold public assets, and cut military spending. These neoliberal "globalization" policies were supposed to stimulate investment and promote growth. But they can work only if investment is made. It seemed a promising strategy because there was a lot of money available in Eurodollar markets, corporate accounts, development agencies, and government aid programs. Open-door policies in peripheral states made it easier for these institutions to invest in or assist peripheral states. The trouble for the periphery was that global investors have been extremely selective. They have been selective in three ways. First, the bulk of global investment finances economic development in the core. And the percentage is increasing. The core received 67.3 percent of direct investment available worldwide in 1960, but it received 75.5 percent in 1983 and 83.1 percent in 1989.[130] Whereas Western Europe and Japan were the chief beneficiaries of investment and aid in the 1950s and 1960s, the United States is now the major beneficiary of global investment flow, which is one important reason why it has improved its competitiveness and grown in recent years.[131] Although most of this money comes from other core countries, a substantial amount comes from the periphery in the form of "capital flight." Domestic investors in Latin America, for example, have invested more than $300 billion in the core, most of it in the United States.[132] In many cases, the measures designed to facilitate the import of capital into peripheral states actually make it easier for capital to exit. In this way, the underdeveloped periphery contributes to the improvement of the overdeveloped core.

Of course, some investment is made in the periphery, though the percentage is diminishing. But this investment, too, is selective. Most of it goes to China. In 1996, China received $42 billion in foreign investment.[133] That's a huge sum, though keep in mind that this would not pay the cost of installing a phone line for every house in China. But this sum dwarfs investment elsewhere in the periphery. In the same year, 1996, Mexico received $6 billion worth of investment, and India, with nearly one billion people, received only $3 billion.[134]

Finally, when money from global financial pools trickles into peripheral economies, it is concentrated in enclaves, in the export-manufacturing and tourist industries. Although these industries create jobs for women and provide hard currencies to states, they create more jobs and larger revenues for the core firms that organize and monopolize peripheral manufacturing and tourism. Workers and states in the periphery have vast needs. But they should not expect that their economic development will be assisted by global investors, whose selective patterns of investment deny them what they require. When peripheral states permitted increased foreign investment and "globalized" their economies, they expected some economic reward. But rewards have not been forthcoming.

The investment that has been available globally has not been distributed widely. It has instead been distributed selectively. As such, it is more appropriate to describe contemporary change as a process of "selective globalization," which contributes to diverging economic circumstances, not converging economic fortunes, as many theorists of contemporary "globalization" suggest.[135]

Of course, development in the capitalist world-economy has always been "selective," contributing to the diverging fortunes of core and periphery, First and Third World. Colonialism was the primary form of globalization for several centuries. After World War II, the Cold War and neocolonialism defined the shape of globalization. Since the onset of the debt crisis and the end of the Cold War, globalization has taken a new form, which we have called selective globalization.

Contemporary global change has not united the world economically. It has integrated different regions in the core and some enclaves in the periphery and semiperiphery, but it has increasingly detached the core from most of the periphery. For centuries, core states conquered, colonized, and compelled slaves, servants, and workers in the periphery to furnish the core with raw material, agricultural products, and industrial goods. Until recently, the core needed to exercise its political and military authority—what was called "imperialism"—to compel workers and, after decolonization, compel states to furnish the goods that the core required. But this relationship has fundamentally changed.

The introduction of new technologies in the core means that the core no longer needs many products from the periphery. In fact, the core requires fewer and fewer goods from the periphery. Economically, this means that the core has little incentive to invest in the periphery, except where essential goods are still produced, manufactured, or procured, or where profitable markets for core goods still exist. These markets are hard to find because worker-consumers in the periphery are generally poor. Core firms would much rather invest in the expansion of markets in the core, where they can access worker-consumers who have credit cards, than worker-consumers in the periphery, whose meager earnings are held in depreciating currencies. Core firms would rather sell expensive running shoes to the 20 million U.S. school children with allowance money in their pockets than furnish inexpensive shoes to every person living in Africa.

Politically, this means that government officials in the core view economic and political events in the postcolonial periphery with increasing detachment and relative indifference. No longer are they willing to invest or intervene in the periphery to secure their geopolitical interests. The core's declining economic and political interest in the periphery has resulted in what we have called "indifferent imperialism."[136] Core states are still sometimes willing to exercise their political and military power where their vital interests are threatened, as they did in Iraq in 1990–1991, but most of the periphery hardly matters at all.

This has important implications for theories of "development." We agree with Peter Drucker, who has argued, "For if primary products are becoming of marginal importance to the economies of the developed world, traditional development theories and policies are losing their foundations."[137] From our perspective, "globalization" is not simply the latest model of "development" for the world at large. It is the *end* of development, in the traditional sense, for much of the world.

As economic, political, and military links between the core and much of the periphery fray, the periphery will find itself increasingly on its own. Women and girls will do much of the work necessary to support households under these circumstances. But this new autonomy is largely a product of developments and decisions that originate in the core. So the periphery's new "autonomy" or "independence" is being forced upon its inhabitants, not chosen by them. Still, because the peripheral areas that do not produce industrial and agricultural exports are being red-lined or marginalized, working people may decide to initiate new forms of economic development.

NOTES

1. John T. Passe-Smith, "The Persistence of the Gap between Rich and Poor Countries: Taking Stock of World Economic Growth, 1960–1993," in Mitchell A. Seligson and John T. Passe-Smith, eds., *Development and Underdevelopment: The Political Economy of Global Inequality* (Boulder, Colo.: Rienner, 1998), 33. This area has been called the "Third World," but also the "developing" world and, more recently, the "emerging" world. Yet whatever it is called, "The great majority of developing countries depend for their welfare and livelihood on the production and export of primary commodities." Alfred Maizels, *Commodities in Crisis: The Commodity Crisis of the 1980s and the Political Economy of International Commodity Prices* (Oxford: Clarendon, 1993), 1.

2. See Robert K. Schaeffer, *Power to the People: Democratization around the World* (Boulder, Colo.: Westview, 1997), passim.

3. Schaeffer, *Power to the People*, 94.

The Submerging Periphery   107

4. See Kevin Bales, *Disposable People: New Slavery in the Global Economy* (Berkeley: University of California Press, 1999).
5. Seligson and Passe-Smith, *Development and Underdevelopment*, 35.
6. Deniz Kandiyoti, *Women in Rural Production Systems: Problems and Policies* (Paris: United Nations Education, Scientific and Cultural Organization, 1985), 62.
7. Maizels, *Commodities in Crisis*, 105–106.
8. Duncan Green, *Silent Revolution: The Rise of Market Economies in Latin America* (London: Cassell, 1995), 16–17.
9. Barbara Dinham and Colin Hines, *Agribusiness in Africa* (London: Earth Resources Research, 1983), 56, 72.
10. Robert K. Schaeffer, *Understanding Globalization: The Social Consequences of Political, Economic, and Environmental Change* (Lanham, Md.: Rowman & Littlefield, 1997), 29–30.
11. Lester Brown, *State of the World 1984* (New York: Norton, 1984), 43–44.
12. Kenneth L. Peoples, David Freshwater, Gregory D. Hanson, Paul T. Prentice, and Eric P. Thor, *Anatomy of an American Agricultural Credit Crisis: Farm Debt in the 1980s* (Washington, D.C.: A Farm Credit Assistance Board Publication, 1992), 23.
13. Barbara Stallings, *Banker to the World: U.S. Portfolio Investment in Latin America, 1900–1986* (Berkeley: University of California Press, 1987), 298; Sue Branford and Bernardo Kucinski, *The Debt Squads: The U.S., the Banks and Latin America* (London: Zed, 1988), 58.
14. Schaeffer, *Power to the People*, 88.
15. Robert K. Schaeffer, "Success and Impasse: The Environmental Movement in the United States and around the World," in Walter L. Goldfrank, David Goodman, and Andrew Szasz, eds., *Ecology and the World-System* (Westport, Conn.: Greenwood, 1999), 201.
16. William C. Smith, *Authoritarianism and the Crisis of the Argentine Political Economy* (Stanford, Calif.: Stanford University Press, 1989), 259; Ernst J. Olivari, *Latin American Debt and the Politics of International Finance* (Westport, Conn.: Praeger, 1989), 8–9.
17. Schaeffer, *Power to the People*, 90.
18. Schaeffer, *Power to the People*, 91.
19. Schaeffer, *Power to the People*, 93.
20. Robert K. Schaeffer, "Technology and Work in the Third World," in Randy Hodson, ed., *Research in the Sociology of Work*, vol. 6, *The Globalization of Work* (Greenwich, Conn.: JAI Press, 1997), 76.
21. Maizels, *Commodities in Crisis*, 17.
22. Maizels, *Commodities in Crisis*, 15.
23. David Goodman, Bernardo Sorj, and John Wilkinson, *From Farming to Biotechnology: A Theory of Argo-Industrial Development* (London: Blackwell, 1987), 2–4, 580.
24. H. Guyford Stever and Janet H. Muroyama, "Overview," in Janet H. Muroyama and H. Guyford Stever, *Globalization of Technology* (Washington, D.C.: National Academy Press, 1988), 5.
25. Umberto Colombo, "The Technology Revolution and the Global Economy," in Muroyama and Stever, *Globalization of Technology*, 26.
26. Niels Thygesen, Yutaka Kosai, and Robert Z. Lawrence, *Globalization and Trilateral Labor Markets: Evidence and Implications* (New York, Paris, and Tokyo: Trilateral Commission, 1996), 85.
27. Schaeffer, "Technology and Work," 78–79.
28. Schaeffer, "Technology and Work," 79.
29. Seth Schiesel, "Fiber Optic Cable Demand Outstrips Supply," *New York Times*, November 4, 1996.

30. Schaeffer, "Technology and Work," 80–81.
31. Jonathan Fuerbringer, "An Icon's Fading Glory," *New York Times*, June 15, 1999.
32. Fuerbringer, "An Icon's Fading Glory."
33. Donald G. McNeil, Jr., "As Britain Sells Some Gold, South Africa Howls," *New York Times*, July 7, 1999.
34. See Schaeffer, *Understanding Globalization*, 183–216.
35. Robert J. Samuelson, "The Trouble with Steak," *Newsweek*, April 7, 1997.
36. See Michael Barratt Brown and Pauline Tiffen, *Short Changed: Africa and World Trade* (London: Pluto, 1992), 32.
37. Brown and Tiffen, *Short Changed*, 32.
38. A. Pitotrowski, "Sugar-Free Gum: A Success Story," in Andrew J. Rugg-Gunn, *Sugarless—Towards the Year 2000* (Cambridge: Royal Society of Chemistry, 1994), 184–191.
39. Jonathan Fuerbringer, "Swamped by Asia's Wake," *New York Times*, July 11, 1998; Alfred Maizels, Robert Bacon, and George Mavrotas, *Commodity Supply Management by Producing Countries: A Case-Study of the Tropical Beverage Crops* (Oxford: Clarendon, 1997), 8; Fuerbringer, "An Icon's Fading Glory"; Jonathan Fuerbringer, "Commodities' Price Slide Victimizes Economies of Several Nations," *New York Times*, December 11, 1998; Jonathan Fuerbringer, "No Refuge in Plunging Commodity Prices," *New York Times*, August 28, 1998.
40. Maizels, *Commodities in Crisis*, 27–29.
41. Calestous Juma, *The Gene Hunters: Biotechnology and the Scramble for Seeds* (Princeton: Princeton University Press, 1989), 143.
42. James G. Brown, *The International Sugar Industry: Developments and Prospects*, World Bank Staff Commodity Working Paper #48 (Washington, D.C.: World Bank, 1987), 2; Simon Romero, "Spoonfuls of Hope, Tons of Pain," *New York Times*, May 21, 2000.
43. G. Hawes, *The Philippine State and the Marcos Regime: The Politics of Export* (Ithaca, N.Y.: Cornell University Press, 1987), 85; Michael Redclift and David Goodman, "The Machinery of Hunger: The Crisis of Latin American Food Systems," in David Goodman and Michael Redclift, eds., *Environment and Development in Latin America: The Politics of Sustainability* (Manchester: Manchester University Press, 1991), 66; Maizels, *Commodities in Crisis*, 38.
44. Henk Hobbelink, *Biotechnology and the Future of World Agriculture: The Fourth Resource* (London: Zed, 1991), 74; Frederick Claimonte and John Cavanagh, *Merchants of Drink* (Penang, Malaysia: Third World Network, 1988), 167.
45. Food and Agricultural Organization, *Agricultural Raw Materials: Competition with Synthetic Substitutes*, FAO Economic and Social Development Paper #48 (Rome: Food and Agriculture Organization of the United Nations, 1984), 7.
46. Juma, *The Gene Hunters*; Suzanne Daley, "Vanilla Farming? Not as Bland as You Might Think," *New York Times*, January 19, 1998.
47. Clifford Krauss, "Pinching Pennies in a Land of Copper," *New York Times*, December 21, 1998.
48. Donald G. McNeil, Jr., "Gold Breaks Its Promise to Miners of Lesotho," *New York Times*, June 16, 1998; Rachel L. Swarns, "A Bleak Hour for South Africa Miners," *New York Times*, October 10, 1999.
49. Agis Salpukas, "Roughnecks of Distinction," *New York Times*, July 8, 1998.
50. Allen R. Meyerson, "Soft Oil Prices Take Their Toll on Wildcatters," *New York Times*, January 2, 1999; Agis Salpukas, "Refining Entrepreneurship," *New York Times*, June 9, 1998.
51. The current trade dispute over bananas illustrates the complex character of change for men and women in different settings. In the late 1990s, the United States demanded that

Western Europe reduce its tariffs on banana imports from Central America, so that U.S. corporations with large plantations in the region could sell more bananas in Western Europe. The Europeans refused to lower tariffs because they imported bananas from independent small farmers in their former colonies in the Caribbean. In gender terms, the Europeans were asked to abandon the 145,000 men and women who grow bananas in the Caribbean and buy bananas instead from U.S. plantations in Central America, which employ men. Larry Rohter, "Where Banana Is King, a Land Revolt," *New York Times*, July 22, 1996; Larry Rohter, "Trade Storm Imperils Caribbean Banana Crops," *New York Times*, May 9, 1997.

52. Lynne Brydon and Sylvia Chant, *Women in the Third World: Gender Issues in Rural and Urban Areas* (New Brunswick, N.J.: Rutgers University Press, 1989), 69.

53. Douglas Jehl, "For Ordinary Saudis, Days of Oil and Roses Are Over," *New York Times*, March 20, 1999.

54. Douglas Jehl, "Where Oil Is Plentiful but Cash Is Short," *New York Times*, January 16, 1999.

55. Jonathan Fuerbringer, "Swamped by Asia's Wake," *New York Times*, July 11, 1998; Sam Dillon, "Loss of 3,000 Mexican Steel Jobs Has an Asian Connection," *New York Times*, July 28, 1998; Kraus, "Pinching Pennies in a Land of Copper."

56. Schaeffer, *Power to the People*, 205.

57. Fuerbringer, "Swamped by Asia's Wake."

58. Schaeffer, *Understanding Globalization*, 171–172.

59. Schaeffer, *Power to the People*, 218–245.

60. Green, *Silent Revolution*, 138–139.

61. Dillon, "Loss of 3,000 Mexican Steel Jobs"; Bill Orr, *The Global Economy in the 90s: A User's Guide* (New York: New York University Press, 1992), 83.

62. Green, *Silent Revolution*, 95; Philip McMichael, *Development and Social Change: A Global Perspective* (Thousand Oaks, Calif.: Pine Forge Press, 1996), 130; Roger Cohen, "Argentina Sees Other Face of Globalization," *New York Times*, February 6, 1998.

63. Reana Jhabvala, "Self-Employed Women's Association: Organising Women by Struggle and Development," in Sheila Rowbotham and Swasti Mitter, eds., *Dignity and Daily Bread: New Forms of Economic Organizing among Poor Women in the Third World and the First* (London: Routledge, 1994), 142.

64. Green, *Silent Revolution*, 72.

65. Andre Gunder Frank, "Soviet and Eastern European 'Socialism': What Went Wrong?" in Barry Gills and Shahid Qadir, eds., *Regimes in Crisis: The Post-Soviet Era and the Implications for Development* (London: Zed, 1995), 105.

66. Frank, "Soviet and Eastern European 'Socialism,'" 105.

67. Cohen, "Argentina Sees Other Face of Globalization."

68. Cohen, "Argentina Sees Other Face of Globalization."

69. PA. F. Mullins, Jr., *Born Arming: Development and Military Power in New States* (Stanford, Calif.: Stanford University Press, 1987), 103.

70. Jeanne Vickers, *Women and the World Economic Crisis* (London: Zed, 1991), passim.

71. Faruk Tabak, "The World Labour Force," in Terence K. Hopkins and Immanuel Wallerstein, eds., *The Age of Transition: Trajectory of the World-System, 1945–2025* (London: Zed, 1996), 111.

72. Calvin Sims, "A Saint Besieged: Heaven Knows, Many Need Help," *New York Times*, August 8, 1997; Diana Jean Schemo, "Economic Detour in Brazil," *New York Times*, September 26, 1998.

73. Schemo, "Economic Detour in Brazil."

74. Susan Tiano, *Patriarchy on the Line: Labor, Gender, and Ideology in the Mexican Maquila Industry* (Philadelphia: Temple University Press, 1994), 19; Ira C. Magaziner and Mark Patinkin, *The Silent War: Inside the Global Business Battles Shaping America's Future* (New York: Vintage, 1990), 319–320.

75. Jorge A. Bustamente, "Maquiladoras: A New Face of International Capitalism on Mexico's Northern Frontier," in June Nash and María Patricia Fernández-Kelly, *Women, Men, and the International Division of Labor* (Albany: S.U.N.Y. Press, 1983), 241; Enrique Martin Del Campo, "The Case of the American Hemisphere," in Muroyama and Stever, *Globalization of Technology*, 95; Patricia A. Wilson, *Exports and Local Development: Mexico's New Maquiladoras* (Austin: University of Texas Press, 1992), 43; María Patricia Fernández-Kelly, "Broadening the Scope: Gender and the Study of International Development," in A. Douglas Kincaid and Alejandro Portes, eds., *Comparative National Development: Society and Economy in the New Global Order* (Chapel Hill: University of North Carolina Press, 1994), 157.

76. Magaziner and Patinkin, *The Silent War*, 322.

77. Tiano, *Patriarchy on the Line*, 24.

78. Tiano, *Patriarchy on the Line*, 24.

79. Wilson, *Exports and Local Development*, 10; Linda Y. C. Lim, "Women's Work in Export Factories: The Politics of a Cause," in Irene Tinker, ed., *Persistent Inequalities: Women and World Development* (Oxford: Oxford University Press, 1990), 101.

80. Wilson, *Exports and Local Development*, 10; Lim, "Women's Work in Export Factories," 101.

81. Helen I. Safa and Peggy Antrobus, "Women and the Economic Crisis in the Caribbean," in Lourdes Benería and Shelley Feldman, eds., *Unequal Burden: Economic Crises, Persistent Poverty, and Women's Work* (Boulder, Colo.: Westview, 1992), 63.

82. Emilio Carillo Gamboa, "Globalization of Industry through Production Sharing," in Muroyama and Stever, *Globalization of Technology*, 97.

83. Kamudhini Rosa, "The Conditions and Organisational Activities of Women in Free Trade Zones: Malaysia, Philippines and Sri Lanka, 1970–1990," in Rowbotham and Mitter, *Dignity and Daily Bread*, 80.

84. Diane L. Wolf, *Factory Daughters: Gender, Households Dynamics, and Rural Industrialization in Java* (Berkeley: University of California Press, 1992), 180.

85. David Harrison, "Tourism, Capitalism and Development in Less Developed Countries," in Leslie Sklair, ed., *Capitalism and Development* (London: Routledge, 1994), 238; Diane E. Levy and Patricia B. Lerch, "Tourism as a Factor in Development: Implications for Gender and Work in Barbados," *Gender and Society* 5, no. 1 (March 1991): 69.

86. Barbara Crossette, "Surprises in the Global Tourism Boom," *New York Times*, April 12, 1998.

87. Crossette, "Surprises in the Global Tourism Boom."

88. Harrison, "Tourism, Capitalism and Development," 233.

89. Harrison, "Tourism, Capitalism and Development," 241.

90. Harrison, "Tourism, Capitalism and Development," 242.

91. Marina Budhos, "Putting the Heat on Sex Tourism," *Ms. Magazine* (March 1997): 10; Andrew Sherry, "For Lust or Money," *Far Eastern Economic Review* (December 14, 1995): 23.

92. Sherry, "For Lust or Money," 12; Elizabeth Olson, "U.N. Urges Fiscal Accounting Include Sex Trade," *New York Times*, August 20, 1998.

93. Aili Mari Tripp, "The Impact of Crisis and Economic Reform on Women in Urban Tanzania," in Benería and Feldman, *Unequal Burden*, 164.

94. Green, *Silent Revolution*, 91; Hazel J. Johnson, *Dispelling the Myth of Globalization: The Case for Regionalization* (New York: Praeger, 1991), 2; Of course, rates of poverty vary con-

siderably, from 22 percent in Costa Rica to 77.5 percent in Guatemala. Patricia Baeza, "Introduction," in Women's Feature Service, ed., *The Power to Change: Women in the Third World Redefine Their Environment* (London: Zed, 1992), 2.

95. John F. Burns, "India's Five Decades of Progress and Pain," *New York Times*, August 14, 1997.

96. Dam Dillon, "Peso Crisis Bites into Mexico's Long-Ruling Party," *New York Times*, July 4, 1997.

97. Larry Rohter, "Once More, Brazilians Tighten Belts for a Rough Ride," *New York Times*, February 14, 1999.

98. Anthony De Palma, "In Mexico, Hunger and Woe in Crisis," *New York Times*, January 15, 1995; William K. Stevens, "3d-World Gains in Birth Control: Development Isn't Only Answer," *New York Times*, January 2, 1994.

99. Stevens, "3d-World Gains in Birth Control."

100. Sam Dillon, "Smaller Families to Bring Big Change in Mexico," *New York Times*, June 8, 1999.

101. Dillon, "Smaller Families to Bring Big Change."

102. Lourdes Benería, "The Mexican Debt Crisis: Restructuring the Economy and the Household," in Benería and Feldman, *Unequal Burden*, 94.

103. "Latin America's Birth Surprise," *New York Times*, June 13, 1999.

104. James Brooke, "Births in Brazil Are on Decline, Easing Worries," *New York Times*, August 8, 1989; Amartya Sen, "Populations: Delusion and Reality," *New York Review of Books*, September 22, 1994, 70.

105. Clifford Krauss, "When Even an Economic Miracle Isn't Enough," *New York Times*, July 12, 1998.

106. Bales, *Disposable People*, 23.

107. Bales, *Disposable People*, 23.

108. Bales, *Disposable People*, 15.

109. Ann and James Tyson, "China's Human Avalanche," *Current History* (September 1996): 277.

110. Seth Mydans, "Indonesia Resettles People to Relieve Crowding on Java," *New York Times*, August 25, 1996.

111. Robert Pear, "Academy's Report Says Immigration Benefits the United States," *New York Times*, May 18, 1997.

112. Safa and Antrobus, "Women and the Economic Crisis in the Caribbean," 72.

113. Deborah Sontag, "A Mexican Town That Transcends All Borders," *New York Times*, July 21, 1998.

114. Jan S. Prybyla, "All That Glitters: The Foreign Investment Boom," *Current History* (September 1995): 275.

115. Edward A. Gargan, "Eclipsed and Fraying Macao Limps toward Chinese Rule," *New York Times*, August 24, 1997; Crossette, "Surprises in the Global Tourism Boom."

116. Ian Jeffries, *Socialist Economies and the Transition to the Market: A Guide* (London: Routledge, 1993), 142; Claude Aubert, "China's Food-Takeoff?" in Stephan Feuchtwang, Athar Hussain, and Thierry Pairault, eds., *Transforming China's Economy in the Eighties*, vol. 1 (London: Zed, 1988), 103.

117. Seth Faison, "Major Shift for Communist China: Big State Industries Will Be Sold," *New York Times*, September 12, 1997; Seth Faison, "Messy Free-Market Plunge Rattling China's Businesses," *New York Times*, October 5, 1997.

118. Patrick E. Tyler, "In China's Outlands, Poorest Grow Poorer," *New York Times*, October 26, 1996.

119. Sheryl WuDunn, "The Layoff Introduced to Chinese," *New York Times*, May 11, 1993; Patrick E. Tyler, "China's Hidden Army of Workers Strives to Adapt," *New York Times*, December 11, 1994.
120. Erik Eckholm, "Joblessness: A Perilous Curve on China's Capitalist Road," *New York Times*, January 20, 1998.
121. Erik Eckholm, "As Beijing Pretties Up, Migrants Face Expulsion," *New York Times*, April 18, 1999.
122. Tyler, "China's Hidden Army"; Seth Faison, "China's Chief Tells Army to Give Up Its Commerce," *New York Times*, July 23, 1998; Harlan W. Jencks, "The Military in China," *Current History* (September 1989): 265.
123. Tyler, "In China's Outlands"; Daniel Southerland, "Gansu Province: 'A Third World' within China," *Washington Post*, November 18, 1988.
124. Elisabeth Rosenthal, "Poverty Spreads, and Deepens, in China's Cities," *New York Times*, October 4, 1999.
125. Edward A. Gargan, "China Already Capitalizing on Hong Kong's Wealth," *New York Times*, December 5, 1996; Seth Faison, "China Applies Brakes on Move toward World Economy," *New York Times*, September 30, 1998; Sheryl WuDunn, "The Tail That Wags the Dragon," *New York Times*, June 27, 1997.
126. Mark Landler, "Hong Kong Tries to Limit Court Ruling on Residency," *New York Times*, May 19, 1999; Elisabeth Rosenthal, "Hong Kong Court Strains Ties with Beijing, Saying It Has Last Word on Local Charter," *New York Times*, February 11, 1999.
127. Erik Eckholm, "Not (Yet) Gone the Way of All Asia," *New York Times*, November 15, 1998.
128. Arthur S. Alderson, "Globalization and Deindustrialization: Direct Investment and the Decline of Manufacturing Employment in 17 OECD Nations," *Journal of World-Systems Research* 3, no. 1 (1997): 5.
129. Bruce Cumings, "The Northeast Asian Political Economy," in Frederic C. Deyo, ed., *The Political Economy of the New Asian Industrialism* (Ithaca, N.Y.: Cornell University Press, 1987), 67.
130. Torry D. Dickinson, "Selective Globalization: The Relocation of Industrial Production and the Shaping of Women's Work," in Randy Hodson, ed., *Research in the Sociology of Work*, vol. 6, *The Globalization of Work* (Greenwich, Conn.: JAI Press, 1997), 118; Alderson, "Globalization and Deindustrialization," 5; Priyatosh Maitra, *The Globalization of Capitalism in Third World Countries* (Westport, Conn.: Praeger, 1996), 93.
131. Satoshi Ikeda, "World Production," in Hopkins and Wallerstein, *The Age of Transition*, 46.
132. Chander Kant, *Foreign Direct Investment and Capital Flight* (Princeton: Princeton Studies in International Finance, no. 80 (April 1996): 1; Christel Lane, *Industry and Society in Europe: Stability and Change in Britain, Germany, and France* (Aldershot, UK: Elgar, 1995), 85.
133. David E. Sanger, "Study Shows Jump in Investing in China and Revival in Mexico," *New York Times*, March 24, 1997.
134. Sanger, "Study Shows Jump in Investing"; Burns, "India's Five Decades of Progress and Pain."
135. Dickinson, "Selective Globalization," 124. See William Greider, *One World, Ready or Not: The Manic Logic of Global Capitalism* (New York: Simon and Schuster, 1997), passim. Brazil in 1999 received foreign investments worth about $26 billion. Simon Romero, "Carrying the Flag for Free Trade," *New York Times*, December 2, 1999.

136. Robert K. Schaeffer, "Free Trade Agreements: Their Impact on Agriculture and the Environment," in Philip McMichael, ed., *Food and Agrarian Orders in the World-Economy* (Westport, Conn.: Praeger, 1995), 267.

137. Peter F. Drucker, "The Changed World Economy," *Foreign Affairs* (Spring 1986): 774–775; N. P. Peritore, "Biotechnology: Political Economy and Environmental Impacts," in N. P. Peritore and A. K. Golve-Peritore, eds., *Biotechnology in Latin America: Politics, Impacts, and Risks* (Wilmington, Del.: SR Books, 1995), 20–21.

Chapter 6

Reverses in the Semiperiphery

Many workers live in low- to middle-income countries that are prosperous and literate, urban and industrial. Their governments have vast bureaucracies and large armies.[1] During the postwar period, this "semiperiphery" included the oil-producing states in the Middle East and in Nigeria and Venezuela, the large industrial countries of South America (Argentina, Brazil, Chile) and Southern Africa (South Africa), the states on the corners of southern Europe (Greece, Portugal, Spain), the communist countries in Eastern Europe and the Soviet Union, and the fast-growing "Tigers" in East Asia (South Korea, Taiwan, Singapore, and Hong Kong).[2] In all of these countries, the reorganization of work has transformed gender relations and workers' political alignments.

We will not focus here on developments in all five regions. For the oil-producing states in the Middle East, Africa, and Latin America, declining commodity prices have been the most significant development in recent years, though this has affected countries with large worker populations (Iran, Iraq, Nigeria, Venezuela) more than it has states with small populations (Saudi Arabia, Kuwait). Although oil is a more valuable commodity than sugar, these countries have been subjected to the same forces that affected commodity producers throughout the periphery, forces that we have already discussed.

For the large states in South America and South Africa, workers have been adversely affected by debt crises, deindustrialization, and falling commodity prices, events also ubiquitous in the periphery.

The states on the corners of southern Europe were more fortunate. The oil crisis in the 1970s led to the fall of dictators in Greece, Portugal, and Spain. These states' subsequent entry into the European Community eased them into the core, albeit as poor relations.[3]

There are, however, two regions in the semiperiphery that deserve closer attention, whose development differs substantially from the periphery: the communist countries in Eastern Europe and the Soviet Union; and the capitalist "Tigers" in

East Asia. Workers in both regions were decisively affected by events in the 1980s and 1990s.

In the Soviet Union and Eastern Europe, economic and political crises in the 1980s led to democratization and sometimes division, as occurred in the Soviet Union, Czechoslovakia, and Yugoslavia. After 1989, the governments of democratizing states opened their economies, sold public assets, and reduced military spending, just like states throughout the periphery. But the deindustrialization that ensued was different in scope and character from deindustrialization elsewhere in the periphery. In the Soviet Union and Eastern Europe, where manufacturing industries were more heavily developed than in peripheral states and most other semiperipheral settings, deindustrialization was much more extensive and severe. Deindustrialization there has been so vast, so extensive, that it has no peacetime equivalent. Only world wars have been as destructive of industry.

Deindustrialization in postcommunist states also differed in two important respects from deindustrialization elsewhere. First, where jobs were lost, it was women who typically lost work. In most other settings in the core, the periphery, and the capitalist semiperiphery, deindustrialization typically resulted in job loss for urban males. But in Eastern Europe and the Soviet Union, it forced women from jobs in industry and government. Second, deindustrialization resulted in the loss of *work*, but not necessarily the loss of *jobs*, for the men employed in industry. Throughout the former Soviet Union, manufacturing industries lost work but retained workers, who were paid, after a fashion, even though they had nothing to do. Workers in these settings survived in jobs where there was no work and little pay because they obtained benefits from a communist state that no longer existed, and because they organized work outside of formal employment to generate income.

In East Asia, states developed domestic manufacturing industries. But unlike most other states in the periphery and semiperiphery, these industries produced goods for export, not for domestic markets. This strategy resulted in rapid growth, often described by economists as "miraculous" during the 1960s and 1970s. But changed conditions in the 1980s appreciably slowed their ascent and led to controlled democratization in South Korea and Taiwan. During the 1990s, investment from Japan stimulated growth in these and other East Asian countries, principally Indonesia, Malaysia, and Thailand. But the expansion of export industries throughout the region created excess capacity and a growing glut of manufactured goods. When exports slowed and trade deficits appeared in the late 1990s, currencies collapsed and crisis ensued, resulting in widespread deindustrialization and job loss for men and women. Women in Asia made up about one-third of the workforce in manufacturing industries. This was a low percentage for export-oriented *maquila* manufacturing but a high percentage for domestic-oriented manufacturing in the periphery and semiperiphery. So job loss in East Asia affected both women and men, though it affected men more.[4] In South Korea, the crisis undid decades of economic gain. In Indonesia, the crisis led to limited democratization but also threatened to return the country to the periphery, likely destinations for Malaysia and Thailand as well.

Let us now turn to developments in these two regions of the semiperiphery.

THE SOVIET UNION AND EASTERN EUROPE

After World War II, the Soviet Union installed communist regimes throughout its sphere of influence in Eastern Europe.[5] To promote reconstruction and economic growth, the Soviet Union and its allies adopted strategies common in both the periphery and the core. Like other peripheral states, they developed domestic manufacturing industries that could produce goods for domestic consumers. Like core states in Western Europe, which were then organizing the EEC and NATO, they organized cooperative institutions among neighboring states to promote mutual development.

The Council for Mutual Economic Assistance (COMECON) was established in 1949 by the Soviets to organize industrial relations and trade among member states. This enabled manufacturing industries to produce goods not only for domestic consumers but also consumers in other communist states, though not generally for wider global export markets. Soviet and Eastern European arms, primarily from Czechoslovakia, were the only manufactured goods sold on global markets, though they were purchased principally by dictators allied with the Soviet Union.[6] The Warsaw Pact, which was established in 1955 to counter NATO, integrated the armies of member states under a single, Soviet military command. By coordinating their industries, trade, and defense, communist regimes created economies of scale, divisions of labor, and monetary savings that they could not have achieved on their own. These collective institutions helped promote growth in the 1950s and 1960s. But these policies were less successful than they were in Western Europe, both because industry was not organized as efficiently in the Soviet sphere as it was in the West and because external investment was not available to reconstruct and modernize industry. The kind of public and private money lavished on Western Europe through the Marshall Plan and U.S. corporate investment was simply not available to communist regimes in the Soviet sphere. The most the Soviet Union could do was provide cheap energy, which it supplied to its allies at prices well below the going, global rate.[7]

By the late 1960s, the economies of regimes in Eastern Europe and the Soviet Union had begun to stagnate. Then in the 1970s, a series of Soviet crop failures confronted communist regimes with a serious crisis. Poor harvests in 1972, 1974–1975, 1977, and 1979–1982 forced the Soviets and their allies to import growing quantities of grain from the West. The Soviets, for example, imported 10.5 million metric tons in 1972, 40 mmt in 1981.[8] While regimes needed to buy imported food from abroad, they had few manufactured goods (save arms) or commodities to sell on export markets. The Soviets had large quantities of oil, but most of it was consumed or wasted by inefficient industries in Eastern Europe and the Soviet Union. To buy food and purchase technologies they hoped would improve industrial efficiency, communist regimes began borrowing from the West, a strategy adopted by states throughout the periphery and semiperiphery. Czechoslovakia's debt grew from $608 million in 1970 to $6.8 billion in 1980; Poland's from $764 million to $24 billion; and the Soviet Union's from $6.3 billion in 1975 to $11 billion in 1980 and $50.6 billion in 1989.[9]

By borrowing money from Eurodollar markets, communist regimes averted a serious economic crisis during the 1970s. But when interest rates rose in the early 1980s, the crisis returned with a vengeance. Because dictatorships in the Soviet Union and Eastern Europe were linked by shared economic, political, and military institutions, crisis for one became crisis for all.

The collective crisis originated in the Soviet Union, where the debt crisis was joined by other serious problems in the 1980s. Although grain harvests recovered somewhat in the 1980s, they remained poor and were insufficient to meet the needs of a growing population. Aging industries could not easily improve their efficiency without a massive reorganization and fresh investment. "Between 1980 and 1985, the rate of economic growth appears to have fallen to zero," one economist observed.[10] But there was no money to invest in agriculture or industry because the Soviet regime devoted much of the country's resources to military spending—as much as 20 to 30 percent of its GNP. Military spending even increased during the early 1980s as the Soviets labored to pay for war in Afghanistan.[11] The Soviets nearly exhausted their reserves of gold and diamonds to finance the war, which cost almost $100 billion between 1979 and 1989.[12]

These economic and military problems were joined by an ongoing political crisis in the 1980s. The deaths, in rapid succession, of Soviet leaders—Leonid Brezhnev in 1982, Yuri Andropov in 1984, and Konstantin Chernenko in 1985—prevented the regime from adopting a coherent response to multiple problems. It was only when Mikhail Gorbachev took power in 1985 that a serious political effort to address the economic crisis was made. But Gorbachev's efforts to reform the society would trigger a crisis for client regimes in Eastern Europe and then in the Soviet Union itself.

When he took power, Gorbachev recognized that the Soviet Union was in "a state of severe crisis which embraced all spheres of life."[13] So he adopted three sets of reforms to revive the moribund economy and promote growth. First, he proposed that agriculture and industry be restructured, a process he called perestroika. But because many people in the party, the bureaucracy, and the army opposed substantive economic reform, Gorbachev decided he needed to mobilize political support for this "titanic job."[14] So he rallied support for economic reconstruction by proposing a second, political reform, what he called glasnost, which encouraged political participation by others. Third, he proposed reducing military spending to the "bounds of reasonable sufficiency," so the money wasted on defense could be used to finance perestroika. It was this last reform that would prove the undoing of regimes in Eastern Europe.

To cut military spending, Gorbachev withdrew the Soviet army from Afghanistan; reduced troop levels along the frontier with China; initiated arms control treaties with the United States and its NATO allies; reduced aid to client military regimes in Ethiopia, Cuba, and the Middle East; withdrew troops from Eastern Europe; and renounced the Soviet Union's "right" to intervene in Eastern Europe to protect client regimes.[15]

For regimes that had long relied on the Soviet military to keep them in power, this new policy was a fatal blow. They already faced a serious economic crisis associated with debt and stagnation. Growing opposition movements like Solidarity in Poland, which consisted primarily of male workers in manufacturing industries, demonstrated that the political power of communist regimes was weak and failing. So in the fall of 1989, they abandoned power, bringing an end to communist party rule in Eastern Europe.

In the Soviet Union, meanwhile, Gorbachev's efforts to reform economic and political life foundered, then failed. For economic reforms to work, the government needed to reduce food, housing, and other subsidies and force workers to pay higher market prices for these goods. But this undermined living standards and antagonized the urban workers that Gorbachev had hoped would support perestroika. They were mobilized instead by Gorbachev's competitors, both by Boris Yeltsin and other anticentrist political leaders based in the republics and by conservative communist leaders who opposed economic reform. These groups effectively blocked serious economic reforms.[16] Gorbachev's political opponents also used political institutions in the Soviet Union's constituent republics to compete with the central government for political power and the allegiance of urban workers. The success of anticentrist politicians in the small Baltic republics, and then in large republics like the Ukraine and Russia, eroded central government authority. The 1991 coup by conservative communists, who were opposed both to Gorbachev's reforms and to the growing political power of anticentrist politicians in the republics, extinguished central-government authority. By the end of 1991, the Soviet Union was dissolved and divided into fifteen successor states.

Like democratizing states throughout much of the periphery and semiperiphery, the civilian governments that assumed power in Eastern Europe and in former Soviet republics adopted neoliberal economic policies. By opening their economies to foreign trade and investment, selling state assets, and reducing military spending, officials hoped to repay debts and build capitalist economic institutions, such as free markets and entrepreneurial classes. But these policies were implemented in a somewhat different context. Virtually all of the economic assets in communist semiperipheral countries had been controlled by the state, and much of the economy had been devoted to the military. So privatization was more extensive and demilitarization more dramatic than it was elsewhere.

Governments in Eastern Europe and the former Soviet Union quickly opened their economies to foreign trade. They soon found, however, that it was easy to import foreign goods, which worker-consumers rushed to buy, but difficult to export their goods to foreign markets, where worker-consumers held products from the East in low esteem. Governments in postcommunist states discovered that their traditional "export" markets in neighboring states had collapsed because consumers there preferred goods from outside the region.[17] Government officials also found that domestic markets had disappeared because domestic worker-consumers refused to purchase goods of their own making. State officials expected domestic manufacturing industries to revive and begin to compete successfully in domestic and foreign markets if they received foreign investment, which could be used to modernize industry. But foreign investment did not materialize. The huge investments made in East Germany ($600 billion in public money and another $400 billion private investment) and China ($200 billion), not to mention the investments made in the United States and other core countries, left little for Eastern Europe and the Soviet Union. Hungary did better than most, receiving $5.5 billion between 1990 and 1994.[18] This sum was greater than the combined foreign investment in Poland, the Czech Republic, Romania, Bulgaria, Slovenia, and Slovakia. It was greater than the amount foreigners invested in all of Russia ($4 billion).[19] In Russia itself, 60 percent of foreign investment was made in just one city: Moscow.[20]

These are paltry sums. Economists estimate that it would take $120 billion just to improve Russia's phone system to the level of Spain's.[21] Overall, economists believe that the former Soviet republics would need investments worth between $571 billion and $1.2 trillion each year for a decade to effectively modernize industry and infrastructure there.[22]

It soon became obvious that substantial amounts of foreign investment would not be forthcoming, despite the adoption of open-door economic policies. In addition, debt repayment and capital flight have made it difficult to preserve or collect the capital resources these countries did possess. Russia's foreign debt tripled from $51 billion to $145 billion in the last decade, and $136 billion was lost to the country as a result of capital flight between 1993 and 1998.[23] The government has used high interest rates to attract and retain capital resources, but high rates (150 percent annually) have made it impossible for businesses or consumers to borrow money, further stalling domestic investment and economic growth. High interest rates did little to persuade foreigners to invest in Russia. "Throwing money at a trillion dollar economy that is sinking in political anarchy, waste and corruption is not a brilliant idea," argued Leslie Gelb in a *New York Times* editorial.[24] Most private investors and public officials in the core have reached the same conclusion, preferring China (by a margin of $200 billion to $4 billion), with a government that is still communist, to Russia, where the government is democratic.

Civilian democrats sold public assets to foreign and domestic buyers. Privatization was most rapid and extensive in East Germany and Czechoslovakia, slowest and most limited in the former Soviet Union. But privatization, too, has had disappointing results. The sale of whole industries—300,000 in the communist semiperiphery alone—glutted financial markets.[25] In East Germany, the government managed to sell only half of the 11,000 large firms it put on the block. Many governments took firms off the market because they could not find ready buyers at any price. States sold some small businesses—restaurants and small shops—to workers and investors within these countries. But workers did not have the means to purchase whole factories, so some governments gave them away to worker-shareholders through voucher programs. State officials had hoped to raise money from the sale of public industries and believed that buyers would invest in improving them. But as one World Bank official observed, "They naturally assume that these huge plants with all that heavy machinery have to be worth millions of dollars. But they have no concept of depreciation. They don't understand that something is worth a lot of money only if someone is willing to buy it." This investors refused to do because "about a third of the industrial sector is not likely to be viable at all," and another third would not produce a sufficiently "positive return."[26]

Democratizing states also slashed military spending. In 1987, the Soviet Union spent $356 billion on defense and kept 5.1 million troops under arms. By 1994, Russia spent only $29 billion on defense, one-tenth as much, and kept only 1.5 million troops in arms.[27] The unilateral disarmament of the "most militarized economy in the world," as Gorbachev put it, lifted the burden of defense spending from the economy. But it also resulted in massive unemployment for male soldiers and wage workers employed in the vast industries that produced military goods. In 1994, production in military industries was only 19 percent of 1991 levels.[28] This also resulted in the collapse of export earnings from arms sales, the only Soviet industry that had earlier managed to sell goods on global markets.

Arms sales fell because it had become evident in the 1980s that Soviet arms could not compete with U.S. or NATO weapons on the battlefield. In addition, demilitarization in other peripheral and semiperipheral states reduced the demand for Soviet arms. Export earnings from arms sales plunged from about $50 billion a year in the mid-1980s to only $3 billion a year in the 1990s.[29] This was also a problem for Czechoslovakia, which saw its annual earnings from arms sales fall from $8 billion to $1 billion in this period.[30]

Economic stagnation and the failure of reform led to economic decline in the Soviet Union and Eastern Europe in the late 1980s and early 1990s. From 1989 to 1993, Hungary's economy contracted by 21 percent, Bulgaria's and Romania's by 30 percent.[31] The Soviet economy declined 20 percent in 1991, "a magnitude of decline not seen since the devastating Nazi invasion [of 1941]."[32] In Eastern Europe, the adoption of neoliberal policies arrested decline but did not greatly improve conditions, so they remained mired in a crisis of Great-Depression proportions. In the former Soviet republics, neoliberal policies did not slow decline, they accelerated it. By 1998, the GNP of the former Soviet Republics had declined by half, "the most abrupt decline in any major industrial country since the Great Depression."[33] In fact, a reversal of this magnitude is unprecedented in peacetime. No peacetime depression in the nineteenth or twentieth centuries has been this severe for an industrial country. It can be compared only to the destruction of Japanese and German industry by U.S. bombing campaigns during World War II.[34]

Whole industries in the former Soviet Union and Eastern Europe simply disappeared. Before 1989, male workers in Eastern European and Soviet automobile industries produced Ladas, Trabants, Zastavas, Polmots, Moskvitches, Skodas, and Wartburgs.[35] Although many of these cars are still on the road, they are no longer being made. Why? Because working-class consumers stopped buying them. In the two years after communists fell from power in Poland, worker-consumers turned to Western European and Japanese imports, buying 500,000 cars from them.[36] Sales of Polish cars collapsed and the domestic auto industry virtually vanished. (Some Polish workers still make cars, but they now make cars for Western European auto makers, and they don't make nearly as many cars as they had before.) Given the fact that the world auto industry has the capacity to produce 79 million cars a year but can find customers for only 58 million of them, "someone is going to have to close more car factories."[37] As it turned out, the auto industry throughout the postcommunist semiperiphery closed its car factories in the 1990s and stopped hiring the male workers who labored in them.

The auto industry was not unique. In Russia, industry after industry was shut down or greatly reduced in the 1990s: coal, iron and steel, machine tool, truck, chemical fiber and fertilizer, paper, cement, television, washing machine, radio and tape recorder, vacuum cleaner, footwear, and refrigerator.[38] The average number of employees in deindustrializing firms in Russia fell from 781 to 126 between 1990 and 1994.[39] The production of grain, meat, milk, and vegetables fell, too, and the region was unable to grow enough food to meet domestic needs.[40] These economic problems affected women and men alike.

Some former Soviet republics have vast natural resources: oil, gold, diamonds. But falling commodity prices mean that the former republics have gained little from the sale of these commodities. Indeed, their efforts to export these commodities, which had long been held back from global markets, helped depress world prices.

"Because thousands of useless Soviet-era plants now lie idle," it should not be surprising that in 1996 "the living standard of the average Russian family had fallen by almost half since the reforms took hold."[41] Some economists estimate that wage income has fallen as much as 60 percent.[42] In Eastern Europe, the loss of income was less severe, 10 percent in the Czech Republic, 18 percent in Poland, 24 percent in Hungary.[43] As incomes fell, poverty rates skyrocketed in the 1990s, from single-digit figures to double-digit rates: 12 percent in Poland, 33 percent in Bulgaria, 39 percent in Russia, 59 percent in Romania, and 88 percent in Kyrgyz.[44]

As we have seen, deindustrialization and the loss of jobs have been common problems in the core, the periphery, and the semiperiphery in recent years. But deindustrialization in the communist semiperiphery was unique in two important respects. First, in Eastern Europe and the former Soviet Union, deindustrialization typically forced women from work, not men. In Eastern Europe, women made up a sizable majority of the unemployed. A UN study in 1999 found that of the 25 million jobs lost in the region during the 1990s, 14 million were jobs that had been held by women. "In the transition to a market economy, the status of women is eroding further," UNICEF director Carol Bellamy reported.[45] Contrast this to deindustrialization elsewhere, where it typically resulted in job loss for urban men.

Second, deindustrialization resulted in the loss of work, but not necessarily the loss of *jobs*, for men employed in residual industries. In Eastern Europe, women and some men lost jobs, leaving between 10 and 20 percent of the workforce unemployed.[46] But in the former Soviet Union, "unemployment" rates remained fairly low—about 5 percent in 1995—this despite massive deindustrialization.[47] Throughout the former Soviet Union, manufacturing industries lost work but retained workers, who were paid, after a fashion, even though they had no work to do.

Worker households survived in a setting where manufacturing industries have stopped producing goods, where workers stay on the job but have no work to do, and where wage incomes have fallen and paychecks arrive late, very late. They have been able to survive with no work and little pay for two reasons. First, they still obtain benefits from a communist state that no longer exists. Second, they organize work outside of formal employment to generate income.

The Soviet state provided important benefits to workers that help households survive today. The government built housing on a large scale for workers. Although accommodations were tight, most workers obtained homes of their own.[48] When the communist state disintegrated, workers retained possession of their homes and obtained title to them through the government's privatization program. As a result, workers pay almost nothing for housing, apart from utilities. This is a significant and enduring benefit, given the fact that most worker households around the world spend 30 to 50 percent of their income on housing. Nor do workers pay much for health care, education, or public transportation. Their incomes were also taxed at low rates, less than 10 percent of their income, compared with 30 percent in the United States.[49] Not only did the Soviet state provide workers with inexpensive housing and public services, it also encouraged workers to save. It did so by providing few consumer goods and by rationing their supply. Because worker-consumers found it hard to shop and difficult to spend, they saved nearly 9 percent of their income, a rate that compared favorably with worker-consumers in Western Europe and that was considerably higher than in the United States (where workers no longer save anything at all).[50] So when their incomes fell, like rain, in the 1990s, workers in postcommunist states could use their rather substantial savings to weather the storm. As the editors of one magazine in Moscow explained, "Almost every normal person has some money set aside for black days."[51]

Of course, worker households have to work hard to curb spending and conserve their savings. For many, this has meant converting their savings into foreign currency—they hold $15 billion in U.S. dollars—buying property or purchasing goods to hoard, which can be sold when supplies run short and prices rise, a skill developed by savings-conscious worker households in the Soviet era.

Generally, worker households have few costs and substantial savings, both legacies of Soviet state policies. This has enabled them to survive job and income loss that would otherwise have reduced them not only to poverty but also to famine. Unfortunately, the decade-long crisis is depleting worker savings.[52] Over time, spending cuts by post-Soviet states have reduced the value of public health care, education, and transportation, which have all appreciably deteriorated. Hospitals, for example, have few medical supplies and patients are asked to bring the medicines and supplies doctors will need to treat them.[53] The Post Office cannot move 1,000 train cars filled with mail because it cannot pay the railway for its services.[54]

Workers, too, have gone unpaid, often for months, sometimes for years. Tatyana A. Maslova, who in 1998 answered phones for a closed Siberian mine, hadn't been paid since 1996. "This way of life doesn't have a name," she said.[55] The government, which still owns many firms, employs workers but cannot pay them, largely because it has been unable to raise or collect taxes effectively.[56] So how do workers survive? How can they live a life that doesn't have a name?

Contemporary workers survive in the same way that British sailors survived in the eighteenth century. The British government then, like the Russian government today, found it difficult to raise taxes and pay sailors impressed into the Navy, even though the empire depended on them. Sailors often went months or even years without receiving their wages. Sailors at sea could survive without wages because they were housed and fed by the Navy, though deplorably. But their wives and families were without these benefits. Fortunately for them, they had the government's *promise* to pay wages due. Families could trade these promises—credit, if you will—to shopkeepers and landlords, though typically at a "discount." This meant that shopkeepers would sell or "discount" goods worth eight shillings on credit but expect ten shillings when the sailor's cash became available.[57] Workers in Russia today do what sailors in Britain did two hundred years ago. They shop with their government's promise to pay back wages. Because nearly everyone is in similar financial circumstances—pensioners, soldiers, factory workers, postal workers, bus drivers, and school teachers—allowances are made, credit extended, discounts taken, gardens are grown, and families share their resources.

Where businesses and governments found it difficult to raise the cash needed to pay workers and suppliers, as was common, workers were also invited to take payment in kind, not in cash. One small Russian airline could not afford to pay its pilots' wages, so it offered them old airplanes in lieu of cash. The pilots sold the airplanes to residents who converted the fuselages into summer homes and storage rooms and used the wings to fence garden plots.[58]

Because the value of benefits provided by the Soviet state are slowly eroding, and income from wages is falling, worker households have also worked hard to generate income from other sources.

The Soviet state long prohibited workers from organizing activities that generated income outside of paid state employment. Perhaps the only exception was the provision of garden plots for urban workers. These plots became important sources of food for urban workers, enabling them to grow food that was not produced by Soviet farmers or available in government stores. Workers could sometimes generate income from the sale or exchange of food on unofficial "black markets." Economists estimate that 100 million workers in Russia tend garden plots, and these microfarms supply 80 percent of the potatoes and 65 percent of the vegetables consumed by worker-households.[59] The worker-organized production of food and embryonic, unofficial black markets emerged in the Soviet era because the state rationed the supply of food and other consumer goods. When the Soviet state vanished, the production of goods for black and other "free markets" expanded dramatically, providing work and alternative sources of income for worker households. Perhaps as much as half of all the economic activity in the post-Soviet states is organized by workers themselves.[60] Earnings from these sources provide more than half of worker incomes.[61] As a result, "most people look to themselves rather than to the state [or large firms] to provide their livelihood."[62]

Income from the production, exchange, sale, and barter of goods in informal free markets has enabled worker households to survive the collapse of formal economic systems. (Some informal markets, like the produce markets in Moscow, are monopolized by crime groups, which means they may be capitalist but also not very "free," so many farmers and gardeners sell produce at freeway exits outside the city to evade gang control.)[63] This income is supplemented by benefits that are the legacy of the now-defunct Soviet state. In a real sense, the communist state provided a safety net that helped worker households survive in a capitalist economy.

Still, many have fallen through the shredded parts of the safety net. For the millions of Russians who migrated from non-Russian republics and abandoned their apartments and garden plots, for those without appreciable savings, for the nine million stranded in the Siberian Arctic who cannot afford to move, for the population of war-ravaged Chechnya, and for the more than one million prisoners who are malnourished and face epidemic disease (particularly drug-resistant tuberculosis), economic change has been catastrophic.[64] One measure of this has been deteriorating public health. Between 1990 and 1995, "fruit consumption dropped one-third; meat, one-quarter; vegetables, one-fifth. Fish consumption was halved."[65] Because they eat less fruit, "20 percent of Russians are critically low in vitamin C—so low they risk getting rickets [or scurvy, like eighteenth century British sailors]."[66] Average life expectancy fell from 69.6 years to 64.[67] So economic change can be said to have taken five years off the life of every Russian worker. "A decline in life expectancy this dramatic has never happened in the postwar period," observed one demographer.[68]

Under these conditions, it should not be surprising that workers drink heavily. Although the social consequences of heavy alcohol consumption are varied, it is telling that the number of drunk Russians who drown every year in the country's rivers and reservoirs (most of them men) is greater than the number of people murdered in the United States.[69]

EAST ASIA

The History: 1945–1993

For many years, some East Asian countries recorded extremely rapid rates of economic growth. This enabled South Korea, Taiwan, Singapore, and Hong Kong, known collectively as the Asian "Tigers," to increase per capita incomes significantly. In South Korea, double-digit annual rates of growth increased per capita income from $87 in 1962, a figure comparable to that of Ghana, to $6,498 in 1991, a level near that of Greece. Taiwan, meanwhile, increased per capita incomes from $153 in 1962 to $7,600 in 1989.[70] Singapore and Hong Kong grew at comparable rates. This kind of growth was exceeded only by Japan in the postwar period. Not surprisingly, economists touted their success as an "economic miracle."

For workers in these countries, rapid growth provided jobs and, in South Korea and Taiwan, also rapid urbanization. But while worker incomes increased, they did not rise nearly as fast as the growth in per capita incomes would suggest.

Although most countries in the periphery and semiperiphery tried to promote growth and increase incomes, few succeeded. How did these Asian countries accomplish what others could not? Because they benefited from Japanese colonial policies before World War II, from U.S. policies after the war, and from domestic policies adopted by their governments.

Korea and Taiwan had both been colonized by Japan (Taiwan, or "Formosa," as it was called by the Japanese, was occupied in 1894–1895; Korea in 1910). Initially, Japan exploited them ruthlessly, much as European empires plundered their colonies in Africa, regarding them as a "source of cheap raw materials, especially rice, for Japan."[71] But in the 1920s, Japanese colonial administrators adopted new policies designed to promote industrial development that would complement Japanese industry. "Japan [was] among the very few imperial powers to have located heavy industry in its colonies: steel, chemicals, hydroelectric facilities," the historian Bruce Cumings has observed. As a result of "colonial enclave" industrialization, Japan and its colonies in Korea and Taiwan all grew substantially, and by 1945, "Korea had an industrial infrastructure that was among the best developed in the Third World."[72]

Some of these gains were lost as a result of civil wars and partition after World War II, but continued Japanese investment after the war helped South Korea and Taiwan survive these crises.[73]

Singapore and Hong Kong were also colonies, though of Great Britain, not Japan. They were among the few British colonies to benefit from investment and infrastructure development. Colonial relations lasted longer in Singapore (1959) and Hong Kong (1997) than in South Korea and Taiwan, but this proved advantageous, not detrimental, to their economic development.

After World War II, the United States took little initial interest in either South Korea or Taiwan. But after the Korean War erupted in 1950, the United States lavished economic and military assistance on both to support them as front-line, anticommunist states. Between 1945 and 1978, the U.S. government provided $13 billion to South Korea and $5.6 billion to Taiwan, a level of spending comparable to Marshall Plan aid to Western Europe and Japan. By purchasing food and other supplies from these countries during U.S. wars in Korea and Vietnam, the United States provided jobs and income for both countries, which were ruled by capitalist dictatorships. The United States also provided cheap food, set favorable exchange rates, and, more important, allowed their goods easy entry into U.S. markets. U.S. policies provided enormous benefits to South Korea and Taiwan, benefits that were not extended to most states in the capitalist periphery or semiperiphery. According to one observer, if the United States had not been as generous, "Taiwan's annual GNP growth rate would have been cut by half, its per capita income would have been reduced by three-quarters, and it would have taken the island 30 more years to reach its 1964 living standards."[74] For South Korea, which received twice as much U.S. aid as Taiwan, U.S. neglect would have had even more serious consequences.

While prewar Japanese policies and postwar U.S. policies spurred economic growth in South Korea and Taiwan, domestic policies also played an important role in their economic success. Unlike most countries in the periphery and semiperiphery, which hardly ever managed to introduce serious land reform without being forced to do so by agrarian revolution, governments in South Korea and Taiwan introduced successful land reform during the 1950s and 1960s. This helped improve agricultural production and created a bedrock political constituency for the government in the countryside. Like their counterparts in the periphery, regimes in South Korea and Taiwan built manufacturing industries that produced goods for domestic markets in the early 1950s. But they soon abandoned these efforts and by the early 1960s were trying instead to push domestic firms to produce goods for export markets, particularly in Japan and the United States. Like Japan, they used high tariffs to prevent domestic worker-consumers from buying imported goods. For many years, a consumer smoking an imported cigarette in South Korea could be sentenced to jail for violating the government's ban on foreign tobacco products.[75]

These export industrialization and trade policies paid huge dividends. Taiwan, for example, recorded its first trade surplus in 1970, which grew rapidly thereafter. By 1990, Taiwan had accumulated foreign exchange reserves worth more than $80 billion, second in the world to Japan.[76]

Like South Korea and Taiwan, Singapore and Hong Kong also adopted export manufacturing. Initially, they produced and exported textiles; later they turned to electronics. They did so as a matter of necessity, because they had no other way to earn the money they needed to pay for imported food and energy.

These four Asian countries benefited not only from colonial and postcolonial foreign and domestic policies but also from what might be called fortuitous political circumstances. All four were detached from large populous hinterlands—Singapore from Malaysia; Hong Kong and Taiwan from China; and South Korea from North Korea—as a result of colonialism, civil war, or partition. This meant that the investment and aid they received was used by small, not large, populations and that the benefits of economic growth were distributed among relatively small demographies. Would Taiwan have increased per capita income from $153 to $7,500 if the 18 million people living there had been yoked politically to China and the one billion people living there? Certainly not. The fact that these relatively small countries—Hong Kong and Singapore are really just cities—are unencumbered by large populations helps explain in part why they have done well.

Still, their ascent into the semiperiphery did not proceed without interruption. In the mid-1980s, South Korea and Taiwan encountered several problems that appreciably slowed their economic growth. In 1985, the United States devalued the dollar to slow imports from Japan, South Korea, and Taiwan. U.S. officials also used trade negotiations to demand that South Korea and Taiwan reduce their tariffs and trade barriers and open their markets to U.S. goods, like tobacco. Changed U.S. policies exerted a downward pressure on South Korea and Taiwan. Their economies were also being increasingly pressed by competition from other Asian countries, which decided to emulate their success and develop export-manufacturing industries of their own. Because firms in Indonesia, Thailand, and Malaysia paid workers even less than firms making the same export goods in South Korea and Taiwan, they could undersell them in markets that South Korean and Taiwanese firms had pioneered. Adding to these difficulties, domestic urban workers and intellectuals in South Korea and Taiwan began demanding a larger share of the benefits associated with rapid growth. Because dictatorships in South Korea and Taiwan had suppressed wages, political dissent, and consumer demand, urban workers and students organized a political alliance, or *minjung* (the "masses"), that demanded higher wages and greater political freedom. Massive demonstrations and widespread strikes in the late 1980s brought the crisis to a head. By 1987, economic growth had slowed to 4 percent, half the 1983 rate, and government officials worried openly that their economies could "collapse like some of the Latin American countries."[77] To prevent this, regimes in both countries called elections and began managing a transition to civilian rule, albeit one that would leave long-ruling elites in power.[78]

Democratization helped solve the domestic crisis, while renewed foreign investment in the late 1980s helped both countries recharge their economic growth. Recall that as a result of the 1985 dollar devaluations, Japan was awash in cash. This pool of money was used to bid up stock and real estate prices in Japan, but much of it was also invested in or loaned to other Asian countries. Although Japanese investment and lending led the way, this money was joined in the 1990s by core investors from the United States and Western Europe who sought opportunities in the "emerging markets." Financial analysts coined this term (*emerging markets*) to persuade investors, who were extremely reluctant to risk capital in a place called the "Third World," to invest in the periphery and semiperiphery.[79]

Much of this capital was invested in the four Asian Tigers, but much of it also made its way to relatively new destinations: China, Indonesia, Malaysia, and Thailand. Although China, as we have seen, received the bulk of investment, Indonesia also received a significant chunk. Indeed, in the early 1990s, Indonesia was seen as the aspirant most likely to join the other Asian Tigers in the semiperiphery.

Indonesia is one of the few Asian countries with substantial oil reserves. Rising oil prices in the 1970s greatly improved its economic fortunes, though its large size—nearly 200 million people—meant that increased oil revenues did not have the same beneficial impact they did in less populous countries like Saudi Arabia. The government also received substantial assistance from the World Bank, which provided $25 billion between 1970 and 1995, and from the U.S. government.[80] The United States and the World Bank provided this aid despite the fact that Indonesia was ruled by a dictatorship that had massacred hundreds of thousands during a 1965 civil war; invaded and annexed neighboring East Timor in 1975, which resulted in the death of tens of thousands more; and funneled much of the money it received from foreign investors into industrial monopolies controlled by the family and friends of President Suharto, the dictator who took power during the 1965 civil war.[81]

Of course, after 1985, oil prices swiftly declined, but new foreign investment and loans after 1985 made good these losses and spurred rapid growth. The government invested heavily in export-manufacturing industries and in domestic industries, even developing its own "national" car called the "Timor," which people there regarded as a cruel joke.[82]

During the 1980s and 1990s, as economic growth accelerated and per capita incomes increased, observers predicted that "any lingering perception of Indonesia as some sort of Southeast Asian backwater will probably fade quickly as this nation . . . completes a transformation intended to create Asia's next economic and political giant."[83] In 1993, the World Bank said that Indonesia would be a "solid middle-income country" by the end of the decade. "In terms of macro-economic management, Indonesia is a role model for the developing world," enthused World Bank representative Nicholas C. Hope.[84]

THE 1990s AND THE ECONOMIC CRASH

But these expectations would be dashed in the late 1990s, when a crisis struck hard at the old and new Asian Tigers. In Indonesia, the crisis would wreck the economy, depose the Suharto dictatorship, and send worker households back toward the kind of poverty they had only recently left behind.

During the 1990s, investment and loans flooded into East Asia. Indonesia, Malaysia, the Philippines, South Korea, and Thailand received $211 billion from the core between 1994 and 1996.[85] Some of this money was invested by subsidiaries of core firms from Japan, Western Europe, and the United States; some by subcontractors in the region; and some by domestic firms, many of them large monopolies controlled by elite families and state officials—what has sometimes been described as "crony capitalism."[86] These firms used investment and loans to bid up stock market and real estate prices, which attracted new investment once prices rose sharply, and to expand production in export-manufacturing industries. These economies looked increasingly like Japan's "Bubble" economy.[87] Unlike Japan, however, these countries had developed export industries but also opened their economies to foreign investment and trade.

The 1997–1998 crisis in Asia, which struck first at Thailand and then at many of the others, began much as it did in Mexico a few years earlier. Domestic consumers—elite, middle-income, and sometimes working households—started buying imported goods as the governments reduced trade barriers.[88] This binge buying occurred at a time when the sale of export goods had begun to fall. Exports slowed because investment in export manufacturing had vastly increased the supply of goods, which increased competition and lowered the prices that producers could get for their products. Exports also slowed because recession in Japan meant that little demand existed for their goods in this important market. Falling prices and sluggish sales reduced export revenues for countries that relied on exports to fuel growth. As imports surged and exports fell, trade deficits appeared, for the first time in decades.

Trade deficits usually force countries to devalue their currencies. By making imports more expensive and exports cheaper, devaluations are supposed to restore trade balances. But when faced with rising trade deficits, governments in Thailand and elsewhere tried to "defend" their currencies at fixed exchange rates. Foreign investors, however, bet that trade deficits would eventually force governments to devalue, so they began selling these currencies and withdrawing the money they had invested or loaned. The abrupt departure of billions of dollars soon depleted the hard-currency savings these countries had stockpiled and forced them to devalue.[89]

As governments ran out of hard currency, the International Monetary Fund (IMF) stepped in, providing money to purchase the imports they needed. But the IMF also demanded that governments raise interest rates to persuade foreign investors to return. Unfortunately, sky-high interest rates triggered the collapse of stock and real estate markets, forced many large banks and businesses into bankruptcy, and ruined consumers who had borrowed money. The result was the most serious region-wide recession since World War II.[90] "This is off the radar screens in terms of severity," said Allen Sinai, a global economic analyst. "It is the single most negative event since the Great Depression in the United States."[91]

Many economists have asked why a crisis in Thailand or Indonesia, "a country whose gross domestic product is roughly comparable to the combined annual revenues of Walmart and Exxon," would have a "contagion" effect, "spreading financial crisis not only to nearby countries in Asia but also to distant Brazil and Russia"?[92]

Some blame the crisis on unregulated crony capitalists in these countries, who made unwise investments or adopted unwise monetary policies. Some, like Malaysia's prime minister Mahathir Mohammed, blame foreign currency speculators, who had defeated government monetary policies and withdrawn their investments.[93] Some also blamed the IMF, which had insisted on using high interest rates to assuage foreign investors, a move that plunged economies into deep recession.[94]

While there is plenty of blame to go around, the spread of crisis is due not to separate causes but to collective decisions. Crisis spread because many countries had simultaneously adopted the same strategy to develop economically. They had all opened their economies to foreign investment and trade and had expanded export-manufacturing industries. They then encountered the same problems: buying binges by domestic consumers, glutted markets for the goods produced by export industries, price inflation in stock and real estate markets, and the abrupt withdrawal of capital by foreign investors and creditors. They were then told by the IMF to adopt the same remedies: devalue their currencies, raise interest rates, and impose austerity programs. Because they had all used the same strategies, encountered the same problems, and adopted the same solutions, the crisis was collectively shared.

Taiwan was perhaps the exception to the rule, surviving its neighbors' crises relatively unscathed. But it differed from its neighbors in some important respects. First, it had accumulated a huge foreign currency reserve—$80 billion—that it could draw on if it faced export declines or trade deficits. Second, it had invested heavily in China, which did not experience these problems. Third, capitalists in Taiwan were organized in relatively small firms, not large monopolies, so if one business failed in export markets, it would not bankrupt other businesses, as happened so often in other Asian states.

Throughout the region, workers have paid heavily for the practices and policies that were adopted without their participation or consent. South Korea is something of the exception. There, democratic leaders apologized publicly for the "bone-carving pain" the crisis has imposed on worker-voters. "I have come here, to beg the forgiveness of the Korean people," South Korea's finance minister Lim Chang Yuel told a televised audience. "Please understand the necessity of the economic pain we must bear and overcome."[95]

The crisis resulted in a widespread deindustrialization of export-manufacturing industries. Millions of workers in these industries—roughly 70 percent of them are men and 30 percent are women—lost their jobs. Wages fell for those who remained, as businesses cut costs to regain their competitiveness.[96] Workers who had borrowed money to purchase a home, open a shop, or buy a rickshaw were badly hurt by rising interest rates and the subsequent recession. During the boom, Mr. Salamet, an Indonesian rickshaw driver living in Mojokerto, borrowed money to buy a rickshaw.[97] At first, he and his household made good money. But as others borrowed money to buy carts, competition increased and his earnings fell. When interest rates rose and business activity slowed, rickshaw drivers were idled. Mr. Salamet and his household could no longer afford to spend $2 a month on painkillers for his dying mother, could not pay the $28 bill for her coffin and funeral after she died, could not pay the son's school fees, and could not keep up the payments on his rickshaw loan. His mother-in-law pawned her sarongs to buy food for his children. As a result of the crisis, the household risked losing its investment and its livelihood.[98]

Meanwhile, the rising price of rice, fuel, school fees, and bus fares, which resulted from IMF-imposed and government-managed austerity programs, has cut real incomes for workers across Asia. In Indonesia, the number of people living in poverty increased dramatically, and "between 40 million and 100 million people now have only one meal a day."[99]

These are not unfamiliar events. Similar developments occurred in Eastern Europe and the former Soviet republics. But an important difference exists between workers in the postcommunist semiperiphery and the capitalist semiperiphery in Asia. Unlike workers in postcommunist settings, workers in Asia have few assets: homes or land of their own. They have meager savings, if any, in part because they have only recently found wage employment, in part because the wages they received were extremely low. They also had higher costs, paying for housing, school, medical care, and transportation out of their own pockets. So when crisis struck, they had few resources of their own to fall back on and no social "safety net" to catch them. "The role of the poor in the boom [was] to create wealth," explained Ji Ungpakorn, a political scientist in Thailand. "Now when the boom turns to slump, some of them will be cast aside, and they have nothing to cushion them at all."[100]

Many rural households in the region depend on the wages earned by family members who worked in export industries. "We came to the city to work and send money home to our parents," explained Song Siwang, a seamstress in a Thai dress factory in Pathum Thani. "Now we are losing our jobs. Who will support my family? If I go home, who will support me?"[101]

Economic change has also created or intensified conflicts among ethnic groups. In Indonesia, for example, austerity programs forced the government to more than double food prices.[102] Because most food shops are owned by ethnic Chinese, who are a minority, ethnic "Indonesian" workers, most of them Muslims, began attacking ethnic Chinese, whom they held responsible for higher prices.[103] Food riots led to the assault, rape, and murder of ethnic Chinese. One three-day riot in Jakarta resulted in the deaths of 1,200 people.[104] Some of this fury was directed against Christians and "ninjas," or sorcerers believed to be assaulting Muslims.[105] This kind of ethnic conflict also became endemic in parts of the postcommunist semiperiphery. In Yugoslavia, Czechoslovakia, and the former Soviet Union, economic crisis divided ethnic groups, leading to the partition of these states and, in some cases, to ethnic conflict and war.[106]

Workers in two regions of the semiperiphery experienced sharp reverses during the 1990s. The collapse of communist states in Eastern Europe and the Soviet Union, and the massive deindustrialization that followed, forced vast regions into the periphery. Ironically, the benefits provided by now-defunct communist states made it possible for workers to survive the harrowing descent into a capitalist economy.

For workers in East Asia, changes in the 1980s stalled economies that had grown at breakneck speed for much of the postwar period. Crises in the 1990s then reversed many of these gains. Because states provided few social benefits, and workers had not accumulated substantial savings, workers in many states were rapidly impoverished by the sudden downturn.

States play important economic roles for workers in the semiperiphery, as they do in the core and periphery. During the postwar period, laboring households around the world came to depend not only on income from wages but also on income and benefits provided by the state. Unfortunately, states the world over have recently cut benefits to workers, reducing their standards of living. For worker households, state cuts have compounded the problems—job loss and falling wages—created by contemporary economic change.

If there is a silver lining in this otherwise dark cloud, it is that economic crisis contributed to the fall of dictators in the Philippines, South Korea, and Taiwan in the 1980s; in Eastern Europe and the Soviet Union between 1989 and 1992; and in Indonesia in 1998.[107] Still, democratization has neither fully transformed the social, economic, and political life of these countries nor made workers full participants in the decisions that affect their lives. And in many countries in the East European and East Asian semiperiphery, elites who were closely associated with fallen and discredited regimes retained considerable power in democratizing states.

Economic change has led to new understandings of work and its gendered components and of possible avenues of social change. Events of the last twenty years have sharpened workers' understanding of the world-economy, gender inequalities, and political democracy.

NOTES

1. For Wallerstein, the semiperiphery consists of middle-income countries with strong state machineries. Giovanni Arrighi and Jessica Drangel, "The Stratification of the World-Economy: An Exploration of the Semi-Peripheral Zone," review, vol. 10, no. 1 (Summer 1986): 13.

2. Arrighi and Drangel, "The Stratification of the World-Economy," 66–69; John T. Passe-Smith, "The Persistence of the Gap between Rich and Poor Countries: Taking Stock of Economic Growth, 1960–1993," in Mitchell A. Seligson and John T. Passe-Smith, eds., *Development and Underdevelopment: The Political Economy of Global Inequality* (Boulder, Colo.: Rienner, 1998), 37.

3. Robert K. Schaeffer, *Power to the People: Democratization around the World* (Boulder, Colo.: Westview, 1997), 57–83.

4. Faruk Tabak, "The World Labour Force," in Terence K. Hopkins and Immanuel Wallerstein, *The Age of Transition: Trajectory of the World-System, 1945–2025* (London: Zed, 1996), 101.

5. Schaeffer, *Power to the People*, 5–31.

6. Schaeffer, *Power to the People*, 163.

7. Schaeffer, *Power to the People*, 160.

8. Daniel Yergin, *The Prize: The Epic Quest for Oil, Money and Power* (New York: Simon and Schuster, 1991), 625; Ernst J. Oliveri, *Latin American Debt and the Politics of International Finance* (Westport, Conn.: Praeger, 1992), 11; Nick Butler, *The International Grain Trade* (New York: St. Martin's, 1986), 55.

9. Schaeffer, *Power to the People*, 176; Robert K. Schaeffer, *Severed States: Dilemmas of Democracy in a Divided World* (Lanham, Md.: Rowman & Littlefield, 1999), 198–199.

10. Richard Sakwa, *Gorbachev and His Reforms, 1985–1990* (Upper Saddle River, N.J.: Prentice Hall, 1990), 22.

11. Sakwa, *Gorbachev and His Reforms*, 335; David Holloway and Michael McFaul, "Demilitarization and Defense Conversion," in Gail W. Lapidus, *The New Russia: Troubled Transformation* (Boulder, Colo.: Westview, 1995), 204.

12. Schaeffer, *Power to the People*, 164–165.

13. Marshall I. Goldman, "The Future of Soviet Economic Reform," *Current History* (October 1989): 329.

14. Anders Aslund, *Gorbachev's Struggle for Economic Reform* (Ithaca, N.Y.: Cornell University Press, 1991), 28.

15. Schaeffer, *Power to the People*, 171–174.

16. Schaeffer, *Severed States*, 204–205.

17. Schaeffer, *Power to the People*, 231.

18. Thomas W. Simons, Jr., *Eastern Europe in the Postwar World* (New York: St. Martin's, 1991), 162.

19. Schaeffer, *Power to the People*, 229.

20. David Remnick, "Moscow: The New Revolution," *National Geographic* (April 1997): 37.
21. Michael H. Bernhard, *The Origins of Democratization in Poland: Workers, Intellectuals, and Oppositional Politics, 1976–1980* (New York: Columbia University Press, 1993), 36–37.
22. Alan Smith, *Russia and the World Economy: Problems of Integration* (London: Routledge, 1993), 219.
23. Timothy L. O'Brien, "Follow the Money, If You Can," *New York Times*, September 5, 1999; David E. Sanger, "Next 'Asian' Crisis?" *New York Times*, May 28, 1998; Michael Specter, "Crisis of Bread and Land Afflicts Russian Farming," *New York Times*, September 19, 1994.
24. Schaeffer, *Power to the People*, 229.
25. Bartolomeij Kaminski, "Introduction," in Bartolomeij Kaminski, ed., *Economic Transition in Russia and the New States of Eurasia* (Armonk, N.Y.: Sharpe, 1996), 9.
26. Gale Stokes, *From Stalinism to Pluralism: A Documentary History of Eastern Europe since 1945* (New York: Oxford University Press, 1991), 214–15; Raphael Shen, *The Polish Economy: Legacies from the Past, Prospects for the Future* (New York: Praeger, 1992), 73.
27. Karen Dawisha, *Eastern Europe, Gorbachev and Reform: The Great Challenge* (Cambridge: Cambridge University Press, 1990), 287.
28. Yevgeny Kuznetsov, "Learning to Learn: Emerging Patterns of Enterprise Behavior in the Russian Defense Sector, 1992–95," in Kaminski, *Economic Transition in Russia*, 317.
29. Holloway and McFaul, "Demilitarization and Defense Conversion," 212; Schaeffer, *Power to the People*, 238.
30. C. S. Leff, *The Czech and Slovak Republics: Nation versus State* (Boulder, Colo.: Westview, 1997), 229.
31. Leonid Friedman, "Russia and the Commonwealth of Independent States in the Emerging Structure of the World Economy," in Kaminski, *Economic Transition in Russia*, 244.
32. William Moskoff, *Hard Times: Impoverishment and Protest in the Perestroika Years: The Soviet Union 1985–1991* (Armonk, N.Y.: Sharpe, 1993, 15; Steven Greenhouse, "U.N. Calls East's Slide at Depression Point," *New York Times*, December 3, 1991; Richard E. Ericson, "The Russian Economy since Independence," in Lapidus, *The New Russia*, 40.
33. Rick Bragg, "More Than Money, They Miss the Pride a Good Job Brought," *New York Times*, March 5, 1996; Judith Thornton, "Restructuring Production without Market Infrastructure," in Joan M. Nelson, Charles Tilly, and Lee Walker, eds., *Transforming Post-Communist Political Economies* (Washington, D.C.: National Academy Press, 1997), 133.
34. Schaeffer, *Power to the People*, 159.
35. See Ward's Communications, *Ward's Automotive International: How World's Auto Makers Are Related, 1990* (Detroit: Ward's Automotive International, 1990).
36. Simons, *Eastern Europe in the Postwar World*, 205.
37. William Greider, "The Real Chinese Threat," *New York Times*, March 5, 1997.
38. Friedman, "Russia and the Commonwealth of Independent States," 247.
39. Alastair McAuley, "Social Policy and Labor Market in Russia during Transition," in Nelson, Tilly, and Walker, *Transforming Post-Communist Political Economies*, 239.
40. Specter, "Crisis of Bread and Land."
41. Michael Specter, "Russians Choosing Today: Either Reforms or the Past," *New York Times*, June 16, 1996.
42. McAuley, "Social Policy and Labor Market in Russia," 237.
43. Barbara Boyle Torrey, Timothy M. Smeeding, and Debra Bailey, "Vulnerable Populations in Central Europe," in Nelson, Tilly, and Walker, *Transforming Post-Communist Political Economies*, 351.

44. Elizabeth Olson, "Free Markets Leave Women Worse Off, Unicef Says," *New York Times*, September 23, 1999; Joan M. Nelson, "Social Costs, Social-Sector Reforms, and Politics," in Nelson, Tilly, and Walker, *Transforming Post-Communist Political Economies*, 250, 274.

45. Lenore B. Goldman, "To Act without 'Isms': Women in East Central Europe and Russia," in Jennifer Turpin and Lois Ann Lorentzen, eds., *The Gendered New World Order: Militarism, Development, and the Environment* (London: Routledge, 1996), 41; Victor Zaslavsky, "From Redistribution to Marketization: Social and Attitudinal Change in Post-Soviet Russia," in Lapidus, *The New Russia*, 132–133; Valentine M. Moghadam, "Gender Dynamics of Restructuring in the Semi-Periphery," in Rae Lesser Blumberg, Cathy A. Rakowski, Irene Tinker, and Michael Monteón, eds., *EnGENDERing Wealth and Well-Being: Empowerment for Global Change* (Boulder, Colo.: Westview, 1995), 23–25.

46. Simon Johnson, Daniel Kaufman, and Oleg Ustenko, "Formal Employment and Survival Strategies after Communism," in Nelson, Tilly, and Walker, *Transforming Post-Communist Political Economies*, 180.

47. Richard E. Ericson, "The Russian Economy since Independence," in Lapidus, *The New Russia*, 46, 62–64; Edgar L. Feige, "Underground Activity and Institutional Change: Productive, Protective, and Predatory Behavior in Transition Economies," in Nelson, Tilly, and Walker, *Transforming Post-Communist Political Economies*, 72.

48. Fred Weir, "The Death of Dreams," *In These Times*, April 11, 1999.

49. Moskoff, *Hard Times*, 114.

50. Moskoff, *Hard Times*, 114.

51. Celestine Bohlen, "Ruble Is on 'Tilt,' but Russians Keep Their Balance," *New York Times*, October 6, 1998.

52. Michael Wines, "What's Going to Happen to Russian Nest Eggs?" *New York Times*, August 18, 1998.

53. Rachel L. Swarns, "For Russia's Cardiac Patients, Little Care and Grim Prognosis," *New York Times*, September 24, 1996.

54. Michael Wines, "At Russian Post Office, Check Isn't in the Mail," *New York Times*, October 3, 1998.

55. Michael Wines, "A Russian Coal-Mine Region Producing Little but Misery," *New York Times*, September 17, 1998.

56. Michael R. Gordon, "I.M.F. May Suspend Huge Loan to Russia," *New York Times*, October 25, 1996.

57. See Robert K. Schaeffer, "The Chains of Bondage Broke: The Proletarianization of Seafaring Labor, 1600–1800" (Ph.D. thesis, State University of New York at Binghamton, 1984), 235–240.

58. Associated Press, "Ailing Economy's Theme: Everything Open to Trade," *San Jose Mercury News*, September 7, 1998.

59. Michael R. Gordon, "Soviet Mindset Defeating Rural Capitalism," *New York Times*, November 30, 1998.

60. Daniel Kaufmann and Alksander Kaliberda, "Integrating the Unofficial Economy into the Dynamics of Post-Socialist Economies: A Framework of Analysis and Evidence," in Kaminski, *Economic Transition in Russia*, 96; Feige, "Underground Activity and Institutional Change," in Nelson, Tilly, and Walker, *Transforming Post-Communist Political Economies*, 29.

61. Kaminski, "Introduction," in Kaminski, *Economic Transition in Russia*, 22; Johnson, Kaufman, and Ustenko, "Formal Employment and Survival Strategies," in Nelson, Tilly, and Walker, *Transforming Post-Communist Political Economies*, 192.

62. Kaminski, "Introduction," in Kaminski, *Economic Transition in Russia*, 22; Michael R. Gordon, "Communists and Workers March to Denounce Yeltsin," *New York Times*, October 8, 1998.
63. Specter, "Crisis of Bread and Land."
64. Moskoff, *Hard Times*, 142–143; Michael R. Gordon, "Forsaken in Russia's Arctic: 9 Million Stranded Workers," *New York Times*, January 6, 1999; Michael R. Gordon, "In War-Ravaged Chechnya, Russia's Presence Is Fading," *New York Times*, November 1, 1996; David Remnick, "More Bad News from the Gulag," *New Yorker* (February 15, 1999): 36; Alessandra Stanley, "Russian's Lament the Crime of Punishment," *New York Times*, January 8, 1998.
65. Michael Wines, "Russians Drown Sorrows, and Selves," *New York Times*, June 28, 1999.
66. Michael Wines, "Lean Times at the Russian Dinner Table," *New York Times*, December 6, 1998.
67. Jeni Klugman, George Schieber, Timothy Heleniak, and Vivian Hon, "Vulnerable Populations in Central Europe," in Nelson, Tilly, and Walker, *Transforming Post-Communist Political Economies*, 325.
68. Schaeffer, *Power to the People*, 241–242.
69. Wines, "Russians Drown Sorrows, and Selves."
70. Il Sakong, *Korea in the World Economy* (Washington, D.C.: Institute for International Economics, 1993), xv; Steve Chan and Cal Clark, *Flexibility, Foresight and Fortuna in Taiwan's Development: Navigating between Scylla and Charybdis* (London: Routledge, 1992), 34.
71. Carter J. Eckert, *Offspring of Empire: The Koch 'ang Kims and the Colonial Origins of Korean Capitalism, 1876–1945* (Seattle: University of Washington Press, 1991), 41.
72. Bruce Cumings, "The Origins and Development of the Northeast Asian Political Economy: Industrial Sectors, Product Cycles and Political Consequences," in Frederic C. Deyo, ed., *The Political Economy of the New Asian Industrialism* (Ithaca, N.Y.: Cornell University Press, 1987), 45, 55–56; Sakong, *Korea in the World Economy*, 1.
73. Giovanni Arrighi, Satoshi Ikeda, and Alex Irwan, "The Rise of East Asia: One Miracle or Many?" in Ravi Arvind Palat, ed., *Pacific-Asia and the Future of the World-System* (Westport, Conn.: Greenwood, 1993), 60; Cumings, "The Origins and Development of the Northeast Asian Political Economy," in Deyo, *The Political Economy of the New Asian Industrialism*, 77–78, 80.
74. Chan and Clark, *Flexibility, Foresight and Fortuna*, 99.
75. Bruce Cumings, "The Abortive Abertura: South Korea in the Light of the Latin American Experience," *New Left Review* (January–February 1989): 13.
76. Chan and Clark, *Flexibility, Foresight and Fortuna*, 40.
77. Tim Shorrock, "South Korea: Chun, the Kims and the Constitutional Struggle," *Third World Quarterly* 10, no. 1 (January 1988): 108.
78. Schaeffer, *Power to the People*, 146–148.
79. Nicholas D. Kristof and Edward Wyatt, "Who Went Under in the World's Sea of Cash," *New York Times*, February 15, 1999; Paul Krugman, *The Return of Depression Economics* (New York: Norton, 1999), 84–85.
80. David E. Sanger, "World Bank Beats Breast for Failures in Indonesia," *New York Times*, February 11, 1999.
81. Philip Shenon, "For Asian Nation's First Family, Financial Empire Is in Peril," *New York Times*, February 16, 1998.
82. Shenon, "For Asian Nation's First Family."

83. Philip Shenon, "As Indonesia Crushes Its Critics, It Helps Millions Escape Poverty," *New York Times*, August 27, 1993.

84. Shenon, "As Indonesia Crushes Its Critics."

85. Nicholas D. Kristof and David E. Sanger, "How U.S. Wooed Asia to Let Cash Flow in," *New York Times*, February 16, 1999.

86. Krugman, *Return of Depression Economics*, 84–85.

87. Krugman, *Return of Depression Economics*, 87.

88. Krugman, *Return of Depression Economics*, 87.

89. Kristof and Sanger, "How U.S. Wooed Asia."

90. Edward A. Gargan, "The Thai Slump at Ground Level," *New York Times*, September 19, 1997; Mark Landler, "Gloom over Asia Economies Spreads as Yen Drops Again," *New York Times*, June 12, 1998.

91. David E. Sanger, "The World Looks at Bali and Sees Krakatoa," *New York Times*, January 18, 1998.

92. Sanger, "The World Looks at Bali"; Krugman, *Return of Depression Economics*, 92–93.

93. Krugman, *Return of Depression Economics*, 92–101.

94. David E. Sanger, "As Economies Fail, the I.M.F. Is Rife with Recrimination," *New York Times*, October 2, 1998; David E. Sanger and Richard W. Stevenson, "Second-Guessing the Economic Doctor," *New York Times*, February 1, 1998; Nicholas D. Kristof, "Has the I.M.F. Cured or Harmed Asia? Dispute Rages after Months of Crisis," *New York Times*, April 23, 1998; Mark Landler, "Malaysia to Be Unlikely Host at Economic Meeting," *New York Times*, November 6, 1998.

95. Andrew Pollack, "Package of Loans Worth $55 Billion Is Set for Korea," *New York Times*, December 4, 1997.

96. Stephanie Strom, "South Korean Unions to Accept Some Layoffs," *New York Times*, January 21, 1998.

97. Kristof and Wyatt, "Who Went Under in the World's Sea of Cash."

98. Kristof and Wyatt, "Who Went Under"; Nicholas Kristof, "World's Ills Are Obvious, the Cures Much Less So," *New York Times*, February 18, 1999; Nicholas D. Kristof and Sheryl WuDunn, "Of World Markets, None an Island," *New York Times*, February 17, 1999.

99. New York Times, "Indonesia's Anguish," *New York Times*, October 16, 1998.

100. Seth Mydans, "Thailand Economic Crash Crushes the Working Poor," *New York Times*, December 15, 1997. Of course, some middle-class and high-income households have substantial savings, which they use to weather economic crises. See Wayne Arnold, "Indonesia's Grocery Revolution: Urban Rich Lure Foreign Retailers and Spur a Recovery," *New York Times*, November 18, 1999. But their numbers are fairly small.

101. Mydans, "Thailand Economic Crash."

102. Seth Mydans, "Indonesians at a Crossroads: Democracy or Chaos?" *New York Times*, December 26, 1998.

103. Seth Mydans, "The Empty Bowls That Fill Indonesia with Fear," *New York Times*, February 26, 1998.

104. Nicholas D. Kristof, "New Freedoms Feed Ethnic Frictions," *New York Times*, May 25, 1998; Mark Landler, "Riots Bare Ethnic Hatreds in Indonesia," *New York Times*, May 9, 1998; Seth Mydans, "New Threats Reported on Rapes in Indonesia Are Investigated," *New York Times*, July 20, 1998.

105. Nicholas D. Kristof, "Fears of Sorcerers Spur Killings in Java," *New York Times*, October 20, 1998.

106. Schaeffer, *Severed States*, 194–241.
107. Seth Mydans, "Once-Buoyant Hopes Sink in Indonesia's Slump," *New York Times*, December 13, 1997; Seth Mydans, "Suharto Steps Down after 32 Years in Power," *New York Times*, May 21, 1998.

Chapter 7
Welfare States Cut Worker Benefits

Workers depend not only on wages and self-generated income; they also rely on income and benefits provided by the state. After World War II, the benefits given workers by "welfare states" in the core and by "developmental states" in the periphery and semiperiphery substantially increased.[1] But in recent years, states around the world have significantly reduced benefits to workers, cutting their incomes and increasing their costs.

The benefits provided workers by states in the postwar period varied considerably. States in different regions of the world provided different levels of benefits and dispensed them in different ways. This reflected the different economic and political capacities of states in the republican interstate system, which was based, after World War II, on nation-state republics.[2]

In the core, welfare states in Western Europe provided generous benefits to workers and distributed them widely. States established "universal" health-care and retirement programs, aided the unemployed and the poor, and provided benefits for housewives, mothers, and children.[3] Some of the programs were quite generous. Pensions were large and workers could retire at an early age—in France, railway workers could retire at fifty-five—and unemployed workers in the Netherlands received 75 percent of their salary, while workers suffering from "stress" received $630 a month in disability payments. In Norway, women with young children on "welfare" could obtain a pension, free day care, subsidized housing and vacations, free medical and dental care, and money for training and education.[4] Pregnant women in Italy were entitled to five months of maternity leave at full salary; unemployed mothers in France had to pay only $33 a month for child care that cost $800 per child.[5] To cement its union with East Germany, the (West) German state provided benefits worth $600 billion to 22 million residents in the East, which had "an economy the size of North Carolina's."[6]

Of course, to pay for generous, widespread benefits, states in Western Europe levied heavy taxes on the rich, corporations, and workers. In 1994, tax revenues amounted to 58.6 percent of the gross domestic product in Denmark; 51.2 percent in the Netherlands; 49.6 percent in France; 46.1 percent in Germany, and 36.4 percent in Britain.[7] On average, states in Western Europe collected 45.5 percent of GDP in taxes, compared to only 31.6 percent in the United States.[8]

During the postwar period, benefits provided to workers in the United States were less generous than those given in Western Europe.[9] With the exception of social security, the U.S. government did not provide the "universal" benefit programs, such as health care, that were widely available to workers in Western Europe.[10] Instead, U.S. officials insisted that benefits be delivered only to particular, "entitled" individuals or groups of workers. Their determination to provide aid only to targeted beneficiaries greatly increased the administrative cost of benefit programs because large bureaucracies were needed to ensure that aid was obtained only by designated groups: veterans, poor single women and their children, the elderly, the ill (either elderly or poor), the disabled, and farmers. Congressional representatives and government officials spent huge sums on bureaucracies to prevent what economists call "free riders" from obtaining any unwarranted benefits from state welfare programs. They were particularly keen on scrutinizing and monitoring benefits to the poor, though they allowed some higher-income workers to self-administer their benefits. For example, the mortgage interest-payment deduction, which allowed homeowners to deduct the interest they paid on home loans from their income taxes, was self-administered by worker-homeowners, though it was reviewed by the Internal Revenue Service when workers filed their tax returns. This large benefit program was not administered by case workers assigned to scrutinize worker finances. The unequal treatment given workers who received state benefits—the costly, heavy-handed administration of benefits for poor workers, and the inexpensive, self-administration of benefits for higher-income workers—illustrates the selective, discriminatory, and segmented approach to worker benefits in the United States. Of course, the relatively high cost of administering welfare programs in the United States reduced their real benefit to workers.

But while U.S. workers received less generous benefits than workers in Western Europe, their tax burdens are also considerably lower: "In 1995, the United States has the lowest tax burden among the advanced industrial economies."[11]

Among core states, Japan has been an anomaly, probably because it joined the core more recently than states in Western Europe and North America. Unlike them, the state in Japan provided few public benefits to workers, and these were not very generous.[12] For example, public assistance to poor workers is available only if they have no families, and then only if they are ill. Poor unemployed workers who have no relatives to assist them cannot claim aid if they are "able to work." Single mothers and the unemployed are expected instead to seek assistance from family members, relatives, or friends. Elderly, bedridden widows without families to support them and the handicapped are the principal beneficiaries of welfare in Japan. In 1994, 880,000 elderly and handicapped individuals received welfare in Japan, compared with 12.3 million recipients of Aid to Families with Dependent Children (AFDC, commonly known as "Welfare") in the United States. "Japan has a welfare system that . . . makes even the new, dismantled American system seem a model of generosity," Nicholas Kristof reported in the *New York Times*.[13]

The Japanese state did provide universal health care and comprehensive day care, but health care in Japan compared poorly to health-care services in Western Europe.

Japan also distributed aid to workers in a manner that contrasts sharply with practices elsewhere in the core. Instead of providing benefits to workers directly, Japan provided large subsidies to businesses, which were then responsible for providing benefits to workers.[14] Companies provided lifetime employment, health care, and pensions to workers. As we have previously noted, these benefits were made available primarily to male workers, which reinforced the dependence of other family members on male household heads. Worker households were in turn expected to provide "welfare" or assistance to family members and relatives who found themselves in dire circumstances or who had retired. In Japan, most worker-households provided benefits for retired family members, and 55 percent of workers over sixty-five lived with their children.[15] Worker households could provide a safety net for worker-relatives so long as unemployment was low, wages were rising, and savings were growing ($79,500 on average in 1997).[16]

Because private businesses administered worker benefits in Japan, and because worker households assumed responsibility for providing the social safety net for relatives, the cost to government of administering worker benefits was extremely low. Although state benefits in Japan were not very generous, official tax burdens for workers, corporations, and wealthy households were also lower than those in Western Europe or the United States. But tax burdens in Japan were not as low as official statistics suggest. Recall that the Japanese government adopted policies that encouraged or compelled workers to save a significant portion of their wages and invest their savings, at low rates of interest, in postal savings accounts and banks. The government used these savings to subsidize businesses, so they could compete in world markets and pay worker benefits. The government also expected workers to use their savings to assist relatives and themselves in times of need. So the real cost to workers of the benefits they received from corporations and the state was higher than tax-burden statistics suggest: they paid for benefits not only out of their income but also out of their savings.

In the periphery and semiperiphery, "developmental states" took a very different approach. Few states could afford the cost of providing generous health, pension, or welfare benefits to workers. Nor could they afford to pay large bureaucracies to administer them. They preferred instead to use their resources to raise armies and hire bureaucracies that would support the dictatorships that ruled most of the states in the periphery and semiperiphery between 1950 and 1980/1989.[17]

Still, states in the periphery and semiperiphery could not wholly neglect to provide worker benefits, particularly where workers were hostile to dictators. So states used some revenues to furnish workers with inexpensive goods and services: cheap staple foods, cooking and heating fuels, primary education, and public transportation. They made these important goods and services universally available, not just to poor workers but also to middle-income and wealthy households. State officials did not worry that "free riders" might also obtain these benefits, because the use of food, fuel, and transportation subsidies cost very little to administer.

Communist states in the periphery and semiperiphery were more ambitious. They not only subsidized consumer goods and services—food, fuel, and transportation—like other peripheral states, they also provided universal health care, housing, pensions, and higher education, similar to welfare states in Western Europe. Although the quality of these programs was not as high as those provided by Western European states, the programs were dramatically superior to those available to workers elsewhere in the capitalist periphery and semiperiphery. Workers in communist states had higher literacy rates, longer life expectancies, and lower infant mortality rates than workers in comparable capitalist states in the semiperiphery.[18]

States in the core, the periphery, and the semiperiphery have all cut benefits to workers. But they have done so at different times, for different reasons. Worker benefits were cut first in the United States during the 1970s, largely as a result of a "tax revolt" supported in part by workers themselves. In the 1980s, the debt crisis forced states throughout the periphery and semiperiphery to slash worker benefits, a development that triggered widespread revolts against benefit cuts there. The collapse of communist regimes, which started in 1989, led to a massive reduction of workers' benefits, subsidies, and universal social welfare programs alike. In the 1990s, recession and the monetary unification of Western European states persuaded officials there to emulate the United States and curb worker benefits. Recession in Japan, meanwhile, forced the state to reduce its subsidies to failing businesses, which jeopardized the benefits of workers employed by them. Finally, the collapse of East Asian economies in the late 1990s forced them to emulate peripheral and semiperipheral states and reduce their modest benefit programs. Let us now examine these events in more detail.

TAX REVOLT AND BENEFIT CUTS IN THE UNITED STATES

After World War II, the U.S. government greatly expanded benefits to workers. Most of the benefits provided by the state were designed to assist specific groups: veterans, farmers, homeowners, and the elderly. In the mid-1960s, benefit increases were extended to poor workers, women, minorities, and children, largely as a result of protests by workers in civil rights movements.

The benefits provided to workers by the state were obscured in the United States by a rhetoric that depicted benefits to poor workers as "welfare" but described benefits for other workers as an "entitlement," which workers had somehow "earned." This rhetoric obscured the unequal distribution of benefits to different groups of workers. In 1994, for example, the state gave $16 billion to 12.5 million poor women and children on "welfare." But it gave an equal sum to only one million farmers, though officials did not describe payments to farmers as a form of "welfare."[19] Nor was the $94 billion worth of benefits given worker-homeowners through the mortgage-interest deduction in 1996 described as a "welfare" program, though it was greater than the cost of all programs designed to aid the poor.[20] Of course, these generous welfare programs were dwarfed by the $400 billion given to retired workers through Social Security.

For workers who received state aid, benefits were an important source of income. But it is difficult to argue, as some have, that workers who received large benefits were somehow more "entitled" to them than workers who received small benefits. After all, homeowners do not "work" for their benefits, and Social Security or Medicare recipients typically receive more in benefits than they paid in payroll taxes. For example, a worker who retired in 1995, after working thirty years at the average wage, paid $30,691 to Medicare but received $80,442 in benefits.[21] This is not to say that poor workers, farmers, homeowners, or pensioners are undeserving of government benefits, only that the distribution of benefits to different groups of workers is unequal and that it is obscured by a rhetoric that rationalizes this uneven distribution. This rationalizing rhetoric is reinforced by the government, which assigns vast bureaucracies to regulate the meager benefits given poor workers but gives higher-income workers large benefits without much scrutiny. In this way, gender, ethnic, and class privileges have been embedded in government transfers to workers.

Early in the postwar period, wealthy households and corporations objected to the expansion of state benefits to workers, largely because high tax rates on wealthy individual and corporate incomes forced them to bear much of the cost. In 1947, wealthy individuals in the top tax bracket paid 91 percent of their income over $200,000 to the government, while corporations handed over half (50.9 percent) of their profits in taxes.[22] During the 1950s, corporations paid about one-third of all income taxes collected by the government. Consequently, the tax burden on workers was relatively low. For example, the tax burden of a median-income worker household was only 10 percent in 1950 and 13 percent in 1959.[23]

In 1963, President Kennedy slashed taxes on wealthy households and corporations. Tax rates for households in the top bracket fell from 91 percent to 70 percent, a level not seen since President Roosevelt raised taxes on the rich during the Great Depression. Corporate tax rates fell from 50.9 percent to 35.1 percent in the same period.[24] Of course, tax cuts for wealthy households and corporations increased the tax burden on worker households, raising it from 13.1 percent in 1959 to 20.9 percent in 1969.[25] Workers did not immediately object to this redistribution of tax burdens because unemployment was low and wages were rising rapidly, doubling between 1950 and 1970. Rising wages increased workers' ability to pay taxes, and this increased tax revenues for the government. The government used higher tax revenues to pay for the war in Vietnam and increase benefits to workers, including, for the first time, poor workers. Although workers did not protest the redistribution of tax burdens in the 1960s, changed economic conditions encouraged workers to revolt against taxes in the 1970s.

In the 1970s, the cost of worker benefit programs began to rise. Social Security benefits rose in 1972 because the Democratic Congress and Republican president Richard Nixon approved a 20 percent increase and linked future benefits to the rate of inflation through annual cost of living adjustments (COLAs).[26] Because inflation soon accelerated as a result of the OPEC oil embargo and poor Soviet grain harvests, the benefits paid to retired workers grew rapidly in the 1970s, running down the surplus accumulated in the 1950s and 1960s. Benefits provided by AFDC also increased rapidly in this period. In 1940, AFDC paid benefits to only 372,000 families. Twenty years later, in 1960, only 803,000 families were enrolled.[27] But during the 1960s and 1970s, the civil rights and welfare rights movements demanded that program restrictions at the state and federal levels be eased, and poor workers were encouraged to apply for benefits.[28] By 1975, the number of families receiving AFDC benefits more than tripled to 3.5 million.[29] It then quadrupled again to 12.3 million in 1995. But while poverty programs like AFDC helped reduce poverty among children from 14.7 million in 1965 to 10 million in 1975, the programs' costs also increased.[30]

As inflation drove up the cost of social security benefits, it also drove up housing prices and local property taxes. The recession made it difficult for workers to raise wages to keep pace with inflation. As wages stagnated, the growing tax burden finally became apparent to workers. Worker-taxpayers might have demanded that tax burdens be redistributed and that wealthy households and corporations again shoulder heavier loads. But this was difficult to do with a Republican president, and it would invite attacks by corporations and the rich on worker benefits. Instead, workers joined a revolt against higher taxes.

The revolt began in California, where conservative elites initiated a ballot measure that promised to cut local property taxes and limit future tax increases. Worker-taxpayers supported Proposition 13 in large numbers and helped it pass into law. They did so because taxes were rising (pushed up by house-price inflation) and wages were falling. Worker-taxpayers believed that tax cuts would increase their real income. Conservative elites immediately recognized that the increasing salience of taxpayer identities among workers, first among home owners and retired workers, could assist them in their ongoing efforts to cut taxes.

Conservative elites quickly mobilized worker-taxpayers, creating a tax-cut coalition that brought Ronald Reagan to power in 1980. But they could not immediately persuade their worker-taxpayer allies to cut worker benefits, except public education, which deteriorated in the wake of property-tax cuts. Although worker-taxpayers supported "tax cuts" in principle, they were reluctant to do so if cuts resulted in any reduction of worker benefits. Congressional Democrats could also block any major reduction in worker benefits during the 1980s. So conservative elites proceeded in two stages. First, during the 1980s, they cut taxes, with crucial support from worker-taxpayers (mostly, white male workers). Then in the 1990s, after tax cuts had created huge budget deficits and mounting national debt, and tax-cut Republicans took control of Congress, conservative elites began cutting worker-benefit programs.

During the 1980s, the Reagan administration and the tax-cut coalition moved first to cut taxes. Tax rates for wealthy households were cut from 70 percent to 50 percent, then to 38 percent, and finally to 28 percent. The Bush and Clinton administrations subsequently raised them back to 32 and then 39 percent, but this rate still represented a 50-percent cut from 1980 levels.[31]

Not only did wealthy households contribute less to government, they also gave less to charities. Charitable contributions by the rich declined by more than one-half during the 1980s, forcing private charities to cut aid to the poor.[32]

Corporate taxes were also reduced, from 37.5 percent to 26.5 percent.[33] Whereas corporations had paid one-third of all income taxes in 1955, they paid only 10 percent in 1990.[34] In what became a recurrent pattern, the large tax cuts for wealthy individuals and corporations were accompanied by only tiny tax cuts for worker-taxpayers. Small tax cuts for workers did little to reduce worker tax burdens, which had increased to 28 percent (up from 20 percent in 1970). As David Stockman, Reagan's budget director, explained, small tax cuts for worker-taxpayers enabled conservatives to pass large tax cuts for the rich: "[Small tax cuts] were always a Trojan horse to bring down the top rates."[35]

While the tax-cut coalition was able to cut taxes at the federal, state, and local levels during the 1980s, it could not immediately reduce workers' benefits because Democrats blocked such efforts. The coalition did, however, manage to reduce the real value of some worker benefits: for example, welfare benefits fell 51 percent in value between 1970 and 1996 because officials did not adjust them for inflation.[36] But tax cuts in this period set the stage for subsequent benefit cuts.

When the Reagan administration cut taxes, it did so while raising interest rates to combat inflation. This deflationary policy plunged the U.S. economy into a recession. Because unemployment grew and wages were stagnant, tax revenues fell dramatically. At the same time, the Reagan administration increased defense spending 50 percent, from $201 billion in 1980 to $311 billion in 1987.[37] Falling tax revenues and increased government spending resulted in massive budget deficits and growing national debt. When Reagan took office in 1981, he promised to cut the $1 trillion national debt, which he described as "a stack of $1,000-dollar bills 67 miles high."[38] But in 1992, the national debt had grown instead to $4 trillion, and Reagan's imaginary stack of $1,000-dollar bills reached 268 miles high.

As budget deficits increased and national debt soared, Republicans argued that "tax and spend" Democrats were to blame. They insisted that Congress adopt balanced budgets, even if that meant cutting worker-benefit programs. So the debts run up as a result of tax cuts in the 1980s were used as the rationale to cut worker benefits in the 1990s. When Republicans supported by the tax-cut coalition took control of Congress in 1994, they moved first against benefits for "undeserving" workers: poor women and children on welfare, and legal and illegal immigrants. Together with President Clinton, a conservative Democrat who had promised to "end welfare as we know it," they slashed benefits for these culturally subordinate gender and ethnic working groups.[39]

The 1996 welfare "reform" required recipients to work at assigned jobs while looking for permanent employment, limited benefits to only five years in a person's lifetime, made recipients submit to fingerprinting and home inspections, and put their benefits at risk if they refused work assignment, showed up late, or could not find child care for their children.[40] "You get, like, nothing, and you have to kiss their boots," complained one recipient on a workfare assignment for New York City's

Sanitation Department.[41] As welfare bureaucracies cracked down, they frequently deterred or prevented workers from receiving other benefits—food stamps and Medicaid—to which they were still entitled.[42]

Under these conditions, the number of poor women workers receiving welfare benefits fell by half. Seven million women and children left, or were forced off, the rolls between 1996 and 1999.[43] Of these, between half to two-thirds found jobs.[44] Low rates of unemployment in the late 1990s made it possible for some workers to obtain minimum-wage jobs. This was easier for white workers than for black and Hispanic workers to do. For many years, the number of white families on welfare was greater than the number of African American households. But by 1998, Black and Hispanic recipients outnumbered Whites two to one.[45] It was also easier for workers who lived in small cities to find jobs and leave welfare than for workers in big cities or rural areas. As a result, the workers still on welfare consisted increasingly of minorities in urban and rural settings, where jobs remained scarce despite economic growth.[46]

Policy makers argued that reforms were a success because three to four million workers found jobs. But another two to three million workers left welfare rolls without finding work. The loss of welfare benefits for this group of poor workers was comparable to the loss of jobs for two million male steel workers in the 1970s and 1980s. But what became of them?

Because the welfare bureaucracy did not track what happened to them, they were regarded as "missing." "We don't know what's happened to people," one economist admitted.[47] But scholars who study the poor believed that many found refuge with relatives, lovers, and friends.[48] In fact, many welfare bureaucrats "urge[d] the needy to rely on relatives," much as bureaucrats have done in Japan.[49] For example, when Maggie Miller lost her benefits in Greenville, Mississippi, "she moved in with her sister, raising the number of children in the two-bedroom house to 15."[50]

Of course, when women and their children seek refuge with relatives and boyfriends, some may find themselves in abusive situations. "My guess is that some [women who have left welfare] have probably moved in with former spouses and boyfriends, of whom some are probably abusing them," said Randy Abbelda, an economist at the University of Massachusetts.[51] Economic deprivation and gender structures placed women in situations where dependency on men is encouraged.

There was also another problem. Many of the workers assigned jobs through the reform's "workfare" provisions were used to replace workers who had been employed by cities and nonprofit agencies. In New York City, the 34,100 people in the city's workfare programs have provided a low-cost workforce that officials used to reduce the city's formal payrolls by 20,000 employees.[52] "We're doing the same job as regular workers [were doing], but we're not getting paid for it," argued Cecilia Mathis, a workfare recipient who cleans buildings for the city's Health Department.[53] She worked twenty-four hours a week and received $62 in benefits, or less than $3 an hour, a rate well below the minimum wage and far below the wages and benefits paid to regular city employees.

The entry of poor workers into minimum-wage labor markets increased competition and depressed wages, making it difficult for unskilled workers to collect an income that could lift them out of poverty. One economist likened it to a game of musical chairs. "What we have is a limited number of chairs, and there are a lot of potential workers circling these chairs, waiting for someone to get up," said Pam Burtless, a Brookings Institution fellow.[54]

A study of welfare reform in Wisconsin, where reform was hailed as a model, found that people who left welfare and found jobs earned $400 a month less than they had on welfare.[55] Researchers also discovered that many people on welfare already worked but did so secretly, so they could keep their benefits from being cut. Kathryn Edin, a sociologist at the University of Pennsylvania, found that AFDC typically provided just 34 percent of the average recipient's monthly income, with another 25 percent provided by food stamps. The other 41 percent came from "boyfriends, charities, relatives and jobs, including under the table work."[56] As another researcher explained, "There's more people working now [as a result of reform], but the difference is not as large as people think because a lot of people were already working under the old system."[57]

Because many people were already working, the reforms designed to make them work did not significantly alter their lives. They just worked more than they had, without increasing their income significantly. Nor did increased workloads boost worker self-esteem. A study by psychologists found that after two years, the average worker still registered levels of depression above the threshold that most psychologists considered cause for clinical referrals.[58]

Of course, the full impact of benefit cuts for welfare recipients has not yet been felt. When the U.S. economy slows or when the five-year limit on welfare benefits begins to expire for the millions of workers on welfare in 1996, the true cost to workers of benefit cuts will be revealed.[59]

The creation of a tax-cut coalition was an enormous political achievement for conservative elites and corporations, who could not have cut taxes or worker benefits on their own. Worker-taxpayers participated in the ongoing tax revolt because they wanted to reduce their own tax burdens, because elites prevented the eventual impact of tax cuts on workers' benefits from becoming immediately apparent, and because elites successfully diverted worker-taxpayers from considering other possible solutions: (1) redistributing tax burdens and increasing taxes for wealthy households and corporations to past levels; or (2) raising wages and thereby increasing workers' ability to pay for benefit programs, as occurred in the 1950s and 1960s.

The tax-cut coalition that first emerged in California during the 1970s enabled conservative Republicans to capture the White House in 1980 and cut taxes dramatically, then seize control of Congress in 1994 and assault worker benefit programs, starting with welfare. They had grown so bold by 1999 that they proposed cutting taxes by $800 billion, slashing capital gains taxes, abolishing the inheritance tax (two long-cherished goals of wealthy elites), and restructuring Social Security. Again, the tax cuts proposed by Congress would have granted large reductions for wealthy households—a couple earning $200,000 would receive tax cuts worth

$2,720—but delivered only tiny cuts to worker-households: A family with an income of $50,000, "which is near the national median, would receive an annual tax cut of $265 [one-tenth as much as the high-income family], less than enough for a movie a week in most cities."[60]

Buoyed by their ability to cut benefits for poor and also immigrant workers, the tax-cut coalition even broached the possibility of restructuring Social Security. When Social Security was first proposed in the 1930s, conservative elites opposed it because they worried that it would reduce the amount of savings available for investment, either through banks or Wall Street. But now they want the government to invest a portion of Social Security trust funds in the stock market and compel worker-taxpayers to invest a portion of their payroll taxes in Wall Street, steps that have been endorsed by Republican and Democratic politicians in the tax-cut coalition.[61]

This partial "privatization" of Social Security would annually direct hundreds of billions of dollars into U.S. capital markets, distributing worker-savings to corporations and their wealthy owners, who control the bulk of stock shares.[62] This approach is not unlike Japan's, where the state collects worker savings and distributes them to Japanese corporations. The difference is that the state in Japan does not rely on the stock market to direct investment but relies instead on banks and state bureaucracies to control savings and direct investment flow.

The idea of directing worker savings toward Wall Street was a daunting prospect even for some elite money managers. Federal Reserve Board chairman Alan Greenspan argued that the proposal to invest a portion of Social Security reserves in the stock market could actually endanger the economy. "I do not believe that it is politically feasible to insulate such huge funds from government direction," he warned. Political pressure, he said, could lead to inefficient investments that, in turn, would result in a lower rate of return for retired people and a lower standard of living for all Americans.[63] Greenspan was joined by Arthur Levitt, Jr., chairman of the Securities and Exchange Commission, which oversees Wall Street, who warned that the "army of novice investors" created by such a plan would be extremely vulnerable to fraud. "We have an obligation to think long and hard about the implications of Social Security reform," he said.[64]

Many worker-taxpayers support the proposed changes because they have seen the stock market soar in recent years, because they don't want their taxes to rise as aging workers retire, and because they don't trust the state to safeguard their benefits.[65] "I trust myself more than I do the Government," said Debi A. Lenox, an interior designer from Atlanta.[66] This sentiment is particularly widespread among young worker-taxpayers. "Frankly, what I'd really like to see is for the Government to give me everything I've put into [Social Security]," said John Zimmerman, a geologist. "Let me manage my own money and I promise you I won't ask the Government for help when I retire."[67]

But the effort to channel workers' retirement savings into the stock market would have adverse consequences for many workers. Even if capital markets rewarded the government and individual investors with generous returns, they would not do so uniformly. Uneven rewards would differentiate workers. It would tend, for instance, to discriminate against women. "Privatization [of Social Security] is a threat to American women," warned Edith U. Fierst, a pension-rights lawyer. "The money accumulated in a personal savings would belong to the person whose earnings were taxed, not to the spouse. Men are still earning more than women, so their accounts would be larger."[68]

This system would be discriminatory, providing larger retirement benefits to some workers than to others. But workers who received smaller benefits would find it difficult to object because their returns would be viewed as a personal failing, the fault of poor individual investment decisions.

Of course, if capital markets failed to deliver the kind of returns that investors have recently come to expect, then government and worker-investors could be collectively devastated. The privatization of Social Security in Chile illustrates the problem with tying pension savings to capital markets. During their first fifteen years, the investment funds that received worker savings provided a 12 percent annual return.[69] But falling copper prices and recession in the 1990s reduced the pension fund's rates of return to a 2.5 percent loss in 1995, a 3.5 percent gain in 1996, and a 4.7 percent gain in 1997. "I may seem calm on the outside, but my stomach is churning," said Fapian Moraga, a computer technician in Chile. "I don't know what will happen tomorrow with these stock markets."[70]

Also missing from the discussion about restructuring Social Security is the impact of Wall Street investment for workers who have not yet retired. We have already seen that relatively modest levels of worker-taxpayer investments through IRAs and 401(k)s fueled a stock-price inflation that resulted in the growing monopolization of U.S. corporations and the downsizing of workers employed by merged firms. Proposals to invest considerably larger amounts would no doubt accelerate this kind of development, which has already had deleterious consequences for millions of workers.

The problem for workers in the United States is that state benefits to poor women and children have been cut, and these cuts have been supported by workers whose identities as taxpayers guide their political behavior. The growth and increasing salience of taxpayer identities among workers in the United States means that further reductions in state benefits, for at least some workers, are almost certain.

DEBT CRISIS: DEMOCRATIZATION AND BENEFIT CUTS IN THE PERIPHERY AND SEMIPERIPHERY

States in the periphery and capitalist semiperiphery provided few of the benefits to workers that core states routinely offered. If they managed to provide workers with a primary education, they congratulated themselves for reducing literacy. But aside from this, most states provided little in the way of worker benefits. Remember that most peripheral and semiperipheral states, both capitalist and communist, were ruled by dictators, military juntas, and one-party regimes between 1945 and 1980/1989.

Most of these dictatorships devoted the bulk of public resources to armies and bureaucracies, which protected the regime and provided employment for loyal constituencies. They did not spend much on programs that assisted urban and rural workers. Communist regimes in the semiperiphery, like dictatorships elsewhere, devoted the bulk of public resources to the military. But unlike other capitalist dictatorships, they also provided substantial benefits to workers.

In the early 1970s, rising oil and food prices created a problem for dictatorships across the periphery and semiperiphery. Rising fuel and food prices increased costs for workers, a development that triggered worker riots in many countries. To prevent rising prices from fueling worker opposition to their regimes, dictators around the world hit upon an ingenious solution: use borrowed money to subsidize the cost of food, fuel, transportation, and sometimes higher education and modest health services.[71] These subsidies insulated workers from global inflation, deflected or deterred worker protest, and provided workers with important, widely available or "universal" benefits at a low administrative cost.[72]

But in the 1980s, when the debt crisis struck, global economic institutions insisted that indebted states in the periphery and semiperiphery adopt neoconservative economic policies, which required them to cut state subsidies and benefits to workers and reduce government payrolls. One 1986 study of ninety-four structural adjustment programs found that most cut subsidies and transfer payment programs, such as social security and unemployment assistance.[73]

Debt crisis forced officials in many states to curb benefits dramatically. Spending on education, for example, fell by a third in Turkey and Mexico, by half in Tanzania and Tunisia, and by 95 percent in Zaire.[74] In sub-Saharan Africa, overall social spending fell, on average, 26 percent.[75] In Jamaica, spending on education, health, and social security fell 44 percent.[76]

The sharp reductions in subsidies and other worker-benefit programs had serious consequences for workers throughout the periphery and semiperiphery, increasing costs and reducing real incomes, developments that were particularly hard on poor workers, women, and children.[77]

When the Indian government increased the price of many staple foods, including cooking oil and onions, the government admitted that these steps would have a serious impact on the poor and on women who did most of the household work. "I must apologize to all housewives," the finance minister said, as he slashed subsidies to working people.[78]

Where subsidies for food, fuel, transportation, and higher education were reduced, and prices rose, workers frequently rioted. Students protesting the structural adjustment policies adopted by the Indonesian government during its crisis in 1998 demanded: "Rice, Sugar, Cooking Oil, and Democracy."[79] After protests continued unabated, the government cut the price of train tickets in an effort to move unemployed and disgruntled workers out of Jakarta and return them to their families in rural areas.[80] In Indonesia, as in Japan and the United States, officials hoped that relatives could provide benefits to assist needy workers when the state could not, or would not.

Protests against falling benefits and rising prices have become so frequent and so ubiquitous that scholars now refer to them as "IMF Riots" because they commonly accompany the reduction of workers' benefits by peripheral states at the behest of global economic institutions.[81]

In the communist semiperiphery, debt and democratization led not only to a reduction in subsidies for food, fuel, and transportation but also to a wholesale reduction of comprehensive benefits: housing, health care, education, social security, and guaranteed employment. After the Soviet Union collapsed, social service spending in Russia fell by half in its first year of independence. In Hungary, the value of pension benefits fell 25 percent.[82] The only bright spot in this gloomy picture was that the free housing workers had earlier obtained under communist rule provided a benefit that helped workers survive.

There was another, more general problem for workers in peripheral and semiperipheral states. The collapse of dictatorships and ongoing economic crises not only reduced specific worker benefits but also weakened the ability of many states to function as "states," what the sociologist John Walton called a "partial state breakdown."[83]

The adoption of structural adjustment programs weakened the ability of state officials to manage their economies by using monetary policies to set exchange rates, stimulate investment, or reduce unemployment. Some state officials have conceded as much, arguing that they should adopt the U.S. dollar as their own national currency because they lack the ability to manage monetary policy on their own. Government officials in Ecuador, after defaulting on the country's $13 billion foreign debt and watching the inflation rate soar and the value of the currency plummet, decided to adopt the U.S. dollar as their official currency in early 2000.[84] The decision prompted massive protests by people without access to dollars (the large indigenous Indian population) and triggered a coup attempt, which ousted the president and installed the vice president in his place. Although the new president argued that "Ecuador is not a banana republic" and would proceed to dollarize the economy, he effectively surrendered the government's sovereign economic powers to another country.[85]

This astonishing surrender of monetary policy is due not to increasing corporate power, as many suppose, but to the increasing power of global economic institutions, which are controlled by core states and state bureaucracies like the U.S. Federal Reserve, not by transnational corporations or capital markets.

The decline of state power in the periphery and semiperiphery is also due to domestic forces. Officials in the former Soviet republics and in states throughout Latin America and Africa have found it increasingly difficult to collect taxes, particularly from the rich, whose widespread refusal to pay taxes amounts to a unilateral reduction in their taxes.[86] In Russia, the government collected half as much in taxes in 1997 as it did in 1992.[87] In Guatemala, "a powerful coalition of agricultural, industrial, and financial groups is simply refusing to pay up and has blocked all efforts at tax reform."[88] In Uruguay, "Nobody pays taxes," U.S. Ambassador Leslie M. Alexander observed.[89] In South Africa, wealthy Whites in many suburbs have collectively refused to pay property taxes to the Black-controlled democratic government, a "crippling weapon of mass non-payment" designed to make towns ungovernable. White business leaders who participated in the nonpayment campaign warned that "property owners are not a bottomless pit from which money can be siphoned off indiscriminately."[90]

Tax revolts in the periphery and semiperiphery, unlike tax revolts in the United States, are organized almost wholly by wealthy elites and corporations, with little participation by workers. Peripheral tax revolts are different, too, because they decisively weaken the state, undermining its capacity to provide services or protection for its citizens. In the United States, by contrast, while the tax-cut coalition has been willing to attack workers' benefits, it has insisted on increased spending for national defense and police protection, which strengthens the state. In Russia, the government's inability to collect taxes has pushed up the cost of borrowing money, which it needs to pay worker salaries.[91] In Argentina, it means that the postal service is so poor and "so unreliable that most businesses use expensive courier and private mail services for local deliveries."[92] In many countries, it means that lawlessness, crime, and corruption have made life more insecure and protection more expensive.[93]

Where states have weakened, as they have in Eastern Europe and the former Soviet Union, or collapsed, as they have in Somalia and Zaire, workers have sometimes mobilized along ethnic lines to demand states of their own.[94] These "separatist" movements imagine that a state of their own would provide economic benefits and political protection for ethnic groups, services no longer provided by existing states. Unfortunately, their effort to divide existing states and secure states of their own generally weakens existing and successor states. Where states have divided in recent years—in Czechoslovakia, Ethiopia, Yugoslavia, and the Soviet Union—the economic and political power of successor states is considerably weaker than their undivided predecessors. In some of these states, the ability of officials to perform even minimal functions has eroded significantly, while residual antagonisms between and among successor states have frequently led to conflict and war. Like the rise of taxpayer identities among workers in the United States, the emergence of ethnic identities among workers in peripheral and semiperipheral states has been generally detrimental for workers, particularly where ruinous conflicts and uncivil wars occur.

RECESSION AND BENEFIT CUTS IN WESTERN EUROPE AND JAPAN

During the postwar period, states in Western Europe provided many generous, universal benefits to workers. Government officials did so initially to prevent workers from supporting communist parties and secure electoral majorities for conservative parties. States were able to provide generous benefits because their economies grew rapidly after World War II; because workers, corporations, and the rich paid relatively high taxes; and because worker wages grew throughout this period. In the

1970s and 1980s, when slowed economic growth and stagnant wages gave rise to the tax-cut coalition and an assault on worker benefits in the United States, states in Western Europe kept on providing generous benefits to workers. They did so because their economies continued to grow, largely at U.S. expense; wages continued to rise; and the political parties and trade unions representing workers and defending state benefits remained intact. These developments prevented elites in Western Europe from cutting taxes or worker benefits, as they had in the United States. But this began to change in the 1990s.

During the 1990s, states across Western Europe took steps to cut social spending and reduce worker benefits. They did so for several reasons. First, the decision to create a common European currency forced states to adopt deflationary policies, so they could meet the criteria established in the Maastricht Treaty. This triggered a recession and rising unemployment. Because unemployment was high and wages stagnant, government revenues fell. So state officials looked for ways to cut spending and avoid budget deficits, which were proscribed under the Treaty. "We don't want to dismantle our system," Sweden's prime minister explained, "but we can't spend where we don't have the income."[95] The fact that the workforce was rapidly aging, and birth rates remained low, meant that states would eventually encounter a crisis of social security programs as well.[96]

Second, state officials argued that cuts were necessary to increase the competitiveness of European firms in global markets. If "benefits" were cut, they argued, workers would "benefit" from the jobs and income that increased competitiveness would provide.[97] "We ran up debts and deficits," President Jacques Chirac of France explained in 1997, "and our country little by little lost its economic rank in the world."[98] Prime Minister Helmut Kohl of Germany agreed. "International competition has become much tougher," he said, when he introduced a $33 billion package of spending cuts in Parliament. "We can maintain our position [only] if we undertake the necessary changes."[99]

Finally, there was a desire, among conservative elites, to emulate the United States and cut both taxes and worker benefits. Helmut Kohl proposed sizable tax cuts for the rich, which would have reduced tax rates from 53 to 39 percent, a figure in line with U.S. tax rates on wealthy taxpayers.[100] His successor, Gerhard Schröder, a Social Democrat, recently advocated austerity measures that would cut spending and freeze pension benefits at current levels.[101] His coalition partners, the environmentalist Green Party, advocated that pension benefits be reduced and corporate taxes cut as part of a "sustainable" economic policy.[102] Meanwhile, Prime Minister Tony Blair, head of a Labour government in the United Kingdom, attacked what he called the "something-for-nothing welfare state." He introduced a plan to reduce welfare benefits and drive recipients from the rolls, saying this would introduce "a new ethic of rights and responsibilities."[103]

These leaders, like their tax-cut counterparts in the United States, have organized political support for policies that would reduce state benefits to workers in a dramatic way. As yet, they have had less success than officials in the United States. They have been less resolute because parliamentary systems allow greater representation to worker-identified political parties, because trade unions are still strong and have organized large and determined protests against reductions in state benefits, and because taxpayer and consumer identities are less salient among workers in Western Europe.[104]

Among core states, Japan is the odd case. The state never provided direct, generous, or extensive benefits to workers of the sort extended by other states in the core. Instead, it provided substantial benefits to business firms, which were then expected to deliver benefits to workers. These benefits took the form of lifetime employment and pensions, which relieved the state of providing comprehensive unemployment or social security programs. Because the state essentially contracted business firms to provide worker benefits, the administrative cost to the state was extremely low.

But while the state in Japan took a different approach to worker benefits, it, too, has come under pressure to reduce the worker benefits it indirectly provides. The collapse of stock and real estate markets in the early 1990s triggered a recession that essentially forced many firms into insolvency. But the state has been reluctant to let them fail, because legal bankruptcy would force firms to fire primarily male workers and eliminate their benefits (bankrupt firms cannot pay pensions unless they have been fully funded). So the state has continued to subsidize bankrupt businesses, a costly endeavor. But pressure is growing on state officials to let businesses fail and allow their worker benefits to lapse. Pressure for changed state policies comes from several sources. First, budget deficits have grown because the state has continued to subsidize businesses during a recession, when neither the economy nor wages are growing. In 1996, Japan's budget deficit amounted to 7 percent of its gross domestic product, the highest among core states. "Japan holds a [budget deficit] time bomb that is expected to explode in a few years, and the bomb gets bigger every year," warned one Ministry of Finance report.[105]

Second, many large firms in Japan would like to see the government cut spending and let domestic competitors fail. Like corporations everywhere, they would like to cut taxes on corporations and wealthy individuals. They would also like to see unemployment rates rise and worker benefits fall, which would increase competition among workers in the labor force and exert a downward pressure on wages. Lower wages would then help them compete in U.S. and other global markets.

Third, U.S. officials have attacked the Japanese state's subsidy policy because they believe it "unfairly aids" Japanese firms that compete with U.S. firms in global markets. If Japan reduced its subsidies, they reason, U.S. firms could capture some of these markets.

So far, officials in Japan have been unwilling to succumb to these pressures and change their policies, though they have forced a few firms into bankruptcy. They have been reluctant to deprive firms of subsidies and allow them to go bankrupt in large number because this would break the link between the state and worker benefits. Because the state has no alternative benefit programs in place, workers who lost their jobs and pensions would be entirely on their own, or they would be forced to seek welfare from family members. Such a step would undo the consensus upon which postwar economic growth in Japan was based. Of that, officials in the conservative government are afraid. Very afraid. As a result, they have been unwilling to reduce business subsidies and worker benefits, even if that means running large deficits and piling up national debt.

Worker households in the core, the periphery, and the semiperiphery have seen jobs disappear and wages fall in recent years. They have also watched states cut benefits, which provided an important source of income for households. As the wages and benefits from private businesses and the state have declined, worker households around the world have had to find alternative sources of income. Their collective efforts have created new kinds of economic activity, transformed gender relations at work and at home, and generated new political struggles over environmental, economic, and social resources. It is to these developments that we now turn.

NOTES

1. According to scholars, the term *welfare state* originated in a report to the British government in 1942, which recommended a comprehensive package of state benefits to workers. The recommendations of the Beveridge Report were adopted after the war by the Labour government. Wallace C. Peterson, *Transfer Spending, Taxes, and the American Welfare State* (Boston: Kluwer Academic, 1991), 1; Sheila Pelizzon and John Casparis, "World Human Welfare," in Terence K. Hopkins and Immanuel Wallerstein, eds., *The Age of Transition: Trajectory of the World-System, 1945–2025* (London: Zed, 1996), 119.

2. Robert K. Schaeffer, *Power to the People: Democratization around the World* (Boulder, Colo.: Westview, 1997), 5–17; Robert K. Schaeffer, *Severed States: Dilemmas of Democracy in a Divided World* (Lanham, Md.: Rowman & Littlefield, 1999), 9–26.

3. Pelizzon and Casparis, "World Human Welfare," 119–120.

4. Youssef M. Ibrahim, "Welfare's Snug Coat Cuts Norwegian Cold," *New York Times*, December 13, 1996.

5. Marlise Simons, "Child Care Sacred as France Cuts Back the Welfare State," *New York Times*, December 31, 1997; Celestine Bohlen, "Where Every Day Is Mother's Day," *New York Times*, May 12, 1996.

6. Edmund L. Andrews, "Bonn's Blank Check Buys Hollow Economy," *New York Times*, April 17, 1997.

7. Nathaniel C. Nash, "Europeans Shrug as Taxes Go Up," *New York Times*, February 16, 1995.

8. Nash, "Europeans Shrug."

9. Dani Rodrik, *Has Globalization Gone Too Far?* (Washington, D.C.: Institute for International Economics, 1997), 51; Michael J. Piore and Charles F. Sabel, *The Second Industrial Divide: Possibilities for Prosperity* (New York: Basic, 1984), 12.

10. Pelizzon and Casparis, "World Human Welfare," 120.

11. Lawrence Mishel, Jared Bernstein, and John Schmitt, *The State of Working America, 1998–99* (Armonk, N.Y.: Sharpe, 1991), 93.

12. Nicholas D. Kristof, "Welfare as Japan Knows It: A Family Affair," *New York Times*, September 10, 1996.

13. Kristof, "Welfare as Japan Knows It."

14. Nicholas D. Kristof, "Empty Isles Are Signs Japan's Sun Might Dim," *New York Times*, August 1, 1999.
15. Sheryl WuDunn, "The Face of the Future in Japan," *New York Times*, September 2, 1997.
16. WuDunn, "The Face of the Future in Japan."
17. Schaeffer, *Power to the People*, passim.
18. Schaeffer, *Power to the People*, 131; Giovanni Arrighi, "World Income Inequalities and the Future of Socialism," *New Left Review* 189 (September/October 1991): 57.
19. Michael Wines, "Taxpayers Are Angry: They're Expensive Too," *New York Times*, November 20, 1994; Tim Weiner, "It's Raining Subsidies," *New York Times*, August 8, 1999.
20. Alan Finder, "In Battle for Low-Cost Housing, Faint Hopes and a Few Bright Spots," *New York Times*, October 11, 1996; Wines, "Taxpayers Are Angry."
21. Robert Pear, "Typical Relief Check in 1996 Was Worth Half That of '70," *New York Times*, November 19, 1996.
22. Robert K. Schaeffer, *Understanding Globalization: The Social Consequences of Political, Economic, and Environmental Change* (Lanham, Md.: Rowman & Littlefield, 1997), 108–109; Lawrence Mishel and David M. Frankel, *The State of Working America, 1990–91* (Armonk, N.Y.: Sharpe, 1991), 60.
23. Frank Levy, *Dollars and Dreams: The Changing American Income Distribution* (New York: Russell Sage, 1987), 37–38, 56.
24. Schaeffer, *Understanding Globalization*, 109; Mishel and Frankel, *State of Working America, 1990–91*, 60.
25. Levy, *Dollars and Dreams*, 56.
26. Schaeffer, *Understanding Globalization*, 115.
27. Levy, *Dollars and Dreams*, 169.
28. Peterson, *Transfer Spending*, 12; Pelizzon and Casparis, "World Human Welfare," 133.
29. Peterson, *Transfer Spending*, 12.
30. Peter T. Kilborn, "Shrinking Safety Net Cradles Hearts and Hopes of Children," *New York Times*, November 30, 1996.
31. Schaeffer, *Understanding Globalization*, 109.
32. Felicity Barringer, "Giving by the Rich Declines, on Average," *New York Times*, May 24, 1992; David Cay Johnston, "Amid High-Tech Wealth, a United Way Is Depleted," *New York Times*, May 16, 1999; Andrew Jacobs, "Even in a Bull Market and Boom Times, the Working Poor Face Steep Odds," *New York Times*, November 30, 1997.
33. Mishel and Frankel, *State of Working America, 1990–91*, 60.
34. Richard W. Stevenson, "Taxing the Treasury's Patience," *New York Times*, June 4, 1999.
35. Peterson, *Transfer Spending*, 104.
36. Peterson, *Transfer Spending*, 115; Pear, "Typical Relief Check in 1996."
37. Schaeffer, *Understanding Globalization*, 116.
38. Schaeffer, *Understanding Globalization*, 105.
39. Jason DeParle, "Success, and Frustration, as Welfare Rules Change," *New York Times*, December 30, 1997.
40. Douglas Martin, "New York Workfare Expansion Fuels Debate," *New York Times*, September 1, 1995; Rachel L. Swarns, "New York's New Strategy Sharply Cuts Welfare Applications at Two Offices," *New York Times*, June 22, 1998; Rachel L. Swarns, "Mothers Poised for Workfare Face Acute Lack of Day Care," *New York Times*, April 14, 1998.
41. Martin, "New York Workfare Expansion Fuels Debate."

42. Robert Pear, "Poor Workers Lose Medicaid Coverage despite Eligibility," *New York Times*, April 12, 1999; Andrew C. Revkin, "Plunge in Use of Food Stamps Causes Concern," *New York Times*, February 25, 1999.

43. Andrew C. Revkin, "Welfare Policies Alter the Face of Food Lines," *New York Times*, February 26, 1999; Michael M. Weinstein, "When Work Is Not Enough," *New York Times*, August 26, 1999.

44. Raymond Hernandez, "More Who Leave Welfare Rolls in New York Are Found to Get Jobs," *New York Times*, August 5, 1999.

45. Jason DeParle, "Shrinking Welfare Rolls Leaves Record Share of Minorities," *New York Times*, July 27, 1998.

46. DeParle, "Shrinking Welfare Rolls"; Alan Finder, "Welfare Recipients in Big Cities Outnumber Jobs They Might Fill," *New York Times*, August 25, 1996.

47. Carey Goldberg, "Welfare's Missing-in-Action," *New York Times*, May 2, 1999.

48. DeParle, "Success, and Frustration."

49. DeParle, "Success, and Frustration"; Rachel L. Swarns, "The Search for Self-Reliance," *New York Times*, February 23, 1999; Jonathan Rabinovitz, "How to Survive Welfare Cuts: Really Trying," *New York Times*, April 28, 1996.

50. Jason deParle, "Welfare Law Weighs Heavily on Delta, Where Jobs Are Few," *New York Times*, October 16, 1997.

51. Goldberg, "Welfare's Missing-in-Action."

52. Steven Greenhouse, "Many Participants in Workfare Take Place of City Workers," *New York Times*, April 13, 1998.

53. Greenhouse, "Many Participants in Workfare."

54. Louis Uchitelle, "Welfare Recipients Taking Jobs Often Held by the Working Poor," *New York Times*, April 1, 1997.

55. Robert Pear, "Panel on Social Security Urges Investing in Stocks, but Is Split over Methods," *New York Times*, January 7, 1997.

56. Pear, "Panel on Social Security."

57. Pear, "Panel on Social Security."

58. Pear, "Panel on Social Security."

59. Michael M. Weinstein, "The New Welfare Rules May Be Tested in the Next Recession," *New York Times*, June 3, 1999.

60. Ann Monroe, "Safe and Secure?" *Mother Jones* (November/December 1996): 10.

61. Pear, "Panel on Social Security"; Richard W. Stevenson, "Bipartisan Group Urges Big Changes in Social Security," *New York Times*, May 19, 1998; Richard W. Stevenson, "Social Security Nudges Onstage," *New York Times*, December 8, 1998.

62. David E. Rosenbaum, "Greenspan Sees Possible Threat in Clinton Plan," *New York Times*, January 21, 1999; David E. Rosenbaum, "Flirting with a Buy Order for $1 Trillion in Stock," *New York Times*, February 7, 1999.

63. Rosenbaum, "Greenspan Sees Possible Threat."

64. Richard W. Stevenson, "S.E.C. Chairman Is Cautious about Social Security Plans," *New York Times*, October 20, 1998.

65. Richard W. Stevenson, "Privatizing Social Security Gains Backers in Congress," *New York Times*, April 6, 1998.

66. Kevin Sack, "Faith Shifts over Secure Retirement Funds," *New York Times*, February 7, 1999.

67. Sack, "Faith Shifts."

68. Pear, "Panel on Social Security."

69. Clifford Krauss, "Pensioners Quiver as Markets Fall," *New York Times*, August 16, 1998.
70. Krauss, "Pensioners Quiver."
71. John Walton and David Seddon, *Free Markets and Food Riots: The Politics of Global Adjustment* (Oxford: Blackwell, 1994), 101.
72. Schaeffer, *Power to the People*, 88.
73. Schaeffer, *Power to the People*, 96: Walton and Seddon, *Free Markets and Food Riots*, 102–103; Duncan Green, *Silent Revolution: The Rise of Market Economies in Latin America* (London: Cassell, 1995), 100.
74. Jeanne Vickers, *Women and the World Economic Crisis* (London: Zed, 1991), 28.
75. Walton and Seddon, *Free Markets and Food Riots*, 139.
76. Helen I. Safa and Peggy Antrobus, "Women and the Economic Crisis in the Caribbean," in Lourdes Benería and Shelley Feldman, eds., *Unequal Burden: Economic Crises, Persistent Poverty, and Women's Work* (Boulder, Colo.: Westview, 1992), 58.
77. Walton and Seddon, *Free Markets and Food Riots*, 322.
78. Celia W. Dugger, "Hindu Party Faces Test as Prices Anger Indians," *New York Times*, November 20, 1998; Celia W. Dugger, "India's Hottest Political Issue: The Price of Onions," *New York Times*, October 12, 1998; Celia W. Dugger, "India's Angry Poor: A Political Question Mark," *New York Times*, April 30, 1999.
79. Seth Mydans, "Indonesian Students Keep Protests Well within the Pale," *New York Times*, March 29, 1998; Julia Preston, "Mexico's New Rebel Students Just Want Careers," *New York Times*, October 3, 1995; Michael R. Gordon, "On the Road to Capitalism, Tax Breakdown for Russia," *New York Times*, February 19, 1997.
80. Seth Mydans, "Newly Jobless (and Newly Angry) Upset Indonesians," *New York Times*, January 29, 1998.
81. Green, *Silent Revolution*, 99, 167–169; Walton and Seddon, *Free Markets and Food Riots*, 43.
82. Christine I. Wallich, "Reforming Intergovernmental Relations: Russia and the Challenge of Fiscal Federalism," in Bartlomiej Kaminski, ed., *Economic Transition in Russia and the New States of Eurasia* (Armonk, N.Y.: Sharpe, 1996), 259; Janos Kornai, "Reform in the Welfare Sector in the Post-Communist Countries: A Normative Approach," in Joan M. Nelson, Charles Tilly, and Lee Walker, eds., *Transforming Post-Communist Political Economies* (Washington, D.C.: National Academy Press, 1997), 283.
83. Walton and Seddon, *Free Markets and Food Riots*, 335.
84. New York Times, "Ecuador's Currency Falls as the Government Examines Its Options," *New York Times*, January 5, 2000; Larry Rohter, "Ecuador's 3 Top Central Bankers Quit over Dollarization," *New York Times*, January 12, 2000; Larry Rohter, "Using the Dollar to Hold the Line: U.S. Currency Becomes Ecuador's," *New York Times*, January 18, 2000.
85. Larry Rohter, "New Ecuadorian President Pleads for Patience after Tumultuous 'Buffoonery,'" *New York Times*, January 25, 2000. Argentina and Russia have also discussed dollarizing their economies. If they did, they would join Panama, currently the only other country outside the United States that uses the dollar as its currency.
86. Green, *Silent Revolution*, 97.
87. Michael R. Gordon, "On the Road to Capitalism, Tax Breakdown for Russia," *New York Times*, February 19, 1997.
88. Larry Rohter, "Where Taxes Aren't So Certain," *New York Times*, March 21, 1999.
89. Rohter, "Where Taxes Aren't So Certain."

90. Suzanne Daley, "Country Club in Revolt over Post-Apartheid Taxes," *New York Times*, January 8, 1997.
91. Gordon, "On the Road to Capitalism."
92. Calvin Sims, "Argentina's Revival Doesn't Include Electricity and Telephone," *New York Times*, October 18, 1994.
93. Seth Faison, "No. 1 Complaint of Chinese: All This Corruption!" *New York Times*, March 11, 1999.
94. See Schaeffer, *Severed States*, passim.
95. Richard W. Stevenson, "Deficit-Cutting's International," *New York Times*, November 12, 1995; Helen Ginsburg, "Fall from Grace," *In These Times*, December 23, 1996.
96. Alan Cowell, "It's Young vs. Old in Germany as the Welfare State Fades," *New York Times*, June 4, 1997.
97. Dan Clawson and John O'Connor, "From Welfare Rights to Welfare Fights: Is the United States an Exception?" *Radical America*, vol. 26, no. 1 (1996): 59.
98. Craig R. Whitney, "The French and Germans Hear Refrain: Tighten Belts," *New York Times*, January 1, 1997.
99. Whitney, "The French and Germans Hear Refrain"; Alan Cowell, "Austerity Plan for Workers Is Approved in Germany," *New York Times*, June 29, 1996.
100. Alan Cowell, "As Bonn Fails at Tax Reform, German Businesses Study U.S." *New York Times*, August 1, 1997.
101. Roger Cohen, "A Ragged Rip in Schroder's Party Is Becoming All Too Public," *New York Times*, August 2, 1999.
102. Martin Hufner, "The Greens vs. Germany's Welfare State," *New York Times*, February 1, 1999.
103. Sarah Lylal, "Britain Plans New Effort to Whittle Welfare Rolls," *New York Times*, February 11, 1999; Sarah Lylal, "Blair's Countercultural Plan for Welfare: Get Work," *New York Times*, May 23, 1999.
104. William Wallace, "The Nation-State—Rescue or Retreat," in Peter Cowan and Perry Anderson, eds., *The Question of Europe* (London: Verso, 1997), 38; Celestine Bohlen, "The Magic Word for Italians: Europe (Pain and All)," *New York Times*, October 26, 1997.
105. Andrew Pollack, "Japan's Road to Bankruptcy Is Paved with Public Works," *New York Times*, March 1, 1997.

Part III

THE CHANGING GROUND FOR WORKING HOUSEHOLDS

Women's work supports the world-economy.

Chapter 8

Households, Class Transformations, and the Emergence of Women-Centered Labor Movements

Midway through this study, we are ready to return to social change and households. From this vantage, we will begin examining working-class transformations and worker protests. These class transformations include proletarianization, deproletarianization, and the new social relations being created outside the world-economy. By *proletarianization,* we mean the process by which households become more dependent on wage labor and market consumption. *Deproletarianization* refers to a declining dependence on wages for households and an increasing reliance on non-wage work. When households do not rely on wages for an extended period of time, they can be regarded as nonproletarian workers. Transformations like these can only be fully recognized by looking at social change in household and informal work settings.

In the first half of the book, we started at the center of a conceptual "figure eight" and traversed through largely macro-level changes in wage work and the state in the zones of the world-economy. During this journey through contemporary history, we showed how changes in formal work and state arrangements affected work and gender. We began to understand the social transitions that cultivated conditions of global and regional rebellion.

To understand work transitions and protests about work and culture, it is crucial to meld macro-level change and micro-level changes. The study of laboring households, emerging communities, and conflicts within the work environment enables us to see how labor's movements have diversified. This chapter, which serves as a theoretical and empirical introduction to the second section of the book, analyzes how micro-level changes in social and "natural" environments have encouraged the emergence of a diverse family of labor movements. By exploring labor's protests against firms and states and labor's attempts to diversify social relations, we will complete a second circuit of empirical and historical inquiry. Then we can consider changes in firms, states, households, and protest movements at the macro- and micro-levels.

THE THEORETICAL AND METHODOLOGICAL IMPORTANCE OF THE HOUSEHOLD

Firms, states, and households all need to be studied if the formation of gender, ethnic, and class relations is to be understood, and vice versa. Most scholars who study class formation overlook the household and its importance for changing class relationships. If class formation, class de-formation, and social transitions are only studied at the aggregate level, without looking at households and informal work, then it is easy to misinterpret some important changes. What may look like proletarianization, or labor's increasing dependence on wages and the global market, may actually turn out to be deproletarianization, or declining dependence on wages and market consumption.

If local communities' and women's protests are seen outside of the global context in which they develop, then a major systemic break may be missed. What may look like the growth of small-scale capitalism and the "development" of the periphery may actually turn out to be widespread indications of systemic demise.

If households are not studied as part of the world-economy, the growth of female wage labor may appear to be proof of globalization, rather than a temporary integration of some female laborers in limited enclaves, a development often accompanied by the marginalization of other household members.

HOUSEHOLDS AND GENDER

In the last twenty years, fundamental changes have taken place in the total work environment of worker households. Household dependence on wage labor has become increasingly insecure, state transfers have declined, and households have relied increasingly on each other for support. Households now create many worker-run political and economic organizations. Many of these global changes cannot be seen if class formation issues are studied at the level of income or ethnic groupings. Nor can they be understood by just considering wage labor organizations such as unions. To appreciate change at the global level, one has to examine change at the level of households and interhousehold networks, where, on any given day, most nonmigrating household members can be found congregating and working.

As part of global change, working people in households have begun to establish alternative relationships and organizations to replace capitalist organizations and institutions. At the heart of these efforts has been workers' need to reduce their dependency on profit-making firms and the state and to define new ways of sustaining themselves. For workers, the household has emerged as a powerful base upon which antisystemic movements can be built.

Households are the place where we can understand how and why female-centered, overlapping labor movements have evolved. Households are the intersection between formal and informal economic relations, between the global and the local, between dominant and subordinate cultures, and between male and female workers. An examination of changes that affect households illuminates the central role that women play in contemporary social transitions and struggles. By examining households, we can see why revolutionary disturbances at the household level, on the one hand, can lead to revolutionary disruptions elsewhere. On the other hand, through a focus on laboring households, we can recognize otherwise undetected, systemic disturbances and revolutionary projects. This world historical and economic framework includes the invisible half of gender relations, the changing organization of household work, and the patterns of wage and other income allocation that shape gender and age groups. To see how society is unfolding, we must look at the systemic building blocks of our current global society and the transformation blocks that are creating one or more future societies. It is only by linking knowledge gained from all capitalist institutions—and this means including an analysis of households—that we can see how the system has been developing, where it is going, and why the whole family of labor movements will define our collective future.

THE TRANSITION FROM MALE-CENTERED TO FEMALE-CENTERED HOUSEHOLDS

Although images of U.S. gender relations are still derived from ideal-typical impressions of male-dominated families before 1970, the engendered world is changing in major ways. Now women are supporting more household members, and the world-economy's structure has tilted toward more female-centered households. Living in a world like this has meant that the level of polarization between adult females and adult males has intensified. In some cases, the gradual growth of female-centered households has also meant that social polarization has increased between female teens and teenage males. More than ever before, adult women keep worker households going without substantial assistance from male partners. Meanwhile, adult men, particularly those who have migrated with the goal of increasing household income, have done less to support their children, spouses, and parents. But the emergence of a more women-centered world does not necessarily mean that all females and all males are becoming polarized. In many cases, children and elders of both genders have affiliated with adult females, while adult males (and sometimes teen males) have separated from females in economic, social, or geographical terms.

It is difficult not to view contemporary developments through male-centered images of the past. During the century between 1870 and 1970 in the United States, men came to occupy a central place at work, in households, and in political life. As capitalist manufacturing firms expanded, they organized work around adult males, providing jobs primarily or exclusively to men. Firms typically paid men 25 percent to 50 percent more than they paid women in manufacturing or in service industry jobs. Male dominance in the workplace and in households was also buttressed by the state. During the many colonial, global, and cold wars of the nineteenth and twentieth centuries, states demanded military service from adult men, not women. States then conferred substantial benefits, privileges, and honors on the men who served. Male entry into military service and men's access to the state benefits associated with it solidified their role as the official conduit between the state and working-class households, strengthening their position as heads of households. This was particularly true for households where male wage income and state benefits provided a "family wage," which covered most of the costs of sustaining and reproducing households. But even where male wages and benefits were not adequate to support whole families—as was the case for most working households in the periphery, many in the semiperiphery, and many poor households in the core—they provided essential resources that strengthened male bargaining power. As a result, pooled income, benefits, and power in most households were distributed unequally, almost always to the advantage of men.[1]

Male control of access to jobs, wage income, and state benefits not only accentuated male power in households, it gave rise to formal and organizational politics that often centered around men, at least in dominant cultures. In this period, most unions organized primarily men in manufacturing industries, which were thought to be more central to capitalism than agriculture or service industries, and working-class political parties relied on organized labor and male constituencies based in manufacturing for their political support. The workplace and electoral struggles of this period were centered around men and aimed at securing higher wages and better state benefits for men. This in turn strengthened men's position as "breadwinners" in the home and distanced women from work, wage income, state benefits, and political power. With the male-headed household as the micro-institutional base of the capitalist world-economy, women rarely controlled economic resources, headed households, or participated fully in shaping labor's political choices. "Fordism," as this set of economic and political relations that emerged in the core during this period is sometimes called, was a profoundly male-centered set of social relations.

But this century-long pattern of male domination in workplaces, households, and politics began to change after 1970, giving rise to new relations in which women took a more central role. Economic, political, and gender relations have changed as a result of two simultaneous and related developments.

First, the male hold on jobs and wage income has weakened. As we have seen, deindustrialization, downsizing, and the redistribution of work around the world has resulted in the loss of jobs and income for men, particularly men in manufacturing. This has weakened the economic strength of unions whose membership was concentrated in manufacturing industries and the clout of political parties that relied on organized labor and male electoral constituencies. The reduction of state benefits, and the declining importance of military service in the core, further weakened the ability of men to act as conduit between family and state. These developments in turn undermined the position of men as heads of households and their claim to unequal privileges within households; men could no longer claim their access to wages and benefits as the basis for privilege and patriarchy in the home. Of course, it is important to note that business practices and state policies played major roles in these developments, first by abetting male-centered social institutions, then by weakening them.

Second, women entered the wage force in increasing numbers. As they did, women gained more political and social power. They achieved political power and social gains despite the fact that they earned 20 to 50 percent less than men.[2] As anthropologist Helen Safa has noted, when women become wage workers, they typically become more assertive at home and at work.[3] When women work, their husbands are also more likely to tell wives what their wages really are and to share their earnings.[4] This should not be surprising, since control over access to jobs and wages has long been a source of power and, often, privilege. Where women have entered the workforce in large numbers, they have sometimes organized unions, just as men did in the earlier period.[5] But women's jobs are changing in fundamental ways, which cannot be grasped by looking at wage employment in isolation from other kinds of household work.

Gender relations and women's work are being recast in ways that are changing the face of working-class politics around the world. Complex shifts are appearing in a number of related areas, and their implications for social change movements are dramatic. Before 1970, women worked, but this work was invisible to themselves and unappreciated by others in the hierarchy. The historical tendency was for the "private" sphere to be increasingly separated from the "public" sphere. In the past, many women remained dispersed in home-based manufacturing and in agricultural work. Although many women worked for wages, manufacturers drew them into the workforce at different times in their lives, particularly during their teen years. This practice, of course, continues. But today women are increasingly expected to support their families, and men are no longer defined as the sole or primary wage earners. The employment of women and reliance on female nonwage labor are now accompanied by the departure of some men from some sectors of the visible public sphere, including manufacturing.

As the world-economy has developed, more aspects of its operations have become public and more operations take place in the public sphere. As women have become increasingly integrated into the public sphere on an ongoing basis, work and political relations have become exposed and are now "out in the open." Open work relations assume a different political and social meaning than ones that are blanketed by ideological and sexist interpretations of private/public distinctions. Capitalist development has so commercialized the home that many of its activities have become the object of overt, international public policies. For example, it became the policy of core countries to collect debts from the periphery by forcing governments there to reduce public benefits and private wages, which requires women to increase their nonwage work burdens. Similar policies have taken hold in the United States and other core countries, where states decided to weaken their social guarantees to poor children and their parents.

When national and international organizations implemented overt policies to make women work harder at home and in informal markets, patriarchy started to break down in ways that the state and capital may never be able to repair. Not only was the state trying to force women to work harder to support a sexist, racist, and core-centered global system, but the system had begun to expel men from many jobs that had allowed them to dominate their families economically and socially. In other words, the global system created a situation that exposed—and opened up attacks on—sexism in the world-system and sexist male authority figures in households. Because states adopted overtly sexist policies that increased the exploitation of women, while capitalists expelled many men from full-time employment, these separate but related actions by state and capitalist institutions started to dissolve both world-systemic and familial patriarchy.

Since 1970, the global order deconstructed household patriarchy, the fundamental base of the whole system. This occurred just when global feminist movements emerged. This was a world historic development, with extremely important consequences. For many years, the relationship between household patriarchy and global patriarchy was blurry. Were they related or separate phenomena? When household patriarchy and systemic patriarchy were tightly intertwined, as they were for the last five hundred years, the global system had a lot of stability. But once global feminism appeared, once capital undermined male power in households, once the state forced women to do more nonwage work, the relation between household patriarchy and capitalist patriarchy was not only exposed but partly severed. By redefining female–male relationships and woman-to-woman relationships, this conjunctural change has provoked many important cultural and political changes.

WOMEN DO MORE WORK AND DESIGN NEW SURVIVAL STRATEGIES

Since 1975, women's workload has increased around the world. But will women bear the growing burden that has been placed on their shoulders? When women do more wage work and carry out more nonwage work, they often have to recruit others to do housework. In both Ecuador and Mexico, the increasing pressure to earn wages has pushed young males into wage work, where they can contribute to household maintenance. In this situation, working women often rely on their teenage daughters to assume part of the burden of nonwage work. But if the combined wages of the young males and adult wage earners is not sufficient, young daughters may have to earn wages, too. In this situation, "the quality of domestic life may well deteriorate to the point that households cannot sustain themselves at all."[6] Because young girls earn the lowest wages, their entry into the workforce produces diminishing returns. Some households try to stop this exploitation, demanding that the state or businesses provide them with "more satisfactory and dignified means of survival."[7] Households also try to design other ways of living through interhousehold cooperation and more inclusive social movements. Growing numbers of women, girls, and other workers have resisted growing workloads, revolting against the increasing burden of work and giving rise to a new kind of politics centered around the reproductive needs of households, evolving communities, and global labor.

A large proportion of the world's female and male workers, who work at low-paying jobs and perform nonwage work, face increasing hardships that relate to the lack of wage employment, the decline in natural resources, and the imposition of country-wide austerity programs. For the last twenty years, the vast middle and lower tiers of workers around the world have seen real wages, wage-related benefits, and state subsidies decline. The growing dependence on women's nonwage work and on women's global wage work in manufacturing, agricultural, and sex-trade and tourist enclaves is related to the decline in some jobs that once were largely given to men. It is also related to the withdrawal of investments from Africa and Latin America and the general lack of expansion in the periphery in the 1990s and early 2000s. There, workers have had to rely increasingly on nonwage income (even as environmental degradation has reduced some nonwage options) and have tried to migrate within countries or across international borders to secure income and obtain democratic rights.[8]

An analysis of women's self-organized work in the periphery reveals that women now do a lot more nonwage work, even where they continue to hold jobs that pay wages.[9] Women's income-earning options are limited because private investments "only selectively fill the gap left by reduced public services."[10] Although most of the South's recent export-oriented production jobs have gone to young women, the growth of female enclave-employment has occurred at a time when male jobs in import-substitutionist manufacturing industries have declined and the informal sector has grown.[11] Any new power that female employees have acquired at Third World factory sites needs to be put in the larger context of the overall changes in women's and men's "formal" employment, the reduction of real wages through salary freezes and subsidy removals, and the decline of support systems and some kinds of subsistence production.[12]

Feminist scholars have reached a common conclusion: Laboring women's work burden has increased throughout the world. It has increased because gender relations have been disrupted by recent changes in factory work, environmental degradation, war, and the implementation of austerity measures. It has increased because households need income from informal work and other household survival strategies: trading, vending, microproducing, and migrating to cities and across national borders.[13]

A continuing problem for women is that while they have found jobs and entered the workforce, their wages are lower than men's wages. Real wages have declined, and the prices of many goods that workers consume have risen. This means that women have to intensify their nonwage work efforts alongside of their wage work, if they want to prevent their standards of living from falling.

Because many scholars focus on women's successful acquisition of jobs in the wealthiest countries, there is a widespread impression that women have made tremendous economic gains. Between 1970 and 1990, the vast majority of the world's women did make gains in life expectancy, schooling, and access to new contraceptive technologies. But it is also true that women generally have lost economic ground. In global terms, it is not the case that women have gained and men have lost. Most women *and* men, and their entire households, have lost ground within the world-economy, which appears to be undergoing systemic dissolution. Men have lost some of their patriarchal power in households, but patriarchy in the capitalist system has remained largely intact. Change has disadvantaged women much more than men. In forty-one countries in the periphery and semiperiphery, more rural women than rural men fell into poverty, and women made up 60 percent of the rural poor by 1988.[14] In the South, feminist scholars have found that women and children are greatly overrepresented in the poorest of the poor.[15]

Female workers rarely receive wages that cover household needs, and many teen girls receive wages that do not cover the cost of their own reproduction. In central Java, for example, female factory workers did not earn enough to even cover the cost of one person's subsistence. Male factory workers, on the other hand, received 50 percent more for their efforts, allowing them to cover the cost of their own subsistence.[16] In fact, families actually supplemented the wages earned by their daughters who worked full-time in factories. Families gave their daughters free food, goods, services, lodging, and cash so that their daughters could afford to do factory work. In this way, laboring households provided a free subsidy to employers, helping to "keep wages down and factory profits up."[17] In return, households received cash, a rare commodity that they needed to survive. Many would interpret this as proof of globalization. But we believe that evidence like this supports the view that deproletarianization and the eventual expulsion of labor from the world-economy are taking place.

Female household heads keep more families going, though they face tremendous economic hardships. Researchers count female household heads in different ways. Some scholars count only women who are the sole adult in a household. Others count women who bring in most of the household income. The first method understates women's economic contribution, the second more accurately reflects women's economic role. In a survey of more than fifty recent studies, the International Center for Research on Women (ICRW) found that female-headed households were poorer than male-headed households. Households headed by women are poorer because, the ICRW explained, they suffer from "persistent sexual discrimination in terms of employment and wages."[18] These female-headed households supported just as many dependents as adult male heads.[19] In India, female household heads "constitute the most disadvantaged and poorest of the rural poor."[20]

Employers suppress wages by taking advantage of the "continual flow of female school-leavers each year."[21] In the strawberry fields around Zamora, Mexico, employers give female heads of households only the lowest-paying work in the fields. Adult women do the grueling work of picking strawberries, while managers reserve processing plant work for young females, who are seen as money "savers." The comparative disadvantage for older female heads of households turns out to be a comparative advantage for agribusinesses.[22]

In low-income households in Latin America and Southeast Asia, when adult females toil for low pay, female and male children and elders, along with adult males, need to earn income.[23] "For the sons and daughters of the impoverished in Latin America, Asia, Africa, and the Middle East . . . work . . . is a must for staying alive," one scholar observed.[24] But because employers discriminate against young workers, it is often hard for youth to find jobs in the Third World.[25] Much the same is true in the core. In England, Wales, and Scotland, young adults have the highest unemployment rates, extending their parents' responsibilities, limiting educational pursuits, and making it very difficult for young people to form households of their own.[26]

Although household patriarchy has been increasingly under attack by women, it remains the dominant cultural norm in many social contexts. For example, even though China has an official policy that women should be treated as men's equals, household patriarchy has remained firmly entrenched. In 1979, rural women in southwest China still generated two-thirds of village income, though the Chinese Revolution increased the agricultural work done by men. Between 1939 and 1979, Chinese women's wages in rural areas increased from 50 percent to 89 percent of male wages.[27] But women were also expected to do extensive nonwage work. While rural men have had limited agricultural responsibilities (hoeing and threshing), women did the bulk of farm work and other independent activities. In one study, researchers met a woman who managed a factory and raised pigs, and a woman who cooked for workers in a factory cafeteria and then worked in the fields after her shift was done. Rural women in China have to cook, wash, care for children, cultivate and harvest vegetables, preserve food, sell vegetables, and raise pigs, cows, chickens, and turkeys.[28]

A study of three Chinese villages in the Shandong province shows that married and widowed women, who are forty years of age and younger, now constitute the core of the agricultural workforce.[29] Although Chinese development strategies have called for the increasing integration of women into jobs outside of the home, officials have not called for women to reduce their domestic workloads.[30] As the economy developed, poor female-headed households became differentiated from richer patriarchal ones.[31] Female-headed households in Shandong often engaged in self-employed, enterprising work.[32]

Because the Chinese state has encouraged the development of the independent household as part of its rural decollectivization plan, rural women do more work. But the state also assumes less responsibility for distributing welfare, and households are now taxed for wages paid. In order to institutionalize the reduction of state responsibilities, officials have urged households to engage in domestic sidelines, including petty producing and marketing. Rural women in China have been defined as "domestic sideline" workers. Parents have often taken girls out of school and enlisted them in a growing number of "female" agricultural chores, which has reinforced the gender division of labor at home.[33] Patterns of social inequality like these will not completely disappear until people make egalitarian social change.

WOMEN TURN HEADS: THE RISE OF FEMALE BREADWINNERS

Feminist scholars place tremendous importance on the increase in female-headed households since 1970. And rightly so. Scholars see this trend as extremely significant for women and men and for their children. As women's workloads increased, more women around the world began supporting household members on their own, without assistance or interference from adult men. Although more women ran households on their own, the rise of female-headed households also meant that the system was increasingly based on the exploitation of women. Women's workloads increased, but wages remained low and market work continued to bring low prices. In the periphery, household work—carrying water, finding forage for goats or cows, and cultivating vegetables—often meant the difference between going hungry and having one meal a day.

In the current period, the increase in female-headed households is not just a cyclical phenomenon, not just a survival strategy associated with economic downturn or depression. It represents instead a secular change, which has already begun transforming gender relations and politics. Capitalism's household work units, most of which were once firmly in the control of adult males, are increasingly directed by women. Within the capitalist world, this is the first time that more than one-quarter of the world's women—who do both low-paid wage work and nonwage work—have run household units.

Female-headed households have risen throughout the world, in rich and poor countries alike. These units have increased as real household income declined, male earnings dropped, and the cost of living rose.[34] Based on census research in twenty-six countries, the Population Council found that a rise in female-headed households has occurred in eighteen of those countries. Council surveys indicate that the rise in female household heads is a global trend.

In the core, where some middle-class men once obtained a family wage that supported the whole unit, the rise of female-headed households is eroding the image that men are household "breadwinners." By 1990, for example, about 57 percent of adult women in the United States worked in the labor force; and in cities like Buffalo and Jersey City, women headed about 36 percent of households with children.[35]

United Nations' officials also found a growing proportion of female heads in eight Latin American and Caribbean countries.[36] The loss of remittances from migrant husbands, abandonment by husbands and children, and the flight or migration of women who supported children all contributed to the rise of female-headed households there.[37] As a result of migration, male death, desertion, and divorce, many women kept families going virtually on their own; and women "shouldered an unequal burden in coping with poverty at the household level."[38] The migration of men does not necessarily mean that women make independent decisions on expenditure and work. Some economically independent women still exhibit social dependence on their spouses. Although increasing rates of marital separation and divorce (partly resulting from urbanization) have changed life for middle-aged and elderly women, they may not alter young women's expectations about partnerships with men.[39]

Even where men remain in the household, many families have come to rely primarily on the income provided by women. So while women are not the only adult in the household, they are nonetheless its "de facto" head. In Buenos Aires, for example, households where women are the main economic contributors now make up one out of every three households.[40] As extended families grow and as more households share living quarters, more married women have become breadwinners.[41] More rural households in China have "virtually become female operated and headed."[42] In the southern African country of Lesotho, two-thirds of households are "de facto female-headed."[43]

Women now head up to one-third of households around the world.[44] A more conservative estimate is that female-headed households constitute 25 to 35 percent of households in some regions. The organization's researchers also note that many of these households are poor, especially those in the South.[45] Indeed, even the one-third estimate may be conservative, if researchers count women who earn most of the household income in all "household" types (including nuclear, single-parent, extended, couple, and domestic network arrangements). For example, the U.S. Women's Bureau has found that, for the first time ever, U.S. wage-earning women now earn most of the household income.[46] This means that while there are a lot of single moms, there are also many men who are now largely dependent on women.

Although women head between one-quarter and one-third of the world's households, a great deal of variation exists between regions. In Mexico, 30 percent of wage-earning women now generate most of the household income.[47] Although some scholars argue that about 20 percent of all African households are female-headed, women in Zambia are thought to head between 30 and 60 percent of households.[48] In Sudan, up to 50 percent of migrant and refugee families are headed by women.[49] Although they have low wages and small nonwage incomes, women typically use their meager earnings to pay for food, shelter, clothes, and education, while husbands withhold "five to six times the proportion withheld by wives."[50]

Along with the recent interest in the steadfastness of extended families, scholars note a significant rise in female-headed extended families. During the five-century rise of wage labor, nuclear families gradually replaced extended families, particularly in the core. But this process seems to be stabilizing, if not reversing itself. According to Sylvia Chant, the ongoing decline of real wages, the loss of access to land, and the shortage of housing may lead to more extended, communal arrangements, sometimes connecting women from two or more households. Although most of the world's extended families are now poor families, more middle-class and single-parent families may become extended, which some observers believe could make household relations more egalitarian and also help reduce domestic violence.[51]

In addition, many extended families today are also headed by women, a pattern that many scholars have neglected. Although households usually become female-headed before adult women join the labor force, women often make a series of adjustments to make work and family life easier. As part of this adjustment process, women in countries like Mexico, Jamaica, Tanzania, Costa Rica, and Ecuador often choose to extend their households. In Querétaro, Mexico, female-headed households (including one-parent and extended families) made up 40 percent of a small, nonrandom sample of households studied in 1986.[52] The extension of households not only increases the well-being of its members, it usually leads to a more equitable sharing of resources and work.[53] Extended families often fare better during economic stress than nuclear ones. By bringing in relatives, adults can increase households' access to wages, reduce the level of expenditures for individual household members, and share the benefits of household members' reproductive work.[54] Furthermore, female networks form the basis of many kinds of production. In Zimbabwe, for example, 63 percent of female cooperative members are heads of households, which solidifies female economic independence and female control of cooperative organizing.[55]

The growth in family dependency on women's work and on female household heads means that women are gaining power in families, communities, and politics. As women run their own family units, and as young women become more autonomous when they move away from home to work in factories, other females learn that they, too, can acquire greater social independence.[56] In some rich and poor countries, boys do more housework, both because mothers have defined new socialization patterns and because fathers have adjusted their work patterns.[57] Just as the dominance of the male-headed household resulted in the articulation of a politics centered around male wage earners, the increase in female-headed households means the growing predominance of a politics based on female wage, and nonwage laborers. For the first time in history, the changes in material life, which were unleashed by global change after 1970, have placed nonwage issues on the political agenda. As one scholar has argued, "Unremunerated work became more vital than remunerated work."[58]

The rise of female-headed households and the growth of female work opened the century with the critical examination of nonwage work issues. We argue that the growth in the proportion of female household heads, the decrease in real incomes for men and women, and the changing occupational and geographical structures of global production served to shift labor's politics from one based largely on wage labor and the state, to one that also includes nonwage work. At the same time, capitalist development and recent actions taken by corporations and the state have exposed the separation between household and systemic patriarchy, allowing women to gain a stronger say in their families and communities. As we shall see, these changes have led to the rise of nonwage political struggles, which developed next to increasingly female-centered politics about employment and the state. Although shifts in the global economy initiated these social and cultural changes, these new political struggles would not have emerged without women's movements and egalitarian ethnic movements. Both of these movements have questioned why society values some work and some people but not others.

THE INCREASING IMPORTANCE OF GENDER IN SOCIAL ORGANIZATION AND POLITICS

Labor's intentional social change efforts, capital and the state's social engineering efforts, and the anarchic workings of the world-economy, which produce unintentional social change, create conditions that have undermined the dominant, male-headed model of household reproduction and introduced a new model based on female-headed households. In highly gender-divided households and social contexts, this global change may increase the separation between male and female household members.

Although ruling-class efforts to maximize global profits during the era of selective globalization, along with household patriarchy and racism, have contributed to this polarization, this change has also been promoted by economic chaos and the ways that labor reacts to new forms of global plunder and corporate desertion. The polarization of gender groups, which separates women, children, and elders from male adults and male teens, has social, cultural, geographical, and political implications. Family members are being raised by women more than ever, and women are playing a larger role in creating family and community culture. Adult males often work and live away from their children, and women are reinventing politics to respond to society and direct the development of social relations. Some adult men and teen boys are becoming even more peripheral to child rearing and elder care.

As part of the formation of enclaves and production centers that rely heavily on female wage workers, the global system has created female-centered enclaves of household reproduction. The formation of this pattern of women-centered wage and nonwage work is developing very gradually, and it may never characterize even the majority of global households. But this new work pattern is so striking that it is hard not to compare it with the "homelands" created by South Africa's apartheid regime. Since 1970, systemic patriarchal relations have established a sexist "homeland model," which may become the dominant pattern of social reproduction. Selective globalization and its particular structure of systemic patriarchy may increase women's workloads and "endow" women with the mixed task of sustaining households on their own.

In this context, it is appropriate to examine the household pattern developed in Lesotho, where reproduction was almost completely centered around female household heads. Work and household reproduction patterns in Lesotho developed because apartheid officials in South Africa only allowed Lesotho's men to immigrate if they worked in mines. Male mine workers were forced to live in single-sex hostels, and they were only allowed annual visits with their families in Lesotho. The state imposed this gender divide to split up families and weaken labor. This class-defined patriarchal structure, coupled with patriarchal culture, encouraged many male mine workers to establish second families in South Africa. Male mine workers who did so often stopped sending their meager remittances to families back home and sometimes stopped visiting their first families altogether. Just as men in Lesotho were courted by mine managers, women in Lesotho looked for urban domestic jobs and export-zone employment. Today, in postapartheid South Africa, officials are trying to dismantle institutionalized gender biases and family-splitting employment policies.[59] But feminists and other critics have questioned whether the new South Africa has significantly improved the lives of its working-class majority and whether it can.

Throughout the world's production enclaves, it is clear that a capital- and often state-sanctioned gender divide is being erected. Gender relations are created through class relations. Just as gender reveals class, class reveals gender. It is important to go beyond recognizing that we do not live in a genderless, classless, or unracialized world; our thinking and scholarship needs consider how gender and class reveal ethnicity and racism, just as racism always reveals gender and class.

When one studies the emergence of the world-economy's ethnic relations, something surprising becomes evident: more of the world's women are defined in ethniclike terms. As adult women become more separated from adult men, and adult and teen females are organized more directly by capital and the state, women and men begin to form more distinct social groups. As more women become directly subordinated by the rules of selective globalization, they are treated increasingly like a subordinate *ethnic* group. Gender is becoming "racialized" in new ways. Racist models for organizing the majority of the world's workers are now being redeployed to organize large groups of female workers as subordinate "ethnic workers." Gender relations are becoming more racist, and racism is broadening to include more working people.

Gender and ethnicity increasingly overlap. In fact, within the global labor force, firms and states have tried to organize gender groups in much the same way that they have tried to organize ethnic groups. This interactive process has been going on throughout the history of capitalism. Males from particular ethnic groups have been mobilized by capital and sent overseas. For example, poor men from China were sent without their families to work on U.S. railroads, and men from Mexico were sent to the United States to work on farms as *braceros*. In the nineteenth century, mill owners brought teen girls to textile factories in New England and utilized them as cheap labor. In export enclaves today, teen girls and young and middle-years women make up the dominant labor force in global sweatshops. Today, women, girls, and male children have been mobilized by capital on a massive scale and sent overseas to work in the international sex trade. In all of these cases, capital has mobilized ethnic groups according to gender criteria or gender groups according to ethnic criteria. Genderization and ethnicization go together.

Firms and states have increasingly inserted gender separators as they organize ethnic groups; eventually, the organization of these overlapping "apartheids" may encourage the rise of cross-group rebellions.

The decline of male-headed households and the rise of female household heads in the last thirty years were first noted in places like Lesotho, where there was the imposition of engendered and racialized poverty. They have also been observed in low-income, urban areas in the United States. The most racist methods of organizing labor in the periphery, like that developed by the apartheid government in Lesotho, are similar to the sexist, racist, inner-city model that has emerged in the core. In the United States, poor, female-headed, African American and Latino households in Detroit or Chicago are organized along similar lines. An examination of the hard, underpaid work done by women in South Africa's apartheid "homelands" and the work done by low-income, urban, African American women in the "inner cities" of the United States provides a glimpse of how female labor may be structured in coming decades.

The social overlap between gender, class, and ethnicity suggests that more of the world's working-class women may be increasingly organized as a subordinate "gendered-ethnic" group. For the first time on a global scale, adult women and teen girls are being separated from adult men. They are being organized as a distinct social group. This current organization of female labor resembles the way ethnic groups have been organized on a world scale. Low-income subordinate ethnic groups have been joined by female working people, many of whom have been historically defined as women of color.

Class relations are expressed not simply in stark, clearly defined class terms, a point made by antislavery scholar Kevin Bales.[60] Instead, class is becoming expressed more often in racist terms. Laboring females, and the households they support, are being defined in the same way that racialized, subordinate groups have been characterized. But while previous racist regimes allowed coupled, adult females and males to sustain households together, global pressures may push many adult females and males apart for long periods of their adult lives. As a result, more adult heterosexual household members will be deprived of regular intimacy and sex, and fewer children will be reared by both biological parents.

If gender does become more "ethnicized," and if class continues to be defined through racism, we may see capital and the state structuring more female labor in ways that resemble racist forms of production and reproduction. If this occurs, we could expect to see more women fighting racism and institutional sexism, not just household patriarchy. As the burdens imposed on women increase, female workers may work harder to eliminate the linked inequities in the world-system. New forms of political struggle for women and men have grown out of the different relationships that workers had with firms, states, and laboring networks. New wage and nonwage work relations are at the heart of new social movements. It is only by examining how households, gender, and ethnic relations have developed since 1970 that we can understand the new global labor movements.

LABOR'S POLITICS AS VIEWED FROM THE HOUSEHOLD

The world today is marked by the widespread emergence of new global social movements. These movements often center around laboring women and their efforts to sustain households through wage work and state transfers and services and through nonwage activities. In the period between 1870 and 1970, when wage labor was dominated by male household heads, development was characterized by the geographic expansion of the world-system. During this period, male-centered labor movements focused on changing the institutions of wage labor and the state. But in the contemporary period, work has changed in significant ways, prompting the emergence of new movements that address wage work and state policies.

New movements have emerged partly because women have assumed a larger responsibility for supporting households. Contemporary movements cannot be understood without recognizing that "work" refers to both wage and nonwage activities.

Movements today often raise issues relating to changes in wage and nonwage work, the declining support of the state for labor, and problems relating to gender and ethnic equality.

It is useful to conceptualize global struggles across a continuum. This continuum can be visualized in the following way. On the left, institutional struggles are directed against capital and the state. On the right, diversifying struggles try to create noncapitalist, democratic, and egalitarian relationships and social networks. In the middle are hybrid varieties of struggles, which have both institutional and diversifying aspects.

After 1970, social movements continued to fight the world-system's formal institutions. Working-class movements that try to change relationships between labor and the formal institutions of the firm and the state are here called *institutional struggles*. For example, institutional struggles include strikes against employers and demonstrations against the state, as movements seek higher wages or increased funding for welfare or education. Historically, scholars have focused their attention on labor's institutional struggles because they deal with central economic and political institutions: capital and the state. Movements challenging these institutions have grown in strength as capital became more concentrated and the state assumed a larger responsibility for ensuring the daily and generational reproduction of labor. Between 1850 and 1970, many institutional movements centered around the male wage and on maintaining or extending white, male privilege.

In general, institutional politics grow out of labor's connections with wage labor and with the state. Movement politics reflect the dominant institutions that have confronted labor during the last five hundred years. Fighting for higher wages, increased state benefits, and a greater say in decision-making have been key demands of laboring communities. As labor's dependency on the capitalist world-economy grew, its politics increasingly reflected its ties with its central institutions. In many cases, labor movement politics expressed worker hopes for a better position within these institutions.

Diversifying politics, by contrast, simultaneously grow out of workers' inability to rely on the global system for their well-being and, equally important, their ability to rely on themselves. In the contemporary world, worker households have been forced to rely on themselves, particularly since they have been deserted by employers and the state. The politics of diversifying movements reflects workers' knowledge that institutional support is weaker than ever and that laboring households and laboring networks largely support themselves. These networks are now beginning to imagine how production could be organized to sustain working people, how political practices could be developed that take worker households' needs and ideas into account. Diversifying politics evolve out of household-based survival strategies and become group or community survival strategies. These politics reflect the sphere of nonwage work and informal community political and practices. Although workers have long practiced diversifying politics (including during periods of colonial conquest and incorporation), they have re-emerged in particularly strong forms in the periphery, semiperiphery, and core since 1970.[61]

Both institutional and diversifying struggles reflect labor's politics. Both types of politics, and their hybrid forms, grow out of worker efforts to reproduce households and create culture and the economy in ways that benefit working people. Both sets of politics will play vital roles in exposing and transforming the hierarchical world-economy.

THE WORLD IS CHANGING; SO, TOO, ARE WORKING-CLASS MOVEMENTS

Although definite similarities exist between the institutional struggles of the pre- and post-1970 periods, the character of many struggles against capital and the state has changed in recent years. With the change in work and gender relations, labor's increasing dependence on female work has altered the political terrain of class struggle, and this is true in both formal and informal arenas. In the formal arena, new social movements have introduced a stronger concern with wage equity for all workers, and these movements often fight for state policies that support families.

The period since the 1970s has also been characterized by the emergence of new nonwage movements and new women-centered movements. These diversifying movements explore the possibility of organizing alternative, noncapitalist relations. Their goal is to create new ways of organizing social, cultural, political, and economic relations. Rather than fighting to change the system's dominant institutions, as do antifirm and antistate movements, contemporary diversifying struggles try to find ways for labor to survive outside the capitalist market, away from the state's jurisdiction and away from class rule. One example of a diversifying struggle is the regional movement to establish worker-run producer cooperatives. Other new, informal movements address the issues of everyday life and emphasize the need for a comprehensive approach to social reproduction. Nonwage work and living conditions, along with domestic violence and environmental degradation, are some of the other issues raised by these movements. Some diversifying movements create new networks that enable households to live more fully outside of profit-oriented, market-driven institutions. Many of these movements believe that work should be reorganized around the reproduction of households and communities, not around employment, the market, and the state.

The post-1970s world is changing how workers live, how workers think about everyday life. Rather than remaining fragmented and bound within nation-states, many labor movements have become global. Both institutional and diversifying movements have a global presence, and they are both increasingly women-centered. Although women and men participate in these movements, many of the movements reflect women's growing presence in work and at home, and they challenge increasing levels of direct and indirect exploitation.

The emergence of labor's new global labor movements is beginning to present a major challenge to capital and the state. Both institutional and diversifying movements can be antisystemic. Institutional movements challenge the world-system from the inside; diversifying movements oppose it from the outside. Their simultaneous efforts disrupt the system.

The growth of women-centered and feminist movements is much more than a gender-based phenomenon: it is also a class-based phenomenon. As movements challenge capital's use of direct and indirect exploitation, they also fight ethnic injustice. Women-centered movements address the reproductive conditions of male labor, just as much as they address the social reproduction of female labor. Women's movements are labor movements. Women's movements form part of global, national, and regional class struggles, and they comprise some of the global efforts to challenge the anarchic world-system.

Since 1970, networks of women have participated in and led broad-based movements that address class inequities. Many women-centered movements, using both institutional and diversifying approaches, challenge the ways that the global system has restricted their social options. Women in these movements are not just fighting for themselves, and they are rarely fighting alone. They are also fighting for men, children, and elders, whose lives intersect in a global production system based on unpaid, unappreciated nonwage work.

As selective globalization has intensified development in parts of the core and halted development in parts of the South, new profit-making structures have wreaked havoc all over the world. In response, laboring people in cities, agricultural areas, export enclaves, and rain forests have fought back and tried to initiate new ways to live. Many movements have opposed the increased exploitation of female labor, the continual creation of cheap labor, what some scholars have called the "feminization" of the global labor force, and the global reduction of workers' wages.

Women-centered movements have criticized transnational agencies that expect women and girls to make up the losses induced by shrinking state programs and subsidies. Feminist movements have also criticized capital's destruction of the environment, which has made it even more difficult to retrieve water, cultivate food, find firewood, and keep children healthy. Women have also searched for ways to stop sex-trade recruiters who entrap young girls.

Selective globalization made it much harder for most workers—particularly those in the South—to survive on an everyday basis. As gender and ethnic hierarchies were recast after 1970, working people recognized that the benefits offered by the world-economy were limited, particularly for women and subordinate ethnic groups.

Although institutional and diversifying movements vary greatly, they all respond to the world-economy's uneven development. Many also respond to social differentiation, sexism, and racism. Both types of movements share common roots that relate to the historical formation of an unequal, gender-, age-, ethnic-, and class-based hierarchy. When contemporary social movements challenge the world-economy's inequality, they alter global choices. Some global labor movements organize working people to change the way the system operates—by raising wages, improving working conditions, increasing workers' power in public and private settings, and increasing state benefits for working families. Other movements organize workers to construct new social relations and then build the frameworks for new societies, which would allow labor to design, control, and benefit from development. When labor movements use the second approach, the diversifying approach, they communicate the idea that the real society does not reside in the formal institutions of the world-economy but is instead located at home, in self-designed networks, where new societies are being built.

Just as the public and private spheres of life cannot be neatly separated, worker movements, which grow out of the overlapping relations between wage and nonwage work, cannot be neatly separated. At one level, these movements are one and the same movement. But social divides often push movements in different directions, sometimes to fight racism and sometimes, unfortunately, to promote it. Although labor's separate efforts are abstractly linked, the global division of labor is pulling adult women and men apart, inhibiting an understanding of the historic connections between the engendered wage and nonwage work hierarchy, and between institutional and diversifying politics.

Many new women-centered movements can be seen as growing out of what Catherine Coquery-Vidrovitch describes as broad working-class traditions. Organized by groups of women, political activities "reflect daily life that includes sharing tasks, concerns and amusements."[62] An increasingly important stage for women-centered movements is not the factory floor in isolation from the home but the factory in relationship to the home. Informal terrains are also important, placing the kitchen, the hearth, the yard, the street, the neighborhood, and labor's informal markets at the center of politics. All these locations are sites where laboring women, men, and households have begun "reclaiming the commons." Mariarosa Dalla Costa has argued that the rise of these reproduction-centered movements are necessary, if people are to reverse the five-hundred-year-old global enclosure process.[63]

A theoretical and potential connection always exists between factory-floor and home-centered protests, whether it is visible or not. There is also an intimate, obvious, and historical connection. Political actions that reclaim the commons through environmental, antistate, and self-empowering actions—creating women-run producing and marketing networks that bypass systemically driven ones—provide a strong base for subsequent actions: confronting employers in large export factories and in geographically dispersed putting-out operations.

As both wage laborers and nonwage workers, adult women and their household members create value that sustains themselves and the world-economy. More than any group of labor, women and girls have occupied both income-generating spheres. Rather than seeing their work lives improve and "modernize," women and girls have found that the level of direct and indirect exploitation has increased. Because women have a double workload, they join together the two spheres of direct wage exploitation and indirect nonwage exploitation. As they work, they can obtain a comprehensive understanding of total work relations. The new emphasis on labor's total workload helps distinguish contemporary political struggles from previous ones.

Contemporary politics grew out of the five-hundred-year development of the world-economy. The world-economy has long been based on the subjugation of labor, particularly on wage labor. Wage labor itself relies on uncompensated and low-paid nonwage work, which has been done primarily by women and girls. Moreover, low-paid wage labor by women and other undervalued ethnic and age groups has been a key component of the system.

During the last century, women have been drawn into wage work during recessions, a cyclical process that has helped fuel the engine of capital accumulation. When the rate of profit falls, the lowest paid workers in the world (women and girls) were drawn into wage work. Their increased participation, along with technological changes, major increases in the consumption of producer and consumer goods, and the reorganization of the global division of labor, helped increase profit levels and recharge the global system, allowing it to survive. In fact, the employment of female labor in alternating periods of long-term structural development recharged the system so much that the reintroduction of adult male laborers generally promoted profitability for a very long time.

In the current period, when expansion has become core-centered and often enclave-specific, employers are trying to use female labor as a way to prevent profits from falling. The utilization of female labor has a new historical meaning in this context. It is unlikely that this strategy of further exploiting female labor will provide sufficient fuel for the engine of global development. What is different in this structural period is that the process of global accumulation is no longer expansive and intensive but selectively intensive. The system is no longer endlessly flexible and relentlessly expansionary; the geographical limits of the world have been reached, and the system is now feeding on its already industrialized regions. The system's limitations are more obvious. Working people, including large numbers of worker households in the core, have learned that they cannot rely on the global system to provide security. More people now question how the system works and ask what its continuation will mean.

Diverse groups of female labor are at the heart of the process of challenging the world-economy's power-holders. This is partly because most women can more easily see the totality of work relations. Laboring women and girls now tend to do increasingly heavy amounts of directly and indirectly exploited work. Because they form this crucial portion of the world's labor force, they can more easily see the connections between wage and nonwage struggles. This ability has helped movements link underprivileged women in the North and South.[64] Women, who typically straddle wage and nonwage spheres, are acquiring the ability to organize links between different ethnic groups and between labor in the periphery, semiperiphery, and core.

As both formal and informal workers, women can more easily see how wage work creates value and how nonwage work creates multidimensional values, which simultaneously support and undermine capitalism. Institutional struggles challenge how capitalist value is produced, and nonwage workers try to change or subvert the terms of its production. They may also try to challenge the power relations that uphold this form of exploitation. Diversifying struggles grow out of the double-sided nature of nonwage work. Traditionally, this work has sustained the system. But as working people organize their own work and develop these independent and/or collective work skills, nonwage workers can also imagine the possibility of organizing their own societies.

Before we explore the many variations of institutional movements that are directed against capitalist firms and states, and the many diversifying movements, it is important to recognize the significance of these movements. In general, we are optimistic about the ability of global labor movements to change social and economic relations. Social relations are increasingly shaped by selective globalization, which ties together some parts of the world around the core but also marginalizes much of the world. As the world becomes more integrated and more fragmented, diverse movements can provide options to workers who have been disconnected from the world-economy and marginalized. Institutional and diversifying movements may help to change social priorities and to create institutional alternatives that are more democratic and egalitarian.

There are a number of reasons why labor's women-centered movements, in particular, may undermine the global system and create new social relations that could replace the anarchic global economy in many parts of the world. The movements that address both wage and nonwage work issues and attempt to subvert the gender and age divisions that separate working-class households into fragmented components are extremely important. Households are divided along gender and age lines. Household members find their age identity and power relationships being redefined as they grow older. These changing social identities have split households and limited their ability to organize against formal institutions. Social movements that undermine the gender divide offer new opportunities to unite workers.

Movements that address wage and nonwage work also provide ways to fight ethnic divides. One way to contest global racism is to address the divide between wage and nonwage workers. Working people involved in women-centered movements understand that wage and nonwage exploitation are connected. These "social reproduction" movements challenge the world-economy's underlying structure, where unequal amounts of nonwage work in the South and North sustain both global accumulators and the laboring class. Because this issue is very important, especially to economically disadvantaged ethnic groups in the North and South—the vast majority of the world's population that needs to heavily rely on nonwage income—total work movements bridge the gap between workers in the South and North.

These comprehensive labor movements also provide a critique of capitalist culture and of the notion that participation in the system will eventually lead to better wages, more generous state benefits, greater democracy, and increasing social equality. This is because many contemporary labor movements develop in contexts where economic and environmental degradation is obvious, and they also provide an environmental critique of the system.

Finally, diversifying labor movements have outlined economic alternatives to global capitalism. These movements conduct social experiments and develop new ways of sustaining households, social networks, communities, and regions. As they design and build noncapitalist relationships that sustain regions, they show others how to grow through multi-ethnic and multicultural connections. The world's labor movements are teaching each other how to design and build the social relations that will form the basis of new ways of living.

Social change takes place through much more than the global labor force and the state. Change occurs through many social constellations, including households, gender and age groups, ethnic groups, work environments, class structure, and labor's social movements. All of these constellations are, of course, always changing. Processes involved with the degradation of work and living environments are analyzed in the next chapter. Subsequent chapters explore the emergence of antibusiness movements, state-directed and antistate movements, and diversifying movements that attempt to build new microworlds to increase political participation and to create work-based equality. An examination of these overlapping movements shows how different laboring groups reshape and restructure the world around them.

NOTES

1. Louise A. Tilly, *Industrialization and Gender Inequality* (Washington, D.C.: American Historical Association, 1993), 4.
2. Sylvia Chant, *Women and Survival in Mexican Cities: Perspectives on Gender, Labour Markets, and Low-Income Households* (Manchester: Manchester University Press, 1991), 16.
3. Helene Pellerin, "Global Restructuring and International Migration: Consequences for the Globalization of Politics," in Khosrow Fatemi, ed., *The Maquiladora Industry: Economic Solution or Problem?* (New York: Praeger, 1990).
4. Chant, *Women and Survival*, 203.
5. Ruth Milkman, "Union Responses to Workforce Feminization in the United States," in Jane Jenson and Rianne Mahon, eds., *The Challenge of Restructuring: North American Labor Movements Respond* (Philadelphia: Temple University Press, 1993), 229.
6. Chant, *Women and Survival*, 218.
7. Chant, *Women and Survival*, 219.
8. See G. Sen and C. Grown, *Development, Crises and Alternative Visions: Third World Women's Perspectives* (New York: Monthly Review Press, 1987); Jeanne Vickers, *Women and World Economic Crisis* (London: Zed, 1991); Lourdes Benería and Shelly Feldman, eds., *Unequal Burden: Economic Crises, Persistent Poverty and Women's Work* (Boulder, Colo.: Westview, 1992); Mercedes Gonzáles de la Rocha, *The Resources of Poverty: Women and Survival in a Mexican City* (Cambridge: Blackwell, 1994); Ann Leonard, ed., *Seeds 2: Supporting Women's Work around the World* (New York: Feminist Press, 1995); William Greider, *One World, Ready or Not: The Manic Logic of Global Capitalism* (New York: Simon and Schuster, 1997).
9. Nora Lustig, *Mexico: The Remaking of an Economy* (Washington, D.C.: Brookings Institution, 1992), 72; Duncan Green, *Silent Revolution: The Rise of Market Economies in Latin America* (London: Cassell, 1995), 103; Winthrop P. Carty and Elizabeth Lee, *In the Shadow of the First World: The Environment as Seen from Developing Nations* (Chicago: Chicago Review, 1995), 155; Lois Ann Lorentzen and Jennifer Turpin, "Introduction," in Lois Ann Lorentzen and Jennifer Turpin, eds., *The Gendered New World Order: Militarism, Development and the Environment* (New York: Routledge, 1996), 8.

Households, Class, and the Emergence of Women-Centered Labor Movements   183

10. Keena Owoh, "Gender and Health in Nigerian Structural Adjustment: Locating Room to Maneuver," in Rae Lesser Blumberg, Cathy A. Rakowski, Irene Tinker, and Michael Monteón, eds., *Engendering Wealth and Well-Being: Empowerment for Global Change* (Boulder, Colo.: Westview, 1995), 192.

11. Valentine M. Moghadam, "Gender Dynamic of Restructuring in the Semiperiphery," in Blumberg, Rakowski, Tinker, and Monteón, *Engendering Wealth*, 22–23.

12. Rae Lesser Blumberg, "Introduction," in Blumberg, Rakowski, Tinker, and Monteón, *Engendering Wealth*, 15; Owoh, "Gender and Health," in Blumberg, Rakowski, Tinker, and Monteón, *Engendering Wealth*, 186; Cathy A. Rakowski, "Conclusion," in Blumberg, Rakowski, Tinker, and Monteón, *Engendering Wealth*, 286–287.

13. Blumberg, "Introduction," in Blumberg, Rakowski, Tinker, and Monteón, *Engendering Wealth*, 286.

14. Mayra Buvinic, "Women in Poverty: A New Global Underclass," *Foreign Policy*, no. 108 (Fall 1997): 42–43.

15. Chant, *Women and Survival*, 10.

16. Diane Lauren Wolf, *Factory Daughters: Gender, Household Dynamics, and Rural Industrialization in Java* (Berkeley: University of California Press, 1992), 117.

17. Wolf, *Factory Daughters*, 195.

18. Buvinic, "Women in Poverty," 45–46.

19. Devaki Jain and Nirmala Banerjee, "Introduction," in Devaki Jain and Nirmala Banerjee, eds., *Tyranny of the Household: Investigative Essays on Women's Work* (New Delhi: Shakti, 1985), xv.

20. Iftikhar Ahmed, *Technology and Rural Women: Conceptual and Empirical Issues* (London: Allen and Unwin, 1985), 331.

21. Aihwa Ong, *Spirits of Resistance and Capitalist Discipline: Factory Women in Malaysia* (Albany: SUNY Press, 1987), 152.

22. Lourdes Arizpe and Josefina Aranda, "Women Workers in the Strawberry Agribusiness in Mexico," in Eleanor Leacock and Helen I. Safa, eds., *Women's Work: Development and the Division of Labor by Gender* (South Hadley, Mass.: Bergin and Garvey, 1986), 191–193.

23. Chant, *Women and Survival*, 220.

24. Peter Tacon, "A Global Overview of Social Mobilization on Behalf of Street Children," in William E. Meyers, ed., *Protecting Working Children* (London: Zed, 1991), 87.

25. Chant, *Women and Survival*, 220.

26. Patricia Allatt and Susan Yeandle, *Youth Employment and the Family: Voices of Disordered Times* (London: Routledge, 1992), 14.

27. Laurel Bossen, "Gender and Economic Reform in Southwest China," in Huguette Dagenais and Denise Piche, eds., *Feminism and Development* (Montreal: McGill-Queen's University Press, 1994), 228–229.

28. Bosen, "Gender and Economic Reform," in Dagenais and Piche, *Feminism and Development*, 234–235.

29. Bosen, "Gender and Economic Reform," in Dagenais and Piche, *Feminism and Development*, 207–208, 210.

30. Bosen, "Gender and Economic Reform," in Dagenais and Piche, *Feminism and Development*, 205.

31. Bosen, "Gender and Economic Reform," in Dagenais and Piche, *Feminism and Development*, 201.

32. Bosen, "Gender and Economic Reform," in Dagenais and Piche, *Feminism and Development*, 215.

33. Elisabeth Croll, "Some Implications of the Rural Economic Reforms for the Chinese Peasant Household," in Ashwani Saith, ed., *The Re-Emergence of the Chinese Peasantry: Aspects of Rural Decollectivisation* (London: Croom Helm, 1987), 111, 124, 129.

34. Helen I. Safa, "Development and Changing Gender Roles in Latin America and the Caribbean," in Hilda Kahne and Janet Z. Giele, eds., *Women's Work and Women's Lives: The Continuing Struggle Worldwide* (Boulder, Colo.: Westview, 1992), 71; Martha Alter Chen, "The Feminization of Poverty," in Noeleen Heyzer, ed., *A Commitment to the World's Women: Perspectives on Beijing and Beyond* (New York: United Nations Development Fund for Women, 1995), 24–26.

35. Michelle Fine and Lois Weis, *The Unknown City: The Lives of Poor and Working-Class Young Adults* (Boston: Beacon, 1998), 190–191.

36. Buvinic, "Women in Poverty," 43.

37. Buvinic, "Women in Poverty," 43.

38. Martha Alter Chen, "The Feminization of Poverty," in Heyzer, *A Commitment to the World's Women*, 23.

39. Sylvia Chant and Cathy McIlwaine, *3 Generations, 2 Genders, 1 World: Women and Men in a Changing Century* (London: Zed, 1998), 114, 99.

40. Buvinic, "Women in Poverty," 45.

41. Safa, "Development and Changing Gender Roles," in Kahne and Giele, *Women's Work and Women's Lives*, 71, 75.

42. Elisabeth Croll, "Some Implications of the Rural Economic Reforms for the Chinese Peasant Household," in Saith, *The Re-Emergence of the Chinese Peasantry*, 126.

43. Alfonso Gonzalez and Jim Norwine, *The New Third World* (Boulder, Colo.: Westview, 1998), 101.

44. Chant, *Women and Survival*, 10.

45. York W. Bradshaw, "Introduction: The Enduring Importance of Education," *International Journal of Contemporary Sociology*, vol. 37, nos. 1–2 (June 1996): 6.

46. "Update to Beijing," TV conference, monitored by Judy Woodruff (Fall 1996); and "Working Women's Summit," Department of Labor, Women's Bureau (1997), TV conference.

47. Brígida García and Orlandina de Oliveira, "Gender Relations in Urban Middle-Class and Working-Class Households in Mexico," in Blumberg, Rakowski, Tinker, and Monteón, *Engendering Wealth*, 198.

48. Janice Jiggins, "Breaking New Ground: Reaching Out to Women Farmers in Western Zambia," in Leonard, *Seeds 2*, 18.

49. Eve Hall, "The Port Sudan Small-Scale Enterprise Program," in Leonard, *Seeds 2*, 66.

50. Judith Bruce, "The Economics of Motherhood," in Heyzer, *A Commitment to the World's Women*, 42.

51. Chant, *Women and Survival*, 25, 215–216.

52. Chant, *Women and Survival*, 19, 25, 214, 137.

53. Chant, *Women and Survival*, 221.

54. Chant, *Women and Survival*, 19.

55. Chant and McIlwaine, *3 Generations, 2 Genders, 1 World*, 223.

56. Lydia Kung, *Factory Women in Taiwan* (Ann Arbor, Mich.: UMI Research Press, 1983), xiv.

57. Chant and McIlwaine, *3 Generations, 2 Genders, 1 World*, 9.

58. Alain Supiot, "Perspectives on Work: Introduction," *International Labor Review*, vol. 135, no. 6 (1996): 611.

59. Gonzalez and Norwine, *The New Third World*, 101; Temma Kaplan, *Crazy for Democracy: Women in Grassroots Movements* (New York: Routledge, 1997), passim.
60. See Kevin Bales, *Disposable People: New Slavery in the Global Economy* (Berkeley: University of California Press, 1999).
61. See Sheila Rowbotham and Swasti Mitter, *Dignity and Daily Bread* (London: Routledge, 1994), passim.
62. Catherine Coquery-Vidrovitch, *African Women: A Modern History* (Boulder, Colo.: Westview, 1997), 233.
63. Women's Day on Food Conference. "Conference Proceedings," November 1996, Rome. Archival tapes. Institute on Theory and Praxis for Subsistence, Cologne, Germany.
64. Caroline Sweetman, *North–South Cooperation* (Oxford: Oxfam, 1994), passim.

Chapter 9

The Degradation of Social and Natural Work Environments

The wages and benefits that businesses and states provide workers have declined in recent years. To replace lost income from private and public sources, worker households have tried to secure wage work or organize nonwage work activities. But the degradation of social and natural environments in many regions has made it increasingly difficult for workers to generate income and obtain the resources they need to survive.

New social movements have emerged to address this situation. Because the burden of nonwage work continues to rest on women's shoulders, many of these movements have been organized by women. Many of the "environmental" movements that have emerged are not just about preserving nature but are also about protecting healthy work and living environments, a prerequisite for worker survival.

The degradation of social environments has been closely linked with the decline of state power in the periphery and semiperiphery. As states have weakened, government officials and nonstate actors have emerged to compete for political power. The corruption and violence associated with the emergence of government "kleptocracies," ethnic independence movements, insurrectionist guerrilla movements, mafias, and vigilantes have created uncivil societies. This has made it difficult for worker households to organize wage and nonwage work on a safe, sustainable basis. This competition has also been particularly disadvantageous for women, who have been subjected to violence and exploitation by men with guns. Indeed, young and adult men have increasingly used weapons to control women, children, and elders.

The decline of state power and the corresponding rise of criminal, warlord, ideological, and interpersonal violence have also contributed to the degradation of natural environments. The inability of states to provide public health infrastructures or reduce pollution has increased workers' exposure to illness and disease. But environmental degradation has also been the result of other developments, chief among them the expansion of commodity exports. The effort by businesses and states to increase the export of agricultural goods, timber products, and raw materials has displaced workers and deprived them of access to land, forests, water, and other natural resources. Where the expansion of commodity exports has led to the displacement of small farmers, which in many parts of the world are primarily women, this has disadvantaged women.

To appreciate these developments, let us look first at the degradation of social environments. Then we will examine developments that have contributed to the decline of natural environments. Both of them undermine workers' ability to survive in a changing world.

SOCIAL DEGRADATION

Economic crisis and political change have weakened states across the periphery and semiperiphery in recent years. Debt crisis, austerity programs, and falling commodity prices have reduced the ability of states to control monetary policy (to fix exchange rates or set interest rates), control trade and capital investment flow, adopt industrial policies, and provide jobs and social services. State officials have surrendered control to global institutions and markets, as well as private entrepreneurs, both foreign and domestic.[1] As a result, states' ability to manage their economies has diminished considerably.

In political terms, widespread democratization in the periphery and semiperiphery has significantly widened workers' participation in public life. Unfortunately, elected officials have less ability to manage public affairs, particularly economic ones, than the dictators and one-party regimes that preceded them. This has been particularly true in countries where democratization led to division, as it did in Czechoslovakia, Yugoslavia, the Soviet Union, Ethiopia, and Indonesia.[2] The twenty-six new states that emerged when these countries were partitioned, perhaps more if Kosovo is detached from Yugoslavia and Chechnya breaks from Russia, all have considerably less economic and political power than the singular states that preceded them. Globalization has undermined weak states in the periphery and semiperiphery much more than strong ones in the core.[3]

Recent developments have made it difficult for peripheral and semiperipheral states to exercise their sovereign rights or perform public functions. Some barely function as states at all. In Africa, the political power of states like Chad, the Congo, Ethiopia, Liberia, Somalia, and Sudan have deteriorated to such an extent that scholars now refer to them as "collapsed states."[4] In the Congo, one scholar has even argued that the state has "become a myth."[5] One indicator of this, Basil Davidson argued, was the fact that the state under Mobutu could not even maintain the country's roads: "In 1960, the authoritarian but well-ordered Belgian Congo has possessed 88,000 miles of usable road; by 1985, the total length of usable road was down to 12,000, of which only 1,400 were paved."[6] The government's 1997 collapse at the hands of a small guerrilla band that traveled down one of the country's few paved roads to the capital demonstrated just how far state power had withered.[7] Since then, the armies of six other African states and nine different domestic rebel militias have joined in fighting across the country, forcing hundreds of thousands of people from their homes.[8] The collapsed state has gone from legend to myth.

Recent economic and political change has weakened states throughout much, though not all, of the world. As state power deteriorated, government officials and nonstate actors have emerged to compete with states for political power. They often usurp functions (taxation), furnish goods (drugs, smuggled consumer goods), and provide services (protection) that states cannot. Three different kinds of actors now compete for power, each with separate social origins: corrupt officials; mafias and vigilantes; and ideological political movements.

Corrupt Officials

Corruption has long been a problem in weak states in the periphery. There, central governments have lacked the means to pay bureaucrats or the authority to control and monitor them. Many governments also allowed cronies and relatives to enrich themselves at public expense to secure their support for dictatorship. The result in many countries was the creation of large, corrupt, but also inefficient, bureaucracies. As Egyptian president Gamal Nasser once explained, "You imagine that we are simply giving orders and the country is run accordingly. You are greatly mistaken."[9]

Although corruption and inefficiency were widespread in peripheral states, the collapse of dictatorships, the rise of civilian governments, and the adoption of neoliberal economic policies have created new conditions that encourage official corruption to bloom and flourish, not only in the periphery but also in the postcommunist semiperiphery. The sale of public assets, or "privatization," by democratizing states has played a central role. Government officials in many states profited from the sale of public assets and secured lucrative enterprises for themselves. Corrupt government officials in Bulgaria, for instance, "stripped state enterprises of their assets . . . and sent the money abroad."[10] Western banks estimated that between $3 billion and $5 billion was looted by corrupt officials and their business partners, leaving the country without any economic resources. "You can't get a country more bankrupt than Bulgaria," one banker observed.[11] In Bosnia, corrupt officials stole $1 billion in public funds and foreign aid.[12] These thefts were, of course, dwarfed by the wholesale looting that went on in Russia and other post-Soviet republics, amounting to tens if not hundreds of billions of dollars.

While high-level government officials and their business allies looted public resources, lower-level bureaucrats and police enriched themselves by demanding bribes and payoffs. This endemic form of penny-ante corruption amounts to an unofficial tax on economic activity. Policemen demand bribes from motorists and payoffs from businesses and individuals who smuggle goods across borders, exacting private duties so that entrepreneurs can evade official tariffs. In the Ukraine, the "shuttle trade," as entrepreneurial smuggling is called, accounted for 11 percent of all imports. Because corrupt customs officials collected private duties on $2 billion worth of smuggled goods, the state lost an important source of public revenue.[13] In 1999, the state countered by firing one of every thirteen customs officers for bribery and the abuse of power, and the director of customs was arrested after he tried to withdraw $1.1 million from a foreign bank.[14] Although states have tried to curb corruption, it has been difficult. In Mexico City, the government fired nine hundred male traffic cops and replaced them all with female officers, hoping that women would be less likely to demand bribes, called the *mordida,* or "bite," from motorists.[15] But these were desperate measures.

In Colombia, almost half of the country's imports, worth nearly $6 billion, were brought into the country by smugglers with the assistance of corrupt officials.[16] In China, meanwhile, officials estimate that corrupt bureaucrats and army officers smuggled goods worth tens of billions of dollars into the country each year.[17]

Of course, the collection of informal taxes by corrupt officials places additional burdens on workers and businesses, who are also subject to official taxes, and deprives states of tax revenue. It also forces some businesses into bankruptcy if their goods are undersold by cheaper, smuggled imports.[18] The growth of male-run illegal enterprises, such as the drug trades; the smuggling of goods and also migrant workers; and the spread of semi-underground sex industries all contribute to official corruption because the entrepreneurs who ply these trades bribe officials to secure their "protection" from harassment and taxation by the state. Drug traffickers in Mexico, for instance, pay as much as $6 billion in bribes every year to corrupt government officials, police officers and, increasingly, U.S. customs and border guards.[19]

Mafias and Vigilantes

Historically, organized criminal gangs emerged in periods of rapid economic and political change, particularly in regions where states were weak. Mafias in Sicily, triads in China, and Yakuza in Japan all appeared first in the mid-nineteenth century, at a time when feudal economic relations and social obligations were dissolving and new capitalist relations were being introduced.[20] States in these peripheral regions were weak, and central authority was restricted and uncertain. Under these conditions, small groups of armed men inserted themselves into economic life, extorting money from merchants, workers, and vendors and providing them with "protection" from violence—in fact, immunity from assault by violent mafias—in return. In addition to providing protection in the absence of fully functioning police and judiciaries managed by the state, *mafias* (a term used generically to describe organized criminal gangs) soon took control of the vice industries: gambling, narcotics, and prostitution. The monopolies they established by their use of force provided the revenue that financed their economic growth and informal political power. Some even migrated to the United States, where they took root in Chinese and Italian immigrant communities.

Some of these activities resemble those carried out today. For example, the exploitation of teen girls and children by the global sex industry is particularly heinous. But the scope of mafia enterprise is much larger today, having gone from a regional to a global phenomenon. The sudden collapse of socialist economic relations and social obligations and the rapid introduction of new capitalist relations have created conditions in which mafias can thrive. This is particularly true where central state authority has been decisively weakened, as it has in Eastern Europe and post-Soviet states. Like their mafia predecessors, contemporary *mafiyas* have extorted money, levied private taxes on economic activity, and seized control of gambling, drugs, prostitution, illegal migration, smuggling, street vending, and a host of "legitimate" business enterprises as well.[21] Their ready use of violence helps them extort money—sometimes through organized kidnapping—secure monopolies, and intimidate state officials.[22]

Mafias have grown so large and powerful in some places that they have virtually usurped power from central governments. Government officials in India recently admitted that Bombay, the country's financial and entertainment capital, "is now dominated by some Mafia groups."[23] In Bosnia and in Albania, official governments barely maintain a presence in countrysides ruled by mafias and armed gangs.[24] And in Colombia, the drug cartels grew so strong that in 1989 they declared war on the state.[25] Their campaign of assassination and bombing resulted in 3,000 deaths and eventually forced the government to rescind its decision to extradite mafioso to the United States for trial.

Where states are weak and unable to protect business from crime, vigilantes have emerged to perform the state's "police" functions. In Brazil, businessmen and police organized death squads that murdered street children, and taxi-cab drivers organized assaults and lynchings of suspected criminals.[26] In South Africa, vigilante business groups, with names like the "Angry 13" and the "Cleaners," "track down known criminals and maim them," torture captives, and kill suspected criminals and street children.[27]

Ideological Political Movements

States in the periphery and semiperiphery face growing competition not only from corrupt government officials, mafias, and vigilantes but also from ideological political movements that organize groups along ethnic or class lines. Although these movements may try to promote a redistribution of resources to long-deprived groups, they may also trigger ongoing irregular warfare, which may destroy resources and put workers throughout the area at risk.

Historically, political movements have mobilized ethnic groups to obtain state power for themselves. When political movements organize ethnic minorities, they frequently demand separate states of their own, a demand that usually requires the partition of an existing state.[28] Karen in Burma, Kashmiris in India, Kurds in Turkey (and in Iran, Iraq, and Syria), Tamils in Sri Lanka, Palestinians in Israeli-occupied territories, Chechnyans in Russia, Armenians in Azerbaijan, Biafrans in Nigeria, and Kosovars in Yugoslavia have all organized ethnic minorities and mobilized irregular armies to secure states of their own. One scholar has estimated that there are 233 "politically active communal groups" worldwide, and about 120 of them are engaged in conflict with the governments of states where they reside.[29]

During most of the postwar period, separatist ethnic independence movements had little success. The only ethnic movement to win its independence from an existing state was the Awami League, which successfully broke from Pakistan and established Bangladesh in 1971.[30] But economic crisis and democratization in the 1990s provided new opportunities for ethnic movements. When dictators and one-party regimes fell in Czechoslovakia, Yugoslavia, the Soviet Union, and Indonesia, ethnic independence movements asserted themselves and claimed states of their own.[31] Their success encouraged widespread emulation. Separatists have since proliferated, presenting growing challenges to states across the periphery and semiperiphery.

When political movements organize ethnic majorities, they have sometimes tried to seize the state or use it to exclude or expel minority populations. Hindu "nationalist" movements in India have sought to exclude Moslems, Moslems in Indonesia have tried to exclude Chinese and Christians, some Jewish movements in Israel have tried to exclude Moslem Arabs and Palestinians, just as Protestants in Northern Ireland tried to exclude Catholics. In some respects, majorities see exclusion as a way to strengthen the state. But the divisive conflicts that exclusion engenders typically weaken central government authority. This is what occurred in Rwanda. There, government officials and political leaders of the Hutu majority undertook to murder the Tutsi minority and consolidate Hutu control of an ethnically homogeneous state. They murdered 800,000 in 1994 before being driven from the slaughter by a rebel Tutsi army. Many Hutu took refuge for a time in Zaire (the Congo), though most eventually returned to Rwanda.[32] The state that survived, led now by the Tutsi minority, was weaker, less representative, and more impoverished than the one that preceded it.

Political movements have not only organized along ethnic lines but have often mobilized class-based identities in their contest for state power. In Latin America, ethnic identities are less salient than in other regions, largely because different ethnic groups share a common language (Spanish or Portuguese) and a common religion (Catholicism). So opposition movements there have more often appealed to class-based identities and have mobilized guerrilla armies to struggle for power. The result has been bitter and protracted civil wars. In the 1980s, they raged in El Salvador, Guatemala, and Nicaragua. In the 1990s, they were waged in Colombia, Mexico, and Peru.[33] All of these struggles disrupted the ability of households to make ends meet, forced men into the service of regular and irregular armies, and displaced working families.

Class-based guerrilla movements are also found in Africa and India. In the Indian state of Bihar, armed irregulars hired by upper-caste landlords and militias organized by a lower-caste Marxist group called the "People's War Group" have clashed in reciprocating attacks.[34] But in many regions, class-based identities are linked with ethnic identities in some fashion.

Where ethnic- and class-based movements contest for state power, where violent conflict erupts, it is extremely difficult for merchants, workers, and farmers to ply their trades. This is particularly true where armed groups levy taxes and seize property to finance their campaigns and seize young men and children to fill their ranks and act as porters and cooks.[35] Violent conflict has forced many people to flee, and the number of political refugees amounted to 27 million in 1995 alone.[36] Flight may save workers' lives, but it deprives them of their livelihoods and forces them into refugee camps, where they are dependent on international relief organizations or subject to control by predatory gangs (usually both).[37] Once they are installed in refugee camps, it becomes difficult to leave, and refugees often languish in camps for years, even decades. In Bangladesh, Bihari refugees have been encamped since 1971; in Lebanon, Palestinian refugee camps date back to the 1940s.[38]

The corrupt officials, mafias, and ideological movements that compete for power in weakened states have separate origins. But they share some common features. First, their activities impose private taxes on workers and businesses. These levies burden workers who must also pay official taxes, and they deprive states of important revenues, forcing officials to raise taxes or cut services. Second, the violence they deploy cripples civil society, undermines the rule of law, puts workers at risk, discourages economic activity, drives people from their homes, and deprives them of their livelihoods. When violence increases, economic activity declines.[39]

Third, these activities are typically conducted by men with guns: police, mafias, vigilantes, and guerrillas. They use violence or the threat of violence to extort taxes, monopolize economic activity, and compete for formal or informal political power. Because they are all organized by men, along rigid gender lines, their emergence is particularly harmful to women. Women are excluded from armed male gangs and are exploited in the industries where they are employed as drug couriers, prostitutes, or indentured migrants.

Drug mafias rely on women to act as couriers, ingesting drugs in tiny balloons to escape detection. The "swallowers," as they are called, risk arrest and death if the packages containing heroin or cocaine burst in their intestines.[40] Mafias also rely on women to work in the industries they control. In the last decade, Russian *mafiyas* have transported as many as 400,000 women from the Ukraine to work in the sex industries of other countries.[41] Once they have been lured abroad, their passports are confiscated, they are threatened with violence by their mafia overseers, and they are forced to work in brothels to repay their "debts." In Israel, where many Ukrainian women labor in Tel Aviv brothels, women who file complaints against their captors are required to remain in jail until they testify. As a result, one Israeli official admitted, "I don't know of a single case where a woman chose to testify."[42]

Chinese mafias have smuggled migrants into the United States, where they work in sweatshops, brothels, and restaurants until they repay the $30,000 "fees" demanded by traffickers. When Gao Liquin, a woman from Fujian province in China, did not repay her debt, mafia kidnappers "raped Ms. Gao, cut off one of her fingers, hit her over the head with a television set and finally strangled her with a telephone cord."[43]

Ideological armies, meanwhile, rape and murder women to demonstrate their implacable determination to seize power. In the civil war in Algeria, Islamic guerrillas singled out civilian women and children for attack. "Often the killers cut victim's throats, burned them alive, gouged out their eyes, or hacked them to pieces."[44] This has been a pattern, too, of paramilitaries in Yugoslavia's civil wars, where assaults on women were designed to terrorize enemies and speed their flight, which facilitated "ethnic cleansing."

The violence directed at women by armed male groups is one of the consequences of declining state power and the disintegration of civil society in many regions. Where states have weakened and groups of armed men have emerged, women workers face increasing exploitation and risk. In extreme cases, they are wholly excluded from private employment and public life and are subjected to assault if they do not comply. In Afghanistan, the Taliban, an armed, male Islamic movement, has forced women from jobs and prohibited them from appearing in public without a male relative to escort them, meting out violence if they disobey. Women widowed by war and those without male relatives cannot easily survive under these conditions. But even where armed men do not take such extreme measures against women, women are vulnerable to their demands for taxes and labor.

Although state power in the periphery and semiperiphery has waned, state power in the core has not appreciably weakened in recent years. States in the core retain control of monetary policy and trade, and they manage efficient bureaucracies that collect taxes and provide substantial, though somewhat diminishing, social services. The police powers of core states have actually increased as a result of domestic "wars" against crime, drugs, and illegal immigrants. Their ability to exercise unilateral military power has also grown stronger, largely because the collapse of communist states reduced international restraints to military intervention by core states.

For workers in the core, the expansion of the state's police powers has been a problem because central and local governments have used their expanded authority to crack down on nonwage work activities. This has made it harder for workers to organize nonwage work, which many need to compensate for lost jobs and income from private firms and public benefit programs.

In the United States, for example, the central government has intensified efforts to deprive workers of income from nonwage work in the drug trades. The U.S. prison population has grown to two million, one-quarter of all prisoners worldwide, largely as a result of the government's war on drugs (two-thirds of federal prison inmates were convicted of drug-related crimes). The government's police power has also been used to curb illegal immigration and force unregistered workers from their jobs and from public benefit programs and schools. This has been the case in Western Europe as well, where states have cracked down on illegal immigration. The goal of the French government has been "zero immigration," reported Interior Minister Charles Pasqua.[45]

But while the federal government in the United States has tried to diminish the scope of some nonwage work activities, local governments have played a more significant role in reducing a wide range of nonwage work alternatives. Local officials have used their police powers to crack down on street vending, recycling, and panhandling, waging determined campaigns against itinerant merchants, squeegee washers, recyclers, beggars, vagrants, squatters, and renters in poor neighborhoods. For example, officials in Washington, D.C., evicted vendors from tourist spots. "I'm trying to do something legit," complained Charles Johnson, a T-shirt vendor. "I ain't out there selling no drugs . . . You've got to make some type of money."[46]

New York City mayor Rudolph Giuliani tried to ban vendors from a 144-block area, and he ordered police to arrest squeegee washers and other workers who plied street trades, saying he was trying to "strike the right balance" between street vendors and licensed businesses, which were losing customers to itinerant merchants.[47] In New York and in cities across the country, local governments adopted tougher antipanhandling laws. A study of 49 cities by the National Law Center on Homelessness and Poverty found that 62 percent passed new laws in 1994 and "one-fourth conducted police sweeps of shopping areas or trendy neighborhoods, and restricted homeless people's use of public places."[48] In some cities, officials seized grocery carts used by homeless people and bulldozed squatter camps.[49] Unlike poor countries, where poor homeless people regularly squat on unused land and build shantytowns, in core states it is virtually impossible for homeless workers to build shelter of their own. And if they find shelter in poor neighborhoods, they may be evicted by local redevelopment agencies that regularly clear "slums" and gentrify neighborhoods in the name of "urban renewal." In Houston, officials bulldozed homes rented by poor and elderly workers in the city's Fourth Ward, replacing their inexpensive housing with more expensive "market-rate" homes and a few subsidized units. "I know a lot of this is that these people rent, so they don't have any say-so," Elizabeth Bailes, the local mail carrier observed. "But it seems to me that if you've been in the same place for 40 or 50 years, you ought to have squatter's rights or something. These people aren't being looked out for."[50]

In one respect, states in the core are becoming more like the old communist states: they vigorously suppress nonwage work and unlicensed migration. Generally speaking, the expansion of the state's police powers and their use by government officials against nonwage workers have adversely affected the nonwage work environment. This has made it more difficult for workers, particularly poor workers in the nondrug trades, to secure income in lieu of formal employment.

ENVIRONMENTAL DEGRADATION

Recent events have also resulted in environmental degradation in the periphery and semiperiphery. Environmental destruction there has made it difficult for workers to obtain the resources they need to generate nonwage income, and it threatens their health and livelihoods. Environments around the world have deteriorated as a result of economic and political change. As the environment is degraded, women and girls have to work harder to help households survive.

Commodity Exports

During the 1970s and 1980s, producers and states across the periphery and semiperiphery expanded their production of export commodities. They did so in the 1970s to take advantage of high commodity prices. In the 1980s, they did so to repay the debts they owed foreigners (see chapter 4). But growing commodity supplies contributed to falling prices. So producers redoubled their efforts. Unfortunately, this only further weakened prices and placed even greater pressure on farm and forest ecosystems.

Recall that commodity prices fell for two reasons. They fell because peripheral supplies increased and because core demand fell, largely because new substitutionist technologies made it possible for the core to do without many peripheral products. While we earlier focused on this latter development, let us now return to the former (increasing supplies) because it more directly affects natural environments.

Producers in the periphery and semiperiphery were able to expand the production of agricultural commodities because they adopted new technologies that had recently become available. New hybrid seeds, synthetic fertilizers, chemical pesticides, and farm machinery—what have been described collectively as the "Green Revolution"—made it possible for farmers to increase yields and grow more food.[51] Unfortunately, the new technologies created a series of problems for farmers and environments, including the destruction of genetic diversity.

First, the new technologies enabled farmers to grow more food with less labor. So workers were displaced from Green-Revolution farms. Second, farmers with access to agricultural credit and loans from the state were able to purchase new technologies and expand their production. They soon bought out farmers who could neither obtain credit nor produce goods as cheaply. As Green-Revolution farmers consolidated their control of land, and farm sizes grew, small farmers were displaced. Third, large farmers typically grew crops they could sell abroad. They grew increasing quantities of feed grains and fruits and vegetables that were exported, not consumed locally. Food exports reduced the supply of subsistence foods and raised the price of staples consumed by domestic workers. As food prices rose, workers ate less. So the Green Revolution increased the quantity of food but also contributed to growing hunger. Fourth, the use of Green Revolution technologies increased pollution, largely because the heavy use of synthetic fertilizers and chemical pesticides contaminated water supplies used by rural and urban workers.

These developments deprived large numbers of workers of their customary access to agricultural land and employment and reduced the availability of subsistence foods. The declining availability of land and water and the degradation of agricultural resources have made it increasingly difficult for workers to generate the produce and income, or obtain the resources, they need to survive. The increasing production of timber, minerals, and hydroelectricity in the periphery and semiperiphery has had similar consequences.

In Papua New Guinea, timber exports grew from 640,000 cubic meters in 1980 to 2.7 million cubic meters in 1992, a four-fold increase.[52] The companies that obtained logging concessions paid villages only $15 million for timber worth $500 million, ruining ecosystems and livelihoods in the process. Topsoil has washed away and loggers destroyed farms with road cuts. Vincent Mutumutu saw his livelihood destroyed when "a bulldozer owned by a foreign logging company came crashing into [his] tiny farm of banana trees and watermelon vines, destroying the only source of income for his family of sixteen. 'I don't know what I will do now,' he said."[53]

Across the periphery, state officials, desperate for revenue, have sold timber, mining, and oil concessions to foreign and domestic firms. Government officials in Surinam sold concessions to Asian firms that opened 40 percent of the country's timber to loggers.[54] In Venezuela, officials adopted new laws that deprived small-scale miners of their claims and awarded gold and diamond concessions to large-scale firms, permitting them entry into ecologically fragile regions.[55] In Nigeria, foreign oil firms have polluted rivers, destroyed crops, and injured the health of Ogoni residents.[56]

The development of hydroelectric dams has also displaced workers and destroyed ecosystems. China's Three Gorges Dam, the largest hydroelectric dam in the world (600-feet high and one mile wide), would create a 400-mile lake on the Yangtze River and displace 1.3 million people.[57] The dam will capture silt that refreshes the topsoil of farms downstream and trap pollution and waste from farms and cities up river, creating what some scientists describe as a toxic "mudpie."[58] One scholar warned that displacement and pollution will create "an explosive social problem, and the dam region will become a hotbed of sustained upheaval for China."[59]

The intensification of agriculture, forestry, mining, and hydroelectric development deprives workers of their access to important natural resources; degrades soils, ecosystems, and water supplies; and drives workers into urban areas, where they confront environmental problems of a different sort.

Declining Public Health Infrastructures

Debts, falling commodity prices, and shrinking tax revenues have forced states in the periphery and semiperiphery to cut back benefits and reduce public spending. This has undermined the public health infrastructures that provide clean water, sanitation, family planning, education, and medical care. The influx of displaced rural workers into towns and cities in recent years has further strained inadequate public health infrastructures. These two developments—declining public health infrastructures and rising urban densities—have increased the incidence of disease and facilitated its spread, exposing worker households to chronic and deadly diseases and crippling their ability to work and survive. The number of people who have no access to a toilet, not even a decent pit latrine, increased in the 1990s to three billion. Even where latrines are available, they often act as breeding grounds for parasites and disease. "When you have a medieval level of sanitation, you have a medieval level of disease," said Akhtar Haneed Kahn, the author of a UN study on sanitation in Pakistan.[60]

Across the periphery and semiperiphery, water polluted by human sewage is a scourge that costs workers their money and their lives. In India, Usha Bhagwani must spend $4 a month to buy the kerosene she needs to boil water for her family.[61] Because this amounts to one-third of her monthly earnings, she cannot afford to boil water on a regular basis. As a result, two of her children died from water-borne disease, and the other two risked death from diarrhea, the most common symptom of water-borne disease. Worldwide, diarrhea kills more than 3 million annually, mostly children like Santosh and Sheetal Bhagwani.[62]

In Nairobi, Kenya, poor families wake before sunrise so they can obtain clean water before supplies run dry. "Getting water is a nightmare," said George Mwangi. "Most of the people here just go without water for up to two days at a time. The problem can only get worse because people keep moving to Nairobi."[63]

Across the periphery and semiperiphery, displaced rural workers are crowding into cities like Nairobi. By 2015, eight of the ten largest cities in the world will be located in the South.[64] Bombay is expected to grow from 15.1 million in 2000 to 26.2 million in 2015; Lagos from 10 million to 24.6 million.[65] Lagos now has a density of 143,000 people per square mile, compared to 11,400 per square mile in New York City.[66] Rapid urbanization is taking place in states where money for public health infrastructures is scarce, even nonexistent.

Even in China, which among peripheral states has recently recorded impressive rates of economic growth, the state lacks the resources or the determination to supplement the country's salt with iodine, resulting in more than 10 million cases of mental retardation caused by iodine-deficient diets.[67] The terrible air pollution associated with massive industrialization and urbanization kills 289,000 annually and reduces the gross domestic product by 3 to 8 percent each year.[68]

As public health infrastructures declined, disease has spread. Malaria and AIDS are the two biggest killers in the periphery, and their spread has wreaked havoc on worker households, with particularly adverse consequences for women and children.

Half a billion people contract malaria each year.[69] With simple precautions, like a $5 mosquito net and medical treatment, malaria is not usually fatal, though drug-resistant strains are increasing fatality rates. Worldwide, three million people who contracted malaria in 1995 died from the disease.[70] The disease can have devastating consequences for poor households, many of which cannot afford to purchase nets or antimalarial medicines. When malaria struck Mr. Jamaluddin's family in northern India, he lost one of his two wives and three of his seven children in a two-week period. He borrowed $350 to pay for medical care and funeral costs and so could not afford to continue leasing his tea-shop. "I don't know if my life will ever get back on track," said Mr. Jamaluddin, who went to work as a day laborer. "I'm completely shattered."[71]

Malaria is particularly hard on women and children. Women weakened by recent childbirth and children are particularly vulnerable to infection. And because many worker households use their scarce resources to treat men and boys rather than women and girls, females tend to have higher mortality rates.[72]

Much the same is true of AIDS. In Africa, women and girls are more vulnerable to HIV infection, both because it is more easily transmitted from men to women than from women to men, and because infected men are more promiscuous and "often coerce girls into sex or buy their favors with sugar-daddy gifts," according to a World Health Organization report.[73] As a result, more women than men are infected with the AIDS virus in Africa.[74]

Africa has been the region hardest hit by AIDS. Of the 30 million people with the disease worldwide, 21 million live in Africa, where states are unprepared or incapable of taking even rudimentary steps to prevent or treat the disease.[75] In sub-Saharan Africa, one of every four adults is infected, and life expectancy, which was 61 years in 1993, is expected to drop to 41 by 2005.[76] "In looking at global epidemics, one has to go back to the 16th century and the introduction of small pox in the Aztec population of Mexico to find anything on [a comparable] scale," said Lester Brown, president of the World Watch Institute.[77]

As the AIDS epidemic gathered force, it orphaned millions of children, 1.7 million in 1997 alone.[78] It has crippled worker households, which try to function with fewer living or working adults, and appreciably slowed economic growth, which was modest or negligible to begin with.[79]

The degradation of natural environments in the periphery and semiperiphery, which has been a product of economic and political change, has made it increasingly difficult for workers to obtain the resources—arable land, clean water, disease-free and nonviolent environments—they need to maintain their health and pursue their livelihoods. Many depend on these resources for their survival because they cannot obtain wage income from private firms or secure benefits from impoverished states. If they are denied access to these resources and medical care, if the quality of these resources or services is degraded, their ability to reproduce as multigenerational household units is seriously compromised. Many movements have emerged to address these social and environmental issues.

NOTES

1. Robert K. Schaeffer, *Power to the People: Democratization around the World* (Boulder, Colo.: Westview, 1997), 218–245.
2. Robert K. Schaeffer, *Severed States: Dilemmas of Democracy in a Divided World* (Lanham, Md.: Rowman & Littlefield, 1999), 195–241.
3. Robert K. Schaeffer, "State and Devolution: Economic Crises and the Devolution of U.S. Superstate Power," *International Journal of Sociology of Agriculture and Food* 4 (1994): 47–63.
4. William I. Zartman, *Collapsed States: The Disintegration and Restoration of Legitimate Authority* (Boulder, Colo.: Rienner, 1995), passim.
5. Basil Davidson, *The Black Man's Burden: Africa and the Curse of the Nation-State* (New York: Times Books, 1992), 257.
6. Davidson, *The Black Man's Burden*, 257.
7. Howard W. French, "Zaire's Power Vacuum Sucks in Neighbors," *New York Times*, March 9, 1997.
8. Ian Fisher and Norimitsu Onishi, "Many Armies Ravage Rich Land In the 'First World War' of Africa," *New York Times*, February 6, 2000.
9. Joel S. Migdal, *Strong Societies and Weak States: State-Society Relations and State Capabilities in the Third World* (Princeton: Princeton University Press, 1988), 204, 208.
10. Jane Perlez, "Looted by Its Own Officials, Bulgaria Faces the Day of Economic Reckoning," *New York Times*, October 28, 1996.
11. Perlez, "Looted by Its Own Officials."

12. Chris Hedges, "Up to $1 Billion Reported Stolen by Bosnian Leaders," *New York Times*, August 17, 1999.
13. Michael Wines, "The Border Is So Near, the Smuggling So Easy," *New York Times*, March 1, 1999.
14. Wines, "The Border Is So Near."
15. Joseph B. Treaster, "Counting on Women to Be More Honest Than Men," *New York Times*, August 15, 1999.
16. "In Colombia Smuggling Is an Old, Old Custom," *New York Times*, November 21, 1996.
17. Seth Faison, "China Attacks 'Hidden' Crime: Smuggling," *New York Times*, July 17, 1998.
18. Anthony Suau, "Shady Customs," *New York Times Magazine*, July 26, 1997.
19. Christopher S. Wren, "Keeping Cocaine Resilient: Low Cost and High Profit," *New York Times*, March 4, 1997.
20. Robert K. Schaeffer, *Understanding Globalization: The Social Consequences of Political, Economic, and Environmental Change* (Lanham, Md.: Rowman & Littlefield, 1997), 321–329.
21. Selwyn Raab, "Officials Say Mob Is Shifting Crimes to New Industries," *New York Times*, February 10, 1997.
22. Steve LeVine, "Get Rich in Chechnya: Kidnap Your Neighbors," *New York Times*, September 5, 1997.
23. New York Times, "India Warns Bombay to Curb Gang Activity," *New York Times*, August 21, 1997; Celia W. Dugger, "As Bombay Piles up Wealth, Gangsters Get Their Cut, Too," *New York Times*, November 12, 1998.
24. Jane Perlez, "Anarchy of Thugs Menaces Albania," *New York Times*, March 12, 1997; Philip Gourevitch, "Zaire's Killer Camps," *New York Times*, October 28, 1996.
25. Schaeffer, *Understanding Globalization*, 337–338.
26. James Brooke, "Brazil's Army Joins Battle in Lawless Rio," *New York Times*, November 6, 1994; Jean Diana Schemo, "Rio Ex-Officer Is Convicted in Massacre," *New York Times*, May 1, 1996.
27. Suzanne Daley, "Blacks in South Africa Turn to Vigilantes as Crime Soars," *New York Times*, November 27, 1995.
28. Schaeffer, *Severed States*, 243–247.
29. Schaeffer, *Severed States*, 244; Ted Robert Gurr, *Minorities at Risk: A Global View of Ethnopolitical Conflicts* (Washington, D.C.: U.S. Institute of Peace Press, 1993), 3; David Binder and Barbara Crossette, "As Ethnic Wars Multiply, U.S. Strives for a Policy," *New York Times*, February 7, 1993.
30. Schaeffer, *Severed States*, 177–183.
31. Schaeffer, *Severed States*, 195–229.
32. Raymond Bonner, "Rwandans Who Massacre Now Terrorize Camps," *New York Times*, October 31, 1994.
33. Diana Jean Schemo and Time Golden, "Bogota Aid: To Fight Drugs or Rebels?" *New York Times*, June 2, 1998; Ginger Thompson, "Where Killings Defiled a Church, No Forgiveness," *New York Times*, December 23, 1998; Larry Rohter, "Andes Battle: Right vs. Left vs. Civilians vs. Troops," *New York Times*, March 26, 1999.
34. Reuters, "Revenge Vow and Funerals after Killings in Indian State," *New York Times*, March 21, 1999.
35. Donna Bryson, "For Mozambique's Stolen Kids, Peace Is Strange," *San Francisco Chronicle*, June 25, 1996.

36. Michael Parfit, "Human Migration," *National Geographic* (October 1998): 16–17.
37. Bonner, "Rwandans Who Massacre Now Terrorize Camps."
38. Robert Schaeffer, *Warpaths: The Politics of Partition* (New York: Hill and Wang, 1990), 238; Barry Bearak, "Stranded Pakistanis Dream of Deliverance," *New York Times*, May 13, 2000.
39. Gerald W. Scully, "Dept. of Gee, Now That You Mention It: Genocide Is Bad for the Economy," *New York Times*, December 14, 1997.
40. Christopher S. Wren, "Drug Agent's Challenge: Heroin 'Swallowers,'" *New York Times*, February 21, 1999.
41. Michael Specter, "Trafficker's New Cargo: Naive Slavic Women," *New York Times*, January 11, 1998.
42. Specter, "Trafficker's New Cargo."
43. Seth Faison, "Brutal End to an Immigrant's Voyage of Hope," *New York Times*, October 3, 1995.
44. John F. Burns, "Unexpectedly, Algerian Peace Seems Possible," *New York Times*, March 7, 1999.
45. Roger Cohen, "France a Match Breaker, Mixed Couples Assert," *New York Times*, February 14, 1994; Alan Riding, "New Law In France Allows Random Identity Checks," *New York Times*, June 12, 1993; John Darnton, "Western Europe Is Ending Its Welcome to Immigrants," *New York Times*, August 10, 1993.
46. "Capital T-Shirt Sellers Get Eviction Notices," *New York Times*, April 16, 1995.
47. Mike Allen, "Giuliani Gives Sidewalk Vendors a Reprieve as He Reconsiders a Ban," *New York Times*, June 18, 1998.
48. Associated Press, "Homeless People in the Middle—Helped or Harassed," *San Francisco Chronicle*, December 15, 1994; Maria Alicia Gaura, "San Jose Regulates Pushcarts," *San Francisco Chronicle*, July 25, 1996.
49. "Police Join Social Workers to Move Homeless," *New York Times*, August 27, 1995; Shawn G. Kennedy, "New York Seeks to Retake Building from Squatters," *New York Times*, October 26, 1994.
50. Sam Howe Verhovek, "Historic Houston Neighborhood Falls to Renewal," *New York Times*, March 15, 1998.
51. Schaeffer, *Understanding Globalization*, 170–174.
52. Philip Shenan, "Isolated Papua New Guineans Fall Prey to Foreign Bulldozers," *New York Times*, June 5, 1994.
53. Shenan, "Isolated Papua New Guineans Fall Prey."
54. Anthony DePalma, "In Surinam's Rain Forests, a Fight over Trees vs. Jobs," *New York Times*, September 4, 1995; Julia Preston, "Nicaragua Sells Off Its Forests," *San Francisco Chronicle*, June 25, 1996.
55. Diana Jean Schemo, "Legally Now, Venezuelans to Mine Fragile Lands," *New York Times*, December 8, 1996.
56. Kenneth B. Noble, "Atop a Sea of Oil, Nothing but Misery," *New York Times*, September 9, 1993; Roger Cohen, "Mobil Spill Bares Ebb Tide of Nigerian Life," *New York Times*, September 20, 1998.
57. Erik Eckholm, "Relocations for China Dam Are Found to Lag," *New York Times*, March 12, 1998; Erik Eckholm, "China Admits Ecological Sins Played Role in Human Disaster," *New York Times*, August 26, 1998; Seth Faison, "Set to Build Dam, China Diverts Yangtze while Crowing about It," *New York Times*, November 9, 1997; Erik Eckholm, "China Shifts on How to Resettle Million People for Giant Dam," *New York Times*, May 25, 1999.

58. Faison, "Set to Build Dam."
59. Erik Eckholm, "Rare Criticism of China Plan for a Big Dam," *New York Times*, March 18, 1999.
60. Barbara Crossette, "Half the World Lacks Sanitation, Says UNICEF," *New York Times*, July 23, 1997; Nicholas D. Kristof, "For Third World, Water Is Still a Deadly Drink," *New York Times*, May 9, 1997.
61. Kristof, "For Third World, Water Is Still a Deadly Drink."
62. Kristof, "For Third World, Water Is Still a Deadly Drink."
63. Donatella Lorch, "Overcrowded, Nairobi Discovers Poverty," *New York Times*, December 12, 1995.
64. Roger Cohen, "Audis and Cell Phones, Poverty and Fear," *New York Times*, January 1, 2000.
65. Cohen, "Audis and Cell Phones."
66. Paul Kennedy, *Preparing for the Twenty-First Century* (New York: Random House, 1993), 26.
67. Patrick E. Tyler, "Lacking Iodine in Their Diets, Millions in China Are Retarded," *New York Times*, June 4, 1996.
68. Edward A. Gargan, "Weakness Seen in China's Economic Boom," *New York Times*, September 19, 1997.
69. Nicholas D. Kristof, "Malaria Makes a Comeback, and Is More Deadly Than Ever," *New York Times*, January 8, 1997.
70. Kristof, "Malaria Makes a Comeback."
71. Kristof, "Malaria Makes a Comeback."
72. Ian Fisher, "Malaria, a Swamp Dweller, Finds a Hillier Home," *New York Times*, July 21, 1999.
73. Lawrence K. Altman, "More African Women Have AIDS Than Men," *New York Times*, November 24, 1999.
74. Altman, "More African Women Have AIDS Than Men."
75. Lawrence K. Altman, "Parts of Africa Showing HIV in 1 in 4 Adults," *New York Times*, June 24, 1998.
76. Youssef M. Ibrahim, "AIDS Is Slashing Africa's Population, U.N. Survey Finds," *New York Times*, October 28, 1998.
77. Ibrahim, "AIDS Is Slashing Africa's Population."
78. Suzanne Daley, "In Zambia, the Abandoned Generation," *New York Times*, September 18, 1998.
79. Donald G. McNeil, Jr., "AIDS Is the Silent Killer in Africa's Economies," *New York Times*, September 15, 1998; Donald G. McNeil, Jr., "AIDS Takes a Toll on Africa, Even after Death," *New York Times*, November 16, 1998.

Part IV
CHANGE AND PROTEST

Protest takes diverse forms.

Chapter 10

Institutional Struggles: Female and Male Workers Challenge Business

Today, workers around the world are struggling against capitalist firms and states, the two central economic and political institutions of the world-system. This should not be surprising because wage workers have challenged business for hundreds of years, ever since capitalism first emerged in Western Europe during the sixteenth century. But while similarities exist between past and present protests, contemporary movements challenge businesses in diverse and sometimes totally new ways. Contemporary protest movements attack both wage and nonwage work structures, and women play a growing role in movements directed at businesses and, as we shall see, states.

During the first two hundred years of capitalism, worker struggles to raise wages and improve working conditions were disorganized, spontaneous, and usually illegal. It was not until the late eighteenth century that the term *strike* entered the vocabulary of class conflict. Sailors in the British navy coined the term when they "struck" their yards and refused to set sail during war with France.[1] The Great Mutinies of 1797, as they were known, were some of the first expressions of self-conscious organization by wage workers on an industry-wide basis.[2] But while strikes soon became a common practice of workers struggling against capitalist firms and states, wage workers did not create permanent organizations (unions) or establish political parties to represent their collective economic interests and press their political demands until the mid- to late-nineteenth century. The American Federation of Labor was founded only in 1886, at a time when workers first organized labor parties and socialist internationals in Western Europe and the United States. These organizations then struggled for decades before businesses and states agreed to recognize collective bargaining as a right; assent to worker demands for shorter hours, higher wages, and better working conditions; or admit worker parties to government. It was only recently, after World War II, that mainstream unions assumed a prominent role in economic life and labor parties played a significant political role in core states.

Contemporary wage workers, trade unions, and political parties still challenge capitalist firms and states, demanding changes that have traditionally been made by male wage workers, particularly those employed in the manufacturing industries of the core. But while it is important to recognize that traditional worker struggles against businesses and states are an ongoing feature of the modern world, we want to focus here on some of the novel features of conflict between labor and capital. In this chapter, we will look at how female and male working people challenge businesses around the world. In the following chapter, we will examine worker struggles against states. After that, we will analyze diversifying movements, worker struggles that have other nontraditional economic and social objectives.

There are two important features of contemporary worker struggles against capitalist firms around the world. First, worker struggles in the core and in the periphery and semiperiphery differ in significant ways. In the core, the redistribution and reorganization of work first *dis*organized wage worker's unions, making it difficult for worker movements to challenge corporations and competitive business effectively. Then, wage workers broadened their organizing efforts in the core, going beyond traditional wage–labor struggles and adopting antibusiness struggles that raised consumer and environmental issues. In the periphery and semiperiphery, democratization has given workers new political opportunities, enabling them to mobilize openly for the first time in generations. But debt crisis and deindustrialization have made it difficult for workers to make economic gains.

Second, workers in both settings have moved beyond "traditional" objectives. They have demanded not only formal recognition, higher wages, and better conditions but have also attacked the social divisions (sexism, racism, and ageism) created by capitalist firms as part of their labor-force management. Many workers now attack sexism and racism at work. This objective reflects, in part, the changing character and composition of wage work. Workers in both the North and South attack the different forms of class-based stratification because relations between workers in both regions have grown stronger. As employers and governments improve communication systems, workers have forged new ties with workers living elsewhere. Many worker movements already hold cyberspace conferences to discuss common interests and develop collective strategies.

Let us look first at anticorporate organizing in the core and then at struggles against business in the periphery and semiperiphery.

ANTICORPORATE ORGANIZING IN THE CORE

The redistribution and reorganization of work by monopolizing firms in the core have *dis*organized workers' long-established ties with businesses and the state. Deindustrialization and downsizing have reduced the number of wage workers in unions and weakened worker claims to the wealth they produce. While corporations have disorganized workers, state officials have discouraged workers by using high interest rates and deflationary monetary policies to limit and constrain worker demands for higher wages. These developments have made it extremely difficult for workers to struggle effectively in battles with migratory capital.

Still, it is important to take a patient, long-term view of change. Recall that it took U.S. workers a generation to respond effectively to the changes introduced by Frederick Taylor and Henry Ford in the first twenty years of this century. It took years before predominantly male wage workers in manufacturing developed organizations like the Committee for Industrial Organizations, adopted tactics like the sit-down strike, and passed laws like the Wagner (1935) and Taft-Hartley (1947) Acts. It was only when they possessed these tools that workers could challenge capitalist firms in some industries effectively. It will no doubt take some time in the current era before workers in the core develop the strategies, organizations, and perhaps even legislation they need to respond effectively to change. Some evidence already exists that wage workers are developing new approaches and adopting wider goals.

New Approaches to Unionizing in the United States

In the United States, labor unions have begun to change the way they organize union members, nonunionized workers, working-class communities, and groups of workers in other countries. In 1996, AFL-CIO leaders began stressing issues that affected all workers, not just their own members, arguing that wages be increased across the board and that the gap between rich and poor be narrowed.[3] In 1997, union officials decided to intensify their efforts to organize working women and immigrants, establishing a presence in California agriculture and in Las Vegas hotels, construction sites, and health-care centers.[4] One year later, AFL-CIO representatives traveled to Mexico to encourage cross-border organizing efforts and demonstrate their support for independent unions that operate outside government-controlled trade federations.[5]

But unions in the United States have had a hard time organizing workers in service and high-tech industries, even where workers had once belonged to unions. Although many of the service workers employed at stores like Walmart were once highly paid, unionized manufacturing workers, unions have found it difficult to organize them effectively, and firms like Walmart have been able to deter unionization drives. Walmart invested so much money to fight a unionization drive by the steelworker's union in Merrill, Wisconsin, that the company "could have paid everyone in the store a living wage for the rest of their lives," said Michael Barkley, a union supporter.[6]

Unions have also had a difficult time unionizing workers in high-technology firms. So the AFL-CIO established its own temporary-employment agency that provides good benefits to high-tech, temporary, and part-time workers in Silicon Valley.[7] Because temporary workers now make up about one-third of the workforce in the computer industry, the unions' temporary-placement agencies could eventually establish a union presence in high-tech industries.

In recent years, unions have departed from their long-standing dependence on white male workers and have organized along cross-gender and cross-ethnic lines.

Rather than pursuing white male union members and ignoring women and economically disadvantaged ethnic groups, the AFL-CIO has reached out to lower-paid segments of the workforce, particularly immigrants in the West and low-income workers in the South.[8] Affiliated unions have organized nursing home workers in Miami and food workers in New Orleans, where the workforces are predominantly female and Hispanic or African American. They have had less success, however, in the institutional nursing care industry and in the poultry industry, which also employ women and minorities.[9] Still, union supporters in Maine have pressed the governor to support egg-farm workers at Decoster (the nation's largest brown-egg producer). The United Paperworkers International Union has made some progress among workers there, many of them immigrants from Central America.[10] The Communications Workers of America successfully organized 10,000 U.S. Airways workers who sell tickets, take reservations, and serve as gate agents, many of them women.[11] In 1999, after ninety-three years of failed unionization attempts, employees at Fieldcrest-Cannon, most of them women, finally joined the Union of Needletrades, Industrial and Textile Employees (UNITE).[12] Meanwhile, high-paid women who play for the Women's National Basketball Association have discussed forming their own union.[13]

Many union activists feared that Cesar Chavez's death in 1993 would inhibit organizing by the United Farm Workers (UFW). But under cofounder Delores Huerta's leadership, the UFW made impressive gains in the 1990s. A number of groups of workers have joined the UFW, including mushroom pickers along the California coast, rose workers in the Central Valley, and winery workers in Washington State. The union also concluded a successful, eighteen-year campaign to organize Red Coach lettuce workers, bringing them gradual raises over the next five years.[14] In 1996, when the Farm Workers began organizing California strawberry pickers, they reached out to young, recent immigrants. Strawberry picker's wages had fallen 25 percent over the last twenty-five years, the workers were denied medical and disability benefits, and they were subjected to arbitrary dismissal procedures.[15] In Florida, the UFW mobilized immigrants from Mexico and El Salvador against large mushroom producers, whom workers said treated them with "disrespect."[16]

Although Cesar Chavez used strikes, consumer boycotts, individual fasts, public marches, and even direct mail appeals to organize workers, UFW leaders have added new strategies to their arsenal. They not only raise bread-and-butter issues, they also confront problems related to racism, sexism, and homophobia.[17] For example, the UFW recently joined a class-action suit brought by female workers who are trying to fight sexist, seasonal-hiring practices. Angelita Melgoza filed the suit after she realized that her husband and other men were hired during the spring picking season, while women had to wait until the summer picking season to find work.[18] The UFW has also raised environmental issues, educating workers and consumers about pesticide exposure and food safety and convincing several supermarket chains to support the right of strawberry workers to organize.[19]

As part of its campaign to organize poor workers and support constituent unions, the AFL-CIO contributed $1 million to the strawberry-worker organizing drive.

UFW president Arturo Rodriguez, who sits on motel floors and speaks to workers, is now seen by the AFL-CIO organizing director as someone who is "a model for the rest of the labor movement to follow."[20] The UFW has demonstrated that multicultural, cross-gender unions can play an important role, not only by organizing low-paid workers but also by developing comprehensive strategies that can be adopted by unions in other settings.

During the 1990s, the pace of union organizing efforts accelerated, and unions began reaching out to new social constituencies. These efforts have not, as yet, increased the percentage of workers that belong to unions. Recall that unions would have to recruit 15 million new members to regain their postwar strength. But their success among workers long excluded from union membership—women, ethnic minorities, and immigrants—in industries where unions have historically made little headway (agriculture, textile, and service industries), suggests that unions are developing new approaches that may assist workers in their ongoing struggles with business.

Job Strikes in the Core

Strikes have long been the most visible and most studied expression of struggle by labor movements. Strikes have often been seen as the only important form of protesting by adult male workers. The number of strikes has risen dramatically in countries that have become the world's new export enclaves. But in recent years, relatively few strikes have occurred in the United States, particularly in the declining manufacturing industries that have long provided jobs to white men. Still, while the incidence of strikes has been low, some large-scale and significant strikes have taken place. In 1997, auto workers struck at seventeen General Motors plants in North America. They opposed the introduction of new technology, arguing that new stamping machines would reduce their job security.[21]

One of the key strikes of the decade was called in 1997 by workers at United Parcel Service (UPS). The Teamster's union opposed management's plans to divide workers into two unequal groups: a well-paid, full-time workforce and a poorly paid, part-time workforce (70 percent of UPS employees worked on a part-time basis). Workers complained that women and other economically disadvantaged groups were being channeled into the poorly paid, temporary workforce. As part-timer Marilyn Lange said, "The men in suits are making all the loot."[22]

Through the Teamsters, workers demanded higher pay and better benefits for part-time workers and insisted that UPS continue to subscribe to the Teamsters' pension plan, rather than create a weaker pension plan of its own.[23] The fifteen-day strike resulted in pay increases for full- and part-time workers, the gradual conversion of 10,000 part-time jobs into full-time positions, and a promise that the Teamsters' pension plan would not be replaced.[24] The strike was significant because UPS, a dominant force in the fast-growing package-delivery industry, relied heavily on part-time workers and a two-tier workforce. The strike was one of the first to challenge this divide-and-rule management practice successfully.

For many years, picket lines were manned primarily by well-paid white males. But many contemporary strikes are now led by women and men who come from economically disadvantaged and immigrant backgrounds. The 1999 strike at IBP, a large meat packing firm in Walla Walla, Washington, was called by female and male immigrants who organized across gender and ethnic lines. Leaders gave speeches in Spanish and English and had them translated into Lao, Vietnamese, and Serbo-Croatian. "'Enough is enough' is something you can understand in any language," observed Maria Martinez, one strike leader.[25] Immigrant workers from different ethnic backgrounds agreed. "There's a lot wrong inside that plant," one Bosnian Muslim immigrant complained. "There's not safety. There's not respect."[26] Although the action began as a wildcat strike, the Teamsters eventually recognized the economic and safety issues raised by workers and endorsed the strike.

The show of public support for striking workers in Puerto Rico, a U.S. dependency, was also significant. In July 1998, 500,000 Puerto Rican workers from 50 unions joined a 48-hour general strike to show support for striking workers at the Puerto Rican Telephone Company. The Puerto Rican Legislature, like governments across Latin America, had voted to privatize the state-controlled telephone company and sell it to GTE, a U.S. corporation based in Connecticut. Workers opposed the sale because they worried that reorganization would result in large-scale layoffs. They were joined by consumers who feared that privatization would increase telephone bills. Many others joined the general strike to protest the sale of public assets to a private firm in the United States. "We're defending the Puerto Rican Telephone Company not only because it's our rice and beans but because it's our national patrimony," argued Annie Cruz, a president of the labor-consumer-nationalist coalition.[27] Many Puerto Ricans are afraid that their governor, who had already privatized other state-owned companies (a shipping company, hospitals, and hotels), was selling Puerto Rican assets so that the U.S. Congress would more readily admit Puerto Rico to the union as a state. During the strike, labor union members shut down shopping malls, banks, and San Juan's airport, and protesters sabotaged phone lines and clogged phone lines with false reports to the police.[28]

Although general strikes in the United States are rare, they are fairly common in Western Europe. Throughout 1996, French public employees stopped work to protest government spending cuts and hiring freezes. Thirty-two percent of French workers joined public employees during the general strike. The year before, 57 percent of French workers had joined a long railway workers' strike.[29] In Germany, municipal and transport workers in key cities called a five-hour general strike in 1998. Strike organizers demanded that the state preserve public service and transit employees' wages and pension benefits.[30] As the adoption of a common European currency approached, the German government, like governments across Europe, tried to reduce the wages and benefits of public employees, cutting back on sick pay and getting rid of free pensions.

Although strikes are less common today than they have been at other times during the postwar period, when workers in the core have gone on strike they have raised some new issues (the treatment of part-time workers, introduction of new technology) and appealed to groups (women, immigrants, and consumers) that have not regularly joined or supported strikes in the private or public sector.

Workers have also joined with other groups—consumers, students—to challenge global change and raise issues about workers in other countries. This is perhaps best exemplified in recent years by workers' struggles against domestic and foreign-based sweatshops.

Sweatshops

In the 1930s and 1940s, clothing was produced primarily at home-based work sites. That changed during World War II, when the U.S. government prohibited home-based manufacturing, arguing that it was too difficult to regulate and permitted widespread abuse of minimum wage, overtime, and child-labor laws.[31] By 1950, production had shifted to large-scale factories. Apparel manufacturing changed again in the 1980s and 1990s, when the industry was reorganized. Clothing was increasingly produced at small-scale shops, both in the United States and abroad. The owners of small shops contracted to manufacture goods for fashion-label firms. Unfortunately, the growing number of small-scale shops, with a dizzying network of contractors and subcontractors, made it extremely difficult for government inspectors to monitor compliance with labor laws. This encouraged widespread abuse of worker rights and facilitated the return of "sweatshop" conditions throughout the industry. It became common for employers to demand long hours, pay below-minimum wages, hire minors, and neglect worker safety.[32]

In 1992, the federal government introduced a program allowing fashion-label firms to monitor wage levels and working conditions at shops run by their suppliers. But private-industry regulation failed to improve sweatshop conditions in the industry significantly. "It's the fox guarding the chicken coop," argued Edna Bonacich, a sociologist who studies the garment industry.[33]

These developments presented a problem for unions, because the move to small-scale shops meant they had to organize tiny groups of workers, most of them women and many of them recent immigrants.[34] Not surprisingly, the number of unionized workers in the garment industry fell by half between 1989 and 1996.[35] These difficulties were compounded by the fact that fashion-industry firms have contracted with small-scale suppliers not only in the United States but abroad, where U.S. labor laws do not apply.

To address the domestic and global issues associated with sweatshops and changes in the garment industry, unions have tried to develop a different approach. In 1996, they joined with apparel industry representatives, government officials, religious leaders, and human rights advocates to discuss ways to curb abuses in sweatshops, both in the United States and abroad.[36] But while some progress was made—the industry established new rules for its domestic and foreign suppliers—participating unions refused to endorse the final agreement because the industry did not agree to pay living wages (it insisted on paying lower "prevailing" wages) and insisted on contracting from suppliers in countries like China, where the government denies workers the right to organize and bargain collectively.[37] Still, union efforts to change corporate practices in the United States and abroad was a departure. "Labor's job is to push the envelope a little further," observed Lenore Miller, a former union president who participated in the negotiations.[38]

While unions have not secured a comprehensive approach to global sweatshops, they have managed to establish that the industry is responsible for conditions it does not itself directly manage, and they have managed to curb abuses in some settings.

In Saipan, which is part of the U.S. commonwealth in the Marianas, labor unions have fought the exploitation of workers in sweatshops on the island. When Chinese workers are recruited, they are told they will be going to work in the United States. But they find themselves transported instead to Saipan and forced to live in barracks that are "ringed with barb wire and patrolled by teams of uniformed guards."[39] One young woman from the Philippines, who eventually escaped from Saipan's assembly line, said "the girls have no freedom."[40] Because workers go into debt to recruiters and employers in Saipan, they are afraid to complain, fight back, or leave the island. "Their conditions are horrendous," Neils Jensen, a Christian missionary from New Zealand, observed. "It certainly has its parallels to slavery or indentured servitude."[41]

Labor lawyers in the United States helped workers file a class-action suit against corporations that contracted with sweatshops in Saipan in January 1999. Eight months later, four U.S. retailers (Nordstrom, Gymboree, Cutter and Buck, and J. Crew) settled the suit with 50,000 current and former workers. They agreed to improve wages and conditions and allow an independent, nonprofit firm to monitor the terms of the settlement. Fourteen other companies refused to settle, so workers pressed ahead with a $1 billion lawsuit against them.[42]

Labor unions, lawyers, and nongovernmental organizations were not the only groups to challenge sweatshops. They have been joined by college students across the United States. Duke University students took the growing sales of their basketball apparel as an opportunity to boycott sweatshop-produced goods, many of them made in China and Indonesia. In March 1998, Duke University adopted a code of conduct that prohibited its apparel manufacturers from using child labor, maintaining unsafe workplaces, prohibiting unionization, refusing to pay a minimum wage, and failing to have factories inspected by independent professionals. "We cannot tolerate having the sweat and tears of abused and exploited workers mixed with the fabric of the products which bear our marks," argued Jim Wilkerson, Duke's director of trademark licensing.[43]

In 1999, students at Duke and Georgetown argued that the Collegiate Licensing Company in Atlanta, which helps more than one hundred schools license and manufacture their apparel, had developed an inadequate code of corporate conduct.[44] They organized rallies and sit-ins to force colleges to adopt a tougher code. Students at Princeton, Harvard, Yale, Brown, and Cornell went further, demanding not only that licensed companies adopt a strong code but also disclose factory locations and open them to inspections so that their compliance with the code could be verified.[45] Within two months, the anticorporate, antisweatshop movement had spread across the country, as students joined the antisweatshop movement and demanded that their schools refuse to produce college goods in global sweatshops.[46] Officials at seventeen colleges and universities agreed to join a Fair Labor Association, charged with developing and monitoring labor codes.[47]

The global antisweatshop movement has joined a growing list of groups that fight transnational corporations, mount divestment campaigns, and urge universities, pension funds, and governments to withdraw their investments from corporations that do business in countries that do not protect worker rights. These efforts grew out of the divestment campaign that was waged against apartheid South Africa in the 1970s and 1980s. This global campaign shaped subsequent struggles in the 1990s. For example, civil rights and other activists have asked pension-fund managers to divest their holdings in transnationals that produce oil in Nigeria, where the dictatorship adopted oppressive, antilabor policies in the oil-producing region.

In Massachusetts, the state government in 1996 adopted legislation barring the state from doing business with companies that trade with Burma (Myanmar), a country where the dictatorship has been cited for extensive human-rights violations.[48] A federal district judge ruled in 1998 that states could not impose sanctions against foreign countries, arguing that they infringe on the federal government's foreign-policy prerogatives. But supporters of the anti-Burma legislation in Massachusetts, and in other states and municipalities around the country, have challenged the ruling. Byron Rushing, a Massachusetts state legislator, defended the sanctions, arguing that if such a ruling had been made during the divestment campaign against South Africa, "Nelson Mandela might still be in prison today."[49]

The campaigns against sweatshops, which have insisted that companies either adopt practices that protect workers or sever relations with businesses and states that are unwilling to comply with fair labor codes, are significant because they extend rights to workers not only in the United States but abroad. By creating networks and alliances with diverse groups—students, administrators, elected officials, pension fund managers, and sometimes even industry representatives—they can more effectively address problems associated with global change.

Workers, of course, do not rely only on unions to challenge corporations. They hire lawyers to sue corporations and file class-action suits to protest job discrimination, health and safety violations, and environmental pollution. They sometimes even sue unions, as immigrant garment workers did in Brooklyn. There, workers sued because they believed the union had compromised their interests in negotiations with fashion-industry firms.[50]

In some cases, workers have demanded that businesses treat them as partners, not opponents, and have pressed them to share profits with worker-employees or sell the business to worker-owners. In Montana, one thousand employees of the Columbia Falls Aluminum Company used a lawsuit to force the company to share its profits with workers and in 1998 were awarded $97 million for their efforts.[51] The McKay Nursery company in Waterloo, Wisconsin, agreed to sell the business to employees, providing them with stock shares and bonuses in addition to wages.[52] Although stock shares are regularly offered to corporate managers as an incentive, they are rarely given to low-paid and semiskilled workers.

The idea that workers are also investors, partners, or owners has gained increasing currency as worker participation in the stock market has grown. Many households have even turned to firms that offer "socially responsible" investments, a growing financial-service industry. Households that do so are seeking to advance their interests as both investors and workers. Although these strategies—worker lawsuits, partnerships, and investments—are still in their infancy, they suggest that workers are beginning to consider new ways to pursue their interests and challenge capital. Any comprehensive approach to the changes wrought by the redistribution and reorganization of work could include a capital-investment strategy by workers in the core. It is unlikely that such a strategy would be developed or managed by unions, if only because few workers in the United States are represented by them. In the past, worker political parties and socialist states tried to develop and manage capital-investment strategies. But the approaches they developed—nationalization of industry, import-substitutionist development, central planning—were unable, in the long run, to advance worker interests or challenge the capitalist firm as a global economic institution. So workers must develop new organizations and approaches in coming years, based perhaps on strategies now in their infancy.

WOMEN'S AND MEN'S ANTICORPORATE ORGANIZING IN THE PERIPHERY AND SEMIPERIPHERY

In the periphery and semiperiphery, workers' struggles against business have taken place in a context that differs, in important respects, from the struggles waged by workers in the core. For most of the postwar period, wage workers confronted dictatorships and one-party regimes in most peripheral and semiperipheral states. Although some of those regimes allowed or required workers to join government-controlled "unions," they did not permit workers to organize independent unions or to bargain collectively, and they typically jailed or killed workers who tried. Moreover, regimes often took over or "nationalized" individual businesses and whole industries, collapsing two institutions (firm and state) into one entity. In Latin America, for example, they nationalized electrical power, oil, mining, banking, and telecommunications industries. For workers, this meant that the struggles they waged in the workplace were simultaneously struggles that challenged the state. As a result, conditions for workers in the periphery and semiperiphery were substantially different from conditions in the core, where workers organized and struggled in a democratic context and confronted capital as an institution that was more autonomous from the state as an institution.

The gains made by workers in the immediate postwar period were quickly reversed, and dictatorships were established across the capitalist and communist periphery and semiperiphery. So between 1950 and 1970, it was extremely difficult for workers to wage effective struggles against firms and states in the periphery and semiperiphery.[53] But this pattern changed after 1970. Dictators and one-party regimes began to experience serious economic crises, and workers organized movements to challenge their control of both the workplace and the government. The most important of these movements emerged in capitalist South Korea, communist Poland, apartheid South Africa, and China.[54] In these countries, workers joined with students and intellectuals to create *minjung* (a Korean term for "the people" or "the masses"), powerful alliances that organized illegal unions, conducted illegal strikes and boycotts, and demanded democracy and widespread social change. Although their activities resembled "traditional" labor-union practices in the core, they had a rather different social meaning because they were not simply economistic but also political, not just about wages and conditions in the workplace but also about freedom and democracy in society. Worker movements in these and other countries, and economic crises across the periphery and semiperiphery, swept dictatorships from power in the 1970s (in southern Europe), 1980s (in Latin America, East Asia, and Eastern Europe), and the 1990s (in the Soviet Union, South Africa, and Indonesia).

But while worker movements played a key role in democratization, which allowed them to organize legally, bargain collectively, and participate electorally, workers soon confronted a new set of problems. When civilian democrats came to power, they were usually forced to impose austerity programs and adopt neoliberal policies that opened their economies to foreign trade and investment and forced them to sell public assets. As we have seen, these developments contributed to falling commodity prices and the widespread destruction of manufacturing industries, which had been created by the import-substitutionist industrialization policies of dictatorships. Massive deindustrialization across the periphery and semiperiphery destroyed the economic base of workers who had struggled for democracy. In Poland, for example, the Gdansk shipyard, the birthplace of Solidarity, was closed and its workers, who had struggled courageously against dictatorship, were discharged.

The civilian governments that working-class people helped bring to power have cut wages and laid off workers, and voters have rejected their leadership. In Poland, voters ousted the government led by Solidarity and replaced it with a government led by former Communist Party bureaucrats. In general, democratization in the periphery and semiperiphery resulted in significant political gains (the right to organize, bargain, and vote), but it also resulted in substantial economic losses (rising unemployment, falling wages).

Working-class people have responded to change in this context in a number of ways. First, many women and men organized protests against austerity programs. Worker struggles against structural adjustment programs became so widespread across the periphery and semiperiphery that sociologists now refer to them as "austerity protests" or "IMF riots."[55] Protests against wage and job cuts, as well as price and tax increases, have become an ongoing feature of democratizing states across the periphery and semiperiphery.

Second, states have "privatized" public assets and manufacturing industries on a massive scale.[56] This has institutionally removed state managers from firms and created strictly market-driven capitalist enterprises where few previously existed. Because privatization was often accompanied by currency devaluations and liberal investment policies, many of these new private firms fell into the hands of foreign corporations. Other public assets were transferred to domestic political elites and economic insiders. In this context, workers have organized protests against the privatization process generally, which creates "new" capitalist firms, both foreign and domestic, and against the reorganization of work—downsizing, deunionization, wage cuts—that this process entails. In some settings, workers have organized general strikes against privatization, of the sort we have already observed in Puerto Rico, which challenge globalization, neoliberal policies, insider corruption, and deteriorating wages and conditions in industry.

Contemporary struggles in Mexico, South Korea, Indonesia, and Russia demonstrate that wage workers challenge capitalist firms in democratizing states across the periphery and semiperiphery. In fact, labor militancy in industrial sites has exploded in the semiperiphery.[57] The semiperiphery is the key zone where working families are caught between a "hope" for further proletarianization and the "fear" of deproletarianization. In this zone, tremendous pressure is placed on migrants, women on the global assembly line, male industrial workers, and girls in the global sex trade by households to maintain wage income and prevent the household unit from losing its access to wage labor. But this is not easy to do, because the jobs that provide households with wage income are subject to elimination and access to them is permitted only on a temporary basis.

In Latin America, government efforts to encourage outside investment and sell public assets have been met with tremendous anger on the part of many workers. For example, government workers in Mexico have opposed administrative plans to privatize Mexico's electric power plants. By relinquishing this source of state power, the PRI, which has controlled the Mexican government for decades, hopes to entice outside investors and enhance Mexico's ability to generate and distribute electrical power. Although Brazil and Argentina privatized their electric industries ten years ago, Mexico held on to its electric industry. Government workers and others are highly suspicious of privatization efforts, particularly because the earlier sale of Mexico's state-owned banks led to a financial fiasco and a major economic crisis, which required a $65 billion bail-out by the United States. In the 1930s, Mexicans celebrated a major political victory over the North when the PRI nationalized Mexico's oil fields and established Pemex as a state-owned oil company. In the 1950s, Mexico and states across Latin America adopted policies aimed at increasing their economic independence. They nationalized major industries, developed import-substitutionist strategies to create strong domestic markets, and passed laws to restrict foreign control of domestic industries and reduce their economic dependence on the core. But debt crisis and privatization have made governments repudiate these policies. And many Mexicans now fear that the sale of the state-owned electric power industry to private investors will eventually be followed by the privatization of the state-owned oil industry.

As in Mexico, workers in Brazil organized popular protests to prevent the government from selling Vale do Rio Doce, a state-owned mining company, to private investors. Opponents were not able to stop the sale in Congress, so they asked the federal court to block it. The sale of the mine, worth $5 billion, would be one of the largest sales of its kind in Latin America.[58] Workers have organized demonstrations and filed hundreds of legal actions to block the immediate sale of the mine. During a protest at the stock exchange in Rio de Janeiro, one demonstrator carried a banner of Che Guevara, and another held up a poster that read: "The sale of Vale is the first step toward the internationalization of the Amazon."[59]

During the 1990s, employed and unemployed Mexican workers, many without any official, government-sanctioned union representation, mounted protests against businesses and the government. In 1996, more than three thousand antibusiness and antigovernment marches took place in Mexico City alone. Nurses at social security hospitals became so angry about the lack of medicine for poor people that they removed blood from their arms with syringes and squirted their blood at the main doors to the state agency. Workers angered at high interest rates and their growing indebtedness to banks hired an elephant and rode it to the Central Bank. To focus attention on their poverty, jobless street sweepers entered the chambers of the National Congress and removed all their clothes. Street sweepers in the State of Tabasco, who brought their struggle to the national capitol, said that their layoffs have been particularly cruel because they have no farms and no land to fall back on. They cannot fish, they say, because the water has been polluted by Pemex. All these labor protests have been dramatized by street sweepers' extended hunger strikes, which went on for between 60 and 97 days.[60]

Workers in Mexico are also trying to organize independent unions that are not closely aligned with the PRI or organized by private companies. A major break with government-controlled unions occurred in 1997, when workers in Tijuana persuaded Han Young, a Korean-owned company, to recognize and bargain with the independent union they had organized. Their efforts were assisted by a consumer boycott of Hyundai cars and by demonstrations in front of Hyundai dealerships in the United States. The union at Han Young was the first time an independent union had managed to represent workers at one of the 2,700 *maquila* plants along Mexico's border.[61]

During the initial stages, *maquila* workers had to fight not only Han Young management but also the governor of Baja California and the PRI's official union, which tried to squash the union organizing drive.[62] During the long cross-border struggle, truck assemblers at the plant in Tijuana confronted the Mexican government when it refused to recognize the union, mounted a 22-day hunger strike when Han Young managers fired 12 of the 119 workers at the plant, and convinced 55 workers to vote for the *maquila*'s first independent union.[63] Independent unionizers at Han Young also forged alliances with U.S. unions, educated U.S. consumers, connected with sympathetic Tijuana lawyers, and linked up with San Diego's Support Committee for Maquila Workers, which publicizes organizing drives via phone and fax.[64] The truck assemblers re-knit their relationship to each other and changed their relationships to the company and the state in the process. "This is a historic victory for our movement," said Enrique Hernandez, an independent union organizer. "For the first time, workers in a *maquiladora* plant have won a fight to choose the kind of union they want."[65]

Alejandra Barrales Magdaleno, a thirty-year-old Mexican labor leader who forged alliances with North American unions, recently helped to establish a new, independent federation of workers, the National Workers Union.[66] Barrales, a young woman who is interested in transnational organizing, helped found the National Workers Union in 1997. She then led Aeromexico's flight attendants into a strike the following year. Before independent unions were organized, many workers accepted wage cuts to save their jobs, and the number of strikes in Mexico declined from 675 in 1982 to only 39 in 1997, partly due to government repression.[67] But the rise of independent unions has renewed worker interest in fighting wage cuts. During the Aeromexico strike, Barrales demanded an 18 percent raise and new retirement benefits. The flight attendants waged a successful campaign even though the government took control of the airline and kept planes flying.[68]

But these recent successes need to be seen within the overall context of wage erosion. In 1980, Mexico's manufacturing laborers made one-fifth of what their counterparts in the United States earned. By 1996, Mexican wages had fallen to less than one-tenth of U.S. wages.[69] New independent unions have to make up a lot of lost ground in Mexico and in other settings across the periphery and semiperiphery.

As real wages declined and the gap between the poor and rich grew, working people in Latin America also protested the austerity measures imposed by peripheral and semiperipheral states. In the wake of debt crises, states have mandated wage reductions, reduced state benefits to workers, increased taxes on workers, and privatized state enterprises to raise money to repay their debts. As with the anti-austerity protests in the late 1970s and early 1980s, many women in contemporary anti-austerity movements have taken the lead in fighting against government-imposed sacrifices. Structural adjustment programs have increased the amount of income that working families transfer to the government and pay to commercial banks based in the core. Women have taken an active role because they have experienced gender discrimination at work, have assumed greater responsibility for feeding and caring for their families, and have seen austerity programs greatly increase the number of women and their dependents who live in desperate poverty.[70]

In 1998, working-class women in Bogota organized a week-long strike against the government's austerity program. Workers in Colombia launched an extended strike directed at the state; foreign companies; international organizations, particularly the IMF and the World Bank; and powerful core states, because workers held these institutions collectively responsible for their growing economic misery.[71] One year later, an anti-austerity coalition of labor unions and social movements called an "indefinite nationwide strike" to protest the Colombian government's austerity program. Across Colombia, schools and some businesses closed down for an extended period.[72]

Worker protests against austerity programs were not confined to Latin America. When South Korea experienced an economic crisis in December 1996, the government took steps to adopt an IMF-sponsored austerity program, and labor unrest spread across the country. Workers argued that employers and the state were trying to make workers bear the burden of economic recession. They objected strenuously when the Parliament passed legislation giving corporate managers more power to lay off workers, change work hours, and forbid multiple unions in one work site, and gave the Agency for National Security Planning expanded police powers.[73] Two major labor confederations organized a nationwide general strike, the largest ever. When workers organized this mass strike, they challenged the growing power given by the state to private corporations and police agencies and challenged the neoliberal policies forced on the government by financial institutions based in the core.[74] Strikers also objected to the legislative process in the "democratizing" state. The ruling party had secretly met at 6:00 A.M., without informing opposition party representatives and in seven minutes passed the law giving companies the power to fire workers more easily.[75] The government hoped that rising unemployment levels would moderate demands for wage increases.[76] "I will strike every day until this is resolved," vowed Chong Mi Sook, a striking female nurse.[77]

Three days after the general strike began, columns of rifle- and tear gas–bearing riot police, backed by armored tanks, unsuccessfully tried to disperse the cross-gender army of striking shipbuilders, car-assembly workers, hospital employees, subway workers, financial employees, and broadcasters that marched in the streets.[78] But the strikers persevered, mounting daily demonstrations for more than three weeks, until President Kim Young Sam agreed to meet with opposition leaders and discuss the new labor laws.[79] At this point, workers agreed to strike only on Wednesdays. On January 21, 1997, President Kim agreed to reconsider the government's new police powers and withdraw its warrants for the arrest of strike leaders. But he indicated that the worker-discharge provisions of the new labor law would not be repealed.[80]

When the United States agreed to send $5 billion to bail out South Korea, adult workers objected to "U.S. assistance" and IMF involvement. Protesters appeared on the streets with signs in Korean and English that read: "Re-Negotiate the IMF Agreement! Citizens Coalition for Economic Justice."[81] General strikes against company efforts to increase job exploitation and against political repression by the state soon evolved into struggles against intervention by global capital managers and the austerity programs they imposed.

In the semiperiphery, anticorporate protests have become a more frequent occurrence. Many of the struggles against business have been organized by groups that operate outside of government control. During the economic crisis that engulfed Indonesia in the late 1990s, unofficial labor groups struck for higher wages, safer working conditions, and an end to dictatorship.[82] In Sierra Leone, civil servants associated with the Sierra Leone Labor Congress went on a two-week strike, protesting low salaries, military control of the government, and the absence of a safe living environment.[83]

In Central Europe and in Russia, working people are engaged in a major struggle against the capitalist firms, democratizing states, and international capitalist institutions that have appeared since communist regimes collapsed. Workers have experienced massive deindustrialization, diminishing state power, rising unemployment, falling wages, the irregular payment of wages, and the destruction of housing benefits and health and education services.

In March 1997, millions of workers went on strike across Russia, demanding the payment of back wages and the restoration of job security and social services. At that time, one in three Russians had been unpaid for at least three months, and many public employees joined the protest by refusing to work. Outside Moscow, hunger was widespread and antistate sentiment became acute.[84] In July 1998, unemployed and unpaid workers blocked roads and railways, took over state buildings, seized their managers as hostages, and waged long hunger strikes to call attention to their plight.[85]

Similar protests took place in Eastern Europe. In an effort to avoid layoffs, prevent plant closings, and obtain a 35-percent increase in their wages, striking miners in Romania climbed over police barricades and marched or traveled to the capital city of Bucharest. While police threw tear gas canisters and canceled and rerouted trains, strikers persisted in their fifteen-day effort to draw attention to their cause. Townspeople who were sympathetic to the strikers' cause even threw stones at the police and beat their cars with metal sticks. State authorities aggressively fought strikers because they remembered that protests by miners in 1990 and 1991 had led to the overthrow of the first post-Communist government.[86] Meanwhile, Polish farmers staged hundreds of demonstrations in the spring and summer of 1999 to protest falling commodity prices, growing competition from Western European farmers, and declining rural incomes. Polish miners also fought against the elimination of government subsidies and rising prices.[87]

Although workers in the core, periphery, and semiperiphery have found it difficult to challenge capitalist firms successfully in the present period, they have begun to develop more inclusive organizations and approaches that may help them confront capital more effectively in the future. Any critical assessment of labor movement efforts would benefit from a patient, long-term view of change.

Using cultural insights gained from feminist and antiracist movements, workers have, of course, not only developed new ways to challenge capital as a central economic institution, they have also confronted the state as a political institution. It is to worker struggles against the state that we now turn.

NOTES

1. Robert K. Schaeffer, *The Chains of Bondage Broke: The Proletarianization of Seafaring Labor, 1600–1800* (Ph.D. dissertation, State University of New York at Binghamton, 1984; Ann Arbor: University Microfilms, 1984), 286–287.

2. Mutinous sailors also raised red flags (the battle signal that "no quarter" would be given and "no prisoners" would be taken), elected representatives to negotiate with the Admiralty, and declared "republics afloat." The red flag was subsequently adopted by radical socialist and communist worker's movements. Schaeffer, *The Chains of Bondage Broke*, 311.

3. Peter T. Kilborn, "With New Military, Nation's Unions Hope to Drive Republicans from Congress," *New York Times*, February 19, 1996.

4. "AFL-CIO Puts Recruiting at Top of Its Agenda," *New York Times*, February 17, 1997.

5. Sam Dillon, "U.S. Labor Seeks Union Support in Mexico," *New York Times*, January 23, 1998.
6. Bill Dedman, "Employees Reject an Effort to Unionize a Wal-Mart 'Family,'" *New York Times*, August 10, 1997.
7. Steven Greenhouse, "Unions Need Not Apply: High-Technology Sector Unmoved by Labor's Song," *New York Times*, July 26, 1999.
8. Mireya Navarro, "Florida Farm a Labor Battleground," *New York Times*, April 15, 1996.
9. David Firestone, "Victory for the Union at Plant in South Is Labor Milestone," *New York Times*, June 25, 1999.
10. "Organizers Are Recruiting Maine Egg Farm Workers for Vote Joining Union," *New York Times*, July 7, 1997.
11. Steven Greenhouse, "Workers Vote to Join Union at US Airways," *New York Times*, September 30, 1997.
12. Firestone, "Victory for the Union at Plant in South."
13. Lena Williams, "Women in Pro Basketball Want a Union of Their Own," *New York Times*, April 12, 1998.
14. Carey Goldberg, "Farm Workers Sign Accord with Lettuce Growers, Ending a Long and Bitter Conflict," *New York Times*, May 30, 1996.
15. Carey Goldberg, "Farm Workers Battle to Organize in California's Strawberry Fields," *New York Times*, July 3, 1996.
16. Navarro, "Florida Farm a Labor Battleground"; Associated Press, "Agreement Is Reached to Halt 10-Month Steelworker Strike," *New York Times*, August 2, 1997.
17. Elizabeth Kadetsky, "Dolores Huerta," *Ms. Magazine* (January/February 1998): 46.
18. Elizabeth Kadetsky, "Young Farmworkers Stand Up to Bias," *Ms. Magazine* (January/February 1998): 40.
19. Steven Greenhouse, "Chavez's Son-in-Law Tries to Rebuild Legacy," *New York Times*, June 30, 1997.
20. Greenhouse, "Chavez's Son-in-Law."
21. Nichole M. Christian, "3,400 Strike G.M. Plant, Assembly Put at Risk," *New York Times*, June 6, 1998.
22. Dirk Johnson, "Angry Voices of Pickets Reflect Sense of Concern," *New York Times*, August 6, 1997.
23. Johnson, "Angry Voices of Pickets."
24. Steven Greenhouse, "In Wake of Strike at UPS, a Crush of Parcels Awaits," *New York Times*, August 23, 1997.
25. Sam Howe Verhovek, "The New Language of American Labor," *New York Times*, June 26, 1999.
26. Verhovek, "The New Language of American Labor."
27. Mireya Navarro, "More Unions Set to Join Strike over Puerto Rican Phones," *New York Times*, June 30, 1998.
28. New York Times, "Puerto Rican Labor Protest Disrupts Travel," *New York Times*, July 8, 1998.
29. Craig Whitney, "French Strike Slows Travel in Protesting Proposed Cuts," *New York Times*, October 18, 1996.
30. Alan Cowell, "Strikes by German City Workers Frame Political Battle to Come," *New York Times*, March 4, 1998.
31. Steven Greenhouse, "Sweatshop Raids Cast Doubt on Ability of Garment Makers to Police Factories," *New York Times*, July 18, 1997.

32. Alan Finder, "Despite Tough Law, Sweatshops Flourish," *New York Times*, February 6, 1995.
33. Greenhouse, "Sweatshop Raids Cast Doubt."
34. Finder, "Despite Tough Law, Sweatshops Flourish."
35. Diana B. Henriquez, "Bitter Dispute Pits Garment Union against Its Workers," *New York Times*, April 27, 1998.
36. Steven Greenhouse, "Two More Unions Reject Pact for Curtailing the Sweatshop," *New York Times*, November 6, 1998.
37. Greenhouse, "Two More Unions Reject Pact."
38. Greenhouse, "Two More Unions Reject Pact." Steven Greenhouse, "Anti-Sweatshop Movement Is Achieving Gains Overseas," *New York Times*, January 26, 2000; Steven Greenhouse, "Banishing the Dickensian Factor," *New York Times*, July 9, 2000.
39. Philip Shenon, "Saipan Sweatshops Are No American Dream," *New York Times*, July 18, 1996.
40. Shenon, "Saipan Sweatshops."
41. Shenon, "Saipan Sweatshops."
42. Steven Greenhouse, "4 Companies Gain Accord in Labor Suit," *New York Times*, August 10, 1999.
43. Steven Greenhouse, "Duke to Adopt a Code to Prevent Apparel from Being Made in Sweatshops," *New York Times*, March 8, 1998.
44. Steven Greenhouse, "Two Protests by Students over Wages for Workers," *New York Times*, January 31, 1999.
45. Greenhouse, "Two Protests by Students"; Associated Press, "Princeton Students Protest over Sweatshops," *New York Times*, February 17, 1999.
46. Steven Greenhouse, "17 Top Colleges Enter Alliance on Sweatshops," *New York Times*, March 16, 1999.
47. Greenhouse, "17 Top Colleges Enter Alliance."
48. Carey Goldberg, "Limiting a State's Sphere of Influence," *New York Times*, November 15, 1998.
49. Goldberg, "Limiting a State's Sphere of Influence."
50. Henriquez, "Bitter Dispute Pits Garment Union against Its Workers."
51. Jim Robbins, "A Broken Pact and a $97 Million Payday," *New York Times*, April 19, 1998.
52. Barnaby Feder, "Harvest of Shares: One Farm's Stock Plans Gives Its Migrant Workers a Stake," *New York Times*, June 26, 1997.
53. Robert K. Schaeffer, *Power to the People: Democratization around the World* (Boulder, Colo.: Westview, 1997), 125–126.
54. Schaeffer, *Power to the People*, 144–146, 152, 158, 170–179, 181, 187, 194, 197–198, 200–201, 209–212, 217, 221.
55. See John Walton and David Seddon, *Free Markets & Food Riots: The Politics of Global Adjustment* (Oxford: Blackwell, 1994).
56. Schaeffer, *Power to the People*, 232–236.
57. Beverly J. Silver, "Turning Points of Worker's Militancy in the World Automobile Industry, 1930s–1990s," in Randy Hodson, ed., *Research in the Sociology of Work, The Globalization of Work*, vol. 6 (Greenwich, Conn.: JAI Press, 1997), 43–71.
58. Diana Jean Schemo, "Brazil's Nationalism Rises over Proposed Sale of State Mine," *New York Times*, May 3, 1997.
59. Schemo, "Brazil's Nationalism Rises."

60. Julia Preston, "A Hunger Strike by Humble Streetsweepers Is Capturing the Angry Mood in Mexico," *New York Times,* January 21, 1997.
61. Sam Dillon, "In a Landmark Case, Workers Triumph in a Tijuana Plant Dispute," *New York Times,* December 14, 1997.
62. "Mexico's Vulnerable Workers," *New York Times,* December 6, 1997.
63. "Mexico's Vulnerable Workers," *New York Times,* December 6, 1997.
64. Dillon, "In a Landmark Case"; Sam Dillon, "Union Vote in Mexico Illustrates Abuses," *New York Times,* October 13, 1997.
65. Dillon, "In a Landmark Case."
66. Sam Dillon, "Aeromexico Strike Marks Transition," *New York Times,* June 8, 1998.
67. Dillon, "Aeromexico Strike Marks Transition."
68. Dillon, "Aeromexico Strike Marks Transition."
69. Dillon, "Aeromexico Strike Marks Transition."
70. Andrew Pollack, "Koreans Not Rushing to Shake the Hand Holding the Bailout Check," *New York Times,* December 5, 1997.
71. Julia Preston, "Student Strike in Capitol Jarring All of Mexico," *New York Times,* June 25, 1999.
72. "Colombia: Strike Called," *New York Times,* September 1, 1999.
73. Nicolas D. Kristof, "Riot Police Clash with Protesters in Strike in Seoul," *New York Times,* December 19, 1996.
74. Associated Press, "350,000 on Strike in South Korea as Unrest Spreads," *New York Times,* December 19, 1996.
75. Andrew Pollack, "South Korean Strikes Expand as President Delivers Appeal to Labor Unions," *New York Times,* January 7, 1997.
76. Andrew Pollack, "Thriving, South Koreans Strike to Keep It That Way," *New York Times,* January 17, 1997.
77. Kristof, "Riot Police Clash with Protesters."
78. Kristof, "Riot Police Clash with Protesters"; Andrew Pollack, "South Koreans Assess Strike and Find the Losses Manageable," *New York Times,* January 21, 1997.
79. Pollack, "South Koreans Assess Strike."
80. Andrew Pollack, "To Mollify Labor Groups, South Korean Leader Yields a Bit," *New York Times,* January 22, 1997.
81. Pollack, "Koreans Not Rushing to Shake the Hand Holding the Bailout Check."
82. Seth Mydans, "For Indonesian Workers at the Nike Plant: Just Do It," *New York Times,* August 9, 1996.
83. Associated Press, "As Sierra Leone Strike Persists, Junta Seeks Regional Support," *New York Times,* June 10, 1997.
84. Fred Weir, "Russian Rumblings," *In These Times,* April 14, 1997.
85. Fred Weir, "Russia: Wage Rage," *In These Times,* July 26, 1998.
86. Associated Press, "Striking Romanian Miners Clash with Police on March," *New York Times,* January 20, 1999.
87. Edmund L. Andrews, "Poland Opens Door to West and Chills Blow Both Ways," *New York Times,* June 21, 1999.

Chapter 11
Institutional Struggles: Workers Challenge States

Laboring people challenge the state as an institution in different ways. Female and male workers organize insurrectionary movements and revolutionary armies that seek to overthrow governments by force. They form political parties representing workers and try to win electoral majorities. And they organize social movements to demand that states provide equality and justice, that they redeem the promises made by democratic republics around the world.

It was only a little more than a century ago, in the 1880s, that worker movements identified the seizure of state power as a primary political objective. Since then, worker movements have tried to seize state power in one of two ways. Some "revolutionary" groups tried to overthrow existing governments by force, while other "reformist" movements tried to win power through the electoral process. Workers have had success with both strategies. Revolutionaries seized power in countries like Russia, China, Cuba, Algeria, and Vietnam. Reformists won power in places like the United Kingdom, Germany, France, and Spain. But while these movements obtained their primary political objective, they were unable, in the long run, to transform the state as an institution of the capitalist world-system. They were unable to promote sustained economic development or provide workers with the political power and economic benefits that nineteenth-century workers' movements imagined would accompany their seizure of power. Looking back, the revolutionary movements that seized power in states across the periphery and semiperiphery betrayed workers in those countries and disappointed workers in other countries who might have wished them well. The reformist movements that won parliamentary majorities in the core were less of a disappointment. They managed to provide substantial benefits to workers for a time, but they, too, found it difficult to transform the state as an institution. In recent years, they were often required to manage the withdrawal of services and retraction of benefits provided earlier to workers in "welfare states."

The seizure of power, whether by force or by peaceful means, is still a primary political objective for many worker movements. Many ethnic independence movements have taken up arms to secure states of their own. But they are generally less interested in transforming the state as an institution than they are in acquiring the state so they can use its institutional levers to provide benefits to themselves, without interference from other ethnic groups. While they subscribe to an idea once thought "revolutionary," ethnic movement efforts to obtain states of their own are hardly novel or radical departures. If they succeed in dividing existing states, they simply miniaturize existing institutions and reproduce relations of hierarchy and inequality in new, smaller settings.

Other workers have recently organized movements to overthrow dictatorships and one-party regimes, many of them established by "revolutionary" worker movements in an earlier period. Their success in recent years has been a welcome and significant political achievement. But it has been something of an economic disappointment because democratizing states have generally been required to adopt policies—austerity programs and neoliberal policies—that have been inimical to workers.

Just as workers have organized movements to challenge capital as an economic institution, workers have organized insurrectionary, electoral, separatist, and democratic movements to seize power and transform the state as a political institution, though with varying degrees of success. Workers around the world have done so for a long time, and their efforts continue today. But rather than focus on these efforts, which are well documented and widely appreciated, we want to focus here on worker movements that are not trying to seize the state but instead want to make the state fulfill its "obligations" to provide equality and justice. This may sound like a "reformist," not a "revolutionary," goal, but it is actually a radical objective because it is extremely difficult for states to provide both real equality and substantive justice and remain functioning institutions of the capitalist world-system. By demanding that the state treat all people equally, feminist and antiracist movements attack the legitimacy of the state and the system itself.

The state is an institution of the capitalist world-system, so there are real limits to its ability to promote equality, redistribute resources, and secure impartial justice. Movements that demand these things of the state, which its defenders cannot easily repudiate without surrendering their legitimacy, may in fact subvert, derail, and transform the state as an institution. In a sense, movements that demand equality and justice are asking the impossible. If the state cannot provide what it says it must, then it may lose its legitimacy, its ability to function as a capitalist institution.

In this context, we want to examine three kinds of worker movements that challenge the state as an institution. First, certain movements demand democracy and equality. In some settings, this means an end to dictatorship, in others it means an end to discrimination and access to education and employment. We will look at the students, homosexuals, and ethnic groups that demand that states fulfill their obligations to provide democracy and equality.

Second, many workers demand resources from the state. Increasingly, workers have made a novel claim on the state's resources. They have demanded that states provide compensation or reparations for past injustice. A growing number of movements hold states liable for damages to workers, even if the states responsible for the injury no longer exist. Jewish, Japanese American, and Native American movements have been pioneers, and their success has encouraged other groups of injured or wronged workers to file claims, seeking to place substantial liens on institutional resources.

Third, workers have organized movements demanding impartial justice. They have called for an end to policies that enhance the state's police powers. They object to the surveillance-prison-punishment practices that states use to enforce hierarchy and inequality, particularly those directed at ethnic minorities. Movements have also demanded an end to extrajuridical violence, which has been used by state surrogates, both by groups of armed men and by individual males, to maintain hierarchy and patriarchy.

As we survey these movements, it is important to keep in mind some of their distinctive features. Many movements make overlapping demands, and the constituents often have multiple social identities and play different political roles. So, for example, women participate in movements to end gender-based discrimination, obtain compensation for past injustice, and demand an end to state-sponsored violence and individual rape. It is perhaps useful to think of a continuum, rather than discrete sets of identifiable actors and separate objectives.

It is important to recognize, too, that many of the worker protests that challenge the "state" are now dispersed. Workers today rarely organize the kind of large, focused, anticentral government protests they once did. In the United States, the Million Man March, the Million Woman March, and the anti-gun Million Mom's March are recent examples of focused protests. But protests against the state are often more diffuse and dispersed in the core, the semiperiphery, and the periphery because the state, as an institution, has recently changed shape and reduced its support for worker households.

States in the core, the periphery, and the semiperiphery have not only reduced worker benefits, they have also "devolved" or transferred powers from the central government to other formal and informal institutions. In the United States, for example, the federal government has in recent years devolved considerable responsibility to state and local authorities and, more important, to nongovernmental organizations (NGOs) or "nonprofit" agencies. These governmental authorities and nongovernment agencies are asked to assume responsibility and provide resources for workers that the central government is no longer willing to offer.

The devolution of central government authority reverses a process that began in the early years of this century. During the early 1900s, nonprofit agencies, sometimes described as "charities," provided important services and resources to workers. At that time they tried to wean worker households from relying on self-sufficient work and their own initiative on the streets and in their homes and instead seek paid employment in shops and factories. Charities provided food, shelter, and counsel to households, both as carrot and stick, to persuade workers to make the transition to "respectable" employment as wage workers.[1] In this capacity, charities acted as informal agents of the state, what might be called parastatal agencies or even surrogates. The role of charities was usurped or taken over by the federal government in the 1930s and 1940s because private parastatals proved incapable of meeting the needs of workers during the Great Depression.[2]

Today, nonprofits are again being asked to provide parastatal services and resources to workers, minorities, women, children, immigrants, and the poor. But they are being asked to perform a rather different role than they did earlier. At the turn of the century, charities tried to discourage worker self-sufficiency and initiative. Today, they are trying to encourage worker self-reliance so they can wean workers of their dependency on the state and employment in industry.[3]

Of course, most of these charitable nonprofits are run by well-meaning people. Today, many consider themselves "progressives," as did their turn-of-the-century predecessors. But the central government's growing reliance on these well-meaning surrogates has two problems. First, they are not accountable to the "clients" they serve. They are responsible only to their boards and funding sources, which typically consist of either private foundations (run by trustees for their wealthy benefactors) or government bureaucracies that disburse public funds to private nonprofits. Second, they lack the resources to meet the growing needs of workers. As we already noted (see chapter 3), charitable contributions have been declining, largely because wealthy households are less willing to pay formal or informal taxes to assist others. When government welfare benefits begin to expire, when workers are laid off in large numbers during the next recession, the demand for services and resources will increase. The ability of nonprofits to meet workers' needs, we expect, will then be severely tested, much as it was during the Great Depression.

For workers in the United States, the devolution of state power has important consequences. It has dispersed state power and, in the process, scattered and deflected worker protest, at least for a time. It has also encouraged workers to become more self-reliant, as we will see in the next chapter. But workers are beginning to demand both accountability and resources from government authorities and their nonprofit surrogates, demands that will increasingly test both.

The reduction of government services for workers is less advanced in Western Europe, but evidence exists that it is underway there as well. It is perhaps even more advanced in Japan, where workers have long been expected to provide benefits and resources to distressed family members (see chapter 7).

In the periphery and semiperiphery, states have not devolved much of their authority to domestic nonprofits. Instead, many have transferred power to foreign NGOs: international relief organizations, UN agencies, and international "peacekeeping" forces. In some countries, like Somalia, where the state has collapsed, NGOs have entirely replaced the state as an institution.[4]

But the problems with the devolution of state power in the periphery and semiperiphery are much the same as they are in the core. When states devolve power to foreign NGOs and global political or military authorities, the institutions charged with providing services and resources to workers are not accountable to workers and they have limited resources. Moreover, unlike formal states, NGOs are unwilling to provide services and resources on an ongoing basis. Global NGOs and institutions typically set deadlines or target dates, after which time they terminate their services and withdraw. States, by contrast, were imagined as permanent institutions. Again, the problem for workers is that it is difficult to develop or focus challenges to the "state" when its powers and resources are distributed and dispersed in this fashion, to institutions run by foreigners and transients.

Nonetheless, workers are challenging states and their foreign and domestic surrogates. It is important, in this context, to remember that the state as an institution does not consist only of "government" but also of the ideological and social practices and organizations that sometimes assist it (schools, churches, the media, nonprofit organizations, and charities), what Antonio Gramsci called "civil society." So worker protests against the state include not only demonstrations against the central government but also protests against nonprofits and NGOs, both foreign and domestic, and global economic institutions and international peace-keeping forces. They also include protests against the armed groups of men that are the state's violent surrogates in many places, and the individuals who deploy violence to maintain the state, defend hierarchy and inequality, and protect patriarchy. The workers who protest extrajuridical violence—ethnic minorities, women, children, immigrants—are challenging not only its perpetrators but also their benefactors in government. Let us turn now to the movements that demand democracy and equality from states.

MOVEMENTS FOR DEMOCRACY AND EQUALITY

Although dictators and one-party regimes were swept from power in many countries during the last twenty years, dictators retain control of some states. So workers have continued to mobilize against them.

After demonstrators were massacred in Tiananmen Square in 1989, the regime in China has carefully squelched worker activism. But the regime has not been entirely successful. In January 1999, for example, thousands of southern Chinese farmers led a large protest, confronting heavily armed police. Angry farmers sought to eliminate or reduce excessive and arbitrary taxes, particularly the school and building fees imposed by the central government and local authorities. On the second day of their protest, farmers were met by five hundred police. Workers elsewhere have protested the nonpayment of pensions by factory managers, investment rip-off schemes, and official corruption.[5] But the most widely discussed movement in China is the Falun Gong spiritual and health movement, whose leader resides in New York. The Chinese government cracked down on this movement because it holds large, unauthorized demonstrations, one with ten thousand participants. Authorities have argued that its spiritual claims, which clash with government dogma, go beyond what government officials say can be proven scientifically.[6] Alternative ideologies can be very threatening to authoritarian regimes. The struggle for freedom of thought in China, as elsewhere, is an important component of the struggle for democracy.

In Burma, the dictatorship recently cracked down on dissidents. Like the regime in China, the Burmese dictatorship slaughtered prodemocracy demonstrators in 1988, one year before the massacre at Tiananmen Square. In 1996, students renewed their protests against the state. In response, the government closed all the universities. Prodemocracy activists led by Aung San Suu Kyi then decided to convene their own "true" national parliament, which declared all of the military government's laws null and void. Opposition party leaders wanted to force the military junta to engage in a dialogue about Burma's future, a future cast into doubt by rising unemployment and growing food shortages.[7] In the fall of 1999, prodemocracy supporters seized the national assembly and captured hostages.[8] The opposition's alternative parliament has begun to institutionalize a second state and to challenge directly the junta's legitimacy.

In African countries, many direct confrontations have erupted between working people and states run by dictators. Some of these have occurred during civil wars and during periods when political power has been transferred or seized. In Kenya, for example, working people tried to persuade the government to adopt constitutional reforms in 1999. Working people argued that reforms were needed to reduce unemployment, eliminate corruption, and prevent health care and schools from deteriorating. Prodemocracy demonstrators blocked the highway leading to Nairobi and were assaulted by police.[9]

Where dictators have fallen and civilian governments have taken over, workers have organized to protest central government policies, particularly austerity programs. In democratizing Latin American and Caribbean countries, this kind of protest has been an ongoing feature of contemporary politics. In Haiti, for example, 160 grass-roots organizations called a general strike in January 1997 to voice their opposition to international austerity measures, unemployment, massive cutbacks in state employment, and police violence. As burning tires blocked traffic, and workers and students stayed home, a group of poor working people tried to loot food from a government warehouse.[10] In Brazil, workers have demanded President Cardoso's resignation, a halt to privatization, and the termination of the government's austerity program. In 1999, Brazilian labor unions and left-wing parties organized one of the largest demonstrations in recent years.[11] In Bolivia, thousands of public transit workers carried out a two-day strike in 1999 to object to rising fuel prices.[12] And a coalition of Ecuador's Indian organizations, labor unions, and opposition political parties organized powerful street demonstrations, protesting against growing poverty, and forced a change in government. Indians in Ecuador, where they constitute one-third of the population, have established their own parallel people's parliament, much like the one created by prodemocracy forces in Burma, and plan to carry out an extended civil-disobedience campaign against the neoliberal government.[13]

Student Movements

Rather than trying to fit into the world as it is, many students around the world are rebelling against the state and society. Universities have often become sites where young adults try, through political activism, to create a better future for themselves and others. As we have seen previously (see chapter 10), students in antisweatshop movements have tried to improve conditions for workers in other locations and change their own consumption patterns to reflect more sustainable ways of living as workers.

In the United States, student and youth movements have grown, largely because students realize that few young people will be able to obtain full-time positions that support middle-class lifestyles. Young people today are the first generation to experience fully the downward mobility associated with the redistribution and reorganization of work in the United States. In September 1999, the Million Youth March, which followed hard on the heels of the Million Man March and the Million Woman March, took place in Harlem. At the march, young African Americans expressed their frustration and anger with the state and inequality.[14] Students at predominantly Black and Latino high schools in California, meanwhile, filed a class-action suit against the State of California because many high schools students in poor districts are never offered the courses that they need to gain admission to California's most selective public universities.[15]

In France, high school students have staged similar protests, arguing that the state does not provide the institutional support they need to gain entry to the university or help them find jobs in the private sector. In 1998, 500,000 French high school students took to the streets and organized sit-down strikes at schools, demanding that the state provide more teachers, add classrooms, bring an end to gang violence, change the curriculum, and reduce the number of classes required for the final examination.[16] As in the United States, many students objected to the racist features of the educational system. High school students most in need of state support are immigrants from North Africa, who live in the suburbs of big cities.[17]

University students in France began demanding more state support for education in 1995. They saw it as a way to increase their chance of finding work after they graduated. The post-1995 wave of student uprisings in France is the first major student movement to emerge since 1968, when student protest rocked the government of Charles de Gaulle. Student protesters have been joined by unemployed young people from low-income suburban neighborhoods. In Paris, students and their nonacademic allies looted stores, burned cars, and wrestled with riot police, a reminder of the 1968 student demonstrations in the Latin Quarter.[18] Although unemployed youth and students did not plan their protests together, the alliance between unemployed and school-oriented youth may mark the creation of a youth movement that joins the privileged with the underprivileged.

In the late 1990s, university students around the world have staged lengthy strikes and protests. Like students in the United States and France, students in other countries have tried to maintain or strengthen educational resources so they can prevent the downward mobility of the working class. Students at the National Autonomous University of Mexico organized a student strike that lasted for almost one year. Because the National University is Latin America's largest university, serving 270,000 students, it sets the political tone for universities in the Americas. So this strike has had a major impact on students across the continent. Striking students demanded that the state rescind tuition increases, which raised the cost of instruction from a few cents to $150 a year, and not prosecute striking students. University officials agreed not to prosecute strikers but continued to insist that students pay higher fees. They also rejected demands that students share power with faculty and administrators and restore open-admission policies, allowing students with minimal high school grades to attend the university.[19] Striking students also demanded that the police stop their surveillance of students and that they dismantle their network of campus video cameras. The fight against rising fees was part of a wider campaign that criticized state officials, who have tried to reduce national debt by demanding more of students and workers. Some students argued that the destruction of public education in Mexico was a result of International Monetary Fund and World Bank policies. "For us, education is not a commercial service," one student leader said, "it is one of the social rights we won in Mexico over the last decades."[20] The nine-month strike ended after university officials conducted a "plebiscite" in which a majority of students voted to end the strike and then called in police to enforce the results and evict striking students.[21]

Prodemocracy university students in Indonesia organized first against the Suharto dictatorship and then against his appointed successor. In their effort to create a "people power" movement with their parents, university students demanded greater participation in decision-making, stable prices, and an end to government corruption. Human rights abuses by the military and food shortages also became key issues. University students held daily protests, and they were joined by students around the country. Students persuaded other workers and their parents to join the protests. For example, local women in Semarang joined two thousand women students in one demonstration. In their effort to change Indonesia, student demonstrators gathered wide support from parents, teachers, news reporters, and workers, and protests by students and other working-class movements overlapped on the streets between April 1998 and February 1999. Peaceful protests often mixed with violent street battles with government security forces.[22] The prodemocracy student movement in Indonesia was accompanied by an anticolonial movement in East Timor, where prodemocracy and pro-independence activists fought successfully for the withdrawal of Indonesian troops that had occupied the country since 1974.

In Iran, tens of thousands of university students poured into the streets in July 1999. Initially, they demanded only that the theocratic government grant more freedom of the press and lift the ban on *Salam*, a daily newspaper that supported Iran's elected president and his efforts to control the state's security forces. The student demonstrations were the largest since the pro-Islamic demonstrations against the Shah in 1979. The state reacted violently to the student protests. Security forces and their vigilantes tear-gassed demonstrators, bludgeoned students, and crammed female protesters into cages mounted on top of police cars. On campus, security forces ran through male and female dormitories, attacking students with clubs and throwing some students out of windows. Student protests generated considerable public sympathy, and some observers shaved their beards to express their solidarity with clean-shaven demonstrators.[23] Eventually, student demands widened. "This is not about *Salam* [press freedom] but about freedom in general," one student said. "We are not even allowed to breathe."[24] Looking at more open discussions about the role of clerics, the editor of the newspaper *Iran el-Farda* remarked, "The talk will continue. The ice is beginning to thaw."[25]

While Indonesian and Iranian university students helped forge new coalitions with workers, students at Seoul National University in South Korea prepared to march to the border with North Korea in August 1999. Students demanded that South and North Korea be reunified. But when students began their march, they were met by eight thousand riot police. South Korean authorities wanted to contain what they called the "leftist" student movement, which has become more active in recent years. Students threw rocks at the police and shouted, "Let's accomplish unification!"[26] During the summer of 2000, officials from the two Koreas began negotiating about possible reunification.

Student protests, which demand greater democracy and an end to downward mobility, now take place all around the world. In Thailand, where family status and not student achievement often provides the ticket to exclusive government-run schools, one mother challenged the school that rejected her six-year-old daughter and began a wider struggle for greater equality.[27] At the University of Cocody in the Ivory Coast, a school where 75 percent of the country's students are educated, students went on strike so many times in 1998 that administrators decided not to count the academic year.[28] When four hundred students in Harare, Zimbabwe, demonstrated in front of the Ministry of Higher Education, demanding that they be provided larger student aid grants, paramilitary police officers clubbed hundreds of students.[29]

Schools and universities are not only a center of student activity; they are also a place where nonstudent groups can meet to demand change. At the University of Antioquia in Colombia, workers and students have fought to clear the campus of left- and right-wing paramilitary groups.

FEMINIST MOVEMENTS FOR GENDER AND SEXUAL EQUALITY

Since the late 1960s, women have demanded that the state recognize the principle of gender equality. Feminist movements have also attacked patriarchy, which they see as linked to capitalist society and the state.

Antipatriarchal movements include those that help create a culture that values women. Feminists have struggled to rid cultures of phallocentric practices that demean women, particularly beauty pageants and swimsuit competitions. In 1996, when the Miss World contest was held in Bangalore, India, women from some feminist organizations announced that they planned to commit suicide to disrupt the pageant. One man, who felt that the beauty pageant degraded Indian women, set himself on fire and died.[30]

The Million Woman March, which was held in Philadelphia in 1997, was directed both at the state and at patriarchy. Marchers encouraged African American and other women to develop stronger bonds of woman-to-woman solidarity and end painful jealousies that have divided friends and communities. The mobilization of African American women was seen as a way to demand more of the state, particularly by improving educational opportunities, and as a way to challenge institutional and household patriarchy. "This march is a way to show it's not a negative thing to be a woman and Black," said Devona Gonsalves. "Or a woman, period."[31]

Many feminist groups challenged the state and patriarchy by mounting public policy campaigns. In Japan, feminist organizations led by Watchguard successfully forced a government official to resign in 1999 after he groped a female employee during a car ride. Women in Persian Gulf countries have tried to reform a number of public policies: giving Kuwaiti women the right to vote and run for office; permitting Saudi Arabian women to drive; and allowing women in the United Arab Emirates to serve as cabinet ministers.

Gender equity movements challenge both public policies and private social practices. The gender hierarchy is not simply a product of public policy; it is also a product of practices at the personal, intergenerational, and household level. Gender-group formation and age-group formation overlap and are both shaped by family relations and by broader social forces. Although gender is widely acknowledged as an oppressive social construct, age is often treated simply as an inevitable biological process. But some groups have challenged the social construction of age-based inequality. Student movements and movements organized by mature adults and elders have demanded an end to age-based inequality. Elder movements, for example, have demanded that the state provide improved health care, job retraining, good housing, an end to elder abuse, and the creation of a more age-tolerant culture. Just as members of the subordinate gender organize to change society, people in subordinate age groups also organize to challenge the state.

The same is true of groups with subordinate sexual identities. About 10 percent of the population consists of people with "gay" or "queer" sexual identities. Like gender- and age-based movements, queer movements can play a crucial part of working people's struggles for personal and social freedom.

Social movements promoting lesbian, gay, bisexual, and transgender rights form an integral part of the struggle for gender and sexual equality. These movements also contribute to workers' struggles against the state. Sexual equality movements push for a more open society through public policy initiatives. The struggle for sexual equality, like the struggle for gender equality, is ultimately a struggle that challenges public policy and private practices.

In the United States, the Vermont Supreme Court ruled in December 1999 that the state legislature had to grant lesbian and gay couples the same legal rights provided to married heterosexual couples. Justice Denise Johnson argued that her colleagues should just legalize same-sex marriage, rather than allow the legislature to consider alternative remedies. In California, meanwhile, Governor Grey Davis signed legislation outlawing the harassment of lesbian and gay students and teachers in public schools and universities. The Servicemembers Legal Defense Network has fought antigay violence in the military and the Clinton administration's "Don't ask, don't tell" policy. In early 2000, the British government passed legislation allowing lesbians and gays to serve in the military. Sexual equity movements have made extensive efforts to create safe spaces where alternative, queer culture can develop and to educate the dominant culture about more tolerant ways of living.

ANTIRACIST STRUGGLES FOR EQUALITY

Racism does not just divide people of "White" European descent from people of "Black" African descent. It also divides the core from the rest of the world. Racism is a product of policies and practices adopted by businesses and states. But it is also a product of practices adopted by dominant ethnic and cultural groups, who believe that they deserve more than members of less powerful ethnic groups and who use the artificial concept of race to defend their advantaged place in the hierarchy.

Antiracist labor movements fight on at least two fronts. First, they challenge businesses and the state, which are the two main institutions that promote racial hierarchy. Second, they fight the racism of dominant ethnic groups. Antiracist struggles, like feminist struggles, are embedded in many of the movements organized by working people.

Contemporary antiracist movements demand that workers abandon racial myths and create a new cultural framework that brings out the best in all people. Of course, battles against racism are subtle and complex. In South Africa, for example, "mixed-race" South Africans organized violent protests to obtain the cheap water and electricity rates that the government had already granted to "Black" South Africans, which had been intended as a remedy to "White" racism.[32]

Antiracist movements challenge not only the government as an institution but also the nongovernmental institutions that comprise the state and civil society. In Brazil, for example, people of African descent have challenged the Roman Catholic Church by following Candomble, a religion created by slaves that embraces both African deities and Catholic saints. Church officials in Rome began attacking Candomble syncretism after the Brazilian government designated a Candomble temple a national treasure. By recruiting and training more Black priests and bishops, the Vatican hoped to wean African-Brazilians from Candomble. But many African-Brazilians stood up to Catholic leaders, demanding that they be allowed to practice their African-defined mixture of animism and Catholicism within the Church. And in a movement against historical and global racism, indigenous people in Brazil occupied a national park to protest the initial Portuguese invasion five hundred years ago.[33]

Brazilians have also challenged the racist practices of Carnival clubs. After an African-Brazilian college student was denied membership at one club in 1999, she filed charges of racial discrimination. Adriana Andrade had been told by Whites that she didn't fit in because "Blacks can't join this block," and a childhood friend asked her, "How many more darkies are you planning to bring around?" Ms. Andrade explained why she filed the complaint: "I couldn't remain silent because it was a question of honor, not just for me, but for all black people. As a citizen and a consumer, I have the right not to be blocked by my color."[34] In response to White racism, many Blacks have formed their own Carnival clubs to protest what they call Brazil's perverse cultural apartheid.[35]

Cultural issues are also extremely important for antiracist movements in other countries. In Guatemala, Mayans from twenty-one different linguistic groups have started to "develop visions of our own identity and question everything, from a colonialist church to our relationship with the state," Demetrio Cojti explained.[36] Mayan groups have demanded the incorporation of Maya spiritual healers into public health-care systems and the development of bicultural public schools.

In Central European countries like the Czech Republic and Serbia, Gypsies (or Roma) have organized to fight discrimination in education, employment, and housing. In an effort to eliminate educational segregation and tracking, Gypsy families have appealed to national courts and to the European Court of Human Rights in Strasbourg.[37] Roma have frequently been assaulted by neo-Nazi "skinheads." In 1997, a neo-Nazi street gang in Belgrade attacked and killed a pregnant Gypsy woman. Gang members then killed a teen boy. According to mourner Berisa Ljuan, the Serbs hate Gypsies because "we are dark . . . and we are not Serbs."[38] Aleksandar Jovanovic, father of the murdered boy, said that Gypsy street sweepers were frequently assaulted. "The gangs grab us and light our hair on fire, beat us or strip us of our clothing and make us walk home naked. We file complaints to the police and they do nothing because we are only Gypsies. If the police had reacted, my son would be alive."[39] Confronting their historical exclusion, Gypsies or Roma have also demanded compensation for Nazi atrocities during World War II.

In India, India's *dalits* (often called untouchables) have joined with other, slightly higher castes (or "Other Backward Castes") to demand that the government uphold provisions in the 1950 constitution that forbid discrimination against lower castes. One thirty-nine-year-old *dalit* woman, Mayawati, mobilized a coalition of lower caste groups and Muslims and was elected the chief minister of the state Uttar Pradesh.[40] *Dalits* in the state of Bihar organized to demand higher wages, obtain access to land, and bring an end to the sexual exploitation of lower-caste women. In response to their demands, fifty upper-caste men encircled the village of Shanker Bigha and massacred twenty-two rural people.[41] Wealthier groups have periodically massacred *dalit* communities and tried to force *dalits* to withdraw their demands for equality and economic resources. But *dalit* communities have not been dissuaded, and they have continued to organize coalitions that transcend caste divisions.

Culturally subordinated ethnic groups are waging pro-egalitarian struggles all over the world. Egalitarian movements that challenge state policies and cultural practices can have an important impact on workers in other countries. In the United States, for example, Latinos have mobilized to fight policies that discriminate against new and established immigrants. In 1996, Latinos marched on Washington. They demanded that the federal government continue affirmative action programs, adopt a higher minimum wage, extend the amnesty program for illegal immigrants, and improve public health services and education for residents and recent immigrants.[42] This movement connected workers across the United States and linked them to workers in and from other countries.

COMPENSATION AND REPARATION MOVEMENTS

In the last twenty-five years, new compensation movements have emerged around the world. Some have obtained partial restitution and apologies for past wrongs and injuries. Compensation activists have also persuaded states and businesses to pay restitution to injured workers. These movements demand not only money but also public apologies for violating group and individual rights. Compensation movements want to "right" historical "wrongs."

Movements that demand compensation or reparations for past injustice and injury are novel in several important respects. They argue not only that the past is present in the contemporary world, a notion at odds with capitalism's focus on the here and now, but that the state as an institution is liable for damages to workers, even if the state responsible for the injury no longer exists.

Why have these movements grown in recent years? They have done so for several reasons. First, the global movements of 1968 persuaded workers to think critically about the state and social injustice.[43] Second, in the last twenty years, states have begun to cut back worker benefits and disclaim any responsibility for worker welfare. By demanding compensation, workers not only seek to obtain important resources from the state but also insist that it assume, not deny, responsibility for the welfare of worker-citizens. Third, the legal and legislative success of some claimants has encouraged other victimized groups to come forward and press their suits.

A number of compensation movements have succeeded, and these movements have spurred other groups around the world to seek some form of redistributive justice. In the United States, Japanese Americans pressed for decades to obtain compensation for their forced internment at inland barracks during World War II. In 1988, Congress granted up to $20,000 per person for losses suffered by the 110,000 Japanese and Japanese American survivors interned during the war. Following this success, Italian Americans organized a movement to obtain an apology for the wartime internment of 1,600 Italians and for the government's campaign to spy on 10,000 Italian Americans. More recently, the 2,000 citizens of Latin American countries who were of Japanese ancestry and were also interned in U.S. camps during World War II obtained $5,000 each and an apology from the U.S. government.

Native American groups and indigenous people in other countries have also been pioneers, demanding compensation for injuries suffered long ago. In 1999, for example, the Oneida Indian nation in upstate New York organized to press its claims against New York state and local governments, which had illegally acquired 270,000 acres of Oneida land between 1795 and 1840 without congressional approval. As a result of these illegal expropriations, the Oneida people were left with only 32 acres. Surprisingly, the U.S. Department of Justice has joined with the Oneida in their battle to regain their land.[44] This land reclamation movement can be considered a compensation movement because the Oneida, like many other movements, seek to use the state to redress past wrongs related to racism and coloniality.

Just as Indian groups in the United States have sought to regain stolen land, more than four hundred Maori tribes have forced the state in New Zealand to make compensatory payments for seized land and to protect burial grounds.[45]

Many compensation movements have forced private and public employers to acknowledge that they discriminate against workers in the workplace. In Canada, for example, the pay equity movement is a compensation movement that has asked the state to address sexist employment practices. In the largest pay-equity settlement in North America, the federal government agreed to pay female employees (and male employees in female-dominated jobs) salaries equal to their male counterparts. This 1999 pay-equity settlement occurred because "equal pay for work of equal value" was written into the Canada's Human Rights Act twenty years ago. The government agreed that workers in an occupation dominated by women (e.g., typist) would be paid the same as workers in an occupation dominated by men (sailor), so long as the occupations were rated at the same level. In order to increase the pay for female jobs to comparable pay levels for males, the government will pay out up to $2.3 billion to 230,000, mostly female, federal workers.[46]

Many movements have demanded reparations for contemporary and historical injustice. In the United States, leaders of African American groups have called on Congress to compensate African Americans for the enslavement of Black people prior to the Civil War.[47] So far, Congress has refused to consider this request. But African Americans have nonetheless successfully pressed smaller claims. Southern Black farm families, for example, forced the U.S. government to provide compensation, about $50,000 per farm family, for discriminatory farm loan practices and poor legal assistance, which forced many Black families into bankruptcy. In 2000, the African American reparations movement took a new direction, when Deadria Farmer-Pullman, a lawyer and archival historian who was inspired by the anti-Nazi compensation movement in Europe, began pressing some U.S. corporations to make restitution for the profits they made from slavery. If successful, it may encourage other compensation movements to attack private enterprises that profited from exploitation.[48]

In January 2000, former inmates at Attica prison in New York were awarded $8 million for injuries they suffered when they were assaulted by state troopers and prison guards, who fired 3,000 rounds at inmates during a 1971 prison riot. The settlement provided about $20,000 to each of the 400 survivors. Back in 1971, Governor Rockefeller had ordered the police to storm the Attica prison yard and fire indiscriminately at the 1,281 prisoners and the guards they held hostage. An investigation after the five-day uprising revealed that the police had killed 39 inmates and hostages, wounding 89 others.[49] Although state officials lied and claimed otherwise, subsequent medical investigators proved that the prisoners did not kill a single hostage. Instead, the hostages had all been killed by police bullets. The Attica prison uprising began after prison officials refused to consider some basic, human demands. Prisoners had asked officials to eliminate overcrowding, provide better medical care and food, permit more than one shower a week, allocate more than one roll of toilet paper a month, grant inmates the right to read the Black Panther newspaper, and allow prisoners to have a Black Muslim minister.[50]

In Oklahoma, an official commission recommended that the state provide reparations to Black survivors of race riots in Tulsa. During the 1921 riot, between forty and three hundred Blacks were killed and hundreds of homes burned by Whites.[51] The commission noted that the Florida legislature paid $2 million to compensate Black survivors of a 1923 massacre in Rosewood, which destroyed the small town and resulted in the deaths of at least six Blacks.[52]

There is also an ideological dimension to compensation movements. In 1996, Southern Baptists apologized to African Americans for their antebellum support of slavery, and in 1999, the United Church of Christ apologized for its members' participation in the slave trade.[53] President Clinton apologized to the Hawaiians for the overthrow of Queen Liliuokalani's monarchy by U.S. marines, and he apologized to the victims of crippling, racist medical experiments conducted at the Tuskegee Institute. British prime minister Tony Blair apologized in 1997 for the government's failure to assist the Irish during the potato famine. In 1998, President Clinton obliquely apologized for America's role in the enslavement of Africans during a visit to Goree Island in Senegal, a notorious slave warehousing fort. Six months later, Japan's prime minister apologized for Japan's colonial occupation of Korea between 1910 and 1945.

Consumer struggles, some centered around women, have complemented the efforts of compensation movements. A women-led movement of workers and community members received company compensation for chemical contamination at Love Canal. Women consumers also won compensation for health problems caused by invasive, unhealthy breast implants. In a similar class-action suit, women won $50 million because the manufacturer failed to warn them about the side effects of the contraceptive Norplant, which included headaches, excessive menstrual bleeding, nausea, dizziness, depression, and excess hair growth. In a more general consumer struggle, cigarette smokers and state governments successfully forced tobacco companies to admit that they knew cigarettes were unhealthy and addictive, leading to various forms of compensation for workers and state governments. These consumer and environmental suits provided important legal precedents and legislative skills to other compensation movements.

One important, crossnational compensation movement gained new strength in 1996 and 1997, when European financial investigators disclosed that many banks had seized assets from Jews killed during the Holocaust. As Swiss and other banks revealed information about the bank holdings of Holocaust victims, compensation movements accelerated their efforts to win compensation for Jews whose assets had been seized, but also for workers who were forced to labor for Nazis and for families of Holocaust victims who had been denied insurance claims. Sustained international pressure forced Swiss banks and Allied countries to admit that much of the wealth stolen from Jewish Holocaust victims had been used to finance the German war machine. The political work of Jewish organizations, particularly the World Jewish Congress and the Jewish Agency, played a crucial role in forcing firms and states to compensate survivors and re-examine institutional racism. Jewish organizations sought restitution from Swiss banks for three reasons: (1) by purchasing gold stolen from Jews by Germany, Swiss banks financed the Nazi's war effort; (2) by turning away Jewish refugees, they sent Jews to their deaths; and (3) by keeping the money deposited by Holocaust victims in Swiss banks and keeping the money paid on their insurance policies, Swiss banks profited from the Holocaust.[54] Archival researchers in Germany, Switzerland, Israel, Norway, France, and other countries have documented widespread theft and helped this movement gain strength.

In January 1999, Holocaust survivors received a $1.25 billion settlement from Swiss banks. Under this agreement, victims of Nazi persecution are defined to include: Jews, Gypsies, homosexuals, mentally or physically disabled people, and Jehovah's Witnesses. Other groups that are eligible for compensation include people who were forced to work for companies that held their money in Swiss banks, people forced to work for companies that used slave labor, and Jews who fled to Switzerland but were then were deported to Germany.[55]

One month later, the German government and German firms announced the creation of a DM 10 billion fund that will be used to compensate slave laborers who were exploited by Nazi industrial and agricultural firms. This fund, which was created to deflect class-action lawsuits against German companies, goes beyond Germany's previous reparation efforts. Germany has already paid $60 billion to individual Jews and the State of Israel. Forced laborers for industries, mostly non-Jews from Eastern Europe who were deported to Germany, and slave laborers in concentration camps finally received $5 billion in compensation funds in 2000. The settlement provided up to $2,500 to forced laborers and up to $7,500 to slave laborers.[56] The government in Poland, which is home to more than 500,000 former slave laborers, will help develop a reparation agreement that will provide remembrance programs and monetary compensation to workers in Europe, Israel, and the United States.[57]

Governments in other countries have developed a number of approaches to compensate Nazi victims. Hungary, a former communist country, created additional government pensions for Jewish elders who survived the Holocaust. Prior to this, Jews who lived behind the "Iron Curtain" did not receive compensation after the war because the Allies feared that it would be stolen by communist governments.[58] In order to "pay" for the property it expropriated during World War II and to "seek a broad, moral reconciliation," Norway came up with a plan to pay $60 million to Norwegian Jews and to crossnational Jewish organizations.[59] In 1998, an Italian insurance company announced that it would pay $100 million in reparations to Holocaust victims.[60] Nazis also imprisoned Americans in concentration camps. These Americans, who were captured during the war or caught before they could leave Europe, have obtained compensation from Germany.[61] Germany has not only provided compensation to victims of the Nazi regime, it has also pardoned hundreds of thousands of people who were convicted under Nazi laws and punished by the Nazi state. Resistance fighters, deserters, conscientious objectors, homosexuals, and disabled people were among those given official pardons.[62] This set of restitution movements has led other groups to address wartime wrongs in other settings. In Spain, for example, the government agreed to make payments and return property to Basques and others, who had been victimized by the fascist government's seizure of Spanish Republican property during the late 1930s.[63]

Although compensation movements are organized by different groups in different countries, these movements have developed in relationship to one another. When movements are relatively successful, other movements adopt this antistate approach. In South Africa, a strong and multifaceted compensation movement has grown rapidly in recent years. The vast Black majority was intensively exploited after White colonizers seized their land following passage of the 1913 land expropriation law. The small White minority seized 87 percent of South Africa's land for itself and prohibited Black South Africans from owning more than a small share. This massive theft of land eventually created the basis for South Africa's strong land compensation movement in the mid-1990s.

Given the widespread poverty and lack of resources among Blacks in South Africa, the National Land Committee in 1994 recommended the following measures: distribute surplus government property to Black farmers; end subsidies to White farmers; reverse land concentration and limit the number of farms a person can own; limit land ownership related to land speculation; and provide substantial government support and bank loans to Black farmers. The Truth and Reconciliation Commission, which was asked to repair the damage caused by racist land ownership and land-use policies, suggested in 1996 that the government return unused land, provide alternative land (if the land has been bulldozed and redeveloped), provide employment, or give land claimants a stake in a nearby industry.[64] One year later, the commission pressed the government to make six annual payments of $3,700 to $5,000 to 22,000 victims. Although the program was small, minuscule really, it was seen as a symbolic way to repair some of apartheid's financial, health, and moral problems.[65] Many South Africans, disgusted at the way brutal police officers have avoided prison terms, have expressed anger because they have not received any substantial and widespread compensation, pensions, job training, medical assistance, or housing assistance. In neighboring Zimbabwe, a land reappropriation movement supported by the state has resulted in the occupation of many White farms by landless rural people.

Another important crossnational compensation movement has been led by women in South Korea, Taiwan, the Philippines, and other Asian countries, where women and teen girls were forced by the Japanese army to serve as enslaved "comfort women" during World War II. Captured by the Japanese military, these women were raped by soldiers all day long, throughout the war. Although these women had to overcome the horrible stigma that goes along with being sexually abused by the soldiers of an enemy power, many of the women came forward and pressed for international acknowledgment of this crime. These older women rebels have demanded both an apology from the Japanese government, which they received in

1996, and monetary compensation. Most women who suffered wartime abuse have refused to accept any compensation that did not come from the Japanese government itself. (Some private firms have offered payment on an unofficial basis.) Following Taiwan's lead, South Korea decided in 1998 to pay $22,700 (plus an additional supplement of $4,700) to the 152 registered, comfort-women survivors in Korea.[66]

In the Philippines, Maria Rosa Henson and six other women sought compensation from the Japanese government. Mrs. Henson, who recently died, has written, "When the soldiers raped me, I felt like a pig. Sometimes they tied up my right leg with a waist band or belt and hung it to a wall as they violated me. I was angry all the time . . . I am an avenger of the dead."[67] These heroic women's actions and words, speaking the truth about violence in war, helped encourage violated Bosnian women to appear before an international tribunal and speak the truth about rape during the recent conflicts in the former Yugoslavia. The forceful battle of Korean comfort women has even shaped the politics of the Herero people in Namibia. The Herero have demanded that Germany, which colonized Namibia, provide land reparations and apologize for forcing Herero women into sexual slavery. One Herero man, Mr. Kerina, was overjoyed to see Japan apologize for sexual slavery during World War II. "I thought, hey, that's my grandmother—a comfort woman," he said. "And, I thought, if the Japanese could pay for that, the Germans could."[68]

The remarkable feature of these movements is that they demand the state as an institution to assume responsibility for governments that disappeared long ago. Japan has been asked to make amends for Tojo's regime, Germany to make amends for both Imperial and Nazi regimes, South Africa for apartheid. The success of some movements has encouraged emulation by others.

SOCIAL JUSTICE MOVEMENTS IN THE CORE

Workers around the world have demanded that states dispense impartial social justice. They have called for an end to official and unofficial police practices—surveillance, imprisonment, the death penalty, torture, and murder—that are used by states and their surrogates to enforce hierarchy and inequality. They have also demanded an end to extrajuridical violence, particularly rape, which has been used by state surrogates, both by groups of armed men and by individual males, to maintain inequality and patriarchy.

In the United States, minority groups have argued that the state has long used its police powers to enforce hierarchy and control minority populations. This repression, they argue, is not only a feature of the past, when African Americans were frequently lynched or killed in Southern jails and penitentiaries, but is an ongoing feature of the present. Numerous human and civil rights' organizations, including Amnesty International, have charged that the police, prison guards, immigration officials, legislators, and court officials have used their police power to abuse people of color, immigrants, and others who come in contact with the criminal justice system, an argument supported by the fact that U.S. prisons now hold two million people, one-quarter of the world's prison population.[69]

Many movements have objected to the increasing police surveillance of low-income, minority communities. Social scientists have found that police surveillance increased just at the time when the state began dismantling the safety net for poor families, eradicated prison-rehabilitation programs and halfway houses, and replaced antirecidivist programs with longer custodial oversight and more jail time. Michelle Fine and Lois Weis, authors of *The Unknown City*, have argued that "sites of 'help' for families in poverty—social agencies, social workers, schools and welfare offices—in fact usually double, today, as sites of scrutiny and intelligence."[70]

Across the country, movements have sprung up to resist the state's increasing scrutiny of low-income and minority workers. In Oakland, for example, the Eviction Defense Center has fought for local tenants and the three million other residents of public housing who have been threatened with eviction by housing authorities. Public housing residents now face increased surveillance and are threatened with eviction if anyone with drugs enters their apartments or visits the building's premises.[71]

High school students have organized to confront police surveillance. In one antisurveillance case, the American Civil Liberties Union represented high school students in Tecumseh, Oklahoma, who challenged a new school district policy that required mandatory drug tests for all students who participated in after-school activities.[72] The Reverend Jesse Jackson demanded that high school officials in Decatur, Illinois, redefine their "zero-tolerance" violence policy and reinstate seven African American students who were expelled from school for two years after fighting during a football game.[73]

Neighborhood groups have also objected to police harassment of African American motorists. In Dearborn, Michigan, the NAACP has led the charge against police abuse. During the 1960s, police in Dearborn were notorious for sweeping Black people out of town at sundown and trying to "Keep Dearborn Clean" (the motto painted on the side of squad cars). In recent years, the NAACP found that police had given 90 percent of all traffic tickets issued to Black motorists.[74] Minority motorists won a major victory in 1999, when the U.S. Justice Department ruled that police in Gloucester County, New Jersey, had regularly harassed Black motorists.

Community groups across the United States have organized to fight police violence. Several hundred people gathered in Riverside, California, after twenty-seven police fired bullets at a young African American woman who was sleeping in her car. At a rally attended by one thousand people two months later, speakers accused Riverside police of acting like a firing squad when they killed Tyisha Miller, who had a gun resting in her lap for "personal protection."

Meanwhile, five thousand demonstrators marched in New York City in February 1999 to protest the slaying of Amadou Diallo by police. Diallo was shot forty-one times while he stood, unarmed, outside his apartment. Groups of New York City residents have repeatedly called for the recruitment of more minority police, and some have even called on local militias to protect neighborhoods from the police. For example, five hundred protesters from the Black Men's Movement led a march through Brooklyn at the end of February 1999. They called both for an end to police violence and for arming neighborhood residents. One week later, Women for Justice rallied one thousand people in an antipolice protest.[75]

In recent years, efforts to eradicate police brutality have been initiated both by local grass-roots and by international criminal-justice and human-rights groups. The Circle of Recovery network, which was started by former convicts and substance abusers in East Palo Alto, California, has grown to include not only African American men but also Native Americans and female victims of domestic violence. In Washington, D.C., members of the Alliance of Concerned Men, which consists of men who have experienced imprisonment, substance abuse, and homelessness, talk to members of the capitol's one hundred gangs and try to find jobs for them. According to two members of the Alliance, "[These kids] are lost, caught up in the wrong thing like we were . . . Our experience and lifestyles have taught us certain things. In a way, we've been preparing for the job all our lives."[76]

Police brutality on the street is reinforced by brutality throughout the criminal justice system. Advocates for an egalitarian society have also called for new sentencing policies. They have demanded an end to "three strikes" sentencing and the death penalty, which have been used with increasing frequency. Movements opposed to the death penalty and other surveillance and imprisonment policies have sprung up across the country. In the last twenty-five years, more than 10 percent of the people sentenced to death have been innocent and wrongly convicted, according to a Northwestern University study. At a 1998 conference at Northwestern University, some of the twenty-eight people freed from death row testified against the death penalty. "Had the state gotten its way, I'd be dead today," Sabrina Butler testified.[77]

A large group has also organized to protest the treatment of Mumia abu Jamal, who was sentenced to the death penalty in Philadelphia after a shoddy trial, where he was accused of killing a policeman. As a writer, Mumia has reached out to a coalition of academic, African American, and young activists. By marching in the streets and raising money for his defense, this coalition has worked for years to secure a new, fair trial.

But this movement speaks to only one of the thousands of silenced people who have been sentenced to death. These grass-roots and national movements against the death penalty have been supported by international movements. In response to the widespread use of the death penalty in the United States, the European Union has discussed an anti–death penalty resolution that would publicly denounce the United States and other repressive states like Iran, Saudi Arabia, and Afghanistan for using the death penalty.

Rather than trying to end social inequality, federal and state governments in the United States have imprisoned large segments of the population. Rather than providing education and decent jobs, the state has expanded the prison industry. The widespread and long-term imprisonment of U.S. residents has become the state's primary strategy for controlling poor and minority communities.

Inmate rebellion and prisoner-rights movements have joined with antisurveillance, antibrutality and anti–death penalty movements to challenge the state and demand impartial justice. Individual victims and groups have also taken on systemic abuse in the prison system. At New York City's jail on Rikers Island, which is known as the "House of Pain," fifteen prisoners won a class-action suit against the City's Department of Corrections because the court found that guards regularly broke prisoners' bones (often following supervisors' orders to assault prisoners) and were engaged in "beating down" handcuffed prisoners.[78] At the overcrowded Durango Jail in Phoenix, prisoners living in tents held eleven guards hostage to call public attention to poor medical care, bad food, police brutality, and poor living conditions.[79]

California's prisons are known as particularly violent places. Between 1988 and 1994, California prison guards killed and wounded more inmates than in all of the other prisons in the country. After a group of Pelican Bay prisoners sued prison officials for illegal violence, a judge ruled that authorities were responsible for "senseless suffering and sometimes wretched misery."[80]

SOCIAL JUSTICE MOVEMENTS IN THE PERIPHERY AND SEMIPERIPHERY

In the periphery and semiperiphery, movements have objected not only to the treatment of workers by police and prison officials but also to the use of violence by majority ethnic groups and by militias, death squads, and vigilantes that act as surrogates for the state. In Iran, for instance, Islamic vigilantes have attacked moderate politicians and young people who do not conform to conservative Islamic rules.[81] In East Timor, Indonesian militiamen and the army attacked pro-independence activists in East Timor and "killed them like animals."[82] Muslim militias in Indonesia assaulted relatively wealthy Chinese women and men and destroyed their shops. And in Mexico, right-wing militiamen massacred forty-five Indians in Chiapas. Hundreds of women, many carrying babies or holding their children's hands, then confronted the Mexican army in Altamiro, Chiapas, yelling, "We don't want any soldiers near our houses."[83]

In the periphery, social movements have emerged that contest state surveillance, police and army violence on the street, and the brutal imprisonment of laboring people. At the Santa Ana Prison in El Salvador, inmates crowded into small prison cells threatened to commit suicide. Rebellious prisoners announced that inmates would draw lots in a "death lottery" and then hang their fellow inmates until officials stopped overcrowding practices. Fortunately, human rights groups mediated an end to the protest.[84] Prison riots led to the closure of Panama's overcrowded, crumbling "Model Prison," which a bishop described as "a cemetery for the living."[85]

In Turkey, the state has imprisoned large numbers of leftist rebels and Kurdish separatists. In 1996, 314 prisoners rebelled against the government's war treatment of political prisoners. These prisoners went on a two-month hunger strike, demanding an end to the practice of sending prisoners to jails far from their homes and an end to abuse by the military police. As the hunger strike went on, 2,070 prisoners in 43 other Turkish prisons joined the fast or participated in prison protests. After the eighth hunger striker died (Ayse Idil Ekmen, a twenty-two-year-old woman), separatist Kurds also joined the fast. Sympathizers in Germany demonstrated in support of the hunger strikers, attacking Turkish properties with fire bombs. In Istanbul and Ankara, demonstrators fought with the police.[86] As part of the antibrutality campaign, the mothers of prisoners held weekly demonstrations and called for an end to the state's involvement in the disappearance of family members.[87]

As in Turkey, working people in Argentina, Brazil, and Chile are still trying to come to terms with the military violence that led to the disappearance and death of so many citizens during the "Dirty Wars" of the 1970s and 1980s, when dictatorships kidnapped, tortured, and murdered dissidents. Women, grandmothers, and other human rights activists have organized campaigns to charge the military officers responsible for these crimes. Activists in Chile have spent years trying to bring Augusto Pinochet, the former Chilean dictator, to trial and charge him with the murder of 3,000 to 4,000 people, including Chilean president Salvadore Allende, during a coup in 1973. According to recent CIA documents, Pinochet led a government that was responsible for torturing at least 200,000 people during his seventeen-year reign of terror.[88] In 1999, Pinochet was arrested on a visit to the United Kingdom. He was then held while the British government considered a Spanish judge's request for his extradition to Spain, where he would have been tried for crimes against Spanish citizens living in Chile. Spain, like any country that signed the Convention Against Torture (signed by Chile in 1988), has the right to issue a warrant for the arrest of men responsible for torture. In January 2000, British officials ruled that Pinochet was too ill to be extradited to Spain for trial. After Pinochet returned to Chile, his senatorial immunity was removed and he may yet stand trial for crimes there.

Once the Spanish court charged Pinochet with international crimes, a large number of his victims formed support groups, prepared testimony for a possible court case, demanded that therapeutic services be provided for the victims of torture, and began a public discussion of torture in Chile. Although victims are now organizing collectively, for many years victims made individual protests. Viviana Uribe, for example, looked up the addresses of her torturers in the phone book, called their wives, and told them how she had been raped and assaulted by these men. Ms. Uribe had been arrested and tortured in the early 1970s because she had been caught putting up wall posters. Pinochet's arrest in 1997 gave many others the opportunity to organize. This has opened up a new political space in Chile for dealing with torture on both the personal and social level. A group of political prisoners has also filed the first criminal charges against Pinochet, and it has asked the government to pay millions of dollars to compensate the victims of torture. Paz Rojas, a neurologist at the University of Chile, has argued that Pinochet's arrest changed the political and social climate in Chile. "Pinochet's arrest was a great catharsis that has begun to break the silence," she said.[89]

GLOBAL MOVEMENTS PROTESTING VIOLENCE AGAINST WOMEN

Since the late 1960s, feminist organizations have struggled to rid the world of rape and domestic violence. Many domestic violence shelters and special state- and community-funded programs have been established to prevent violence against women, but far too little has been done to challenge the violence associated with patriarchal culture. Rape is a misogynist crime used by groups of armed men and by individual males to maintain patriarchy and inequality. It is used to assault women, their families, their communities, and their class and ethnic group. Rape is most often committed as a violent act of power by husbands, family members, and male friends and acquaintances. In other words, the men closest to women are the ones who tend to assault them. Women and girls report only about one of every ten rapes, largely because male-dominated society and state institutions defend male prerogatives. In Mexico, for example, feminists have organized to support Claudia Rodrigues Ferrando, a thirty-year-old woman who was imprisoned for defending herself when she shot and killed a rapist. Because the rapist was drunk at the time of the assault, the judge decided that Ms. Ferrando had more control over the situation and should have escaped. But Mexican feminists have argued that this ruling imposed a double legal standard on women. In Mexico, where poverty and crime (including rape) are rising, feminist movements have established both longer prison sentences for rapists and new centers for investigating crimes against women. Feminist groups have also tried to curb police violence against women. Investigators recently discovered that five policemen had been involved in the rapes of nineteen young women.[90] A dramatic and symbolic victory against police violence in Mexico was made in Tepatepec, where villagers seized sixty riot police, disarmed them, stripped and bound them, and made them kneel in the village square for hours before releasing them. Local residents seized the policemen after hearing reports that police had raped a woman. The police had been called into town to evict student demonstrators from a local teacher's college.[91]

Feminist movements that fight rape and male violence, both by individuals and groups of armed men, are important. Rape committed by men during war has finally been recognized by international conventions and courts as a crime against humanity. The ethnic-economic wars of the 1990s demonstrated the cruelties of patriarchal rape as a weapon of war. The public testimonies of female rape survivors in Rwanda and Bosnia made people around the world recognize what state-sanctioned, armed male violence meant for women and girls and for their families and communities. In Rwanda, hundreds of thousands of Tutsi women and teen girls were gang raped, and many of them then mutilated and murdered. Many women were forced to become the sexual slaves of male soldiers and militiamen. Leonille M., a Tutsi mother who became pregnant after being raped in Rwanda, said that a Hutu soldier found her at night and ordered her to have sex with him. She told him, "I'm miserable now. All my people are dead. I don't want you to do what you want. Kill me if you want to." But he forced me, she said. "Two others came after him. It was night, but I remember they were all soldiers." During the genocide, Leonille's husband was killed and her house destroyed, leaving her with five children. She has struggled to feed them and has had to tell them where her youngest son came from. "When he is old enough, I'll tell them what happened to me. What can I do? I had to love him."[92]

Armed military groups in other countries have frequently used rape as a weapon of terror and social domination. In Algeria, Islamic rebels raped secular females. In Indonesia, government security forces raped Chinese women. In Kosovo, Serbs raped Albanian women. All of these instances resemble the terror inflicted by some Hutu men on Tutsi women.

Alongside the fight against rape and domestic violence, women around the world have redoubled their efforts to ban female genital mutilation. Although this harmful practice is often carried out by older women, they do so on behalf of male household heads. This practice permanently injures two million girls each year. Feminist organizations and local women's groups have tried to persuade states to outlaw the practice, something they have achieved in Egypt and Senegal. The Egyptian Society for Prevention of Harmful Practices to Woman and Child played a major role in broadening public understanding of Islamic law and culture. A Senegalese women's organization, Tofhan, which means "breakthrough," led a successful national campaign to outlaw the ritual cutting of girls' genitals. Tofhan began its grass-roots campaign against genital mutilation after women in literacy classes and human rights discussions identified genital cutting as their most pressing concern.[93]

In an effort to complement national struggles, global feminist groups like Equality Now have tried to establish asylums for women fleeing communities where female genital mutilation is practiced. Following the footsteps of Togo refugee Fauziya Kassindja, who was granted U.S. asylum on the grounds of sex-based persecution, Adelaide Abankwah of Ghana was finally granted U.S. asylum after immigrant rights groups and New York legislators protested her detention and the government's initial refusal to grant her petition for asylum.[94] Ablavi Haden of Togo also sought asylum in the United States. Her lawyers argued that genital mutilation was a form of torture, which is forbidden by U.S. and international law. Women refugees from repressive states continue to press U.S. courts to define patriarchal spousal abuse as torture and to define the deportation of an abused woman as a return to the torturer.[95]

All these antistate movements form an integral part of the global labor movement. It will be difficult for states in the capitalist world-economy to redistribute wealth or provide justice on a widespread scale. But if states do not redistribute wealth and power or promote equality and justice, labor movements demanding change will continue to emerge.

Together, this wide group of labor movements is cultivating increased resistance to many oppressive aspects of the current global system. By advancing a wide array of issues related to wage, nonwage, and extrasystemic work, movements have resisted class inequity and authoritarian rule. In many of these movements, female rebels have directed attacks that undermine and delegitimize the state.

NOTES

1. Torry D. Dickinson, *CommonWealth: Self-Sufficiency and Work in American Communities, 1830–1993* (Lanham, Md.: University Press of America, 1995), 38–47, 66–69, 91–106.
2. Dickinson, *CommonWealth*, 129–147.
3. Dickinson, *CommonWealth*, 196–97, 205–209.
4. Alex De Wall and Rakiya Omaar, "Doing Harm by Doing Good? The International Relief Effort in Somalia," *Current History* (May 1993): 198–202.
5. Elisabeth Rosenthal, "Thousands of Farmers Protest in China: 1 Dies in Police Clash," *New York Times*, January 16, 1999.
6. Erik Eckholm, "Health Sects in China Thrive, If Authorities See No Threat," *New York Times*, December 28, 1999; Mark Landler, "Beijing Detains Leaders of Sect, Watchdog Says," *New York Times*, July 21, 1999; Erik Eckholm, "China Sentences 4 in Spiritual Group to Long Jail Time," *New York Times*, December 27, 1999.
7. Seth Mydans, "Burmese Opposition Issues Risky Challenge to the Junta," *New York Times*, September 15, 1998.
8. "End of Burmese Hostage Standoff in Thailand," *New York Times*, October 3, 1999.
9. Reuters, "Kenya: Police Fire at Protesters," *New York Times*, July 8, 1999.
10. Associated Press, "Protests Erupt across Haiti as Leaders Push Austerity," *New York Times*, January 17, 1997.
11. Larry Rohter, "Brazil: Protesters on the March," *New York Times*, August 27, 1999.
12. Clifford Kraus, "Bolivia: Nationwide Strike," *New York Times*, December 18, 1999.
13. Larry Rohter, "Dollar May Buy a Reprieve in Ecuador," *New York Times*, January 16, 2000.
14. David Barstow, "Police in New York Set to Limit Tactics at Rally in Harlem," *New York Times*, September 3, 1999.
15. "The New Affirmative Action," *New York Times*, August 9, 1998.
16. Marlise Simons, "On the Streets of Paris, School Protests Turn Violent," *New York Times*, October 16, 1998.
17. Craig Whitney, "French Youths Strike for the Right to Study Hard," *New York Times*, November 5, 1998.
18. Simons, "On the Streets of Paris"; Whitney, "French Youths Strike."
19. Joseph B. Treaster, "Days before New Term, Mexican University Remains in the Hands of the Strikers," *New York Times*, August 13, 1999; Sam Dillon, "Mexico: New University Chief," *New York Times*, November 19, 1999.
20. Julia Preston, "Student Strike in Capitol Jarring All of Mexico," *New York Times*, June 25, 1999.
21. Julia Preston, "University, Mexico's Pride, Is Ravaged by Strike," *New York Times*, January 20, 2000; Julia Preston, "Big Majority Votes to End Strike at Mexican University," *New York Times*, January 22, 2000.
22. Nicholas D. Kristof, "People Power Unrest on Indonesian Campuses," *New York Times*, April 29, 1998; Mark Landler, "Protesters in Indonesia Find Allies in Parents," *New York Times*, May 12, 1998; Associated Press, "Hundreds Riot in Indonesia," *America Online*, September 14, 1998; Seth Mydans, "Shock and Sorrow in the Aftermath of Timor's Violence," *New York Times*, September 26, 1999.
23. Reuters, "Iran Leader Holds Crisis Meeting as Protests by Students Intensify," *New York Times*, July 11, 1998; Douglas Jehl, "Issue in Iran Democracy Debate: Cleric's Power,"

New York Times, October 15, 1998; Elaine Sciolino, "For Once, the Veil That Hides Conflict Slips," *New York Times*, July 18, 1999.

24. Reuters, "Iran Leader Holds Crisis Meeting."
25. Jehl, "Issue in Iran Democracy Debate."
26. Associated Press, "Seoul Police Block March to the North," *New York Times*, August 16, 1999.
27. Seth Mydans, "In Debris of Economic Crash: Thailand's Faith in Authority," *New York Times*, August 10, 1999.
28. Norimitsu Onishi, "Ivory Coast: University Year Invalidated," *New York Times*, August 4, 1999.
29. Reuters, "Clashes in Zimbabwe," *New York Times*, March 10, 1998.
30. Associated Press, "In India, Man Sets Himself on Fire to Protest Beauty Pageant," *New York Times*, November 15, 1996.
31. Felicia R. Lee, "Thousands of Women Share Wounds, and Celebrate," *New York Times*, October 27, 1997.
32. Suzanne Daley, "Mixed-Race South Africans Riot over Utility Rates," *New York Times*, February 7, 1997.
33. Larry Rohter, "Catholics Battle Brazilian Faith in 'Black Rome,'" *New York Times*, January 10, 2000; Larry Rohter, "Indian Tribe Wants Brazil's Plymouth Rock Back," *New York Times*, December 1, 1999.
34. Larry Rohter, "Brazil: Carnival's Fabled Amity May Hide Bigotry," *New York Times*, December 12, 1999.
35. Rohter, "Brazil: Carnival's Fabled Amity."
36. Larry Rohter, "Maya Renaissance in Guatemala Turns Political," *New York Times*, August 12, 1996.
37. "To Gypsies, Czech Special Schools Are a Lesson in Bias," *New York Times*, July 25, 1999.
38. Chris Hedges, "Another Victim, 14, in Serbia's War on Gypsies," *New York Times*, October 22, 1997.
39. Hedges, "Another Victim."
40. Cheryl Bentley, "Lower Castes Flexing Muscles in Indian Politics," *San Francisco Chronicle*, March 4, 1996.
41. Daley, "Mixed-Race South Africans Riot."
42. Carey Goldberg, "Hispanic Groups Prepare to March to Washington," *New York Times*, October 9, 1996.
43. See Giovanni Arrighi, Terence K. Hopkins, and Immanuel Wallerstein, *Antisystemic Movements* (London: Verso, 1989).
44. James Dao, "Anxiety Growing over Indian Claim in New York State," *New York Times*, January 13, 1999.
45. Dao, "Anxiety Growing over India Claim."
46. James Brooke, "Equity Case in Canada as Redress for Women," *New York Times*, November 19, 1999.
47. See Randall Robinson, *The Debt* (New York: Dutton, 1999).
48. Stephen Carpenter and Randi Ilyse Roth, "Family Farmers in Poverty: A Guide to Agricultural Law for Legal Service Practitioners," *Clearinghouse Review* (April 1996): 1092–1095; "How Slavery Fueled Business in the North," *New York Times*, July 24, 2000; Ron Nixon, "Peculiar Profits: The Reparations Movement Pursues Slavery's Blue-Chip Beneficiaries," *Mother Jones* (July/August 2000).

49. Clyde Hoberman, "Attica: Exorcising the Demons, Redeeming the Deaths," *New York Times*, January 9, 2000.

50. David W. Chen, "$8 Million Offered to End Attica Inmates' Suit," *New York Times*, January 5, 2000.

51. Jim Yardley, "Panel Recommends Reparations in Long-Ignored Tulsa Race Riot," *New York Times*, February 5, 2000.

52. Yardley, "Panel Recommends Reparations."

53. Gustav Neibuhr, "Denomination to Repent Its Ties to Slave Trade," *New York Times*, June 26, 1999.

54. Alan Cowell, "Switzerland and Banks Agree to a Fund for Holocaust Victims," *New York Times*, January 24, 1997.

55. Barry Meier, "Swiss Banks and Victims of the Nazis Nearing Pact," *New York Times*, January 23, 1999.

56. Edmund L. Andrews, "Germans to Set Up $5.1 Billion Fund for Nazi Slaves," *New York Times*, December 15, 1999; Edmund L. Andrews, "Germany Accepts $5.1 Billion Accord to End Claims of Nazi Slave Workers," *New York Times*, December 18, 1999; Roger Cohen, "German Companies Set Up Fund for Slave Laborers under Nazis," *New York Times*, February 17, 1999; "German Parliament Backs Fund for Nazis' Slave Workers," *New York Times*, July 7, 2000.

57. Barry Meier, "Poland Seeks Role in Fund for Nazi Forced Laborers," *New York Times*, February 15, 1999.

58. Jane Perlez, "Hungary to Pay War's 'Forgotten' Jews," *New York Times*, July 27, 1997.

59. "Norway Plans to Pay Jews $60 Million Compensation," *New York Times*, June 27, 1998.

60. Edmund L. Andrews, "53 Years Later, Lawsuit Is Filed on Behalf of Hitler's Slave Labor," *New York Times*, September 1, 1998.

61. Neil A. Lewis, "Time Running Out on Compensation Deal for Americans Held in Nazi Camps," *New York Times*, January 24, 1997.

62. Alan Cowell, "Germany Pardons en Masse Thousands Persecuted by Nazis," *New York Times*, May 29, 1998.

63. "Spain Agrees to Pay Back Parties Looted in Franco Era," *New York Times*, December 28, 1997.

64. Suzanne Daley, "Apartheid's Dispossessed Seek Restitution," *New York Times*, June 25, 1996.

65. Suzanne Daley, "Some Victims of Apartheid May Receive Financial Aid," *New York Times*, October 24, 1997.

66. Stephanie Strom, "Seoul Won't Seek Japan Funds for Army Brothel Women," *New York Times*, April 22, 1998.

67. Seth Mydans, "Inside a Wartime Brothel: The Avenger's Story," *New York Times*, November 12, 1996; Maria Rosa Henson, *Comfort Woman: A Filipina's Story of Prostitution and Slavery under the Japanese Military* (Lanham, Md.: Rowman & Littlefield, 1999).

68. Donald G. McNeil, Jr., "Its Past on Its Sleeve, Tribe Seeks Bonn's Apology," *New York Times*, May 31, 1998.

69. Robert K. Schaeffer, *Understanding Globalization: The Social Consequences of Economic, Political, and Environmental Change* (Lanham, Md.: Rowman & Littlefield, 1997), 342; Elliot Currie, *Reckoning Drugs, the Cities, and the American Future* (New York: Hill and Wang, 1993), 10, 12, 33.

70. Michelle Fine and Lois Weis, *The Unknown City: Lives of Poor and Working-Class Young Adults* (Boston: Beacon, 1998), 200, 202.

71. Frank Bruni, "A Battleground without Winners in the War on Drug Abuse," *New York Times*, June 28, 1998.
72. Dirk Johnson, "Jackson Arrested in Protest over Expulsion of Students," *New York Times*, November 17, 1999.
73. Johnson, "Jackson Arrested."
74. "Racism Charge Reminds Dearborn of Its Ugly Past," *New York Times*, January 5, 1997.
75. Salim Muwakkil, "No Cop Accountability: What Will It Take to Stop Police Brutality?" *In These Times*, April 11, 1999; Don Terry, "Unanswered Questions in a Fatal Police Shooting," *New York Times*, January 9, 1999.
76. Michael Janofsky, "Old Friends, Once Felons, Regroup to Fight Crime," *New York Times*, March 10, 1997.
77. Don Terry, "Survivors Make the Case against Death Row," *New York Times*, November 16, 1998.
78. Associated Press, "Jail Inmates Riot, but Then Talk to Sheriff," *New York Times*, November 19, 1996.
79. Associated Press, "Jail Inmates Riot."
80. Evelyn Nieves, "California Examines Brutal, Deadly Prisons," *New York Times*, November 7, 1998.
81. "Iranian Orders a Crackdown on Vigilantes," *New York Times*, September 6, 1998.
82. Associated Press, "Militiamen Backed by Indonesia Kill 25 in East Timor, Cleric Says," *New York Times*, April 8, 1999.
83. Julia Preston, "Mexican Indian Women Protest Army's Search for Weapons," *New York Times*, January 12, 1998.
84. Mario Murillo, "Beating Swords into Leg Irons," *In These Times*, November 11, 1996.
85. Larry Rohter, "With a Bang, Panama Is Erasing House of Horrors," *New York Times*, December 6, 1996.
86. Alan Cowell, "With 8 Dead in Jail Fasts, Anger at Turkey Is Rising," *New York Times*, July 27, 1996.
87. Alan Cowell, "Hunger Strike in Turkish Jails Lays Bare Country's Divisions," *New York Times*, July 28, 1996.
88. Philip Shenon, "U.S. Releases Files on Abuses in Pinochet Era," *New York Times*, July 1, 1999.
89. Clifford Krauss, "Pinochet Case Reviving Voices of the Tortured," *New York Times*, January 3, 2000.
90. Julia Preston, "A Woman's Shooting of Attacker Rivets Mexico," *New York Times*, February 5, 1997.
91. Julia Preston, "A Mexican Village, in Clash, Brings the Police to Their Knees," *New York Times*, February 21, 2000.
92. James C. McKinley, Jr., "Legacy of Rwanda Violence: The Thousands Born of Rape," *New York Times*, September 23, 1996.
93. Barbara Crossette, "Senegal Bans Cutting of Genitals of Girls," *New York Times*, January 18, 1999.
94. Amy Waldman, "Asylum Won by Woman Who Feared Female Genital Mutilation," *New York Times*, August 18, 1999.
95. Susan Sachs, "Women Newly Seeking Asylum," *New York Times*, August 1, 1999.

Chapter 12

Diversifying Struggles: Redefining Work and Society

Workers already organize much of the work they need to survive. The nonwage work they do in their homes and on the streets, the subsistence work they do in households, and the sharing they do with others make it possible for them to survive as a group. As employers cut wages and states cut benefits, workers have had to organize even more of their own work. Many have realized that it may no longer be useful or necessary to rely on wage labor or the state to provide for their needs, but instead they must rely on themselves and others. They also recognize that they must fight to protect their ability to work on their own, outside the capitalist system. Their efforts to create economic and political spaces where they can organize independent work and social relations can be described as "diversifying movements."

Writing 150 years ago, Karl Marx made an important observation. He noted that large-scale production in factories made it possible for capital to expand the production of commodities and profits. But by bringing together large numbers of workers and subjecting them to its control, capital made workers aware of their exploitation and created conditions that fomented worker rebellion against capital. Since then, activists and scholars using this insight have identified male industrial workers as the key agents of social change. Then, as the benefits provided workers by states increased, and states assumed a larger role in the organization of economic and political life, activists and scholars recognized that worker struggles against the state also contributed to social change. Unfortunately, historians, social scientists, and labor activists typically neglected another important site of worker struggle: the household. At the household level, workers have been organized in relation to the gender divide. But workers have also been brought together to work cooperatively outside of paid employment, to help each other survive and struggle together as a group.

Feminist and world-system scholars have tried to remedy the neglect of household analysis and provide a class analysis of housework and worker struggles in households. Scholars who study households have emphasized the struggles of women against patriarchy, and some have combined their interest in household patriarchy with a study of capitalist patriarchy and the relation between them.[1] By piecing these studies together, we maintain that global capitalism was able to expand because it simultaneously promoted patriarchy on a global scale and nourished patriarchal authoritarianism within laboring households. Sexism in the household provided a fairly stable foundation for sexism at large, and vice versa. Feminist and world-system scholars not only provided critical insights into the double-sided character of patriarchy, they argued that just as the shop floor was a site of class-based oppression and rebellion, nonwage work sites were places of oppression and resistance. Household-centered movements reflected not only worker struggles against the social system but the struggles of working women against sexist, working-class men in households. The struggles of nonwage workers and women in patriarchal households have been an important, but neglected, component of global labor struggles.

Nonwage work sites in households and communities have been places of oppression and rebellion. Much of the nonwage work done in households and communities has been shaped indirectly by capitalism and directly by men in households. Nonwage work sites have been places where household workers have rebelled against the capitalist system and against authoritarian males. Because household work sustains working people and supports the world-system, workers cannot simply stop work or go on strike in this setting. But rebellious workers in households can redefine the meaning of nonwage work and change the relation between nonwage work and the world-system. They can defend and expand the space needed to conduct these activities. Their efforts to redefine work and household relations and their struggles to defend these activities have contributed to economic and political diversity. By expanding the economic and political options available to workers, diversifying movements make it possible for workers to develop new economic and political institutions that may form the basis of future societies.

Because women do most of the nonwage work and try to sustain their families, women have been at the center of efforts to defend these activities and develop social-change strategies. Around the world, households have organized collective strategies designed to: (1) increase nonwage income and even withdraw household members from wage labor and their dependency on income from wage labor; (2) develop participatory decision-making practices and create small centers of economic and political power outside the control of businesses and the state; (3) organize more nonwage work in a cooperative fashion so that alternative forms of producing and redistributing goods and services can be developed outside the capitalist market; and (4) develop new economic and political plans for regional and crossregional development, which would connect worker households, in both the South and the North, in more egalitarian relationships.

Rather than trying to persuade capitalist institutions—businesses and states—to meet the needs of working people, workers in diversifying movements have instead tried to redefine nonwage work and cultural relations so that they meet the economic and political needs of working people. These diversifying struggles have established alternative ways to work and live wholly or partially outside the economic and political institutions of the world-economy. Because diversifying struggles create new social relations, they broaden the kind of struggles organized by worker movements.

Worker movements that challenge businesses and states generally take these institutions as "given," and they try to persuade them to change. Workers in diversifying movements take a different view. They do not accept these institutions as given but instead imagine new ways to organize work and politics. This does not mean that institutional and diversifying movements are at odds with one another. In fact, while they take different approaches, both kinds of movements can challenge capitalist institutions, one from the inside and the other from the outside. Indeed, institutional and diversifying movements are joined by workers in households, who perform wage *and* nonwage work and participate in institutional *and* diversifying movements that challenge capital *and* the state, from the inside and the outside. By presenting alternative visions of work and politics, diversifying movements take the first steps toward creating new economic and political microworlds. While institutional movements try to redistribute wealth and power, diversifying movements typically reorganize economic and social life at the grass-roots or regional level, and show workers how to create new relations based on economic equality and political democracy. By designing and running new economic and political relations on a small scale, what might be called "mini-worlds," diversifying movements broaden the range of social possibilities.

Institutional movements grew out of working people's formal subsumption to wage labor and a capitalist state. Diversifying movements grew out of labor's self-sustaining, nonwage work, which was structurally imposed by the world-economy on working-class households. The capitalist world-economy has never provided worker households with the jobs, income, or benefits they needed to survive. So workers have had to perform nonwage work in their homes and on the streets to make do. It was through these improvising activities—petty producing, interhousehold reciprocity and exchange, and informal market operations—that worker households learned how to organize some of their work activities and create cooperative social and political relations. Workers conducted these activities because the world-economy did not or could not meet all of labor's basic needs. In the process, working people acquired important economic and political skills from their nonwage work activities, skills that eventually prepared them to confront wage work and the global system.

When working-class feminists and other activists realized that nonwage work was more than just "housework," home-based work became defined as a part of a larger cooperative effort. Conceptually and politically, this was a major transformation. This qualitative jump in understanding was made possible because workers recognized the value of women's work, unpaid work, and informal work and appreciated the importance of collective survival skills. If workers in the South and North had not learned to value the economic and political skills they had collectively acquired, if they had not come to appreciate the political strength of local communities and cultures, diversifying movements would not have grown as they did in the 1980s and 1990s. Workers have come to recognize this: they are already doing much of the work needed to survive, so they might as well try to work entirely for themselves, not for others. As employers cut wages and states cut benefits, more workers increasingly realized that they could and should rely on themselves and organize their own work relations.

Groups of households that are undergoing deproletarianization and sometimes expulsion from the world-economy, along with some proletarianizing households, are increasingly establishing alternative, extracapitalist work relations. Organizations that do this provide a political context where working families can redefine work and build new work relations. Diversifying movements enable households undergoing deproletarianization and extrusion to survive at a time when the dominant economy offers insecure wage employment, decreasing state support, and little hope for the future. These new collective organizations are developing largely outside of the world-economy, though many household and collective aspects of work life still remain within it. For example, India's Self-Employed Women's Association (SEWA) is an established and sustained diversifying movement. Through their cooperative, SEWA's women are organizing self-employed workers and developing a comprehensive set of alternative work, self-governance, and household support relations. The explicit goal is to provide support that crosses the boundaries of home and work.

Before 1970, diversifying movements had largely consisted of workers who refused to be incorporated into the world-system, who did not want to become more dependent on wage labor and market consumption. During the first centuries of capitalism, groups of indigenous people, slaves, and peasants refused to participate in the expanding world-system, and they fought or fled to escape it. Other groups of workers, who had been incorporated, tried to rely on their own initiative as much as they could.

In the nineteenth and early twentieth centuries, workers organized diversifying movements to resist the ways that employers, states, and charitable agencies closed off self-sufficient work options, forced worker households to seek employment, and persuaded them to purchase more goods and services from the market.[2] In the core, some diversifying movements tried to maintain nonwage work activities that were not organized by employers. But during the late nineteenth century, it became increasingly difficult for workers to access nonwage work resources, find open land, or run informal, curbside markets. These nonwage activities had often made it possible for workers to sustain themselves during the big railroad and mining strikes. By 1870, male-centered movements began dominating worker politics, a development that obscured the importance of nonwage and worker efforts to preserve some of their economic and cultural autonomy. But few diversifying movements, with the exception of early utopian efforts such as the Oneida community, promoted the idea that the producing and decision-making skills associated with nonwage work gave workers a way to imagine an alternative to, and exit from, the dominant social system. Nonwage activities remained absolutely essential until 1945, providing almost one-half of household income for one-third of the families in the United States. But the growth of the welfare state, the commodification of survival resources, and the rise in wages after 1945 gradually reduced nonwage work and weakened diversifying movements.

In the 1980s, however, diversifying movements became important again, providing work alternatives as wage work and state benefits declined. It is important to note that these movements addressed both how work could be done in a different and more egalitarian way and how decisions could be made in a more democratic way. Work and decision-making alternatives emerged from diverse cultural frameworks, which expressed visions of a better society from various cultural perspectives. As diversifying movements emerged, the framework for social change broadened. Worker movements suddenly moved beyond efforts to confront businesses and states. They now began to formulate how worker communities could create more egalitarian and democratic societies.

Many political activities that leaned toward diversifying politics were still informed by institutional considerations, and the complex elements of antifirm, antistate, and independence-seeking, diversifying movements remain highly intertwined. Some movements seeking to create independence from wage labor have even sought and secured institutional resources. Diversifying movements have sometimes received support and encouragement from odd places. The World Bank, for example, has encouraged workers to develop supplemental income sources because this helps workers survive with smaller wages and fewer state benefits and thus helps stabilize the world-economy. The diversifying movements organized by workers—like the micro-credit loans provided by the Grameen Bank in India—have been described both as "reformist" because they increase workloads for women and as "revolutionary" because they help workers organize new, more inclusive social relations. It is important to recognize that contemporary entrepreneurial projects like the Grameen Bank, which are sometimes funded by the World Bank, have characteristics that help maintain the system, as well as features that undermine it.

Once alternatives to working for capitalist employers are created, then many new possibilities are imagined. Diversifying movements help incubate new social relations and more egalitarian social structures. Even if their initial efforts fail, they provide experience that can be used by movements to develop more sophisticated strategies.

This chapter explores some of the key expressions of contemporary diversifying movements. We will look first at land, property, and resource reclamation movements. These movements have protested the expropriation of land and resources by businesses and states and demanded access to the social and environmental resources that worker households need to survive. We will then examine the diversifying movements that have attempted to transform civil society and create new economic and political structures. Civil society is the set of social relationships that is created by the dominant social institutions. In capitalist states, firms, states, classes, gender groups, ethnic groups, and households are the important social institutions. Still, social relations are not entirely shaped by these dominant institutions. Workers have the capacity to create some social relations of their own. Nonwage work, collective survival networks, and informal markets have always been used by workers to create civil societal spaces of their own. The social spaces that workers have created have emerged as an important area of political protest. Many woman-centered movements operate in the spaces associated with civil society.[3]

In this second historical section, we will also examine worker efforts to create a more open civil society. Workers have redefined education; built collaborative credit, savings, and exchange programs; developed alternative and collaborative forms of agricultural and industrial production; and established alternative, participatory political structures.

ESTABLISHING A BASE FOR WORKERS: LAND RECLAMATION AND ENVIRONMENTAL MOVEMENTS

Worker households need access to forests, common lands, and public resources to survive. But it has become increasingly difficult for workers to access private land and "the commons," resources that working families have traditionally used. In the South, women have typically collected food, fuel, and water from forests and village commons, which have customarily been available to working people. But in recent years, deforestation, the growing control of forests by states, and the privatization and exploitation of village commons by private companies and privileged groups have led to a dramatic decrease in labor's access to forests and village commons. In the United States, for example, Native Americans in Alaska, where treaties had guaranteed their access to subsistence foods, have seen their resources taken away from them by Whites. The U.S. government has been forced to step in and allocate fishing and hunting rights on federal lands to protect Native American access to the commons.[4]

The corporate expropriation of plant genes has privatized the commons in many regions. Large companies based in the core have removed fertile seeds from the commons (which working people have nurtured and cultivated), and then patented and marketed these resources as private, corporate goods.[5] In the North, the commons have been attacked when private companies mine public resources at agricultural research universities for products they can profitably expropriate, patent, and market. In both the South and North, workers have fought to prevent private industry from seizing land, plants, and agricultural knowledge, which were originally cultivated and nurtured by working people.[6]

Village commons have allowed low-income households to generate income and obtain survival resources: wild vegetables and animals, water, animal fodder, and cooking fuel. Workers have used the resources gathered from the commons as an important form of nonwage work and source of income. Access to a village commons has allowed landless households to obtain income and subsistence goods from shared resources. In seven Indian states, for example, poor households generated between 10 and 25 percent of their income from village commons, and village commons provided almost all of their firewood and fodder.[7] Access to village commons has been particularly important for poor and secluded women, who have few resources and little access to markets, education, employment options, or decision-making institutions.[8]

In recent decades, two important changes have reduced labor's ability to use local resources. First, landowners have seized and converted the commons into land for commercial use, denying labor access to the village commons. As cash crop production increased, subsistence production declined. When large-scale agricultural estates expanded, many women and their families were displaced, resulting in hunger and sometimes famine. Equally important, community land and natural resources have been degraded and depleted. There has been a rapid loss of clean water, wild foods, fertile soils, and forest lands, particularly in Central and South America.[9] Air, water, and soil have been contaminated by toxic industrial pollutants.[10] As natural resources are degraded and access to land is restricted, women spend more hours gathering water, food, medicinal plants, firewood, and fuel. According to Bina Agarwal, as women walk greater distances to gather these items, their total work day lengthens and their incomes decrease, particularly since they have less time to grow their own food. Furthermore, as households become more dependent on market goods, they need to generate more cash income.[11]

Oil companies can have a devastating impact on common resources because they pollute large tracts of land around oil reserves. But some workers have fought back, trying to maintain the environments they need for nonwage and subsistence work activities. In Colombia, the Uwa Indians near the city of Chuscal have opposed oil exploration on their reservation, even though the government gave Occidental Petroleum an oil concession in 1992. The Uwa have threatened to commit suicide if the oil company takes steps to prospect for oil or import oil workers. The Uwa, who were not consulted by the government, have fought the oil companies because oil production threatens their livelihood. "Our wood has been exploited, and so have our traditional medicines. The river is angry with us and might overflow. The earth is tired and violated," explained one Uwa leader.[12]

In a similar protest against oil producers in 1997, the Ashuars in Ecuador seized two scientists until an Argentine oil company agreed to pull out of the region.[13]

In northern Brazil, the Macuxi have burned bridges, blocked roads, and sabotaged work sites to defend their claim to a tract of land the size of Connecticut. The Macuxi have fought to keep away settlers, who have tried to stake mining claims and promoted the construction of a hydroelectric dam in Macuxi territory. The Macuxi argue that the Brazilian constitution protects their claim to ancestral lands. Rural Brazilians can sometimes win title to land if the land they occupy has not been used to serve its social function. This law has enabled tens of thousands of working families to secure land. But land occupiers often face violent opposition from absentee landowners, and more than one thousand occupiers have been killed by police and landlord paramilitaries.[14] Although Brazil worked with the Group of Seven to design and fund the protection of 40,000 square miles for indigenous groups, fiscal pressures led Brazil to cut funding for this project in 1999.[15]

Workers have organized resistance to logging concessions in many parts of the South and North. In Nicaragua, where the government told foreign lumber companies that they could log an indigenous area the size of Rhode Island, the Sumos sued the Chamorro government and lodged a complaint with the Organization of American States. In 1992, Nicaraguans protested a Taiwanese logging concession, while thousands of Hondurans successfully fought a logging concession made to Stone

Container, a Chicago paper company.[16] Indigenous groups in Bolivia have fought loggers that felled trees on their lands. And in Surinam, a country plagued by environmental problems, civil war, inflation, and rising unemployment, the government has been trying to raise revenues by selling concessions to logging firms, a development that many environmentalists think will lead to widespread environmental devastation.[17] In Papua New Guinea, where the land belongs to the people who live on it (not to the government), workers have responded to logging companies in different ways. Some see logging as a source of revenue, others see it as a process that destroys their common resources.[18]

In the United States, a coalition of environmentalists and Latino farmers in San Luis, Colorado, blocked the roads and stopped logging trucks six times in 1996 and 1997. Small farmers have opposed deforestation because it has had deleterious consequences on the watershed and irrigated lands.[19] Because logging forests pollutes water, kills fish, triggers landslides and floods, and re-routes rivers and streams, U.S. environmental groups have fought hard to prevent the construction of any new logging roads, which are now two and one-half times longer than the national highway system.[20] Logging and land development, together with monocultural farming and ranching, have also brought 30 percent of the plants in the United States to the edge of extinction, a terrible waste of common genetic resources.[21]

During the last two decades, large agricultural estates and global logging companies have cut down huge swaths of the world's remaining forest lands. In Latin America, both indigenous groups on ancestral lands and landless laborers have battled to protect land from loggers, miners, and ranchers. These workers have struggled either to defend their ownership of land or to maintain their access to land, which they have utilized for subsistence work. As logging, mining, and ranching companies expropriate new territory, sometimes with state approval and often illegally, indigenous people and poor workers have fought back. Throughout the world, reclamation or reappropriation movements have seized land and other property from property owners who have expropriated land and resources. Many egalitarian ethnic organizations and women-centered movements have tried to reverse the closure of the commons and fight to maintain or reclaim community property. It is important to recognize the significance of ethnic group land claims and women's efforts to reclaim and restore the land. After all, workers need access to land if they want to set up independent production and detach themselves, at least in part, from the world-system. And if households want to escape high rents, control of land is vital. In Mexico, for example, "women have become key actors in resisting attempts by state officials to evict *colonos*, residents of communities where workers built homes from recycled construction materials.[22] Even if egalitarian ethnic groups simply want to produce on their own, they provide others with a political alternative. In an era when mass communication reaches across the globe, reclamation movements can encourage other diversification movements.

In Southern Africa and Zimbabwe, where Black majorities have seen White colonial and apartheid governments seize their ancestral lands, movements to seize land have been a very important form of protest. Although the postapartheid governments in both countries have promised to redistribute wealth and land, growing poverty and political conflicts have impeded the redistribution of land and housing. So squatters in urban settlements near Johannesburg and farm reappropriators in Marondera, Zimbabwe, acted initially on their own. But government support for land reclamation soon followed.[23] Both groups have tried to diversify the ways that workers and consumers make goods and define work, expanding the ways that work and markets are structured. By doing this, they have created social alternatives.

Like most African National Congress leaders, Michael Sutcliffe argues that squatting in unused private or open public spaces is not "theft of land" but "reclaiming land that was stolen earlier."[24] According to Mike Foulds of the South African Housing Trust, "We're going to see the continuation of land invasions and see violence escalate on the account of this." He sees this as "pretty frightening for South Africa."[25] Reverend Frank Chikane makes the argument that big businesses should compensate the victims of apartheid.[26]

Land reclamation movements have sprung up around the world. Many indigenous groups in Latin America have fought to maintain control over the rain forests. Landless rural people have demanded that the government provide them with land. In Gravatai, Brazil, for example, 500 rural workers occupied land owned by General Motors and protested the government's failure to redistribute land to 1,500 farm families.[27]

In the United States, Native American groups have tried to control the economic activities they conduct on their land. In 1997, for example, 1,000 Seneca Indians confronted New York state police on the thruway and demanded that the state stop collecting taxes on Indian cigarette and gasoline sales. "We are a sovereign nation and we have the right to govern ourselves. We were here before the white people got here. [Moreover] the state is trying to destroy us," one Seneca leader explained. And Indian groups in New York State—the Onondoga, Iroquois, Oneida, Cayuga, Seneca, and Mohawk—have advanced large-scale land claims, which are expected to transfer land from White owners to Indians.[28]

Indian nations have also opposed congressional legislation that would eliminate sovereign immunity and deny federal money to any of the 554 Indian groups in the United States if they earned over a certain amount. Debra Doxator, chairwoman of the Oneida in Wisconsin, has argued that the new law would effectively abrogate U.S.–Indian treaties: "We gave up vast amounts of land in return for sovereignty and certain obligations by the federal government. Now they want to throw that out. It would be devastating for us."[29]

Native Americans have not been the only groups to demand land or property. Squatter movements are also widespread in the core and periphery. Although New York mayor Rudolph Giuliani has painted squatters as being "dishonest, cheating people who are trying to chisel," fifty squatters who took over three city-owned buildings argued that they had a right to housing.[30]

In another case, a group of immigrants from the Dominican Republic first squatted in an abandoned building in New York City, then fixed it up and made arrangements to buy the property.[31]

By challenging private property, squatters, land appropriators, and land users have challenged the system and questioned its legitimacy. In Paris, 126 members of a tenants group occupied an empty school on the Rue du Dragon until the city government found vacant apartments for them.[32] In Israel, a large group of Palestinians contested an Israeli settlement in the West Bank by invading the settlement and seizing settler weapons. They then petitioned the Israeli court, asking that the land be returned to its original owners.[33]

After the communist regime fell in Albania, squatter settlements sprang up in Tirana. In many squatter settlements, workers engage in now-legal capitalist operations and illegal criminal activities, particularly drug smuggling.[34]

Diversification movements may have different social meanings, depending on the context in which they emerge. In communist China, diversifying movements try to protect socialist agricultural collectives against encroachment by capitalist land-use practices. In communist Cuba, they may try to open community market spaces for the sale of garden produce and break the economic hold that agricultural collectives and state-run markets have on economic life. So for some workers, economic and political diversity may mean defending "collectives"; for others, it may mean weakening "collectives" and creating new economic and political spaces.

During the period after 1970, land was privatized across the capitalist and communist periphery and semiperiphery. In this context, movements demanding access to land and water have grown, as workers have fought to maintain their right to important resources. People who work or spend time out-of-doors have also organized to maintain their right to access lakes, rivers, and beaches. In Britain, for example, "ramblers" or hikers do not challenge land ownership, but they do fight to maintain open access to public trails that cross private property. "It's my birthright to walk here," said Jed Trewin of Mawgan, Cornwall. His group has opposed landowner efforts to block ramblers from footpaths through private lands.

ENVIRONMENTAL DEGRADATION: WORKERS FIGHT INDUSTRIAL PRODUCTION AND ENVIRONMENTAL CONTAMINATION

In the urban-industrial areas of the South and North, large producers have destroyed natural environments, setting the stage for diversifying movements. For example, workers in twelve countries in the periphery have sued six transnational corporations based in the core because they used a banned U.S. chemical that caused sterility among workers employed in their factories.[35] In 1990, the Ogoni people living in the Niger Delta basin drew up an "Ogoni Bill of Rights" to protest the widespread pollution that resulted from oil production in the region. Their fight was widely publicized when the Nigerian dictatorship executed Ken Saro-Wiwa, a leader of the Movement for the Survival of the Ogoni People, in 1995. The Ogoni have tried to change a 1979 Nigerian law that gives all mineral rights to the government and does little to protect the people living in oil-producing areas. In 1998, after Mobil spilled oil in the Niger River Delta, worker communities along the river rioted. In an effort to reverse this degradation, UN General-Secretary Kofi Annan recently persuaded some major corporations, including Shell Oil in Nigeria, to make commitments to improve the environment and work conditions in the region.[36]

In historical terms, starvation was common when new areas were incorporated into the world-economy. Today, in the stage of selective globalization, hunger has again become a common feature for workers in many parts of the world. As real wages drop, part-time work increases, and nonwage resources disappear, many workers face hunger and starvation. In 1997, for example, millions of North Koreans faced food shortages, hunger, and famine after drought and floods destroyed crops.[37] To survive, rural Koreans foraged for wild, edible roots and grasses: "Farmers in Sangdan Ri said that some varieties, such as chok, a long, bitter, fibrous root, hadn't been eaten since the desperate days of 1951, during the Korean War."[38] By November 1998, a U.S. congressman who visited North Korea said that millions of people had starved in the preceding two years, and that for food, survivors relied on dried leaves and straw, which they ground into flour and made into noodles.[39]

Workers in many regions of Africa face severe shortages. In Somalia, food shortages in the countryside pushed many women and children into the port city of Kismayu in 1996.[40] And in 1998, the Sudanese government banned food imports for six months in an effort to starve rebels who opposed the government and wanted to make the southern part of Sudan an autonomous political entity.[41] In Niger, where drought, desertification, poverty, and a drastic reduction of First World aid have combined to limit survival options, people walk five or ten miles to obtain water.[42] In Ghana, the 1998 drought meant that hydroelectric dams generated less energy, which crippled agricultural and industrial production and created near-famine conditions. As the relationship between work, income, and the environment become more precarious, political protests about these life-and-death issues will likely intensify.

Worker movements not only make claims on land and natural resources, they also claim other kinds of goods and property. Of course, many of the movements are often spontaneous, disorganized, and violent. Workers, for example, have frequently rioted and looted to obtain food, clothing, and consumer goods. One rioter in Indonesia defended widespread looting, saying, "It's the only way of getting the government's attention" and persuading the state to rescind fuel price increases.[43] In Mexico, more than four hundred needy farm workers seized forty tons of corn from a train.[44] As conditions for workers deteriorate, more looting, train assaults, and food reclamation riots will occur. Although they may often be violent and disorganized, these reclamation movements all increase the independent social resources available to workers and allow them to pursue the nonwage work activities they need to survive.

RESTRUCTURING CIVIL SOCIETY

Workers have begun to develop alternative self-governance structures, which diversify the ways that people participate in work and politics. It takes a long time to transform a society. But diversifying movements have put in place some of the building blocks needed to achieve this end. Worker efforts to share the benefits of work and make collective decisions can create a new civil society. To this end, workers have organized movements to redefine education, generate resources to support work, diversify political practices, and create alternative ways to produce goods and make political decisions in agricultural and urban settings.

Education

Workers have made numerous attempts to redefine formal and informal education so that it more readily meets their needs. In the last decade, activists have come to appreciate the contributions made by community-based education, which is also known as "community-action" or "participatory-action research." This approach, which was developed by Paolo Freire and others, emphasizes the importance of involving workers in the potentially radicalizing process of defining and addressing their problems. For example, when the government failed to open a school in Bhumlairi, Pakistan, poor farmer parents established their own school. They even figured out how to train the teacher, the only young woman in the village to receive a secondary education. In South Asia, school-planning projects like this have often mobilized low-income people and prepared them to take on other community projects.[45]

Culturally marginalized groups have redefined education and encouraged working-class students to solve community and regional problems. The addition of Women's studies, Black studies, ethnic studies, anticolonial studies, critical multidisciplinary programs, global studies, and environmental studies to curricula in high schools and universities has helped workers explore historical developments and contemporary social trends that affect them. Increasingly, civil education or service learning has been added to high school and university education, helping students integrate community service with academic courses and stimulating problem-solving, leadership development, and visionary thinking about real-world problems.

Resource Generation, Micro-Credit, and Cooperatives

In the world-system, most workers have few resources. But some worker movements have been able to provide limited resources to worker households, often to women, which enable workers to become more economically independent from wage work and capitalist market goods. The movement to encourage savings, credit, and swapping has taken many forms. Some critics have argued that these efforts have not substantially changed the character of everyday life but instead simply made women do more work. Yet if we look at this diversifying movement from a long-term perspective, it is evident that the skills and relations that workers develop may shape future societies in significant ways. This resource-generating movement has played an important role (1) because it has recognized that workers create value on their own, outside of paid employment, which helps them survive as workers, and (2) because the exchange of goods and services has helped workers reduce their dependence on the money economy. Barter systems, where different kinds of goods or services offered by workers can be exchanged, have emerged in England, through the Local Exchange Trading System (LETS), and in the United States. In St. Louis, for example, low-income workers can access services (baby-sitting or a ride to the doctor's) by exchanging household staples or by providing a service like reading to a blind person.[46] In a similar way, food- and resource-sharing schemes have been adopted by Nigerian workers as a way to cope with rising food prices.[47] Almost two hundred local currencies (such as Ithaca dollars) have been established by communities in the United States. These currencies give value to volunteer work and encourage workers to buy goods from local producers. The creation of local currencies has also provided credit to local people who want to start a business or cooperative without obtaining a bank loan.

Civil society has been reconstructed slowly by micro-credit programs like Bangladesh's Grameen Bank, which provides revolving loans to poor, landless women. The First Women's Bank in Islamabad has provided ways for low-income, "credit-risky" women to acquire resources, manage their work, and, significantly, gain greater control over the benefits of their work.[48] Elsewhere, nonprofit organizations have provided start-up support for young people who want to control their own work and its benefits.[49]

Workers need credit, but they also need to generate savings. Nonprofit organizations have worked to encourage low-income households to save, so they can invest in a start-up business, finance their education, or purchase housing. U.S. immigrants often start savings groups. In one Bronx neighborhood, Mexican immigrants contribute $200 a month to their savings group.[50] To help each other obtain low-cost housing, many laboring groups employ a "sweat-equity" strategy, where they agree to repair or build homes collectively so they can reduce their housing costs. Neighborhood groups have also encouraged workers to develop and share the resources made available through community gardens.

It is difficult to collect the resources that workers need to gain more control over their work and life choices. And it is even more difficult to create new social relationships and alternative institutions that can make alternative production and decision-making organizations sustainable. But workers have tried to establish new ways to work and govern in settings around the world. The social change models that workers have established in one place have often influenced the development of alternatives elsewhere. Many of the innovations developed by workers in the last decade have been related to agriculture and household-run micro-enterprises. Rural workers in Liberia, for example, have responded to the chaos of civil war by developing techniques to grow food more quickly. Members of self-organized work groups go to each other's farms to speed planting and harvesting.[51] In Zimbabwe, Chief Mabhena, the first woman chief of the Ndebele, helped establish pig and poultry cooperatives. In North America, more than six hundred community-supported agriculture projects (CSAs) have been started since 1985. This movement, which gets urban consumers to support local farm families and reduce their economic risks, first began in Japan around 1970 and then spread to England in 1982. Urban consumers, who are shareholders in agricultural ventures, help farm families plan crops and expenditures. Later, they get a share of the harvest. Farm families that are a part of these urban/rural linkages benefit from volunteer workers and from the consumers, who pay in advance for summer vegetables and fruits.[52]

Many farm families have tried to establish face-to-face connections with consumers and pull away from the giant fertilizer, seed, butchering, and marketing companies that dominate agricultural economies. But this is difficult to do. When one Canadian farm family tried to sell its grain directly to buyers in North Dakota, a sale that bypassed the monopolistic Canadian Wheat Board, the Canadian government sentenced the farmer to prison.[53] Many farm families on the prairie have explored ways to establish small-scale, sustainable farm practices, which would enable communities to become more self-sufficient and less dependent on large-scale, global producers and marketing firms. In Kansas, farm families that have broken away from consumer networks and become self-sufficient producers and consumers have described their action as "getting off the grid."

The establishment of cooperatives has been an important way that workers have tried to diversity social relations in civil society. Fair trade organizations, which have linked consumers in the core with producers in the periphery, have grown rapidly since 1975. Some of these alternative trade organizations (ATOs), like Equal Exchange in Canton, Massachusetts, are themselves worker cooperatives that use their collective resources to support the development of worker cooperatives in the periphery. One recycling cooperative in Belgium, which deals in used clothing, bags, and shoes, donates almost all of its $10 million annual profits to finance the start-up of cooperatives in the periphery.[54]

Other cooperatives have redefined culture and persuaded low-income workers to question inequality. Some have even challenged male violence and patriarchy. Mayan Women's Strength, a collective of indigenous female playwrights, has challenged local workers to reassess historical events (the Spanish conquest) and contemporary developments (rebellion in Chiapas). This collective not only produces plays, it holds literacy classes and theater workshops, runs a sewing- and job-skills center, and helps young, poor women deal with abusive lovers and husbands.[55]

ESTABLISHING ALTERNATIVE GOVERNMENTS

Diversifying movements have organized two kinds of self-governing political structures that may develop into alternatives to existing states: nongovernmental organizations and guerrilla movements. Nongovernmental organizations (NGOs) have sometimes assumed roles usually reserved for official states. The Urban Poor Coalition in Indonesia, directed by social activist Wardah Hafidz, has fought for human rights, worker protection, legal aid, political freedom, and environmental protection. Together with Indonesian student groups, the Urban Poor Coalition and other NGOs have fought to change civil society and to improve social relations.[56] In many respects, they resemble embryonic states. NGOs like the International Campaign to Ban Land Mines, which was awarded the 1997 Nobel Peace Prize, are quasi-governmental agencies that try to provide communities with peace and security, services that states traditionally provided.[57]

Nonprofit organizations and community-based organizations also have been involved in self-governing efforts to fight racism. For example, twenty-five years ago, Morris Dees started the Southern Poverty Law Center, which has campaigned against racist organizations like the Ku Klux Klan (KKK) and the racist militias that emerged in the 1980s and 1990s. In this respect, they have tried to enforce the rule of law, a function that has long been the responsibility of states.

The NGOs and nonprofit groups organized by workers have provided regional, national, and international leadership in self-governance. Because future societies will, no doubt, evolve from current social relations, the organizations that are now attempting to build new civil societies may be erecting institutions that will form the foundations of governments in the future.[58]

Of course, the movements that are now creating political alternatives may not build the foundations of new, egalitarian, or democratic civil societies. Some "diversifying" movements may do just the opposite. In Burma, opposition to the military dictatorship runs so deep that when a plane carrying military officers and their families crashed in an area held by opposition forces, male rebels tortured, gang raped, and butchered the survivors.[59] Around the world, desperate groups have lashed out at the state, often by attacking civilians. In China, for example, rebels planted bombs on buses in the Xinjiang capital, Ürümqi, killing nine people and injuring seventy-four more.

Guerrilla movements, however, are still the most dramatic expression of worker efforts to redefine or replace state power. In Chiapas, for example, the Zapatistas have established autonomous administrations at villages across the region, organizing indigenous people to resist central government authority.[60] The Zapatistas differ from classic guerrilla movements (in China, Vietnam, or Cuba), in that they have not tried to seize central state power. Instead, they have fought to win municipal power and regional autonomy vis-à-vis the central Mexican state. For a time, the Mexican government allowed them to create their regional political alternative. But the Mexican government cracked down in 1998, sending troops into the region and encouraging paramilitary vigilantes to attack Zapatista supporters. In one attack, paramilitary forces massacred forty-five unarmed civilians.[61] To a large extent, the Zapatistas are an antistate movement that attempts to diversify modes of democratic and economic participation. It is an anti-institutional and a diversifying movement because it both challenges the existing state and creates democratic political alternatives to the state. Moreover, it is organized along both class and ethnic lines. The Zapatistas have also forged links with the National Indian Congress of Mexico. The Congress, which represents Mexico's ninety-six Indian groups, has demanded that the Mexican constitution recognize their ancestral lands and traditional political and legal practices. "We must struggle so that indigenous people can live like human beings and not the way the powerful have kept us, like animals," a Zapatista leader told the Indian Congress.[62] Following the defeat of Mexico's long-dominant party, the PRI, voters elected a pro-Zapatista candidate as governor of Chiapas.

The Popular Revolutionary Army (PRA), Mexico's second major guerrilla movement, first emerged in 1974 and then went underground until 1995, when guerrillas appeared publicly at a memorial service for seventeen rural workers massacred by police. Unlike the Zapatistas, this Marxist-inspired movement has not enjoyed much popular support in its home state of Guerrero. The guerrillas have said that they want to avenge police killings, free political prisoners, overthrow Mexico's government, and establish an elected workers' state.[63] In this regard, they are like traditional antistate guerrilla movements. In secret talks with journalists, PRA officials have said that the group is a coalition of fourteen leftist groups and includes students, urban and rural workers, and Indians. Guerrilla group members are part-time revolutionaries who have regular jobs as agricultural workers, industrial laborers, and schoolteachers.[64]

In August 1996, the PRA took its campaign against the Mexican state to the streets, carrying out five carefully planned, simultaneous attacks in four states. The assaults resulted in thirteen deaths and twenty-three injuries.[65] A month later, insurgents cut highways or fought with police and attacked military outposts in the same states. Although the insurgent group claimed that it attacked two army vehicles in Michoacan, state authorities claimed that the attack was made by drug traffickers, which suggested a possible link between the guerrillas and drug lords.[66]

State officials then moved quickly to contain the insurgency, sending fourteen people from Oaxaca to prisons in Mexico City and Hidalgo State.[67] The state's antiguerrilla tactics may have been effective because there has been little mention of this insurgent group since 1996.

Guerrilla movements have also been active in Colombia. In the late 1990s, Colombia's guerrilla groups raised money by kidnapping wealthy people and travelers and holding them for ransom, trafficking in cocaine and heroin, and extorting money from oil companies. Oil companies have spent heavily to purchase protection from the Colombian military and from guerrilla groups. As one oil executive explained, "You've got high taxes, low security and an unstable government. You've got yourself a time bomb."[68]

Colombia's two largest insurgent organizations are the National Liberation Army and the Revolutionary Armed Forces of Colombia (FARC), one of the oldest and largest Marxist guerrilla groups in the world. Right-wing paramilitary organizations are also active in Colombia. Government officials in Colombia have negotiated with FARC and allowed it to administer four states, which together are the size of Switzerland.[69] FARC leaders have said that they want to promote social justice, seize state power, nationalize industries, outlaw foreign investment, and stop the United States from supplying weapons and money to the government.[70] In this context, guerrilla movements and drug lords have created alternative centers of political power in Colombia. But instead of creating a more civil society, they have contributed to uncivil wars. The president recently said that Colombia had been "divided into three irreconcilable countries, where one country kills, the other dies, and a third, horrified, scratches its head and shuts it eyes."[71]

Other guerrilla movements have been organized throughout the world. Most of them seek to seize state power, which has long been an objective of institutionalist "revolutionary" movements. Where they have failed to overthrow the state but persist in the attempt, they have "diversified" political power by establishing autonomous or alternative political institutions. But with the exception, perhaps, of the Zapatistas, these diversifying movements have done little to transform civil society or create egalitarian or democratic political practices. Instead, they have typically degraded, not improved, the social environment.

Throughout the world, labor activists have simultaneously developed institutional movements that have challenged the authority of businesses and states and diversifying movements that have created new economic and political relations and institutions, some democratic and some authoritarian, that have provided workers with economic and political alternatives to capitalism. In many respects, these activists have assumed more responsibility for defining economic and political relations in the future.

But if the world-system is breaking up, if criminal and authoritarian groups occupy the social spaces that capitalism leaves behind, workers' diversifying movements will have to discover how to challenge the capitalist institutions that remain, how to weaken the hold of criminal and authoritarian groups on workers and consumers, and how to build egalitarian and democratic societies using the resources that they can access or create.

NOTES

1. Margaret Benson, "The Political Economy of Women's Liberation," in R. Hennessy and C. Ingraham, eds., *Materialist Feminism* (New York: Routledge, 1997); Helene Saffioti, *Women in a Class Society* (New York: Monthly Review, 1978); Mariarosa Dalla Costa, "Women and the Subversion of the Community," in Hennessy and Ingraham, *Materialist Feminism*; Maria Mies, Veronica Bennholdt-Thomsen, and Claudia Von Werlhof, *Women: The Last Colony* (London: Zed, 1991); Helen Safa, *The Myth of the Male Breadwinner: Women and Industrialization in the Caribbean* (Boulder, Colo.: Westview, 1995); Joan Smith, Immanuel Wallerstein, and Hans D. Evers, eds., *Households and the World Economy* (Beverly Hills: Sage, 1984); Joan Smith and Immanuel Wallerstein, eds., *Creating and Transforming Households* (Cambridge: Cambridge University Press, 1992).

2. See Torry D. Dickinson, *CommonWealth: Self-Sufficiency and Work in American Communities, 1830 to 1993* (Lanham, Md.: University Press of America, 1995).

3. Miguel Diaz-Barriga, "Beyond the Domestic and the Public: Colonas Participation in Urban Movements in Mexico City," in Sonia E. Alvarez, Evelina Dagnino, and Arturo Escobar, eds., *Culture of Politics, Politics of Culture* (Boulder, Colo.: Westview, 1998), 260, 273.

4. Sam Howe Verhovek, "Alaska Torn over Rights to Live Off the Land," *New York Times*, July 12, 1999.

5. Vandana Shiva and Radha Holla-Bhar, "Piracy by Patent: The Case of the Neem Tree," in Jerry Mander and Edward Goldsmith, eds., *The Case against the Global Economy: And for a Turn to the Local* (San Francisco: Sierra Club, 1996).

6. Vandana Shiva, *Stolen Harvest: The Hijacking of the Global Food Supply* (Cambridge, Mass.: South End, 2000).

Redefining Work and Society

7. Yaakov Garb, "Lost in Translation: Toward a Feminist Account of Chipko," in Joan W. Scott, Cora Kaplan, and Debra Keates, eds., *Transitions, Environments, Translations: Feminisms in International Politics* (New York: Routledge, 1997), 192–193.

8. Garb, "Lost in Translation," in Scott, Kaplan, and Keates, *Transitions, Environments, Translations*, 192–193.

9. V. Spike Petersen and Anne Sisson Runya, *Global Gender Issues* (Boulder, Colo.: Westview, 1999), 134, 148–149.

10. Ted C. Lewellen, *Dependency and Development: An Introduction to the Third World* (Westport, Conn.: Begin and Garvey, 1995), 193–197.

11. Garb, "Lost in Translation," in Scott, Kaplan, and Keates, *Transitions, Environments, Translations*, 194–195.

12. Pamela Mercer, "A Conflict of Indians vs. Oilmen in Colombia," *New York Times*, October 6, 1996.

13. "2 to Be Freed in Ecuador," *New York Times*, February 22, 1997.

14. Diana Jean Schemo, "In Brazil, Indians Call on Spirits to Save Land," *New York Times*, July 21, 1996; "Brazil's Rural Violence," *New York Times*, June 14, 2000.

15. Diana Jean Schemo, "Brazil Slashes Money for Project Aimed at Protecting Amazon," *New York Times*, January 1, 1999.

16. Julia Preston, "Nicaragua Sells Off Its Forests," *San Francisco Chronicle*, June 25, 1996.

17. Anthony DePalma, "In Surinam's Rain Forests, a Fight over Trees vs. Jobs," *New York Times*, September 4, 1995.

18. Philip Shenan, "Isolated Papua New Guineans Fall Prey to Foreign Bulldozers," *New York Times*, June 5, 1994.

19. James Brooke, "In a Colorado Valley, Hispanic Farmers Try to Stop a Timber Baron," *New York Times*, March 24, 1997.

20. Carey Goldberg, "Quiet Roads Bringing Thundering Protests," *New York Times*, May 23, 1997.

21. William K. Stevens, "One in Every 8 Plant Species Is Imperiled, a Survey Finds," *New York Times*, April 9, 1998.

22. Diaz-Barriga, "Beyond the Domestic and the Public," 259.

23. Sudarsan Raghaven, "Rural Black Squatters Battling Homeowners: South Africa's Homeless Problem," *San Francisco Chronicle*, January 3, 1996; Donald G. McNeil, Jr., "Zimbabwe Squatters: Land Claims on White Farms," *New York Times*, June 22, 1998.

24. Bill Keller, "Squatters Testing Limits as Apartheid Crumbles," *New York Times*, November 14, 1993.

25. Raghaven, "Rural Black Squatters Battling Homeowners."

26. David Goodman, *Fault Lines: Journeys into the New South Africa* (Berkeley: University of California Press, 1999), 351.

27. "Brazilian Peasants Demand Farmland," *New York Times*, July 23, 1997.

28. William Glaberson, "For Indian Leaders, Fighting a War on Two Fronts," *New York Times*, April 22, 1997; David Chen, "Battle over Iroquois Land Claims Escalates," *New York Times*, May 16, 2000.

29. Timothy Egan, "Senate Measures Would Deal Blow to Indian Deal," *New York Times*, August 27, 1997.

30. Thomas J. Lueck, "New York Police Evict Squatters from Three City-Owned Tenements," *New York Times*, August 14, 1996.

31. David M. Halbfinger, "For Homesteaders, Prospect of a Rare Victory," *New York Times*, May 31, 1998.

32. Alan Riding, "French Abbe Aids Homeless and Politicians Genuflect," *New York Times*, December 22, 1994; Craig R. Whitney, "Homeless Man Finds Niche: The Car's Last Caretaker," *New York Times*, February 9, 1995.

33. Serge Schmemann, "Settler Killed, Palestinian Wounded in Clash Overland," *New York Times*, April 20, 1998.

34. Jane Perlez, "In a Land Adrift, the Albanian People Drift Too," *New York Times*, July 16, 1997.

35. Diana Jean Schemo, "Pesticide from U.S. Kills the Hopes of Fruit Pickers in the Third World," *New York Times*, December 6, 1995.

36. Roger Cohen, "Mobil Spill Bares Ebb Tide of Nigerian Life," *New York Times*, September 20, 1998.

37. Barbara Crossette, "Relief Teams Say North Korea Faces Vast Drought Emergency," *New York Times*, August 5, 1997.

38. Trevor Pope, "Flood Waters Come and Go. Misery Endures," *New York Times*, May 26, 1996.

39. Nicholas D. Kristof, "A U.S. Visitor Fears Famine Is Decimating North Koreans," *New York Times*, November 15, 1998.

40. James C. McKinley, Jr., "Famine Threat Drives Thousands of Somalis from Homes," *New York Times*, June 19, 1996.

41. James C. McKinley, Jr., "Sudan Hinders UN Aid as South Faces Famine," *New York Times*, March 18, 1998.

42. Joseph R. Gregory, "In the Dust and Drought, a Sultan in His Splendor," *New York Times*, April 21, 1998.

43. Nicholas D. Kristof, "To Some of Indonesia's Poor, Looting Gives Taste of Power," *New York Times*, May 18, 1998.

44. Karen Lehman, "Global Uprisings for Bread," *Earth Island Journal* (Fall 1996): 17.

45. Barbara Crossette, "Third World Fills a Void as Villagers Run Schools," *New York Times*, May 10, 1998.

46. Peter T. Kilborn, "Promising Trade-Off for the Needy," *New York Times*, September 29, 1996.

47. Stephen Buckley, "In Somalia, an Unlikely Boom Town," *San Francisco Chronicle*, March 5, 1996.

48. Edward A. Gargan, "Women at Last Get Their Due Credit," *New York Times*, November 26, 1991.

49. Paul Wisenthal, "For Young Entrepreneurs, a Step Past the Classroom," *New York Times*, March 7, 1999.

50. "Mexicans Seek a Toehold on City's Crowded Ladder," *New York Times*, July 28, 1997.

51. Buckley, "In Somalia, an Unlikely Boom Town."

52. Molly O'Neill, "Urban Living Off the Land," *New York Times*, July 9, 1997.

53. Anthony DePalma, "On Canada's Prairie, a Farmers' Rebellion Flares," *New York Times*, January 3, 1997.

54. Marlise Simons, "Gold in the Streets (Some Call it Trash)," *New York Times*, January 4, 1994.

55. Robert Myers, "Mayan Women Find Their Place Is on the Stage," *New York Times*, September 28, 1997.

56. Seth Mydans, "Activists Thrust Agendas into Post-Suharto Void," *New York Times*, June 28, 1999.

57. Paul Lewis, "Not Just Governments Make War on Peace," *New York Times*, November 28, 1998.
58. Kevin Sack, "A Son of Alabama Takes on Americans Who Live to Hate," *New York Times*, May 12, 1996.
59. Associated Press, "Myanmar Survivors Tortured," *American Online*, September 20, 1998.
60. Julia Preston, "Both Carrot and Stick Fail in Chiapas," *New York Times*, May 17, 1998.
61. Ian Fisher, "Anguished Mexican Village Buries Its Dead," *New York Times*, October 13, 1996; Julia Preston, "Mexico's Overtures to Zapatistas Bring Tensions in Chiapas to a New Boiling Point," *New York Times*, March 6, 1998.
62. Julia Preston, "A Dying Chief of Zapatistas in Mexico City," *New York Times*, October 13, 1996.
63. Dam Dillon, "Shadowy Rebels Pose New Problems for Mexico," *New York Times*, July 17, 1996.
64. Julia Preston, "Mexico's Wary Crackdown on Rebels," *New York Times*, October 16, 1996.
65. Sam Dillon, "Rebels Strike in 4 Mexico States, Leaving 13 Dead," *New York Times*, August 30, 1996.
66. Dillon, "Rebels Strike in 4 Mexico States."
67. Preston, "Mexico's Wary Crackdown on Rebels."
68. Diana Jean Schemo, "Oil Companies Buy an Army to Tame Colombia's Rebels," *New York Times*, August 22, 1996.
69. Larry Rohter, "A Colombian Rebel Group Gains Notice, Loses Sympathy," *New York Times*, June 31, 1999.
70. Diana Jean Schemo, "Colombian Rebel Chief Is Absent as Peace Talks Start," *New York Times*, January 8, 1999.
71. Schemo, "Colombian Rebel Chief Is Absent."

Part V
CONCLUSION

Social change is hard work.

Part V

CONCLUSION

Chapter 13
Fast Forward

The world is in a period of rapid and comprehensive change. But working women and men in the South and North have been affected in different ways. The forward momentum of the world-economy, with its simultaneous processes of core-centered integration and peripheral disintegration, has fundamentally transformed work patterns, gender relations, and labor's resistance activities.

In the first part of this book, we argued that while change is all-embracing, the process and course of change is contradictory and has differed in the three zones of the world-economy during the last thirty years. In the second half of the book, we showed how working people have responded to change and reshaped social relations in new directions. We have argued that three simultaneous processes of working-class transformation are now taking place: proletarianization, deproletarianization, and the expulsion of worker households from the world-economy. We have also argued that working people, from both wage-dependent and expelled households, have organized movements that have both destabilized capitalist institutions and created new social alternatives.

WORKING CLASS FORMATION, DE-FORMATION, AND TRANSFORMATION

After we concluded our research, we reread relevant literature to see how our findings related to current debates about global social change. We differ with many globalization scholars who argue that world capitalist organizations and markets are growing unchecked. Still, globalization scholars provide theoretical support for and documentation of the dual process of proletarianization and deproletarianization. Their writings suggest that many workers have become increasingly reliant on wages while, at the same time, other workers have become less reliant on wages.[1] Their use of the term *globalization* overemphasizes the strength of the global capitalist class and minimizes the contradictory character of the development process.

In general, few scholars have suggested how working-class reproduction is changing, though Maria Mies and other anti-imperialist and environmental feminists have provided some guidelines. By arguing that labor's nonwage work is increasing, that proletarianization is an ongoing process that continues long after workers first enter the capitalist economy, Mies has gone beyond most other globalization scholars. We essentially agree with Mies, Bennholdt-Thomsen, and Werlhof that women form the "last colony."[2] We also agree with Samir Amin, who has warned that the "newly industrializing countries of the South (and of the East?) are already the very core of tomorrow's periphery."[3] He is right, we think, to suggest that wages from global assembly-line work disguise household deproletarianization and impoverishment.

There is an important emerging debate among scholars who address issues related to proletarianization and deproletarianization and/or systemic breakup and demise. The debate is influenced by the different ways that political economists measure wage dependency. The expansion of jobs in particular countries and industries, such as the growth in the number of women's jobs in export-manufacturing enclaves, has been used by some as proof that proletarianization is increasing. But these jobs may be increasing simply as a result of a redistribution of work, not a real increase in total employment. Scholars often take the simple appearance of women in manufacturing enclaves as evidence that labor is earning more and spending more. But there is no examination of how long these women have had jobs or changes in other household members' contributions. Scholars who study changes in household income measure proletarianization in a more comprehensive way.

According to Giovanni Arrighi and Beverly Silver, "greater proletarianization" and "increasing feminization" of the labor force will contribute to a new wave of social conflict.[4] In *Chaos and Governance,* they link increasing feminization to global restructuring and the decline of the core's male-dominated, mass-production, labor aristocracy. After World War II, Arrighi and Silver argue, women moved from household work to office employment only in the core, not in the poorer countries.[5] By emphasizing the increasing proletarianization that resulted from urbanization and factory relocation, they argue that the search by multinational corporations for cheap, flexible labor has resulted in "new and powerful mass-production working classes."[6]

Arrighi and Silver agree with Eric Hobsbawm that one of the most important changes in the last fifty years has been "the death of the peasantry."[7] But while the movement from small towns and the hinterland to mid-size and larger cities has been dramatic, migration rarely moved workers from subsistence work to capitalist work. Peasant households were already dependent on wage labor in the countryside before they migrated to urban settings. Although migrating peasants might have become more dependent on wages when they moved to cities before 1975, since then some feminist ethnographers have argued that urban migrants in the periphery have been forced to secure more income from informal work activities, which means that deproletarianization is taking place today in both urban and rural settings.[8]

Hobsbawm argues that globalization and the relocation of production facilities have led to the integration of most workers within the world-economy. Although most scholars inflate the extent of income redistribution from export production, Hobsbawm notes that industrialization in the export-oriented areas of Hong Kong, Singapore, Taiwan, and South Korea involved less than 2 percent of the Third World population. If workers in these countries are, in fact, becoming more proletarianized, Hobsbawm sees workers in the newly industrialized countries within the context of a growing gap between the world's rich and poor countries. Hobsbawm suggests that the world-economy could continue to function very well even if it discarded countries with low profit rates and dumped very poor people in countries the world over, if there were enough consumers buying high-ticket items. If economic trends and class polarization continue, there may be some countries "in which one quarter of the population [work] gainfully, and three quarters [do] not."[9] But Hobsbawm suggests that the polarization of the world's workers could be reduced, if people developed and used new ways of making decisions about reallocating resources. This would change the world-economy and stop it from being "an increasingly powerful and uncontrolled engine."[10]

Rather than creating a fully proletarianized working class, Immanuel Wallerstein argues, the world-economy has "flattened the variation of the degree of proletarianization across core-periphery and urban-rural differences."[11] His argument that the system works because it relies on workers who are not fully commodified is a critique of many assumptions made by globalization scholars. With the downturn that accompanied the decline of U.S. hegemony, "there was an expansion of the numbers of wage-workers worldwide," he argues. But at the same time, he says, there were reductions in "the average wage level" and "the average percentage of total work time in wage work."[12] In other words, some workers were drawn into wage labor for the first time after 1970 (a process of proletarianization), but workers' dependence on the wage generally declined, indicating that global deproletarianization has also occurred. Yet in the near future, Wallerstein expects that an economic upturn will bring "new proletarianizations" and "the increase in social benefits acquired as a result of the renewed class struggles," which are both changes that sustain demand levels and lead to global accumulation.[13] Ultimately, however, he sees the world-economy as a tinder box, with acute and growing social conflicts and intense class polarization, which will ignite systemic chaos.[14]

WORK-BASED CHANGES IN THE ZONES OF THE WORLD-ECONOMY

With these debates in mind, let us review our findings. We have argued that, in the core, the redistribution and reorganization of wage work resulted in deindustrialization, downsizing, and debt for worker households in the United States. Although the redistribution of work initially assisted wage workers in Western Europe and Japan, its reorganization in recent years has subjected them to many of the problems—job loss and falling incomes—experienced first by working-class households in the United States. Many working families have relied on a combination of credit and indebtedness, and on income from part-time jobs and additional household work.

When households have not been able to make gender patterns more flexible and equal, women and girls have often taken up the slack.

In the periphery, falling commodity prices, spurred in large part by the adoption of new technologies in the core, have resulted in job loss and falling incomes, not only for wage workers but also for farmers and independent commodity producers. Although some new jobs have been created in export-manufacturing (*maquila*) and service industries, these jobs have rarely provided sustained economic stability to workers and their multigenerational households, let alone to the region. In the tourist and sex industries, women workers and their children in particular have suffered from incalculable economic, social, and cultural hardships in terms of their daily and generational well-being, health, and security.

In impoverished urban and rural areas, which rarely see states take steps to protect workers' security, many women have taken the lead in developing alternative agricultural, industrial, and marketing relations. Nonwage work, which needs to be generated on a daily basis in uncertain circumstances, often provides the most stable source of income for those households that still count on some wage income.

For other households, household-organized work has become the sole source of income. For these expelled households that have been pushed out of the global economy (or have chosen to seek other pathways), "nonwage" work is no longer defined in relation to wage labor. In these cases, nonwage work has become transformed into a different kind of work that takes place totally outside the system.

In the semiperiphery, massive deindustrialization in postcommunist states and sudden economic crisis in East Asia resulted in massive job loss and declining wages, reversing the gains made by workers under the communist and capitalist regimes of the earlier postwar period.

Meanwhile, states in all three zones have reduced worker benefits. This has deprived women and men of an important source of income.

Contemporary change, which has taken different regional forms, has had a common result for working people the world over. We argue that, within the contemporary context, falling commodity prices, deindustrialization, falling wages, and reductions in state support for workers are all indications that laboring households rely less on wage income. We believe that these changes provide evidence that substantial deproletarianization can be found in all zones of the world-economy, especially in the periphery.

Change has eliminated jobs in the paid labor force, suppressed or reduced incomes from wage work, and curbed state benefits to workers in the core, periphery, and semiperiphery. As income from wage work and state benefits declined, laboring people—and especially females—have had to work harder. They work harder for others in paid employment and they have intensified their nonwage work activities (subsistence, sharing, and entrepreneurial kinds of work) so they can survive and reproduce in households. In the current period, the old worker aphorism "More work, less pay" accurately depicts the thrust of change, so long as it is understood that "work" refers to a broad range of wage and nonwage activities, and "pay" refers to wages from private firms and benefits from states.

These developments are gendered, as well as racialized. Unequal gender arrangements in paid employment and at home are an integral part of the global system. As work in the world-economy has become restructured through processes of selective globalization, change has altered gendered work relations, placing more burdens on female nonwage and wage workers in particular. Widespread deindustrialization, either as a result of the redistribution and reorganization of wage work in the core or the collapse of import-substitutionist manufacturing in the periphery and semiperiphery, has resulted in the exit of many men from wage work. At the same time, women have entered the paid labor force in large numbers, particularly in expanding service industries, though some, too, in export-manufacturing enclaves. Of course, women who find wage work nonetheless continue to perform nonwage work, which is essential if households want to maintain overall income levels and standards of living in the face of change. These developments have altered gender relations in public and private spheres.

Two crucial components of contemporary change are: (1) the "feminization" of wage work (or the increased female participation in the paid workforce at the overt level and decreased wages for all at the covert level); and (2) the "feminization" of nonwage work (women assuming increased responsibility for generating nonwage income in their homes or on the streets), developments that contribute to the rise of female-headed households. These developments, when combined with related changes in male work and in the reduction of workers' survival options, altered workers' social movements and protests.

Because it is increasingly difficult for laboring people to obtain jobs and income from private firms and benefits from states, worker households, particularly women, have intensified their nonwage work activities. The problem for workers is that their efforts to initiate and organize nonwage work activities have been undermined by the deterioration of social and natural environments, making it more difficult for workers to make do on their own. In the core, states actively discourage, prohibit, and punish worker efforts to generate nonwage income on the streets or in their homes. In the periphery and semiperiphery, states may permit it, but government officials, mafias, and insurrectionary armies tax workers' produce, disrupt worker enterprise, and threaten workers' lives. Moreover, the ongoing destruction of natural resources, particularly arable land and forests; the pollution of environmental commons (air and water); and the spread of disease make it difficult for workers to obtain the resources they need to pursue nonwage work activities and maintain the health of household members. So while laboring people turn increasingly to nonwage work to survive, nonwage work and extrasystemic work are increasingly difficult to pursue.

SYSTEMIC CHANGE AND GLOBAL PATHWAYS

The transition from the capitalist world-economy to one or more new social systems can be seen most clearly at the level of laboring households and interhousehold networks.

By studying changes in households' income sources, it is possible to trace three simultaneous processes in all zones of the world-economy: proletarianization, deproletarianization, and the expulsion of households from the global system. Although proletarianization is still the dominant process in the core, all three processes transform working people's lives, even in the richest countries. These transformative processes typically involve households over a three-generational cycle, and they cannot be understood on an individual level or outside of a historical context. For well-off households in the core, the rising dependence on female wages may often mean that households are being proletarianized. But in most parts of the periphery and the semiperiphery, the growth in female wage earners often (and perhaps typically) represents the deproletarianization of large groupings of multigenerational households.

On the surface, it may seem that, over the household's sustained income-generating cycle of twenty years, the general rise in female wage workers serves to increase household income. But this is not actually the case, given the global, historical context that we have described. When histories of female workers are examined in the poor periphery and semiperiphery, where six-sevenths of the population lives, changes in female wage labor can often be seen as providing evidence for deproletarianization and expulsion from the world-economy.

The labor of teen girls and women can serve as a short-term, stop-gap measure that may not be able to prevent their households from dropping into desperate poverty. Although parents and grandparents may hope that young women will be able to contribute enough wages to support impoverished, landless, rural households, young workers may not earn enough to support even single individuals. Young females earn the lowest wages, and adult women do not earn much more. Moreover, most female jobs provide short-term employment and little job security. Work in the sex industry is notoriously short-term because sex workers contract diseases and live short lives. Female heads of households often sustain units largely on their own. Although people generally assume that female wages supplement male wages, female wages actually serve as a substitute for male wages in many cases. The growing reliance on low-cost female labor has driven down male wages and global wage levels. The growth of female wage labor was designed as a strategy to lower wages. Under these circumstances, the only way households can survive is by doing more nonwage work. In this sense, low-paid female wage labor creates greater dependency on nonwage work and reduces consumption through the capitalist market. Household dependency, therefore, both reflects deproletarianization and contributes to it.

While some highly paid workers in the core have become more dependent on wage income, state transfers, and consumption through the market, most working households have become somewhat less dependent on wages, state benefits, and market consumption. Some poor households in the core are facing rapid deproletarianization, being marginalized much like poor households in the periphery.

In the periphery, a growing group of households is being expelled from the world-economy. These households rely less and less on wage labor, market consumption, and state benefits. Households that face deproletarianization are heavily represented in refugee and migrant populations. Some refugee and migrant households try to reverse their impoverishment by moving to the North, where they hope to find wage work. Households that appear to be the most likely candidates for making a permanent transition out of the capitalist world-economy have been disengaging from wage labor for the past ten to twenty years. If economic contraction continues indefinitely in the periphery and in many areas of the semiperiphery, then large numbers of deproletarianizing households will certainly be cast out of the global system altogether in the not-too-distant future.

In addition, there is a hard-to-define set of laboring, expelled households and capitalist households that rely on some income from criminal or illegal work activities. Profit-making through global and state-level criminal activities has always been a regular part of the world-system. Today, these criminal activities flourish. Some laboring households are becoming more proletarianized as they engage in illegal wage labor, and some that are tied to this kind of work are undergoing deproletarianization. This is an important issue because many workers who try to establish producer collectives are preyed upon by other desperately poor workers. Households that are trying to develop income-generating alternatives to the world-economy will have to address this problem. Meanwhile, illegal enterprises, corrupt governments, and global crime syndicates may develop their own nonsystemic alternatives, which would be cruel and corrupt in their own fashion.

PROTEST: LABOR MOVEMENTS PROMOTE SYSTEMIC CHANGE

Social movements have already started to shape the future and are a powerful force for change in the global arena. Over the last thirty years, labor movements have developed diverse strategies for confronting global institutions: business, the state, the household, racism, sexism, and ageism. In addition, labor movements have been challenging dominant cultures and establishing new ways of working and making collective decisions. Although these movements have grown out of the rebellions of the late 1960s and early 1970s and therefore can be seen as "new," previous working-class protests, cultural developments, social alternatives, and cumulative working-class knowledge have also shaped contemporary movements.[15]

Whether movements' actions will shape future history in a decisive way is not known. Much will depend on how many people become directly involved in change, how soon they become involved, whether their involvement is sustained, how much they learn from other people and related movements, and what they decide to do at key historical conjunctures. Labor movements, all of them, will have a powerful say in shaping whether one new system develops or whether many systems will emerge.

What will be particularly crucial is how diverse movements affect each other and interact with the institutions that they are individually and collectively decomposing and transforming. A very complex and very unpredictable social structure is now forming, given the fragmentation of the working class and also the ruling class. Global capitalist society is being restructured and foundations for future societies are being laid simultaneously. The institutions of the world-economy are being attacked by social movements, and internal workings and contradictions of the system are beginning to undermine its own continuation.

Systemic change cannot be understood if individual movements are analytically removed from the historical development of the family of movements. Individual movements should not be judged on the basis of arbitrary criteria, such as whether they have global connections or adopt class-based identities. We do not believe that movement activists will have time to develop a comprehensive theory of capitalist development and a unified theory of world revolution, before they can act.[16]

In *The Spiral of Capitalism and Socialism* Terry Boswell and Christopher Chase-Dunn call for the development of a global theory that can be adopted by social movements. They criticize "globalization from below" as an inherently weak social change strategy because global grass-roots activists fail to attack nationalism. But they fail to recognize that local-to-global grass-roots movements attack some but not all pillars of the system and that other movements attack other supports.[17]

Labor's power to change the world rests with the development of a diverse family of labor movements that both destabilizes systemic operations and capitalist ideologies and creates sustainable, alternative institutions. These alternative institutions might develop first at regional levels. There is no reason to believe that labor movements could move directly from a global class society to a global classless society. Participation in movement action, not theory construction alone, may be the best way to learn how to develop future societies. Laboring people's knowledge about how to change the world will undoubtedly evolve, and, within a decade or two, the global system and the global family of movements may be seen in a very different way. What different groups of protesters are doing now and tomorrow will matter in unforeseen ways.

Given the changes in work that we have outlined, it should not be surprising that growing numbers of laboring people the world over have protested the direction the system has taken. And it should be no surprise that laboring people have expressed opposition at its five-hundred-year mark, when the world's masses have largely given up any hope for widespread, postcolonial reforms.

But workers have not done so with one voice. Recall that laboring people occupy diverse economic positions and have different levels of income and debt, which are a product of global and local divisions of labor. They also have different and multiple social identities, as wage and nonwage workers, taxpayers, beneficiaries, consumers, and investors; as members of different gender, age, and ethnic groups. Because laboring people have separate economic interests and different social identities, it is difficult for them to act in concert. Nor should we expect them to protest change en masse. Instead, worker efforts to protest global, systemic developments are necessarily diverse, often complementary but sometimes at odds, in both a short- and long-term sense.

Around the world, working people have adopted familiar and novel strategies to protest change, wrest income and resources from private firms and states, and find ways to subsist outside the ambit or control of these institutions. Given the fact that women (who may function as heads of households) do more wage, nonwage and extrasystemic work, it is important to note that women have also assumed a central role in social change movements. The result has been a "feminization" of protest and politics, which actually suggests that global cultural transitions are already taking place. As part of this embedded gender revolution, we now see the potential severing of informal household work from the global system of production. The removal of "indirect exploitation," and its support of global profit-making, from the world-economy will likely stimulate the social transition process.

In the second half of the book, we surveyed protest movements in different settings. Although we noted the traditional struggles of wage workers—strikes by labor unions, for example—we highlighted protests made by wage and nonwage workers, women as well as men, across a wide social spectrum: struggles against private firms, struggles against states, and struggles that attempt to redefine economic and social relations.

During this postcolonial phase of selective globalization in the world-economy, we found that contemporary protests generally have several novel features. First, although workers make economic demands and attempt to wrest income and benefits from private firms and states, they also demand political and environmental change, arguing that democracy, equality, justice, and environmental quality are crucial to their well-being as workers. Second, many movements now take a broad, historically grounded view of households as collective units that are shaped by sexist practices; they try to find ways to meet the needs of women as well as men, and those of children, youth, and elders. Third, while movements may try to take control of or increase workers' participation in the economic and political institutions of the world-economy, they also try to create new social relations and institutions outside of their control. These three novel features are partly based on the widespread integration of feminist thought and practices within regional and global movements.

Today's labor movements, which go far beyond addressing wage labor issues, call for new relations of social and cultural reproduction that include: equitable wage and household-based work relations, gender and age equity, ethnic equity, good health care and housing conditions, a healthy environment and healthy food, adequate state support, quality education for all, democratic security and policing policies, democratic participation in governing bodies, and peaceful global and regional relations. In order to do these things, the collective body of labor movements has called for restitution for past wrongs by governments and corporations, the fulfillment of the promise of democracy, strong international unions, an end to new forms of enslavement, the international boycott of authoritarian regimes, the establishment of parallel governments, an end to materialism and global exploitation, the reclamation of land by laboring groups, and the creation of new work, market, and political relations.

Will these regional and global protests be successful? Will they be able to stop or deflect the thrust of structural change in the world-economy? Which ones are the most likely to succeed? It is extremely difficult to answer these questions for two reasons. First, the analytic tools available to scholars are not so well developed or "scientific" that they can be accurately used to determine the outcome or consequences of struggle in advance. We agree with Antonio Gramsci, an Italian writer, who cautioned, "One can 'scientifically' foresee only the struggle, but not the concrete moments of the struggle. . . . One can 'foresee' [only] to the extent that one acts, to the extent that one applies a voluntary effort and . . . contributes concretely to the result 'foreseen.'"[18]

Second, the idea that one can or should determine which protest is most likely to effect change and that therefore it should be widely adopted by workers everywhere is, we think, mistaken. Because workers have different interests and identities, we think it best if movements do not try to develop a unitary organization or uniform strategy. The conspicuous failures of the First, Second, and Third Internationals should deter contemporary efforts to develop universalistic models of protest and change. Diversity, we think, has real advantages. Movements should be able to learn from each other without being constrained by each other.

After surveying these diverse movements, we are optimistic about their prospects. This optimism stems in part from a recognition that it takes time for movements to organize effective protests against structural change. Recall that it took years, even decades, before workers responded to previous reorganizations of the workplace and of the global division of labor. Moreover, workers' movements have not started from scratch. The fact that workers have already established relatively durable labor, women's, social justice, and environmental organizations means that the global family of antisystemic movements can draw on resources and build upon ideas that already exist.[19]

Today's workers have benefited from the movements in the late 1960s that criticized global imperialism, classism, sexism, heterosexism, racism, ageism, ableism, authoritarian "socialism," and other forms of inequality and hierarchical rule. These critiques developed only after labor had the opportunity to see how the system would play itself out after a series of promising, but ultimately disappointing, historical transitions had taken place, including the end of plantation-based enslavement, the granting of women's suffrage, and the granting of political self-determination to colonies in Asia and Africa. It turned out that global class relations were expressed through a variety of oppressive relations imposed on divided working people. Seeking greater freedom for particular groups did not eliminate global inequality, which continued to manufacture global divisions.

But the 1990s movements split off from the post-1968 movements in a significant way. Although the 1960s and 1970s movements all called for revolutionary actions that would dissolve social inequities and eliminate barriers to full democracy, these movements assumed distinct identities. There was the women's movement, the lesbian and gay rights movement, the Black liberation movement, and the antiwar movement, among others. Interactions between thinkers and activists in these movements were often full of conflict, even when they acknowledged each other's importance.

When social activists addressed more than one issue, the relationships between these movements became apparent. Activists began criticizing the notion of a "hierarchy of need," and they began discussing all movements against oppression. It became less common to see a single movement described as the most important one, and priority was given to incorporating knowledge from all movements. Eventually, academics started to incorporate this new acceptance of multiple social identities and struggles into their research and teaching. Today, the social movements of the later 1960s have become intertwined, feminism has become embedded in many movements, and the gender revolution has become an integral part of workers' regional and global struggles.

SOCIAL PROTEST AND SOCIAL CHANGE

This book is about work, gender, and protest. But it is also about social change generally. Whenever change occurs rapidly, it produces disorder, even chaos.

For some observers, like Immanuel Wallerstein and Terence Hopkins, the "disorder, considerable disorder" that results from contemporary global change signals the breakup of a unitary, universal, capitalist world-system.[20]

Chaos abounds in today's world. No one is in charge. No country, no international organization, and no social movement directs all of the changes that are taking place. But that has been the case for the last five hundred years; the capitalist world-economy has always been a system of anarchy. What is different now is that the global system may be splitting apart at its seams, and there are few sustained egalitarian and democratic networks and organizations to replace it. This may turn out to be the transformation task of people who live during the next fifty to one hundred years. At this point in capitalist history, the development of equal, inclusive, and participatory societal alternatives is greatly needed.

Labor cannot fully control how its actions will impact society or predict how social change processes may evolve, given the complexity and interaction of worldwide and regional events. Some global chaos stems from the fact that groups of households are seeking new ways to live. Some are migrating, some are joining criminal networks, bandit groups, and guerrilla units. Some are trying to establish new economic and political relations. In addition to these sources of chaos, social chaos is created by environmental degradation, regular and irregular wars, migrant and refugee movements, and the expulsion of some working households from the capitalist system. Then, too, there is also the combined impact of workers' social movements, which may act in complementary or oppositional ways. When the mix of global forces is taken together, the direction of social change becomes even more unpredictable.

One central feature of contemporary change has been that the system's component parts have diverged. Regions in the core have experienced a rapid integration of economic, political, and cultural life, what has commonly been called "globalization," and this has contributed to continued economic growth in the core. But while the core has integrated, the periphery and semiperiphery have "disintegrated." That is, deteriorating economic conditions have distanced these regions from the core and, at the same time, degraded the economic and political institutions in these zones. The component parts of the system—core, periphery, and semiperiphery—are no longer bound together as they once were. Instead, they are beginning to go their separate ways.

In the past, the component parts of the system experienced boom and bust together. The Great Depression was an economic disaster experienced by both core and periphery. Likewise, the postwar expansion was an economic boon for all three zones, though, of course, at different rates. But today, boom in the core is accompanied by bust in the periphery and semiperiphery. As a result of diverging trajectories, economic cycles are out of phase, different zones are out of synch. Although they share a common past, we argue that the zones of the world-economy may no longer share a common future. If this internal splintering of the global system is taking place, this parting of the ways is a novel development, a new departure.

If the component parts of the system go separate ways, and the unitary, global system breaks up, what will take its place? It is unlikely, in our view, that another single or universal system will soon emerge. Instead, we think that during the long period of transition that accompanies the breakup of a five-hundred-year-old system, the world in the twenty-first century may soon look something like it did in the eighteenth.

Rather than the system expanding, as it did when the core continually seized new people and land, the system may shrink, as the core discards people and land, especially in the periphery and semiperiphery. During the eighteenth century, the capitalist world-economy was based in a European core. But capitalist firms and states controlled enclaves and entrepots around the world, integrating them into a single, global division of labor. Although the capitalist system in that period was a unitary, global system, it did not include huge populations and vast regions of the world. People in many parts of the world did not meaningfully participate in the capitalist world-economy but instead organized their lives in very different ways. Recall for a moment the diverse cultures of eighteenth-century Japan, Polynesia, China, Afghanistan, central and southern Africa, western North America, and Ottoman lands. Of course, the diverse cultures around the world in the eighteenth century disappeared as the capitalist world-economy based in Europe subsequently expanded, colonized, "globalized." By the twentieth century, the "capitalist world-economy" had become a universal world.

But today, as a result of what we have called "selective globalization," capitalist firms and states in the core have begun to retreat from vast regions of the world, abandoning their interests in the economic welfare or political well-being of people living there. Of course, they still retain control of enclaves and entrepots across the periphery and semiperiphery. These agricultural, manufacturing, tourist, sex-industry, and financial enclaves are tightly integrated into a single, global division of labor. They are "globalized" while their populous hinterlands and vast interiors are "marginalized," excluded from meaningful participation in the world-economy. The world-economy is no longer synonymous with the planetary world. In the marginalized regions, people are beginning to organize their economic and political lives in different ways. In some respects, the world in the twenty-first century increasingly resembles the world in the eighteenth. The difference is that in the eighteenth century, diversity would soon disappear. Today, it is uniformity that is vanishing.

If the global capitalist order disappears, how will people's work and political lives be organized? We do not know, and, at this transitional point in history, nobody can know, at least for a while.

To try looking into the future, one needs to take into account the whole system, including trends in the North and the South. In the core, more working classes are becoming indebted, and they are working harder to try to pay off their mounting debts. As a result, as in the 1960s, workers may build strong movements against consumer culture and materialism. Coupled with the eventual inability of credit card–holding consumers to fuel economic expansion in the core, this antimaterialism may bring a quick halt to corporate profit-making in the United States and in Western Europe and Japan. Many workers in the North—single mothers, immigrants, inner-city residents, low- to moderate-income elders and youth, and displaced farmers—will be denied the "privilege" of materialistic consumerism and may experience rapid deproletarianization.

Over the next twenty-five years, we expect that a growing proportion of workers undergoing deproletarianization will fall out of the world-economy's orbit. It is possible that a sizable proportion of the earth's surface will be organized outside of the legal operations of the world-economy and perhaps even out of the reach of semi- and overtly corrupt governments. Many regions will exhibit noncapitalist ways of living. We do not expect to see one worldwide government emerge in the immediate future or even within the next fifty years. An egalitarian and democratic production and decision-making system that spans the globe probably could take another century to emerge, and we may not see one for considerably longer, if at all.

Egalitarian and democratic social change will not spring from an idealistic theory, but it will come from people reflecting on their efforts to shape the world around them and applying this knowledge to social change. Because we have lived in a global society, our imagination has been shaped by our acceptance of a worldwide system. Perhaps if we imagine other ways of living that may not be global but that fully meet our social, economic, and political needs, today's movements can become more involved in the process of creating other ways of living.

In many respects there are troubling developments in today's world, but the variety and intensity of social movements also introduce more equitable and democratic ways of living together. In many regions, militias, mafias, and men with guns have filled the void, and growing "diversity" is frequently associated with cultures of violence and corruption, economic deterioration, and environmental degradation. But change also creates opportunities, which can be seized by movements seeking to create new economic and social relations. This requires considerable effort and hard work. Fortunately, women and men the world over know quite a lot about hard work. And it is this capacity to work hard for change that gives us hope.

NOTES

1. Jerry Mander and Edward Goldsmith, eds., *The Case against the Global Economy* (San Francisco: Sierra Club, 1996); Jeremy Rifkin, *The End of Work* (New York: G. P. Putnam's Sons, 1996); Richard J. Barnet and John Cavanagh, *Global Dreams* (New York: Simon and Schuster, 1994); Saskia Sassen, *Globalization and Its Discontents* (New York: New Press, 1998); William Greider, *One World, Ready or Not* (New York: Simon and Schuster, 1997).

2. Maria Mies, *Patriarchy and Accumulation on a World Scale* (London: Zed, 1986); Maria Mies, Veronika Bennholdt-Thomsen, and Claudia von Werlhof, *Women: The Last Colony* (London: Zed, 1991); Maria Mies and Veronika Bennholdt-Thomsen, *The Subsistence Perspective: Beyond the Globalised Economy* (London: Zed, 1999).

3. Samir Amin, "The Challenge of Globalization: Delinking," in *The South Center, Facing the Challenge* (London: Zed, 1993), 133.

4. Giovanni Arrighi and Beverly J. Silver, *Chaos and Governance in the Modern World-System* (Minneapolis: University of Minnesota Press, 1999), 228.

5. Arrighi and Silver, *Chaos and Governance*, 285.

6. Arrighi and Silver, *Chaos and Governance*, 286.

7. Arrighi and Silver, *Chaos and Governance*, 286; Eric Hobsbawm, *The Age of Extremes* (New York: Pantheon, 1994), 289–291.

8. Rae Lesser Blumberg, Cathy A. Rakowski, Irene Tinker, and Michael Monteón, eds., *Engendering Wealth and Well-Being* (Boulder, Colo.: Westview, 1995); Noeleen Heyzer, ed., *A Commitment to the World's Women* (New York: United Nations Development Fund for Women, 1995); Caroline Sweetman, *Women and Urban Settlement* (Oxford: Oxfam, 1996).

9. Eric Hobsbawm, *The Age of Extremes: A History of the World, 1914–1991* (New York: Pantheon, 1994), 571, 573, 577.

10. Hobsbawm, *Age of Extremes*, 572, 577–583. A related argument was made by Fred Block at the Political Economy of the World-System Mini-Conference, Washington, D.C., August 11, 2000. He argued that families have been seeing their wage income halved every three, five, and sometimes ten years. We see this as an indication of deproletarianization.

11. Immanuel Wallerstein, "The Global Picture: 1945–1990," in Terence K. Hopkins and Immanuel Wallerstein, eds., *The Age of Transition* (London: Zed, 1996), 224.

12. Wallerstein in Hopkins and Wallerstein, *Age of Transition*, 214.

13. Wallerstein in Hopkins and Wallerstein, *Age of Transitions*, 228.

14. Wallerstein in Hopkins and Wallerstein, *Age of Transition*, 243.

15. James Green, *Taking History to Heart* (Amherst, Mass.: University of Massachusetts Press, 2000).

16. Terry Boswell and Christopher Chase-Dunn, *The Spiral of Capitalism and Socialism* (Boulder, Colo.: Rienner, 2000), 9.

17. Boswell and Chase-Dunn, *The Spiral of Capitalism and Socialism*, 12, 238.

18. Quentin Hoare and Geoffrey Nowell-Smith, eds., *Selections from the Prison Notebooks* (London: Lawrence and Wishart, 1971), 438.

19. The "worldwide family of antisystemic movements" is a concept introduced by Immanuel Wallerstein. Immanuel Wallerstein, *Historical Capitalism* (London: Verso, 1996), 109.

20. Terence K. Hopkins and Immanuel Wallerstein, "The World-System," in Hopkins and Wallerstein, *Age of Transition*, 8, 10. According to Terence Hopkins and Immanuel Wallerstein, 1967/1973 marked the beginning of systemic crisis, bringing "disorder, considerable disorder" (p. 10). Global crisis and resulting disorder has occurred because the world-system's cyclical rhythms lost their ability to restore long-term (relative) disequilibrium" (p. 8). This

crisis is a real crisis, a transitional one that lasts several generations. "[This crisis] happens only once in the life of any system, and signals its historical coming to an end" (p. 8).

Impending chaos is seen in different ways by scholars. See for example, Arrighi and Silver, *Chaos and Governance*. Giovanni Arrighi raises the possibility of permanently reverting to a "precapitalist" chaos, which may be an especially intense type of chaos, one that may operate on a scale never experienced by humanity. Giovanni Arrighi, *The Long Twentieth Century: Money, Power, and the Origins of Our Time* (London: Verso, 1994), 356.

But Wallerstein takes a different view. According to him, a new order will emerge from chaos. Immanuel Wallerstein, *After Liberalism* (New York: New Press, 1995), p. 268.

Selected Bibliography

Anderson, Bridget. *Doing the Dirty Work? The Global Politics of Domestic Labor.* London: Zed Books, 2000.
Arrighi, Giovanni, Terence K. Hopkins, and Immanuel Wallerstein, eds. *Antisystemic Movements.* London: Verso, 1989.
Arrighi, Giovanni, and Beverly J. Silver. *Chaos and Governance in the Modern World System.* Minneapolis: University of Minnesota Press, 1999.
Benería, Lourdes, and Shelly Feldman, eds. *Unequal Burden: Economic Crises, Persistent Poverty, and Women's Work.* Boulder, Colo.: Westview Press, 1992.
Black, Jan K. *Inequity in the Global Village: Recycled Rhetoric and Disposable People.* West Hartford, Conn.: Kumarian Press, 1999.
Boris, Eileen, and Elisabeth Prügl, eds. *Homeworkers in Global Perspective.* New York: Routledge, 1996.
Chant, Sylvia, and Cathy McIlwaine. *Three Generations, Two Genders, One World: Women and Men in a Changing Century.* London: Zed Books, 1998.
Clark, Alice W., ed. *Gender and Political Economy: Explorations of South Asian Systems.* Delhi: Oxford University Press, 1993.
Corr, Anders. *No Trespassing: Squatting, Rent Strikes, and Land Struggles Worldwide.* Cambridge, Mass.: South End Press, 1999.
Cox, Kevin R., ed. *Spaces of Globalization: Reasserting the Power of the Local.* New York: Guilford Press, 1997.
Dalla Costa, Mariarosa, and Giovanna F. Dalla Costa, eds. *Paying the Price: Women and the Politics of International Economic Strategy.* London: Zed Books, 1995.
Davin, Anna. *Growing Up Poor: Home, School and the Street in London 1870–1914.* London: Rivers Oram Press, 1996.
Ferber, Abby L. *White Man Falling: Race, Gender, and White Supremacy.* Lanham, Md.: Rowman & Littlefield, 1998.
Frankenberg, Ruth, ed. *Displacing Whiteness: Essays in Social and Cultural Criticism.* Durham, N.C.: Duke University Press, 1997.
Fullinwider, Robert K. *Civil Society, Democracy, and Civic Renewal.* Lanham, Md.: Rowman & Littlefield, 1999.
Gallin, Rita S., Anne Ferguson, and Janice Harper, eds. *The Women and International Development Annual, Volume 4.* Boulder, Colo.: Westview Press, 1995

Ginsburg, Faye D., and Rayna Rapp, eds. *Conceiving the New World Order: The Global Politics of Reproduction.* Berkeley: University of California Press, 1995.

Green, Charles, ed. *Globalization and Survival in the Black Diaspora: The New Urban Challenge.* Albany: State University of New York Press, 1997.

Green, James. *Taking History to Heart: The Power of the Past in Building Social Movements.* Amherst: University of Massachusetts Press, 2000.

Hopkins, Terence K., and Immanuel Wallerstein, eds. *The Age of Transition: Trajectory of the World-System, 1945–2025.* London: Zed Books, 1996.

Jacobs, Susie, Ruth Jacobson, and Jennifer Marchbank, eds. *States of Conflict: Gender, Violence and Resistance.* London: Zed Books, 2000.

Kempadoo, Kamala, ed. *Sun, Sex, and Gold: Tourism and Sex Work in the Caribbean.* Lanham, Md.: Rowman & Littlefield, 1999.

Korn, David A. *Exodus Within Borders: An Introduction to the Crisis of Internal Displacement.* Washington, D.C.: Brookings Institution Press, 1999.

Krugman, Paul. *The Return of Depression Economics.* New York: W. W. Norton, 1999.

Meyer, Mary K., and Elisabeth Prügl, eds. *Gender Politics in Global Governance.* Lanham, Md.: Rowman & Littlefield, 1999.

Mies, Maria. *Patriarchy and Accumulation on a World Scale: Women in the International Division of Labour.* London: Zed Books, 1998.

Mies, Maria, Veronika Bennholdt-Thomsen, and Claudia Von Werlhof. *Women: The Last Colony.* London: Zed Books, 1988.

Momsen, Janet H., and Vivian Kinnaird, eds. *Different Places, Different Voices: Gender and Development in Africa, Asia and Latin America.* London: Routledge, 1993.

Pettman, Jan J. *Worlding Women: A Feminist International Politics.* London: Routledge, 1996.

Sassen, Saskia. *Globalization and Its Discontents: Essays on the New Mobility of People and Money.* New York: The New Press, 1998.

Scott, Alan. *The Limits of Globalization: Cases and Arguments.* London: Routledge, 1997.

Scott, Alison MacEwen. *Divisions and Solidarities: Gender, Class and Employment in Latin America.* London: Routledge, 1994.

Shiva, Vandana. *Staying Alive: Women, Ecology and Development.* London: Zed Books, 1988.

Sklair, Leslie, ed. *Capitalism and Development.* London: Routledge, 1994.

Smith, Susan E., and Dennis G. Willms, ed. *Nurtured by Knowledge: Learning to Do Participatory Action-Research.* New York: Apex Press, 1997.

Stephen, Lynn. *Women and Social Movements in Latin America: Power from Below.* Austin: University of Texas Press, 1997.

Tarrow, Sidney. *Power in Movement: Social Movements and Contentious Politics.* Cambridge: Cambridge University Press, 1998.

Turpin, Jennifer, and Lois Ann Lorentzen. *The New Gendered World Order: Militarism, Development, and the Environment.* London: Routledge, 1996.

Van Hear, Nicholas. *New Diasporas: The Mass Exodus, Dispersal and Regrouping of Migrant Communities.* Seattle: University of Washington Press, 1998.

Vannoy, Dana, and Paula J. Dubeck, eds. *Challenges for Work and Family in the Twenty-First Century.* New York: Aldine de Gruyter, 1998.

Varano, Charles S. *Forced Choices: Class, Community, and Worker Ownership.* Albany: State University of New York Press, 1999.

Wallerstein, Immanuel. *Historical Capitalism.* London: Verso, 1983.

―――. *Mentoring, Methods, and Movements: Colloquium in Honor of Terence K. Hopkins.* Binghamton, N.Y.: Fernand Braudel Center, 1998.

Walton, John, and David Seddon. *Free Markets and Food Riots: The Politics of Global Adjustment*. Oxford: Blackwell, 1994.

Wichterich, Christa. *The Globalized Woman: Reports from a Future of Inequality*. London: Zed Books, 1998.

Wieringa, Saskia, ed. *Subversive Women: Women's Movements in Africa, Asia, Latin America and the Caribbean*. London: Zed Books, 1995.

Young, Gay, Vidyamali Samarasinghe, and Ken Kusterer, eds. *Women at the Center: Development Issues and Practices for the 1990s*. New York: Kumarian Press, 1993.

Index

Aegon TransAmerica-Deutsche Telekom, 71
Aeromexico, 218
Agarwal, Bina, 258
Afghanistan, 31, 117, 193, 243, 286. *See* Taliban
AFL-CIO, 207–9
Africa, 10, 25, 39, 90–91, 104, 125, 150, 167–68, 191, 197–98, 262, 284, 286
African Americans, 27, 52, 59, 145, 174, 208, 230, 232–33, 237–38, 241–43
African National Congress, 260
AIDS, 98, 197–98
Aid to Families with Dependent Children (AFDC), 139, 143, 146
Airbus, 56–57, 72
Albania, 190, 261
Algeria, 192, 224, 247
Allende, Salvadore, 245
Alliance of Concerned Men, 243
alternative trade organizations, 265
Amazon, 100, 217
American Civil Liberties Union, 242
American Federation of Labor, 205
American Productivity Center, 65
Amnesty International, 241
Andropov, Yuri, 117
Annan, Kofi, 262
Arab–Israeli War (1967), 85
Argentina, 44, 89, 94–95, 114, 151, 216, 245
Armenians, 190

Arrighi, Giovanni, 276
Attica prison, 237–38
Asia, 10, 25, 129–30, 168, 284
AT&T, 39, 88
Aung San Suu Kyi, 229
Australia, 37
Awami League, 190
Azerbaijan, 190

Baghdad, 39
Bahamas, 87
Bales, Kevin, 100, 175
Bangkok, 25
Bangladesh, 24, 99, 191–92, 264
Bank of England, 89
Basques, 240
Beijing, 39, 102
Belgian Congo. *See* Congo
Belgium, 56, 89, 265
Bennholdt-Thomsen, Veronika, 276
Bentson, Margaret, 32
Berlin Wall, 53
Biafrans, 190
Bihari, 191–92
Black Men's Movement, 243
Blair, Tony, 152, 238
Boeing, 56–57, 72
Bolivia, 86, 100, 229, 259
Bombay, 190, 197
Bonacich, Edna, 211
Bosnia-Herzegovina, 24, 188, 190, 246
Boswell, Terry, 282

295

Bracero Program, 96
Brazil, 36, 40, 87, 90, 93–95, 100, 114, 129, 190, 216, 229, 234–35, 245, 258, 260
Bretton Woods, 51
Brezhnev, Leonid, 117
British navy, 36, 123, 205
Brown, Lester, 198
Bulgaria, 119–21, 188
Bundesbank, 68
Burma, 190, 213, 229, 266
Bush, George, 143

Canada, 91, 237; Human Rights Act, 237; Wheat Board, 265
Candomble, 234
capital flight, 86, 104
Caribbean, 39, 91, 97–98, 170, 229
Caterpillar, 64
Catholic Church, 40, 90, 100, 234
Catholics, 191
Central Africa, 100
Chad, 187
Chant, Sylvia, 170
Chase-Dunn, Christopher, 282
Chavez, Cesar, 208
Chechnya, 124, 187, 190. *See also* Russia
Chernenko, Konstantin, 117
Chicago, 57, 174
Chile, 91, 114, 148, 245
China, 39, 93, 100–3, 105, 117, 119, 126–27, 129, 169, 171, 174, 189, 192, 196–97, 210, 212, 215, 224, 228–29, 261, 266, 286
Chinantlan, Mexico, 101
Chinese Revolution, 169
Chirac, Jacques, 152
Chrysler, 56
Circle of Recovery, 243
Citicorp Equity, 94
civil society, 42, 228, 256, 262–63
Clinton, Bill, 143–44, 233, 238
Coca-Cola, 87
Cold War, 60, 73, 105
Collegiate Licensing Company, 212
Colombia, 99, 189, 190–91, 218, 232, 258, 267
Columbia Falls Aluminum Company, 213

colonialism, 105. *See also* indifferent imperialism
Committee for Industrial Organizations, 207
Communications Workers of America, 208
Congo, 84, 187. *See also* Zaire
Coquery-Vidrovitch, Catherine, 179
Corning Glass, 88
Costa Rica, 171
cost of living adjustments (COLAs), 142
Council for Mutual Economic Assistance (COMECON), 116
crony capitalism, 128
cross-border corporations (XBCs), 71. *See also* transnational corporations
Cuba, 25, 28, 39, 100, 117, 224, 262, 266
Cumings, Bruce, 125
Czechoslovakia, 115–16, 119–20, 131, 151, 187, 190. *See also* Czech Republic; Slovakia
Czech Republic, 89, 121, 235. *See also* Czechoslovakia; Slovakia

Dalla Costa, Mariarosa, 179
Davidson, Basil, 187
Davis, Grey, 233
de Gaulle, Charles, 230
de Soto, Hernando, 26
Dees, Morris, 266
deindustrialization, 54, 57, 73, 86, 93, 102–3, 115, 121, 131, 277–79
dematerialization, 87
Denmark, 138
deproletarianization, 161, 175–78, 280–81, 287
Detroit, 56, 71, 174
Deutsche Telekom, 69
Diallo, Amadou, 242
Dirty Wars, 245
diversifying politics, 176
Dominican Republic, 260
Dow Jones Industrial Average, 63–64
downsizing, 63, 65, 70
Drucker, Peter, 106

East Asia, 98, 115
Eastern Airline, 57
Eastern Europe, 10, 53, 69, 114–16, 118, 120–21, 130–31, 151, 215, 220, 239

Index

East Germany, 53, 68, 93, 119, 138. *See also* Germany; West Germany
East Timor, 127, 231, 244. *See also* Indonesia
Egypt, 38, 99, 247
Egyptian Society for Prevention of Harmful Practices to Women and Child, 247
El Salvador, 25, 191, 208, 244
England, 169. *See also* United Kingdom
Equador, 150, 166, 171, 229, 258
Equal Exchange, 265
Equality Now, 247
Ethiopia, 117, 151, 187
Eurocurrency market, 73. *See also* Eurodollar market
Eurodollar market, 85, 92, 104, 117. *See also* Eurocurrency market
Europe, 27
European Community, 114, 116
European Court of Human Rights, 235
European Union, 69, 243
Eviction Defense Center, 242
Exxon, 129

Fair Labor Association, 213
Falun Gong, 228
family, 28. *See also* household
female genital mutilation, 247
Fine, Michelle, 242
Ford, 56
Ford, Henry, 207
Fordism, 72
Ford-Volvo, 71
Formosa, 125. *See also* Taiwan
Fortune 500, 65
France, 56, 97, 138–39, 152, 205, 210, 224, 230, 239
Frank, Andre Gunder, 94
Freire, Paolo, 263

General Agreement on Tariffs and Trade (GATT), 60. *See also* World Trade Organization
General Electric, 51
General Motors, 55, 209, 260
Germany, 69–70, 138, 152, 210, 224, 239, 241, 245. *See also* East Germany; West Germany

Ghana, 124, 247, 262
Giuliani, Rudolph, 194, 260
glastnost, 117
global capital, 16
globalization, 275–76, 282, 286. *See also* selective globalization
global labor, 17
Gorbachev, Mikhail, 117–18, 120
Grameen Bank, 256, 264
Gramsci, Antonio, 42, 228, 284
Great Bengal Famine, 41
Great Britain, 125. *See also* United Kingdom
Great Depression, 43, 52, 70, 90, 120, 129, 142, 227, 286
Great Mutinies, 205
Greece, 53, 114, 124
Green Party, 152
Green Revolution, 92, 195
Gross National Product (GNP), 30
Group of Seven, 14, 258
GTE, 210
Guatemala, 150, 191, 235
Guest Worker, 53
Guevara, Che, 217
Gypsies (Roma), 235, 239

Haiti, 229
Head Start, 30
Herero people, 241
high-fructose corn sweetener (HFCS), 87–90
Hobsbawm, Eric, 276–77
Holocaust, 238
Hong Kong, 39, 102–3, 114, 124–26, 277
Hopkins, Terence, 285
household, 28, 162–63
Huerta, Dolores, 208
Hungary, 119–21
Hutu, 191
Hyundai, 217

IMF Riots, 150, 215, 218. *See also* International Monetary Fund; structural adjustment; World Bank
import substitution, 84, 86, 92, 279
India, 99–100, 104, 149, 168, 190–91, 196, 232, 235, 255–57

indifferent imperialism, 106. *See also* colonialism
Individual Retirement Accounts (IRAs), 43–44, 63–64, 70, 148
Indonesia, 39, 41, 84–85, 92, 99, 115, 127–31, 149, 187, 190, 212, 215–16, 231–32, 244, 265
informal economy, 25–26
institutional struggles, 176
International Campaign to Ban Land Mines, 265–66
International Monetary Fund (IMF), 13, 73, 89, 93, 129–30, 218–19, 231. *See also* IMF Riots; structural adjustment; World Bank
Iran, 114, 190, 231–32, 243
Iraq, 114, 190
Ireland, 69. *See also* Northern Ireland
Iron Curtain, 239
Israel, 39, 190–92, 239. *See also* Jews; Palestinians
Italian Americans, 236
Italy, 25, 53, 69, 97, 138
Ivory Coast, 232

Jackson, Jesse, 242
Jamaica, 86, 149, 171
Japan, 10, 37, 49–54, 56, 60, 62–63, 67–73, 87–88, 93, 98, 104, 115, 124–28, 139–41, 145, 147, 149, 153–54, 227, 233, 238, 240–41, 264, 277, 286–87; Ministry of Finance, 153
Japanese Americans, 226, 236
Jewish Agency, 239
Jews, 226, 238, 239. *See also* Israel
Johnson, Lyndon, 54
just-in-time production, 56

Karen, 190
Kennedy, John F., 54, 142
Ken Saro-Wiwa, 261
Kenya, 197, 229
Keynes, John Maynard, 43
Kim Young Sam, 219
Kindercare, 30
Kohl, Helmut, 152
Korea, 52, 125; Korean War, 262. *See also* North Korea; South Korea

Kosovars, 190
Kosovo, 187. *See also* Yugoslavia
Ku Klux Klan, 226
Kurds, 190
Kuwait, 114, 233
Kyrgyz, 121

Lagos, 197
Latin America, 10, 26, 39, 56, 60, 84, 91, 93–95, 97, 99, 104, 114, 127, 150, 167–68, 170, 191, 214–18, 229, 259–60
Latinos, 235, 259
Lebanon, 192
Lesotho, 171, 173–74
Levitt, Jr., Arthur, 147
Local Exchange Trading System, 264
Lockheed, 57
London, 72, 89

Maastricht, 69
Maastricht Treaty, 152
Macao, 103
Macuxi Indians, 258
Madagascar, 91
mafias, 189–90, 192, 287
Maizels, Alfred, 86
Malaysia, 115, 126–29
Mandela, Nelson, 213
Maori, 237
maquiladoras, 82, 95–98, 115, 217, 278
Marshall Plan, 50, 116, 125
Marx, Karl, 42, 44, 254
McDonnell Douglas, 57
MCI-British Telecom, 71
Medicaid, 145
Medicare, 142
Mercedes-Chrysler, 71
Mexico, 29, 36–37, 86, 91, 93–94, 96–97, 99, 105, 128, 149, 166, 170, 174, 189, 191, 198, 207, 216, 218, 231, 244, 246, 259, 262; Chiapas, 244, 266
Mexico City, 24, 38, 189, 217, 267
Middle East, 114, 117, 168
Mies, Maria, 276
Miller, Tyisha, 242
Million Man March, 226, 230
Million Mom March, 226
Million Woman March, 226, 230, 232

Million Youth March, 230
minjung (the "masses"), 127, 215
Miss World, 232
Mohammed, Mahathir, 129
Moscow, 39, 119, 122, 124, 220
Moslems, 191
Movement for the Survival of the Ogoni People, 261; Ogoni Bill of Rights, 261
Mullins, A. F., 95
Mumia abu Jamal, 243
Munich, 71

Namibia, 241
Nasser, Gamal, 188
National Academy of Science, 101
National Autonomous University of Mexico, 230–31
National Indian Congress of Mexico, 266
National Law Center on Homelessness and Poverty, 194
National Liberation Army, 267
National Workers Union, 218
Native Americans, 226, 257, 260
Netherlands, 69, 138–39
New York City, 24–26, 37, 40, 57, 101, 144–45, 194, 228, 242, 260; Department of Corrections, 244; Harlem, 230; Health Department, 145; Manhattan, 37; Sanitation Department, 145
New York, state of, 68
New Zealand, 212, 237
Nicaragua, 86, 191, 258
Niger, 262
Nigeria, 85, 92, 114, 190, 196, 213, 261–62
Nikkei Index, 67–68
Nixon, Richard, 54, 85, 142
Nobel Peace Prize, 265
Nordstrom, 212
Norplant, 238
North Africa, 230
North Atlantic Treaty Organization (NATO), 14, 51, 116–17, 120
Northern Ireland, 191. See also Ireland; United Kingdom
North Korea, 126, 232, 262. See also Korea; South Korea
North Sea, 87
Norway, 87, 138, 239

Occidental Petroleum, 258
Ogoni people, 261
Oneida community, 255
Oneida Indian nation, 236–37
Organization of American States, 258
Organization of Petroleum Exporting Countries (OPEC), 54, 85, 87, 104, 143

Pakistan, 190, 196, 263
Palestinians, 190–91, 261. See also Israel
Papua New Guinea, 92, 195, 259
People's War Group, 191
Pepsi, 87
perestroika, 117–18
Peru, 86, 91, 99–100, 191
Philippines, 90, 94, 98, 101, 128, 131, 212, 240–41
Pinochet, Augusto, 245
Poland, 86, 91, 116, 118, 121, 215, 220, 239
Polynesia, 286
Popular Revolutionary Army, 267
Population Council, 28–29, 170
Portugal, 53, 114
potato famine, 238
Prebisch, Raúl, 84
proletarianization, 161, 275, 277, 280–81. See also deproletarianization
Proposition 13, 143
Puerto Rican Telephone Company, 210
Puerto Rico, 210, 216

Queen Liliuokalani, 238

Reagan, Ronald, 63, 143–44
Renault-Nissan, 71
Revolutionary Armed Forces of Colombia, 267
Rodriguez, Arturo, 209
Romania, 119–21, 220
Roosevelt, Franklin D., 142
Russia, 25, 36–37, 39–40, 44, 91, 118, 120–21, 123–24, 129, 150–51, 187–88, 190, 216, 219–20, 224. See also Chechnya; Soviet Union
Rwanda, 191, 246

Safa, Helen, 165
Saipan, 212
Saudi Arabia, 92, 114, 127, 233, 243
savings and loan associations (S&Ls), 61
Schor, Juliet, 42, 66
Schröder, Gerhard, 152
Scotland, 169. *See also* United Kingdom
Second World, 36
selective globalization, 72, 103–6, 178, 283, 286. *See also* globalization
Self-Employed Women's Association, 255
Sen, Amartya, 31, 41
Seneca Indians, 260
Senegal, 238, 247
Seoul National University, 232
Serbia, 235. *See also* Yugoslavia
Servicemembers Legal Defense Fund, 233
Shell Oil, 262
Siberian Arctic, 124
Sicily, 189
Sierra Leone, 219
Silicon Valley, 207
Silver, Beverly, 276
Singapore, 93, 114, 124–26, 277
Slovakia, 119. *See also* Czech Republic; Czechoslovakia
Slovenia, 119
Smith, Adam, 27
Social Security, 63, 142, 146–48
Solidarity, 118, 215
Somalia, 151, 187, 227, 262
South Africa, 13, 89, 91–92, 114, 150, 173, 190, 213, 215, 234, 240–41, 259; bantustans, 13; Housing Trust, 260; National Land Committee, 240; Truth and Reconciliation Commission, 240
South Asia, 25, 91
Southern Poverty Law Center, 266
Southeast Asia, 168
South Korea, 38, 93, 98, 104, 114–15, 124, 126–28, 130–31, 215–16, 218–19, 232, 240–41, 277; Agency for National Security Planning, 219
Soviet Union, 25, 52–54, 62, 69, 114–21, 131, 150–51, 187, 190, 215. *See also* Russia; Ukraine
Spain, 53, 56, 69, 97, 114, 119, 224, 240, 245

Sri Lanka, 84, 190
Starving Oil Worker's March, 91
Stockman, David, 144
structural adjustment, 86, 93, 150, 167, 187. *See also* International Monetary Fund; IMF Riots; World Bank
Sudan, 171, 187, 262
Support Committee for Maquila Workers, 217
Surinam, 84, 196, 259
sweatshops, 211–13
Sweden, 152
Switzerland, 238–39
Syria, 190

Taft-Hartley Act, 207
Taiwan, 93, 98, 102, 104, 114–15, 124–27, 129, 131, 240–41, 277
Taliban, 31, 193. *See also* Afghanistan
Tamils, 190
Tanzania, 94, 99, 149, 171
Taylor, Frederick, 207
Teamsters, 209–10
Thailand, 84, 86, 98, 100, 115, 127–31, 232
Third World, 15, 26, 36, 73, 89, 105, 127, 167, 169, 277
Three Gorges Dam, 196
Thurow, Lester, 66
Tiananmen Square, 102, 228–29
Tilly, Charles, 28
Tilly, Chris, 28
Togo, 247
Tokyo, 67–68
Toyota, 71
transnational corporations (TNCs), 71, 86
triads. *See* mafias
Trinidad and Tobago, 90
Tunisia, 149
Turkey, 53, 149, 190, 244–45
Tuskegee Institute, 238

Ukraine, 118, 188, 192. *See also* Soviet Union
Union of Needletrades, Industrial and Textile Employees, 208
United Arab Emirates, 233
United Church of Christ, 238

Index

United Farm Workers, 208–9
United Kingdom, 69, 87, 89–90, 97, 139, 152, 224, 234, 245, 261, 264. *See also individual countries*
United Nations, 36, 39, 121, 170, 196; UNICEF, 121; World Health Organization, 197
United Paperworkers International Union, 208
United Parcel Service, 209
United States, 10–11, 23, 25, 29–30, 36–37, 39–43, 49–56, 59, 62–63, 67–73, 83, 87–88, 91, 93, 97, 99, 102, 104, 117, 119, 122, 124–29, 139–41, 148–52, 163, 165, 170, 189–90, 192–93, 205, 207, 209–10, 212–14, 218, 226–27, 230, 233, 235–37, 241, 243, 247, 257, 259–60, 264, 267, 277, 287; Aid to Families with Dependent Children, 139; Civil War, 237; Congress, 143–44, 146, 210; Department of Justice, 236, 242; Department of Labor, 27; Federal Reserve Board, 147, 150; Immigration and Naturalization Service, 39; Internal Revenue Service, 139; Medicaid, 145; Medicare, 142; Securities and Exchange Commission, 147; Social Security, 142, 146–48
University of Antioquia, 232
Urban Poor Coalition, 265
Uruguay, 150
U.S. Airways, 208
U.S. Steel, 54
Uwa Indians, 258

Venezuela, 114, 196
Vermont Supreme Court, 233
Vietnam, 52, 54, 58, 100, 125, 224, 266
Volkswagen, 55
Volkswagen-Rolls Royce, 71
von Werlhof, Claudia, 276

Wagner Act, 207
Wales, 169. *See also* United Kingdom
Wallerstein, Immanuel, 277, 285
Wall Street, 63, 73, 147–48

Walmart, 129, 207
Walton, John, 150
Ward, Kathryn, 29
Warsaw Pact, 116
Watchguard, 232
Weis, Lois, 242
welfare, 141
welfare states, 138
Western Europe, 10, 13, 31, 37, 49–54, 56, 60, 62–63, 67–68, 70–73, 85, 88, 104, 122, 127–28, 138–41, 151, 153, 193, 205, 210, 220, 227, 277, 287
West Germany, 56, 68, 138. *See also* East Germany; Germany
Wilson, William Julius, 31
Wolf, Diane, 96
Women for Justice, 243
Women's National Basketball Association, 208
work, types of, 23
World Bank, 29, 52, 73, 92, 100, 119, 127–28, 218, 231, 256. *See also* IMF Riots; International Monetary Fund; structural adjustment
World Health Organization, 197. *See also* United Nations
World Jewish Congress, 239
World Trade Organization, 13. *See also* General Agreement on Tariffs and Trade
World War II, 10, 13, 40, 50, 57–58, 67, 71–73, 85, 105, 116, 120, 125, 129, 138, 141, 151, 205, 210, 235–36, 239–41
World Watch Institute, 198

Yakuza. *See* mafias
Yangtze River, 196
Yeltsin, Boris, 118
Yom Kippur War, 85
Yugoslavia, 53, 131, 151, 187, 190, 192, 241. *See also* Kosovo; Serbia

Zaire, 149, 151, 187, 191. *See also* Congo
Zambia, 91, 170
Zapatistas, 266–68
Zimbabwe, 172, 232, 240, 259–60, 264

About the Authors

Torry Dickinson is a professor of women's studies at Kansas State University. She is the author of *CommonWealth: Self-Sufficiency and Work in American Communities, 1830 to 1993* (1995).

Robert Schaeffer is a professor of global sociology at Kansas State University. He is the author of *Understanding Globalization: The Social Consequences of Political, Economic, and Environmental Change* (1997).